MW01492750

Songs in the Morning

Feel free to be inspired

A Daily Devotional inspired by
A variety of songs, Biblical scriptures, and
Real life stories.

Susan!
Be inspired!
You are fierce!
♥ Starr Himmel
Prov. 3:5-6

Starr Himmel

Songs in the Morning
By Starr Himmel
ISBN -10: 0615932398
ISBN -13: 978-0615932392
Copyright © 2013 by Starr Himmel

All Rights Reserved. No part of this publication may be reproduced in any form or by any means, including scanning, photocopying, or otherwise except for brief quotations in printed reviews, without prior written permission of the copyright holder.

DISCLAIMERS: Included in this book are references to songs that have inspired daily writings. The names of individuals or bands attached to the song titles serve as a reference only as someone who has performed the piece or is connected with it and may or may not be the actual writer or composer of same. In each case an effort has been made to use the common and appropriate song titles.

While all attempts have been made to verify information provided in this publication, the Author and Publisher assumes no responsibility for errors, omissions, or contrary interpretation of the subject matter herein. Any perceived slights of specific persons, peoples, or organizations are purely unintentional.

Unless otherwise indicated, all Scripture quotations are taken from the New King James Version of the Bible. **NKJV**: Scripture taken from the New King James Version®. Copyright © 1982 by Thomas Nelson, Inc. Used by permission. All rights reserved.

Scripture quotations marked (AMP) are taken from the Amplified Bible, Copyright © 1954, 1958, 1962, 1964, 1965, 1987 by The Lockman Foundation. Used by permission.

Verses marked CEB - Scripture taken from the Common English Bible®, CEB® Copyright © 2010, 2011 by Common English Bible.™ Used by permission. All rights reserved worldwide. The "CEB" and "Common English Bible" trademarks are registered in the United States Patent and Trademark Office by Common English Bible. Use of either trademark requires the permission of Common English Bible.

Verses marked ERV -t aken from the HOLY BIBLE: EASY-TO-READ VERSION © 2001 by World Bible Translation Center, Inc. and used by permission.
Verses marked KJV – are taken from the King James Version of the Bible.

Verses marked MSG - Scripture taken from *The Message*. Copyright © 1993, 1994, 1995, 1996, 2000, 2001, 2002. Used by permission of NavPress Publishing Group.

Scripture quotations marked (NIrV) are taken from the Holy Bible, New International Reader's Version®, NIrV® Copyright © 1995, 1996, 1998 by Biblica, Inc.™ Used by permission of Zondervan. All rights reserved worldwide. www.zondervan.com The "NIrV" and "New International Reader's Version" are trademarks registered in the United States Patent and Trademark Office by Biblica, Inc.™

Scripture quotations marked (NIV) are taken from the Holy Bible, New International Version®, NIV®. Copyright © 1973, 1978, 1984, 2011 by Biblica, Inc.™ Used by permission of Zondervan. All rights reserved worldwide. www.zondervan.com The "NIV" and "New International Version" are trademarks registered in the United States Patent and Trademark Office by Biblica, Inc.™

Scripture quotations marked (NLT) are taken from the Holy Bible, New Living Translation, copyright © 1996, 2004, 2007 by Tyndale House Foundation. Used by permission of Tyndale House Publishers, Inc., Carol Stream, Illinois 60188. All rights reserved.

Cover Design by Sean Himmel, copyright ©2013. All rights reserved

Proofing assistance by Carol Prose

Special appreciation to all those who followed my blog through this process.

Printed by CreateSpace, An Amazon.com Company

First Printing, 2013   Printed in the United States of America

Dedication

First and foremost, I thank God for giving me a song each day and gifting me to write.

Thanks to my adorable, Godly husband, Steve for sharing this amazing life with me. He has always been supportive, encouraging, and inspiring.

Thanks to my wonderful sons, Sean and Ryan, for being great young men of God and for offering inspiration for many pages in this book.

Thanks to all three of you guys for letting me tell stories about you!

Thank you to my incredible pastors, Pastors David and Kim Blunt, for your faithfulness to teach the uncompromised Word of God, lead, and mentor and for your consistent example of giving, serving, and prayer.

Thank you to my college-town pastors, Pastors Lecil and Fran Frink, for your obedience to God in leadership and for your welcoming arms and your strength shown to me at a pivotal point in my life.

Thank you to my youth pastor, Rev. Jeffrey Carr, for showing me what to do next when I felt the call of God on my life.

Thanks to my high school friend, Jim Armistead, for caring enough to take me to the church service where I received Jesus in my heart.

Thank you to the pastor of my childhood, Rev. Clarence P. Folkins, for first teaching and exemplifying God's love to me.

And thank you to my parents, Richard and Katherine Hampel, for raising me in a loving home.

Songs in the the Morning

Feel free to be inspired

Introduction

For several years now, I have had a song on my heart when I first wake up in the morning. It's almost always been an inspirational song. It occurred to me lately that I was taking that daily gift for granted, so sharing it seemed to be a great idea. My hope is that those who read will be inspired by the songs, both old and new, and will be encouraged daily by them as I am. In turn, perhaps, you will start to hear your own songs each day.

Just to be clear, this is not a song I pick each day. The song picks me. Really, I believe God speaks to me through something that works for me. Lately, up until a few weeks before I started this project, when I woke up in the middle of the night my thoughts would be filled with the cares of life, regrets, dread, failure, and fear. I'm not exactly sure what changed. It may have been a message from my pastor, a scripture I read, a song I heard, a word from my husband, or simply an answer to prayer. In the stillness of the night I began to listen. Listen for the song God had for me. Rehearsing it in my head, I faded back to sleep undaunted by what had kept me awake before. Following is the compilation of a year's worth of "Songs in the Morning" written one day at a time. They include real life illustrations, personal examples, scriptures, and encouragement for your daily living.

Feel free to be inspired.

1 January I remember when our cat had kittens. She was a year old and became the proud mama of five 'cute-as-a-button' babies. When the birthing process started, I was there, excited and concerned that everything would go well. The first one seemed to be a surprise to mama, but she quickly figured it out and by the delivery of number two, she was a pro. All five were healthy. We kept three with the mama cat and gave two away. They have grown up to be great companions and mousers.

Today's song is, "New Season" ~ Israel Houghton. This song reminds me that it's a new season and a new day. There is fresh anointing, power, and prosperity coming my way. As a new season breaks, things will be changing. It's a time to get a breath of fresh air. Time to evaluate the past, but time to reach forward to the greatness that this New Year offers. It may contain some surprises at first, but you will figure it out. It will be a year of growth. It will be a year of opportunity. It will be a year like none other...if you make it that way. You have the choice to live this year as a new and different year or repeat the year past. Philippians 3:12-14 (MSG) says, "I'm not saying that I have this all together, that I have it made. But I am well on my way, reaching out for Christ, who has so wondrously reached out for me. Friends, don't get me wrong: By no means do I count myself an expert in all of this, but I've got my eye on the goal, where God is beckoning us onward—to Jesus. I'm off and running and I'm not turning back." This is the time to believe the best about the year ahead. Believe that power and prosperity are yours. It is time for a fresh anointing. Making goals is not enough. Good intentions are not enough. Resolutions are not enough. Time to create new habits, new methods, new relationships, new ways that will help you fulfill the destiny that God has planned for you. This year, set your goals and complete them. Philippians 1:6 says, "...being confident of this very thing, that He who has begun a good work in you will complete *it* until the day of Jesus Christ" Don't be just a good starter, be a good finisher. You may be concerned that everything will go okay, but hang in there. You will birth something wonderful! Something exciting is coming your way! You may discover something new and even more than you thought was possible!

2 January Tenacity – that persistence that says, "I will not quit." So, I have decided to work harder and smarter this year. My business success depends on it. Wouldn't you know that this morning when I was scheduled to be at a business meeting that I just wanted to stay in bed! I was tired. I was comfortable where I was. I didn't feel good. I didn't get enough sleep. Boo Hoo. Poor me. BUT I got up. I got ready. I got on my way and I went to that meeting. Keeping my commitment is more important than all my excuses. I am so glad I went.

Today's song, "I Will Not Be Moved" ~ Natalie Grant. This song proclaims that on Christ, the Solid Rock, I will stand and I won't be moved. Other ground is like sinking sand. When it comes to commitment, promises, and decisions, you cannot be just a talker. You must be a doer. What good are your intentions if you do not follow through? You decide, and by your decisions, you display to others just how serious you are. You show them how they should treat you and your claims. When it comes to your spiritual walk, your commitment to Christ is serious. Be committed. God has called you. He will equip you to do all that He has for you. You cannot be moved from your decision to follow Christ. Why? Because it has made a difference in you. It's baffling to see 'committed' people who are offended and walk away from God, their Pastor, their Church, their friends. Walking away is like entering a field of sinking sand. It may look good on the surface, but it is deadly. Proverbs 14:12 and 16:25 say the exact same thing… "There is a way which seems right to a man, but its end is the way of death." (We should pay more attention to something when it is said twice.) God really wants you to see how the error of making your own way can have severe consequences. Christ is a solid rock - a support system for all your activities, business, relationships – your life. Don't decide each day, "I will follow Christ" Decide once for the rest of your days, just do it. Your commitment will bring you through. Sometimes it will be hard. You may be tired. You may be too comfortable where you are. You may not feel good. But get up, get going and you will see God work on your behalf, because you are persistent and because He is consistent. Go where you are supposed to be. You will be glad you did.

3 January As my son has progressed in his juggling skills, he has added more dangerous equipment. When he got his torches, some one asked what his mom thought of them. He told him, "She ordered them." Later he added knives to his repertoire. Could be kind of scary, but I approved. It's okay, because I trust him. I trust his skill level. I know what he can do. I trust him to be responsible with his juggling props. He's really good. And I have to tell you that I love to tell people that my son juggles knives and fire!

Today's song is, "In Christ Alone" ~ Michael English. This song says that in Christ alone I place my trust. I find glory in the power of the cross. In every victory, people will say that I got my strength and hope in Christ. This is a defining song in my life. Trust in the Lord has been so important. From my high school days when I asked Him into my heart, and all these years after, He has been a part of who I am. Proverbs 3:5-6 (KJV) says, "Trust in the Lord with all your heart, and lean not on your own under-standing; in all your ways acknowledge Him and He shall direct your paths." Think about when you sit down in your favorite chair. Do you examine it? Do you question whether it will hold you? Do you wonder if it's really there? No. You trust it. You just sit down. You get comfortable. You rest in it. That's how you should be with the Lord. Stop questioning. Stop wondering. Stop examining. He's really there. Trust Him. Sit down, get comforta-ble, and rest in Him. Proverbs 3:5-6 (MSG) says, "Trust God from the bottom of your heart; don't try to figure out everything on your own. Listen for God's voice in everything you do, every-where you go; He's the one who will keep you on track." You can trust the Lord today and what He can do in your life. He knows what He's doing. He's good. You should love to tell people what He has done for you and through you. When victories come, know He has a hand in it. When trials come, know He is there for you. Even when it's kind of scary, He will bring you through. He is your source of strength and your source of hope today. Lean on Him. He will show you what to do next.

4 January Did you ever see a 'plate spinner' at the circus? They always fascinate me. They have the ability to keep so many plates spinning on sticks at the same time. When one slows down, they run back to it and get it going fast again. My brief research revealed that in addition to spinning, these performers have a lengthy list of tricks they can present involving plates, sticks, throwing, catching, passing, balancing, under the leg, behind the back, stick on stick, two on a stick, exchanges, etc. etc. etc. In other words, there's a lot more to it than one would suppose. It's amazing to see.

The song for today is, "The Solid Rock" ~ Edward Mote. "His oath, his covenant, his blood supports me in the whelming flood. When all around my soul gives way, He then is all my hope and stay." God's promise to you is one of support. Deuteronomy 31:6 (MSG) says, "Be strong. Take courage. Don't be intimidated. Don't give them a second thought because God, your God, is striding ahead of you. He's right there with you. He won't let you down; He won't leave you." When you get the 'plates' of your life going, your family, your career, your home, your friends, relatives, church, and personal growth, it can be overwhelming. An overwhelming flood. You want to be in so many places at one time, but you are one person. So you get to choose which plate to spin next. Sometimes you can pass, throw, and put two on a stick. You can get creative. You can wait on some of them. God gives you courage and strength to know what to do. He is going ahead of you. He sees down the road. He knows your path. You just need to walk in it and be confident of what He has planned. It is for your good. To prosper you. To give you a hope and a future. (Jeremiah 29:11) You may have many responsibilities today. Look at each one and ask God to show you what is next. Where do you spin, where do you wait, what do you let drop? He can be a constant in your life when things are changing, when people let you down, when bad things happen. Keep Him involved. Keep Him right beside you. Don't whine, don't quit. Remember His goodness and what He's already done for you. When there is so much going on, your head is spinning, take heart – God is right there, and He's amazing.

5 January As my sons were growing up there were opportunities for them to be in costume for church and school events. Usually it was October. I liked making the costumes. Most of them were Biblical characters. Over the years we had a tiger, Samson, Lazarus, Silas, Naaman (the leper), The boy with 5 loaves and 2 fish, a child carried by Jesus, and my personal favorite, Nicodemus in a tree! The Nicodemus costume was an illusion costume. My son was a tree from the waist down and Nicodemus from the waist up. False legs hung over a fabric and wire tree limb attached with a belt and held by his hand. He really looked like he was sitting in a tree! It was a trophy winner!

Today's song, "Jesus in Disguise" ~ Brandon Heath. This song asks if you ever get something in your head that you haven't heard or read. Or have you ever felt like you been somewhere before? My son's costume the year he was Nicodemus was not what it appeared to be. There are many things like that in life. You can't just judge by what it appears to be. You can't always take it at face value. These are the times that the Lord shows you in your spirit what is really going on. He guides with a thought, a confirmation, of what to say or do. In Exodus 4:12 (CEB), God converses with Moses saying, "Now go! I'll help you speak, and I'll teach you what you should say." Moses was depending on God. God was assuring him that He would be there with guidance and instruction. It's important that you recognize the source of your guidance. Sometimes it seems so subtle. It's just a thought or a nudge, a feeling, intuition, an idea…it is from God when it's directed toward something good, profitable, or helpful. It is not when it leads to hurt, destruction, or loss. God gives that inkling that urges you forward. It's sometimes hard to describe. The important thing is to be open to it. When you seek God, His presence is a part of your life. Today, listen with your spiritual ears; see with your spiritual eyes by paying attention to those things that may not be as they appear. Get quiet. Settle yourself. Take notice when you seem to know something you wouldn't otherwise have known. It's that insight. That familiarity. That confirmation. Get yourself in tune with God's leading. He will direct you. Things may not be as they first appear, but He will show you and you will find yourself to be a winner too.

6 January I am not a chef by any means, but I am a good cook. I really love to cook. The creativity and hands-on work appeals to me. It's fun to take individual ingredients and meld them into something different. I especially enjoy taking left-overs and remaking them for a new dish. It's amazing! (I am so humble too.) The result is often much better than what I had imagined!

Today's song is, "Me Without You" ~ TobyMac. This song acknowledges the grace of God in that He saved me and remade me, admitting that I am not sure where I would be without Him. I don't know where I would have ended up had I not decided to follow Christ. When I was in high school a friend invited me to a youth retreat. Then my Christian boyfriend took me to a revival. I asked Jesus into my heart. God made something new out of me. My grades were A's, my behavior exemplary, and my family intact. I was not abused, neglected, nor abandoned. God just wasn't really a part of my life. I didn't know the saving grace that comes through Jesus. 2 Corinthians 5:17 says, "Therefore, if anyone *is* in Christ, *he is* a new creation; old things have passed away; behold, all things have become new." I am thankful for the people in my life that cared enough to get me to a place where I could learn of Christ. People who knew that just being a good person was not enough. Accepting the Lord was and still is the avenue to life eternal in Heaven. How rich a life I have because of them. If you haven't decided, decide. This is the day. Ask Jesus into your heart. Then make sure you tell a Christian friend or pastor. If He has saved and remade you, first of all, rejoice. Be glad you took that step today, yesterday, last week, last year, a long time ago, whenever it was. Who in your life has not made that decision? Don't give up on them. Don't let them think that being a good person is enough. Romans 3:23 (CEB) says "All have sinned and fall short of God's glory." With overwhelming sin in our lives, we all fall short. There's only one way to get to that new life. John 14:6 says, "Jesus said to him, 'I am the way, the truth, and the life. No one comes to the Father except through me.'" More of the recipe is found in 1 John 1:9 and Romans 10:9-10. These words in scripture are for you and can help you show others the way. You can be the influence that helps them to be remade. The end result will be better than you can imagine!

7 January In the movie, "The Wizard of Oz", Dorothy and the Scarecrow happen upon the Tinman who has rusted from time and rain. His request, "Oil can." The reply, "Oil can what?" So, they squirt some oil on him and he loosens, able to move and walk easily in no time. He joins the journey and becomes a part of the quest for what he felt he was lacking – a heart.

The song today is, "Who You Are" ~ Unspoken. This song tells you to let the ashes fall wherever they land and come back to Jesus, because you can change who you are. Change is progressive. You may want to dramatically change. Realize that one workout will not get you to your goal weight. One well balanced meal will not make you healthy. One day of work will not make you successful. One of anything will not make enough of a difference. Mike Murdock said that the 'key to your success is hidden in your daily routine'. Habits. Day in, day out, day after day. Overnight successes have been working for years, people just don't notice until they are approaching their summit. My pastor says that 'inch by inch, it's a cinch.' Tackling the big battles in life is done by taking on each daily challenge. The little wins add up. So, where you find yourself should not be where you want to be. It's time to come back from where you have been and lay the junk of your life at the foot of the cross. Romans 12:1-2 (MSG) says, "So here's what I want you to do, God helping you: Take your everyday, ordinary life—your sleeping, eating, going-to-work, and walking-around life—and place it before God as an offering. Embracing what God does for you is the best thing you can do for Him. Don't become so well-adjusted to your culture that you fit into it without even thinking. Instead, fix your attention on God. You'll be changed from the inside out. Readily recognize what he wants from you, and quickly respond to it. Unlike the culture around you, always dragging you down to its level of immaturity, God brings the best out of you, develops well-formed maturity in you." This is the path to take. It may not be the Yellow Brick Road, but it does lead to your success and all God has for you. Where you are rusty today, seek the oil of God's anointing so everything will work as it should. You will find yourself moving forward. One day at a time. Your quest will be clear and your heart will be full.

8 January A lot of my friends were leaving for California for a business trip I could have been on… If I had done the work, I could have gone. So I missed it, it made me sad. But the opportunity for this trip has passed. I can mope about it or make sure I go the next time!

The song today is, "Blink" ~ Revive. This song reminds me that life happens in a blink and a flash. Things happen in the time it takes you to look back. Every day opportunities are coming to you or passing you. Things happen quickly. You don't always have time to think about it. You don't always have time to analyze it. You don't always have time to examine, research, chart, compare, schedule, dissect, organize, catalog, or wait. Prepare now for what's coming. Get ready. Do what you can, when you can so you will be able to do what you need to, when you need to do it. If you lay down to go to sleep at night and you don't know where the day went, then you have wasted the day. You have missed an opportunity to prepare. You have missed an opportunity to act. My friend told me that when she goes to sleep at night she wants to be tired because she worked and helped someone else, not because she sat around and drank coffee. Some one else said that we should rest so we can work instead of the other way around. The story in Nehemiah is a favorite of my pastor's wife. She recounts Nehemiah's determination with his goal and his mission, in Nehemiah 6:3 when from the wall of Jerusalem he says, "I'm doing important work, so that I cannot come down." He knew what he was doing was important. He was focused. He was driven. What are you focused on today? What are you thinking? What are you preparing? What are you planning? You do not want to get to the end of the year, the month, the week or even the day and say, "Oh, what opportunities I missed." You must rise up. Be purposeful. Be about the work that God has called you to do. Things can happen in a blink. Make the moments count. Don't be a spectator in life today. Build. Create. Accomplish. Don't mope. Don't give up. You are in charge of what you do.

9 January When I was a youth, we used to play a game called 'Sardines'. It was a hide-n-seek type game where the one person who was 'it' went to hide while all the rest counted. Then they headed in all directions hunting for him. When he was found, the person who found him would hide there as well. This process continued until almost everyone joined in the hiding place. It took patience and silence to remain concealed. The last one would then discover them all! One time we squished about eight people in a bathroom stall at my church!

Today's song, "Forever Reign" ~ Hillsong. This song says that God is true, even when I wander away. Sometimes you can be looking for something and not see it even when it's very close. You may wander around, searching and not find it. That is the time to stop and ask God. "Where is it? Help me find it." And He does. God can show you even when it seems that all your friends have found their way, joined the group, accomplished the goal, come to the revelation, changed their habits, and leaped forward in their lives and you're not quite there yet. He can show you what He wants to do in you. He can show you what the next step is. He is the constant in a world of change. He stays the same. Malachi 3:6 says, "For I am the Lord, I do not change..." He is the same yesterday, today, and forever. So, you can wander, try it on your own, but He continues to be there for you. He waits. He is patient. You must find Him. Then you must trust Him.

Have you wandered today from what God wants for you? Are you searching for something and you just can't put your hand on it? Or wrap your mind around it? Do you question more than trust today? You can find Him when you seck Him. He may have been in a hidden place in your life, but it's time to bring Him to the forefront. Fulfill what He has for you. You'll be excited about what you find!

10 January When my son was little, he ran out on the concrete driveway barefooted. Yep, he stubbed his toe. It was a bloody mess. So I cleaned it up and bandaged it. Several days went by and it was pretty much healed. Confident as he was (and still is), he ran on outside barefooted and you guessed it, he stubbed it again! Ouch! Got to get some shoes on that boy!

Today's song, "The Hurt & The Healer" ~ Mercy Me. This song declares that I am alive even though part of me has died. God takes my heart and breathes life into it. I fall into His arms. That's when hurt and the healer collide. If you haven't been hurt in life, get ready. It will happen. Or it has happened and you are lying to yourself. People let you down. They disappoint. They break promises. They are people. Numbers 23:19 says, "God is not a man, that he should lie; neither the son of man, that he should repent: hath he said, and shall he not do it? or hath he spoken, and shall he not make it good?" God will not let you down. He will do what He says He will do. What do you do when you are hurt? Do you bandage it? Take that bloody mess and clean it up? Or do you stay there and bleed? Do you cry and pout? Do you have a fit? How do you really handle hurt? Be excited to know that God will heal your hurts today. You can trust Him. You can go to Him like a child goes to a parent when they are hurt. Psalm 147:2-6 (MSG) says, "God's the one who rebuilds Jerusalem, who regathers Israel's scattered exiles. He heals the heartbroken and bandages their wounds. He counts the stars and assigns each a name. Our Lord is great, with limitless strength; we'll never comprehend what he knows and does. God puts the fallen on their feet again and pushes the wicked into the ditch." I like every bit of that passage! Here's what it shows you…God will rebuild. He will gather what has been scattered. He will heal your broken heart. He will bandage your wounds. He pays attention to detail. He knows your name. He is strong – especially when you are weak. He goes above and beyond what you will ever realize. He will get you back on your feet again. And He will punish your enemies! With God, you can't lose. Romans 8:31b says, "If God be for us, who can be against us?" If you've been hurt, you can get up and go again. God is there for you. He's your healer. He's your advocate. Run to Him with open arms today. He can bring your heart back to life.

11 January The swinging bridge. There's one at the amusement park we like. If you go on it alone, you can have a nice walk. But we go together and there are other people and the boys jump and the swinging gets wild. It's hard to walk. And awkward. And bouncy. And jerky. It can be frustrating or fun.

Today's song is, "Feels Like I'm Losin'" ~ Tenth Avenue North. This song asks God to forgive people because they don't know what they have been doing. We all have a choice to make in life. When the people in your life start bouncing around making the whole thing swing, you have a choice to make. Do you get upset, angry, frustrated? Or do you go with it, cope, function, adapt? Sometimes you may think, "Hey, you messed up my plan!" but then you have to take a breath and think, "Okay, how can I deal with this?" It may even turn out better. A great book is 3 Seconds: The Power of Thinking Twice by Les Parrott, PhD. He says, "Just three seconds. The time it takes to make a decision. That's all that lies between settling for 'Whatever' ... or insisting on 'Whatever it takes.'" People do things without thinking. They do things for their own benefit. They can be selfish. They can also be mean. Stop saying, "oh well" and say, "what now?" You can move toward success with a proper attitude. A wrong attitude can stop you in your tracks. When your bridge gets invaded and things start swinging, take a breath. Forgive others. Get a fresh perspective. Keep going. Sometimes you have to hold on tighter. Sometimes you have to step a little differently. Sometimes you have to lighten up. Sometimes you have to laugh. Stay with it. You will make it. You can enjoy it and you can bring others with you.

12 January I remember when my boys were little. I just wanted to get them the super hero toys, but no "bad guys" my son said, "Mom, without the bad guys there is no one to fight so they can BE super heroes!"

The song today is, "Blessings" ~ Laura Story. This song asks if your blessings may come through rain drops or your healing through tears? Without a test, there is no testimony. Stuff happens in life. Things can hurt. You can grow through it. It helps you to be stronger if you let it. Your response is the key. A runner who wins the race keeps training so he can win the next race. A runner who loses the race keeps training so he can win the next race. So, if you win or lose this time, either way, you keep training. You keep training because you want to win. You can win against circumstances. You can win against negativity. You can win against deception. You can win against stress. You can win against disappointment. These are the villains of life. And there are no victors without the villains. When things are rough, hang in there. It can change over night. Blessings can come in ways you never imagined. Romans 12:21 (MSG) says, "Don't let evil get the best of you; get the best of evil by doing good." This is a great action plan. Doing good will help you overcome what is troubling you. It will open up opportunity for blessing. Find a focus that is bigger than your problem. Get wisdom on the matter. Respond to it, do not react. Check that visceral response. If you have a solid foundation in your faith, your gut reaction will be good. You will say and do the right things. Your victory will be a testimony to others. An example for them to follow. So I say, fight those bad guys today so you can be a super hero. Battle on! You will be victorious!!!

13 January When I was a girl I liked to have "clubhouses". One of my favorites was under the basement stairs in our house. There was a steamer trunk there. I put a blanket on top of it and hooked up a string of Christmas lights. I could take a book there and read or just relax. There were no elaborate toys or games there. It was quiet. A curtain there served as my door. No one else could fit in that place but me. It was a place of solitude. It was my spot.

Today's song is, "Who You Are" ~ Hillsong. This song reminds me to bask in God's presence by thinking of the good things He has done. To wait patiently to hear His still small voice. He is Holy, righteous, and faithful. Savior, healer, redeemer, and friend. I should worship Him for who He is. There's a place you can go to worship. A place to reflect. A place to relax. A place to be quiet before God. It may be a room, a church, a park, or a road. God is not limited by four walls. But it's that place where you feel like you fit. A favorite place. In Psalm 46:10 (AMP) it says, "Let be *and* be still, and know (recognize and understand) that I am God. I will be exalted among the nations! I will be exalted in the earth!" Sometimes being still and waiting, listening for God seems impossible! You think, "I'm too busy for that." If that's the case, then you are too busy. God wants to speak to you each and every day. He wants to show you things. He wants to tell you the great plan He has for you. He wants to help you with your decisions. He wants to be a part of your life. You have to position yourself to hear Him. Choose to make time for Him. Choose to get still. Choose to listen. Choose to thank Him. Choose to worship. Worship Him not only for what He has done in your life, but also for who He is. Have your place with God. He wants to meet you there. You don't have to have anything elaborate there. It's not a time to play games. It's time for you and Him to build your relationship. Fellowship. Discipleship. From this time with God you will be able to gain the most from each day. Then, step by step you will reach your destination. The place where you are destined to be.

14 January I remember a time when my boys would want my attention while I was working on some project. They would say, "Mom, Mom, Mom…" and when I was really concentrating on the other thing, I wouldn't respond. But then one would say, "Starr" and I responded. At the time I had only been 'Mom' for a short time. I have been 'Starr' all my life. Now I respond to 'Mom' too.

Today's song, "At Your Name" ~ Tim Hughes. The lyrics I'm hearing today are addressing God. In His name, mountains shake and crumble, the oceans roll and tumble. The angels will bow. The earth will rejoice, and His people will cry out, filling up the skies with praise. What happens when someone says your name? You respond. You pay attention. You're thankful they remembered you. Some one said that the sweetest thing you'll ever hear is the sound of your own name. So just think about when you call the name of Jesus. When you cry out to God. When you shout His name. There is power in the name of Jesus. Acts 4:10 (CEB) says, "…you and all the people of Israel need to know that this man stands healthy before you because of the name of Jesus Christ the Nazarene…" Because of the name. John 20:31 says, "but these are written that you may believe that Jesus is the Christ, the Son of God, and that believing you may have life in His name. " Life in His name. In the book of Acts, people were delivered and healed by the name of Jesus. And when we call upon God, His names: Jehovah, Elohim, El Shaddai, (there are many more) it will bring us into His presence. The key is to call the name that will arrest His attention for your situation. Is He Provider today? Healer? Victory? Peace? He's all of that and more. He's had these names since the beginning. He will respond when you call. Jeremiah 33:3 says, "Call to me and I will answer you…" Your praise, your worship touches the heart of God. You become engaged with His power and authority in your life. You can get excited. Shout. Tell others of His goodness, His mercy, His ability, His love for you. Fill the skies with praise today.

15 January When we were in youth ministry and my oldest son was about three or four years old we would come home from youth events and he would have lots of coins in his pockets. We found out that the teens were giving him their change. We aren't sure why. They just gave it to himand he received it gladly.

Today's song, "Speechless" ~ Israel & New Breed. This song says that I need and receive God's grace and it amazes me so much that I am speechless. He takes my breath away. God's grace is His unmerited favor. You don't earn grace. You can't buy grace. You can't always explain it, but it is yours when you have a relationship with God. Psalm 84:11 says, "For the Lord God is a sun and shield: the Lord will give grace and glory: no good thing will he withhold from them that walk uprightly." You may have had those times when you get to go to the front of the line, or something is free, or discounted, or there's a connection with someone who brings you business. Those are the times you think, "That's amazing." But even more amazing is His grace that will save you. His grace that will restore you. His grace that will heal you. His grace that will forgive you. His grace that will align you. Ephesians 2:8 says, "For by grace you have been saved through faith, and that not of yourselves; *it is* the gift of God." In both the spiritual and natural areas of your life, your pockets can be full. 2 Corinthians 12:9 says, "And He said to me, 'My grace is sufficient for you...'"He has enough of all you need. There is no lack in Him. If you had to do it on your own, it wouldn't be possible. You just aren't good enough. You aren't blameless. You aren't worthy. Christ paid the debt you couldn't pay. He paid with His life. So, today, think of all the things God has done for you, provided, protected, given, opened, handed, extended, and recovered for you. Be thankful. Know that God wants to bless you. He wants to give to you as a parent gives to his children. Matthew 7:11 says, "If you then, being evil, know how to give good gifts to your children, how much more will your Father who is in heaven give good things to those who ask Him!" He is good. No matter what the people in the world say or think, He is good. Good does not harm. Good does not abandon. Good does not fall short. Rejoice today. His grace is yours. Receive it, you need it. It's so amazing. It will leave you speechless; it will take your breath away.

16 January There was a time when I had to confront someone. It made me nervous just to think about it. So, I played it out in my head. I imagined the scene, the conversation, the argument, the rebuttal. I was prepared for all they had to hurl at me. I knew it could be messy and loud, and definitely emotional. I might even yell or maybe cry. But I was ready for all of it. Then, we met. Surprisingly, it was short and sweet. They apologized quickly and it was over. I thought, "But, but, but....I had it all rehearsed! I say this, you say that. What happened?" At first I felt cheated, and then I was glad it wasn't a knock-down, drag-out brawl. Sometimes it's not as bad as you make it out to be. Thank God.

The song for the day is, "Redeemed" ~ Big Daddy Weave. This song tells me to stop fighting a fight that's already been won. And that I am redeemed because Jesus set me free. A runner doesn't run another 10 miles right after he's won the race. A football player doesn't keep running through the goal posts repeatedly after a touchdown. A boxer doesn't keep fighting when his opponent is out cold. That would be silly. Yet, many times you continue to fight on a matter when God has already obtained the victory. You struggle, you strive, and you work at it even when it's been settled. I Corinthians 15:57 says, "But thanks be to God, who gives us the victory through our Lord Jesus Christ." No matter what it looks like today, you can be victorious through Jesus. Winning is inevitable. Though battles may not go as you thought, the final outcome will be to your favor. It's like with God the deck is stacked. It's a sure thing. But it's your choice to take advantage of it. How? Get quiet before God. Listen. He will guide and direct you. He will work on your behalf, behind the scenes. Look at what He has to say about the situation in His Word, the Bible. Do what you are prompted to do. Get help if you need it. Rejoice at the outcome even before it happens. Remember the promise that you are redeemed. You have been changed. You are free. The truth of Christ has set you in that place. See the enemy defeated. See him (the devil) out cold. You don't have to keep fighting, claim your victory today and thank God for it.

17 January One time, we remembered a movie that we had seen 'back in the day'. It was a cute movie about a gopher at a golf course. It had a catchy song. There was a funny scene with candy. So we thought, "That would be a fun movie to watch with our boys." We sat down with some popcorn and were ready to share some great laughs. Well, apparently we had selective memory. As we began to watch, we realized – this is not a family movie! Turning it off, our conclusion was that we had changed. That junk just wasn't so funny any more.

Today's song, "Jesus Friend of Sinners" ~ Casting Crowns. This song tells us to let our hearts be led by mercy and reach out with open hearts and open doors. Jesus is the friend of sinners. Our heart should break for what breaks His. It happens gradually. You can get immune over time to the things of this world. What is funny? What is acceptable? What is proper? What is polite? The lines get blurred unless you are diligent to keep them clear. Feeling like it's not a big deal is a dangerous place to be. Feeling like you don't care is precarious. So what, if you laugh at a dirty joke? So what, if you tell one next time? So what, if you watch that provocative movie? So what, if you have that drink? So what, if you are mean to someone because it's just funny? So what, if you...? It starts small and before you know it you have become a sad, mean, dependent, empty person. Wow, that's depressing. The key is to turn it around before it gets bad. You have to come to a place where you see what you've become. You have to see that it's breaking God's heart. And you have to see all those who are deceived into thinking poor behavior is okay. You can be the one who lifts them back up. Be an example. More than living your life as pleasing to God, you also must look at those who are not living that life as He sees them. He loves them. He believes that they deserve a second chance. Revelation 3:20 (MSG) says, "Look at me. I stand at the door. I knock. If you hear me call and open the door, I'll come right in and sit down to supper with you." That's Jesus. He's right there knocking on the door. Matthew 18:14 says, "...it is not the will of your Father which is in heaven, that one of these little ones should perish." God doesn't want to lose anyone. Be mindful of that, reach out to people. Be an influence for good. Be full of compassion. Soon, the junk in life won't be the same to you, because you have changed.

18 January I was excited to try a new recipe. It was a cake. With all the ingredients mixed and in the pan, it would only be a few more minutes until it was ready. Out of the oven and cooled just a little, I decided to taste it. Yuck! What happened? After a bit of detective work, I realized that I had left out the sugar. It's just not the same when something is missing.

The song today is, "Me Without You" ~ TobyMac. This song asks where I would be without you. Relationships are important. They can make such an impact on your life. There are different kinds of friends. Some people are friends because of business. Some people are friends from church. Some are friends because the children are friends. Some friends were classmates. Some friends you see occasionally. Some friends you see often. Some are close friends, some are just acquaintances. They are all ingredients in your life. They have had an influence, shaped the way you think. Your friends will determine your future. Your friends have helped you. They have been there for you. At times they have taken care of you. Watched out for you. Put up with you. Proverbs 18:24 (MSG) says, "Friends come and friends go, but a true friend sticks by you like family." There is great value in having and being a true friend. Proverbs 27:17 says, "Iron sharpens iron; so a man sharpens the countenance of his friend." Your relationships with your friends can make you sharper. They can make you better. Of course, the very best relationship you can have is that relationship with Jesus. That is the one that can sharpen you the most. That is the one that saves you from destruction. That is the one that makes the biggest difference, the one that is the key ingredient. Without Him, life can be 'Yuck!'

Take a look at your relationships today. Are they adding to your life? Are they like sweet ingredients to you? Are you being a good friend? Do you have a relationship with Jesus? What kind of friend is He? Occasional? All the time? Close? Acquaintance? Or best? Time to be honest. Time to be active in your relationships. Time to sharpen. Help your friends. Be mindful of all they've done for you. Thank them and then be their true friend. Be a part of their life. It won't be the same without you.

19 January This morning a song came to me at 2am. It was still there at 6am and 8am. Then when I got up, I got distracted. Had a cup of coffee. Looked at my calendar. When I sat down to write, the song was gone. I knew a couple lyrics but the tune escaped me. I settled in on this song, but I am not convinced it is the right one. So, here's today's song, "There Will Be A Day" ~ Jeremy Camp. It says that there will be a day when we'll see Jesus face to face.

Sometimes when you struggle to get it right and you don't think it's quite there, you need to realize that God is still with you. He's at your shoulder. He's guiding, giving wisdom, because it is not in your own strength that you accomplish what He has called you to do. Zechariah 4:6 says, "…'Not by might nor by power, but by My Spirit,' Says the LORD of hosts." You can rack your brain looking for the answer. If you would just be still and listen, His voice will speak to you. Today, He said to me, "Just use this song, I will help you." It's not the song that is the key, it is the message brought about by it. If you spend your time struggling, you will lose the point. If you get distracted, you must center yourself again.

There will be a day when you see Jesus face to face. He will be there and what can you say? That you were too busy striving to get it all right that you didn't have time to hear what He had for you? Or that you gave yourself a 'time out' to think about, pray about, and listen to Him? He will be there and you want Him to say you did well. If you feel like you've missed it today, just go ahead. Don't be stalled out. Push forward, but listen more. Search more for what He wants for you. Be brave. Be bold. Dive in. God will be there to show you. To guide you. To give you wisdom on how to proceed. 2 Corinthians 12:9 says in part, "My grace is sufficient for you, for My strength is made perfect in weakness." God shines even when you are weak. So don't fret today over getting everything just perfect. Let God give you a boost. When you reach for Him, there's nothing you can't do. Then when that day comes, you will be so happy to stand before Jesus – face to face.

20 January We took Ernie to Tulsa with us for a conference. Ernie was a stuffed toy. He belonged to my son. Somehow, Ernie got lost. We could not find him. So he stayed back in Tulsa, even though he was from another street. Amazingly, Ernie returned on Christmas Day! Back from his vacation, in a brand new box! I always liked Ernie's 'sticky up' hair. He was quite a character, and my son was glad to see him back.

Today's song, "The Hurt & The Healer" ~ MercyMe. This song reassures that I'm alive, even though a part of me has died. God takes my heart and breathes it back to life. When something or some one is lost from your life it can hurt. There may be tears. There may be blame. There may be emptiness. That sense of loss can change you. I've had some losses in my life. My parents and in-laws have all passed away. A good friend was killed by a drunk driver. Had my purse stolen three times. Been betrayed, lied to, talked about, and... Well, I have my own list, I'm sure you have yours. Dwelling on it can give you a hopeless feeling. But God can take your heart and breathe it back to life. Luke 4:18 says, "The Spirit of the LORD *is* upon Me, Because He has anointed Me To preach the gospel to *the* poor; He has sent Me to heal the brokenhearted, To proclaim liberty to *the* captives And recovery of sight to *the* blind, *To* set at liberty those who are oppressed;" and in The Message verse 19 says, "and to announce, 'This is God's year to act!'" What a great message it is! God will act on your behalf this year. He wants to restore what has been stolen. He wants to bind up your wounds. He wants to bring healing to your spirit. He wants you to be free this year from depression. It can be like Christmas for you as that which was lost is returned and in even better condition than when it left your life. It can be a thing, a relationship, or an attitude. Whatever it is you've lost in your life, seek God in the matter and He will turn it around for you. If you have gone away from God, now's the time to return, (even if you don't have it all together, or have 'sticky up' hair) He will be glad to see you back.

21 January My youngest son's first word was "ball". When he was just a couple years old he liked to sing "Take Me Out To The Ball Game". I use the word 'sing' loosely. Actually he shouted the entire song at the top of his lungs. Then he added a 4th strike to the lyrics before "...and you're out at the ole ball game!" He would sing it over and over – as long as he had an audience. That should have been a clue to me about his future as a performer.

The song this morning is "The Top of My Lungs" ~ Phillips, Craig & Dean. This song expresses such gratitude for all that God does. Because of that, I will sing Hallelujah at the top of my lungs! When I recount the life I have lived, my childhood, my marriage, my children, friends, family, faith, I am thankful. You can never feel embarrassed about being blessed. You need to boast on God's goodness. It's not so you can say, "Na na, look at what I got!" It's so you can say, "Look at God! If He can do it for me, He can do it for you." You should want to help others raise their belief level, not make them jealous. Just so, you cannot be jealous when others are blessed. Don't think that if someone is rich it's because they stole it or because they're just lucky. Don't expect them to give you some just because they have more. You should not be mad because you may have been overlooked. Rejoice! Your good attitude toward them will open up the opportunity for you to receive from God. In Luke 15 there are two examples of people who asked their friends to celebrate with them over their blessings. Then in Roman's 12:15 it says, "Rejoice with those who rejoice, and weep with those who weep." It's the right thing to do. Celebrate. Tell of God's goodness and how He had His hand on the situation. Give Him the credit, the glory for everything He has done. Realize His grace and His mercy are for all who call on Him. Reach for it, receive it, and then shout about it. Be happy for others. Don't be discouraged. You haven't messed up too much to get blessed. He will give you another 'strike'. You won't be out, you will be safe. Remember people are watching. God is too. How you respond will be a clue to your future.

22 January Do a strenuous activity and your heart rate increases. Then when you stop to rest, your heart is supposed to recover within about two minutes. Your heart recovery rate indicates your rate of mortality. So, the quicker your heart can recover, the healthier you are and the longer you are expected to live. I believe that a quick recovery is a good thing!

The song today is, "The Hurt & The Healer" ~ MercyMe. This song asks Jesus to come and break my fear, awaken my heart and take my tears away. There is more I am getting from this song today than in previous days. When something stressful happens, it affects your heart. Your spirit can be wounded. You can be devastated. It's okay to grieve. It's okay to feel the loss. You don't have to deny it. But, you do need to recover. Get back up on your feet and go on. Your life depends on your recovery. Your recovery depends on your view of the future. It's hope. Jeremiah 29:11 (CEB) says, "I know the plans I have in mind for you, declares the Lord; they are plans for peace, not disaster, to give you a future filled with hope." You must look forward and overcome the obstacles you see in your path. Those obstacles can be treated like barricades – made to stop you, or as hurdles – made to be jumped! Let the Lord wake up your heart today. Let Him wipe away your tears. If something has been stopping you because you are hurt, wounded, or lost, it's time to let Him take away your fears and your pain so that you can run again. All lives experience stressful events. You can't always avoid them. You can heal though. You can recover. And quick recovery means you're healthy!

23 January I didn't realize how perfect this song would be today when I heard it in my head about 4 am. Why perfect? Because I have had a weak day. Not feeling well. On the couch. Yuck. Writing now is even a chore, yet I write...

Today's song, "Lift Me Up" ~ The Afters. This song says that the Lord will lift me up when I am weak. His arms wrap around me. His love catches me so I can let go. This is truly a day when my reliance on God is paramount. My body has been letting me down, but my spirit is encouraged because God's love is a part of my life. I think of all the things I needed to do today, all the things I wanted to do, and I see that the most important thing right now is to just rest in Him. I think about something we used to do in youth group when I was a teen. It was called a 'trust fall'. You stood with your eyes closed, relaxed and fell backward. You trusted that someone in the circle surrounding you would catch you. They did. So, today it was a forced relax time. I trusted God. I know that I will be better soon. His arms wrap around me like a warm blanket. It's that feeling that you can have when there isn't a hand to hold or a shoulder to lean on. But God. He is there. He's that voice that says, "Everything's going to be okay." Psalm 29:11 says, "The Lord will give strength to his people; the Lord will bless his people with peace." This you can rely on. He will give you strength in the weak days. He will give you peace. Rest in Him. Fall into His arms of love today. If you know someone who is experiencing a time that is weak in their lives, share with them about His love and care for them. It doesn't have to be a 'yuck' day.

24 January In the movie, "The Sound of Music", there is an iconic scene of Julie Andrews on the mountain, spinning with her arms in the air and singing that 'the hills are alive with the sound of music'. That's what I picture this morning...

The song for today is, "At Your Name" ~ Tim Hughes. This song announces to the Lord that we'll shout His name and fill up the skies with endless praise. Imagine the perfect day. Imagine being extremely happy. Imagine peace. Imagine that feeling of bliss. What does it feel like? What does it sound like? Where are you? Who is with you? No matter the circumstances today, you can take yourself to that place. It's not just imagining, it's an attitude adjustment. It's a time to get your mind off your issues and look at the one who has had the answers all along. God. Praise Him today. Look to Him. Talk to Him. Ask Him. Reach out to Him. He will restore you to that place where you feel like singing and dancing on the mountain again. Remember Jonah. He was in the belly of the fish. Not a happy place. In Jonah 2:1-8 (MSG) He cries about it. In verse 9 it says, "But I'm worshiping you, God, calling out in thanksgiving! And I'll do what I promised I'd do! Salvation belongs to God!" He turns his crying into praise. Now look what happens in verse 10, "Then God spoke to the fish, and it vomited up Jonah on the seashore." Changing your attitude from pouts to praise can get you delivered from your situation! It really can be that easy. You must decide which place you want to be in today. In the dark, smelly belly of the fish or on the top of the mountain. Psalm 30:11-12 (MSG) says it wonderfully! "You did it: you changed wild lament into whirling dance; You ripped off my black mourning band and decked me with wildflowers. I'm about to burst with song; I can't keep quiet about you. God, my God, I can't thank you enough." Read that again. Then encourage yourself in the Lord today. He wants to change your situation. It all starts with your attitude.

25 January When our boys were little, we took them to the mall and met some friends and their son and daughter there. We went into the toy store. That was where we revealed the surprise to our children that we were all going to a famous theme park in Florida! They were thrilled! It was an exciting time of anticipation for them over the next several days. The trip was a great memory maker. It was wonderful!

Today's song is, "The Solid Rock" ~ Avalon. This song affirms that my hope is built on nothing less than Jesus' blood and righteousness. My pastor was teaching on 'Hope' and hope is the confident expectation that something good is going to happen. He said that Bible hope is confident. Those children were excited about an amazing trip they were going on. They didn't question thinking, "Are they lying to me?" or "Are we really going?" They expected that since we told them we were going, that we were going. Plain and simple. They knew something good was going to happen and they didn't act otherwise. Their confidence was in their parents. Their hope was in us. They could trust us. So where is your hope today? If it is built on Jesus, then you can trust Him. Your expectation can be high. When you check what Jesus said, you can certainly stand on the fact that He did not lie. Philippians 1:6 says, "Being confident of this very thing, that He who has begun a good work in you will complete it until the day of Jesus Christ." He's not going to walk away from you. You can expect Him to do a work in your life. Your attitudes and your expectations are the key. Be excited for all that is to come. Your best days are ahead.

26 January In the movie "Elf" Buddy encounters a wood-
land creature that is not happy to see him. He reaches out his
arms to the fuzzy raccoon and asks if he needs a hug. Unfortunately the critter is not receptive and chooses to attack.

Today's song is, "Closer/Wrap Me In Your Arms" ~ William
McDowell. This song asks God to draw me closer than ever before and wrap me in His arms. Sometimes you just need a hug.
Maybe it's been 'one of those days' or maybe you just don't feel
too great. Hugs are nurturing, comforting, settling, and convey
affection. They can be a stabilizer. They can be very healthy!
Drawing close helps to balance you. As important as human hugs
are, more important are the moments when you draw close to
God. He is the one who can heal your broken heart. He is the one
who can take away the pain. He is the one who can truly comfort
you. Psalm 71:21 says, "You shall increase my greatness, and
comfort me on every side." God will bring you to a better place. A
higher place. A place that is great. And He will comfort you in
every situation. The key is to seek Him. Reach out for Him in your
time of need. He will be there. You have to be receptive. Do not
attack God; He is the one who wants to hold tight to you. He loves
you. It's that closeness that will bring you through the trials and
issues of life. It's that closeness to God that will settle you. It will
nurture you and it will confirm that God has a great affection for
you. So, find someone who needs a hug today. Hopefully they're
not a nasty raccoon. And reach out for God today. He's reaching
to you saying, "Does somebody need a hug?"

27 January The 'Missing Man Formation' is a salute to someone who has been lost. Often performed by jets like the Blue Angels, it's a 'V' formation that passes over the site of a memorial service and one plane abruptly pulls away leaving a space in the group, signifying the person who died. If you have ever seen it, it is a moving tribute. Just thinking about it brings tears to my eyes. To think of the sacrifice made by those who serve our country. To know that so many have given their lives for our freedom.

The song for today is, "The Hurt & The Healer" ~ MercyMe. Part of this song talks about the moment when humanity is overcome by the majesty of God. Your mortal flesh is capable of a limited amount of things. You can push your flesh, but still there are limits. You are human. When God steps in, He can overcome the limitations of this life, exceeding the bounds of what you can do. His majesty is overwhelming. It should make you thankful. It may make you cry. You can look at God and be amazed. I am really thinking of sacrifice today. What is the point of sacrifice for all of us? It's that place of surrender. It's that place of dedication. It's that place where you stop trying to make it on your own. It's that place where you bring yourself before the altar of God and say, "I am yours." It's that place where He can overcome your humanity with His majesty. Hebrews 13:15 says, "By him therefore let us offer the sacrifice of praise to God continually, that is, the fruit of our lips giving thanks to his name." You bring the sacrifice of praise and thanksgiving. God sacrificed the life of His Son. And by Him you have been set free. You can enjoy that today, but you must remember the sacrifice - the one from God and the one of your own. You must make it significant. Praise should not be a second thought or an after thought. It should be a lifestyle. Your life of praise will be a tribute to the one who gave His life. Jesus.

28 January We were 17. We liked each other, but we weren't really ready to admit it. He and I were at a leadership retreat. It was winter. It was icy. When I slipped, he reached out for my hand. He said he didn't want me to fall. So I held on to him. That was our beginning. When we were 24 he became my husband. I was glad he was there for me. And he has been all these years.

The song this morning is "Right Beside You" ~ Building 429. This song reassures that I will be here through everything, just hold on, don't let go of me. Hold on, when you're ready to fall. I'll carry you. I won't leave you and I'll lift you if you do fall. I am so thankful for the incredible relationship I have with my husband. We have been together a majority of our lives. I know that he will be there for me when I need him. He likes to hold my hand. He is a great encourager. He is a great provider. He is a great husband. I would never want to be without him. He's amazing. Even more amazing is the relationship I have with the Lord. This song is about the way that God wants to be there with you through it all. He wants to hold your hand. He wants to be there when you fall, and even carry you when you need it. John 15:5 (AMP) says, "I am the Vine; you are the branches. Whoever lives in Me and I in him bears much (abundant) fruit. However, apart from Me [cut off from vital union with Me] you can do nothing." Without that connection with the Lord, you can't accomplish what you are called to do. You want Him to be there. You want Him to be a part of your life. There are great opportunities and possibilities when you do. Luke 1:37 says, "For with God nothing will be impossible." and Philippians 4:13, "I can do all things through Christ who strengthens me." The question is not what you can do on your own, but what can you accomplish with God? Anything! Don't run away from Him today. Reach out your hand and your heart to him. He loves you. Do you love Him too? Admit it. He is there for you and has been the whole time. He will never leave you. You don't want to be without Him.

29 January When we were camp directors we would have a day of 'messy games'. The teams of youth would play and cheer. They would get gooey and dirty and messy! It was so fun to watch as all the campers participated, laughed, competed, and enjoyed the events. Of course the winners always celebrated the loudest.

The song today is, "Stand Up, Stand Up for Jesus" ~ George Duffield, Jr. & George J. Webb. This song commissions Christians to stand up for Jesus as soldiers of the cross. His banner must be lifted and victorious. He will lead His army, vanquish every foe, and establish Christ as Lord without doubt. When we had the games at camp, we didn't let the kids just sit out and watch. Everybody played. No bystanders. It's the same with life. You can't just stand by and watch things happen. You can't stay out of the fight. The fight of faith. The fight for right. The fight for all that God has for you. You've got to get into the game. Choose a side. Be loyal to the team. Give it all you've got. Then give the rest. I'm talking about your spiritual fight. Your will. Your resolve that says, "I will do all I can." Keep the fight in you today that says, "I will not lose, I am not a loser" You must travel from victory to victory and triumph to triumph. 1 Corinthians 15:57 says, " But thanks *be* to God, who gives us the victory through our Lord Jesus Christ." God will give you the victory in your situation today. It may get messy. It may get dirty. But you must get going. The battle is to be won. Do not give up. Do not quit. Do not sit idly by. Do not observe from a distance. You are a part of the answer to the problem today. People need you. People are looking to you for what God wants to do through you. He will give you a strategy and He will give you a plan. Don't whine, WIN! Then you too can celebrate the loudest!

30 January It was exciting the year our baseball team won the World Series. We only had three tickets, so my husband and my two sons went to the game. I sat at home and watched it on TV. There I sat on the couch with my snacks and my giant foam hand gesturing the #1 sign, cheering them on. It was great! When they won I cried. I cried for two reasons, first because they were #1 and second because I wasn't there. It was great to hear all the stories when the guys got home, but it's never the same as when you get to experience it first hand.

Today's song is, "You Are God Alone" ~ Phillips, Craig & Dean. This song declares that from before time began, God was on His throne. He is God alone. God. The one true God. The Eternal God. He's always been there. Even when people have looked to other things as their source, He was there. He was the source whether they knew it or not. Whether they acknowledged it or not. God wants to be the only God in your life. Exodus 20:3 says, "You shall have no other gods before Me." When you get distracted and place your trust in things or people, you come up short. Matthew 6:33 says, "But seek first the kingdom of God and His righteousness, and all these things shall be added to you." When you have your priorities straight, things come your way. There is no lack. Being on the throne speaks of being in authority. You should look to God for your authority today. He will establish you. You must give Him the #1 place in your life. When you do that, you are surely a winner. But you want to experience it first hand. You don't want to observe from afar. It's not the same.

Make sure you are putting God first in your life. Don't leave Him behind. You may know the stories, but it's so much better to be in His presence. Hebrews 10:25 (CEB) says, "Don't stop meeting together with other believers, which some people have gotten into the habit of doing. Instead, encourage each other, especially as you see the day drawing near." Keep getting with other people of faith so that you can encourage and be encouraged. When you spend time putting God first together you will be able to cheer!

31 January One of my favorite quotes from Jim Rohn is, "If you spend five minutes complaining, you have just wasted five minutes. If you continue complaining, it won't be long before they haul you out to a financial desert and there let you choke on the dust of your own regret." It's a bleak picture for a complainer!

Today's song, "We Bring The Sacrifice Of Praise" ~ Kirk Dearman. This song tells about bringing the sacrifice of praise into God's house. We offer up the sacrifices of thanksgiving and the sacrifices of joy. Sometimes praise is a big sacrifice. Why? Because you absolutely do not feel like it. You want to go to bed and pull the covers up over your head. You'd rather pout. You fuss and whine. You think that's better. But it's not. People will hurt you, misunderstand you, and disregard you. They will be mean and unfair. They will be selfish, hurtful, and insulting. That's just how people are sometimes. That's when you throw up your hands and say, "God, I praise you anyway!" Make your energy positive. Make yourself smile. Be fascinated with the fix you are in. Don't be frustrated. Don't complain. It's a waste of time. Be thankful. Be joyful. There is a bright side, sometimes you need to look just a little harder for it. Hebrews 13:15 says, "Through Him, therefore, let us constantly *and* at all times offer up to God a sacrifice of praise, which is the fruit of lips that thankfully acknowledge *and* confess *and* glorify His name." If you have gotten into the habit of complaining, time to break it. You must replace it with words of praise. Make a list if you need to. A 'cheat sheet' if you will. Write some positive confessions to refer to when things or people get a little crazy in your life. You will find that things will begin to turn around for you. Your outlook determines your outcome. Keep praise on your lips. You don't want to get stuck in the desert and you don't want to choke on your regrets. Your joy, your thankfulness, and your praise will be the oasis you need!

1 February When the private school where I was principal was small, we went on monthly field trips in a huge group. Sometimes there would be up to 13 vehicles in a caravan driving to the destination. One key guideline on the road: Stay together! Another: If there's strife in your car, you must pull over until it's settled, and every car pulls off with you. It was amazing how we stayed together and the students learned to resolve disputes quickly and get along. After all, no one wanted to be the cause of the whole group being delayed. We had a lot of fun, successful outings those years. I was so proud of the students, teachers, and parents who went along all those times.

The song today is, "Whom Shall I Fear" ~ Chris Tomlin. This songs tells me who goes before me and who stands behind. It's the God of angel armies and He's always on my side. To stay in a caravan you have to pay attention to who is in front of you. You also need to check who is following so that you can stay together. Otherwise, you'll be lost. You've got to be in the right company. If you start following the wrong person, you will end up at the wrong destination. Just so in life, you have got to know who you are following. You've got to know who is on your side. You've got to know who to fear. Who to respect. Who will cause you delay and who will take you forward. When God is the one that is for you, no one can be against you. Romans 8:31 (MSG) puts it this way, "So, what do you think? With God on our side like this, how can we lose?" Having God on your side is a sure win. Don't be afraid of what might come, because He is working for your good. He is going before you to prepare your tomorrow. Exodus 23:20-22 (MSG) says, "Now get yourselves ready. I'm sending my Angel ahead of you to guard you in your travels, to lead you to the place that I've prepared. Pay close attention to him. Obey him. Don't go against him. He won't put up with your rebellions because he's acting on my authority. But if you obey him and do everything I tell you, I'll be an enemy to your enemies; I'll fight those who fight you." It's important to be obedient. Don't let strife in your life. Stay with the God who will fight for you. He will go before you. Do not let anything separate you. When you stay together, He will lead you to your destiny.

2 February When my oldest son was about three he would run into our bedroom early in the morning and declare, "The sun is up!!" He was so excited for the day to begin!! We sometimes were a little sleepy-eyed, but his enthusiasm could be contagious.

Today's song is, "What Life Would Be Like" ~ Big Daddy Weave. This song reminds me that Jesus made the lame walk and the dumb talk, opened blinded eyes to see. The sun rises on His time, yet, He knows what you need. Sometimes you can look at all that God does for other people and be amazed. It's big stuff. Financial breakthroughs, incredible healings, restoration of relationships. People's lives are dramatically changed. On an even grander scale He makes the sun to rise. (For the technically minded – He causes the Earth's rotation.) He truly has the whole world in His hands. He's not just 'The man upstairs', He's the God everywhere. And He's not the 'man behind the curtain', He's the God who rent the curtain of the temple in Matthew 27:51, signifying covenant fellowship with Him. So, even with all of this, God can still be present in your life personally. He can reach you on an intimate level. He's not too big for your life. He knows your needs. Matthew 6:8b says, "For your Father knows the things you have need of before you ask Him." and Ephesians 3:20 says, "Now to Him who is able to do exceedingly abundantly above all that we ask or think, according to the power that works in us." Not only does He know your needs, but He is able to work on your behalf – even more than you could imagine! However, He can do only according to the power that works in you. How big is He in you? How big is your faith? You know He can make the sun rise, but do you believe He can heal you? Do you believe He can restore you? Matthew 9:29 says, "Then He touched their eyes, saying, 'According to your faith let it be to you.'" You can have all that you believe. Do not think that you are insignificant to God. You are significant! He is ready to change your life today. Jesus' resurrection is proof that He is able to revive and restore you too. Look to Him, your Father, with enthusiasm and say, "The Son is up!" Your faith will be contagious and you can look forward to each and every day.

3 February One night we had a surprise snow storm. The snow is beautiful, but during the white-out my oldest son was traveling. Only ten miles from home, he decided to stop and wait in a gas station parking lot. When he called he assured me to not worry. He had warm clothes, food, and his phone. He could also go inside if need be. So he sat in his car and waited. Waited for the trucks to come blade the roads, for the snow to subside, and until he could see more clearly. He safelyarrived at home about an hour later.

Today's song is, "Good To Be Alive" ~ Jason Gray. This song declares that right here and right now, while the sun is shining I want to live like there's no tomorrow and love like I'm on borrowed time, because it's good to be alive. The storm wasn't too bad however; being out in the midst of it was a dangerous situation. Slick roads and low visibility made it treacherous. Timing was everything. When it was time to get on the road, the journey was much simpler. So, in considering the decisions you make in life each day, timing is important. You have to know when it's time to go and when it's time to wait. At some points, proceeding can be treacherous, and the journey can be tough. You may have to wait until your path is clear. We have been praying for a friend of ours, knowing that God would move on his behalf. Today he woke up and he knew things were different. There has been an inward change, not just with his health, but with his perspective. He said, "This is going to be a great testimony!" God has brought him through this storm. He didn't give up or give in to fear or disbelief. He did all he knew to do. And God was there all along. He showed up and showed off. What have you been waiting for today? Is it time to set out? Are the roads clear? Remember, they may not be perfect, but they may be safely passable. Don't be afraid. Don't worry if you have to wait. As long as you have God's provision, you will be okay. Philippians 4:19 says, "And my God shall supply all your need according to His riches in glory by Christ Jesus." His timing is perfect. Don't second guess, but stay in faith. Make decisions based on what He is speaking to your spirit. Not on what you think or feel. You will be on solid ground. You'll make it home safe, on time, and alive. And it's good to be alive!

4 February

"If at first you don't succeed, try, try again." I heard another take on that… "If at first you don't succeed, find out what 2nd place gets." There's no shame in 2nd place. There's shame in not wanting 1st. Settling for less. How much have you settled for 'good enough'? Too many times. There is always room for improvement. Why not go for 'best'? Did you ever hear a runner that was getting ready to run say, "I definitely do not want to win this one. I only want 2nd place." You would want to tell them to just go sit down. 1 Corinthians 9:24 (MSG) says, "You've all been to the stadium and seen the athletes race. Everyone runs; one wins. Run to win. All good athletes train hard. They do it for a gold medal that tarnishes and fades. You're after one that's gold eternally." Be driven. Be motivated. Be excellent. Be quality. Be ahead of the pack today. Stand up and stand out. Be noticed. Be a voice, not an echo. Be a presence, not a shadow. Be forward thinking, not reminiscent.

Today's song is "Whom Shall I Fear" ~ Chris Tomlin. This song admits that my strength is in Jesus' name. He saves, delivers and gives me victory. How do you strive for 1st? How do you reach for 'best'? Your strength is in the Lord. He enables you to go on when you think there's nothing left of you. He helps lift you up when you're weak. There is no substitute for your relationship with the Lord. Anything else is second best. Education alone won't make you smart enough. Lifting weights alone won't make you strong enough. It is God who will cause you to triumph. 2 Corinthians 2:14 (MSG) says, "…in Christ, God leads us from place to place in one perpetual victory parade." That is exciting! Psalm 18:32 (CEB) says, "Only God! The God who equips me with strength and makes my way perfect." He's the answer today. He has the plan. Choose to serve Him. Lean on Him. Search His word. He wants you to succeed. He wants the best for you. Don't settle for anything less. Keep going. Keep reaching. Keep advancing. Keep igniting your passion for best today. God will be there every step of the way and your race will be won.

5 February When my father passed away, my nephew up-on seeing 'Grandpa' in the casket asked, "Why does he have his glasses on if he's sleepin'?" Explaining death to a child can be interesting. Later comes the understanding. My dad had a heart attack and died two months before our wedding. I was devastated. I was mad at God. It paralyzed my faith. I felt lost. I felt betrayed. I felt like God had walked away from me. That was my dad! How could He do that? But, God did not take my dad. John 10:10 talks about the thief coming to steal, kill, and destroy. That thief is the devil. Not God. I got away from everyone, I went to the lake, I cried out to God. He spoke to me that day. He showed me His love. He showed me His promise. I realized that He wanted to bring me through this situation. My heart was softened and I understood. 1 Corinthians 15:36b (ERV) says, "When you plant something, it must die in the ground before it can live and grow." Now that doesn't mean a person in your life has to die before you will have a new life in Christ. It means that the selfish, carnal you must be laid aside, die, so God can do a new work in you. Something has to change. My return to God was complete when my pastor's wife asked me to tell my story. She knew by the Holy Spirit what had transpired in my Christian walk. I was so glad that I was in church that day.

Today the song is, "Great I Am" ~ New Life Worship. This song says that I want to be close to God's side. Heaven is real; death is a lie. Closeness to God is what you want whether times are good or times are bad. No life is without heartache. No life is without struggle or trials. Those times will come. But they do not have to stay. If they have come to dwell with you, it's time to tell them to move out. Your promise from God in John 10:10 is that He comes to give you life and life more abundantly. That is quality and quantity. You can have an amazing life and assured eternity in Heaven when you have Christ in your heart. John 3:16 (ERV) says, "Yes, God loved the world so much that he gave his only Son, so that everyone who believes in him would not be lost but have eternal life." Make Heaven real in your life today and share it with someone else. When trials come don't let them stay. When hurts happen, let them heal. When someone dies, find your life. Keep God close to your side.

6 February A couple of my friends discovered the power of energy drinks during a business trip last fall. They were so excited. Something new! They tasted good! So fun! But then, when they got ready to go to sleep, guess who couldn't stop talking? When I heard this story I had to laugh, because these gals are talkers without the extra caffeine. There was still a lot of chatter about it the next morning. I joked with the sister who introduced them to these new libations that she had truly created a monster! We were wondering if they would ever calm down....but it certainly made for an entertaining day.

Today's song, "Word Of God Speak" ~ Mercy Me. This song asks God to speak and pour down like rain. Let me see His majesty. Let me rest in His holiness, knowing that He is in this place. Energy drinks or not, life can get hectic, busy, and fast-paced. You can feel like you are running a marathon or on a merry-go-round. People can be coming at you from all sides. You are making fast decisions. You are organizing, working, traveling, working, running, working, and administrating your life. You want to do things when it's less busy, but it doesn't get less busy. So you have to make yourself stop for a moment and breathe. Catch your breath. Calm yourself. Take a break. Give yourself a 'time-out'. Psalm 46:10 says, "Be still, and know that I *am* God;" You should let go of your concerns. Then you will know that He is God. It's a call to relax. Settle. Listen. Listen to God speak to you. Get quiet before Him. Let Him wash your eyes of all the clutter in your life so you can see how great He is. Stay and rest in Him for awhile. You will find yourself spiritually energized. Hang out with God. You will find yourself strengthened. You will be refreshed and calm, ready to take on all that God has for you.

7 February My mother often told me that if I have a bad dream that I should flip my pillow over because there are always better dreams on the other side. And you know, even now it works. I think of her every time I find myself flipping that pillow.

Today's song, "Great I Am" ~ Phillips, Craig & Dean. This song tells of the power of God; He is the great 'I Am'. The mountains shake before Him, demons flee, and there is nothing in hell or anyone who can stand above His power and presence. When you have a nightmare, it's just a dream. Not real. Sometimes you aren't sure if it really happened or not. Your mind works over-time to build concepts, ideas, and scenarios both positive and negative during waking hours as well as in sleep. You have to navigate what is real and what isn't. It can affect you. Sometimes the thoughts can be overwhelming. They can be scary. They can become obstacles. But God is the Great I AM. God will shake those mountains of uncertainty for you. God will stand up for you. God will be present when you need Him. It reminds me of another song by Carole King titled "You've Got A Friend" This song says to call out my name and wherever I am I'll come run-ning. In every season, call and I'll be there. That's God. He's a 'right now' God. The demons flee when you mention His name. The air clears. You can see better spiritually. You can breathe that sigh of relief. You can rest. As you gather your thoughts, your focus on God will reveal your destiny. The obstacles will be moved. The path will be open. The road will be ahead of you. Banish the nightmares. Banish the negativity. Banish all that would come against God's plan for you. Flip your pillow (change how you're thinking) and find the dreams God has for you. They are so much better than the nightmares. Proverbs 3:24 says, "When you lie down, you will not be afraid; Yes, you will lie down and your sleep will be sweet." You will have a good night's sleep and you will wake up refreshed and powerful!

8 February Take a magnifying glass outside on a sunny day, angle it just right and you can burn stuff. Technically, you are concentrating energy to a single point which creates high localized energy, which will actually ignite the object of focus. Like I said, you can burn stuff. We did it when I was growing up, maybe you did too. It's a great science experiment, but also fun. Of course, as long as no one gets burned in the process.

The song for today is, "You, You Are God" ~ Gateway Worship. This song recognizes God as the King of everything. He is Lord, who I live for and praise with my life. Focusing on God is concentrated energy. When you seek Him with all you have, love Him with all you have, there is a supernatural energy that you can tap into. Mark 12:30 says, "And you shall love the Lord your God with all your heart, with all your soul, with all your mind, and with all your strength. Then in The Message it says, "… so love the Lord God with all your passion and prayer and intelligence and energy." It's the part of you that says, "I will pay attention to what God has for me." It's the part of you that will ignore the naysayers, the pouters, the people who just want to complain. It's the part that disregards the mess and looks for the miracles. It's the part that presses forward when you just want to quit. It's that passion. That drive. That humility that seeks the Father, the Lord, in every situation because you know you can't do it on your own. Philippians 4:13 says, "I can do all things through Christ who strengthens me." The possibilities. The opportunities. The favor. All can ignite in your life when you are focused on your true power source, the One who strengthens you. It's that power that assures you that 'You Can'. So, today look at where your focus lies. See what you are really living for. Is it people? Things? Success? Prestige? Riches? Position? Or is it God? Matthew 6:33 says, "But seek first the kingdom of God and His righteousness, and all these things shall be added to you." When God is first place in your life, the other things will follow. Right priorities will always pay off. You may have been burned in the past, but today is a new day. Refocus. Look to God, He is the author and the finisher of your faith. He is the King of everything. He's worth living for.

9 February The news reports that some one is 'offended' every day. Whether it is because of religion, race, sex, morality, politics, finances, taxes, laws, healthcare or something else, they are offended and feel like some one should accommodate them. Matthew 10:16 (MSG) gives us, as Christians, a strategy... "Stay alert. This is hazardous work I'm assigning you. You're going to be like sheep running through a wolf pack, so don't call attention to yourselves. Be as cunning as a snake, inoffensive as a dove." It's important to walk in wisdom, because the Kingdom of Heaven is your real home. Your job here is to be an influence, love God, and love people. You may wonder why the people of God are so persecuted. 2 Timothy 3:12 (MSG) says, "Anyone who wants to live all out for Christ is in for a lot of trouble; there's no getting around it. Unscrupulous con men will continue to exploit the faith. They're as deceived as the people they lead astray. As long as they are out there, things can only get worse." Don't be depressed, be of good courage because John 16:33 says, "These things I have spoken to you, so that in Me you may have peace. In the world you have tribulation, but take courage; I have overcome the world."

The song today is, "Jesus In Disguise" ~ Brandon Heath. This song asks God to open my eyes wide. Open your eyes to see by the spirit what is really going on in the world. If you focus on all that is bad and evil in the world, you will lose hope. Stay off of the band wagons of offense. Be motivated by love, compassion, and care for others. Psalm 119:165 says, "Great peace have they which love thy law: and nothing shall offend them." People are so offended is because they do not love God's law. The issue is their salvation, not what they are offended over. Pray for and become a positive testimonial for those who are lost. But don't think that persecution will go away. Just have the assurance that shows up in Romans 5:20 that, "Moreover the law entered that the offense might abound. But where sin abounded, grace abounded much more," God's grace will abound in your life; it will overtake the sin. Don't fret over the condition of the world. Test the condition of your own heart. Ground yourself in the Lord. He will sustain you and cause you to succeed. Approach it with open eyes to see Him always working on your behalf. Be wise in your dealings and you can draw people into salvation and peace.

10 February Mysteriously, my husband's shirts acquire recurring stains while traversing through the laundry. I don't know what it is. They can be pre-treated and washed out but stains reappear. It's interesting. It's quite possible that my laundry techniques would not have detected the stains in the first place. Could it be in the water?

The song this morning is, "Nothing But The Blood" ~ Matt Redman. This song asks and answers, what can wash away our sins and make us whole again? Only the blood of Jesus. Morning rain is a reminder of how God's spirit can wash over you. It's a cleansing. It's a refreshing. It's a calming feeling. Though your life may be stained with the sin of your past, it can be washed clean. 1 John 1:9 says, "If we confess our sins, he is faithful and just to forgive us our sins, and to cleanse us from all unrighteousness." God doesn't just pre-treat, He cleanses it all. The stains of those sins don't reappear. How can this be? Because of Jesus. He knew no sin, yet became sin for you. He paid the price you could not pay. He bridged the gap between you and God by His crucifixion and resurrection. Jesus was the sacrifice that was more than the judgment. It took care of the transgressions. It started a clean slate for all who believe. Today, don't be hampered by the thought of whatever you have done wrong. Don't be stalled by any mistakes. Don't be hindered by sin or your past. Turn to Jesus. His blood sacrifice has cleansed you. When you confessed, it was done. So, get on with what God has for you. What you have come through will be a tool to help others. You will know first hand how to handle what they are going through. As you stand clean before God, He will clothe you. Isaiah 61:10 says, "I will greatly rejoice in the Lord, my soul shall be joyful in my God; for He has clothed me with the garments of salvation, He has covered me with the robe of righteousness, as a bridegroom decks himself with ornaments, and as a bride adorns herself with her jewels." Picture yourself completely clean before God and Him helping you get ready for one of the most important days of your life. Start each day that way. You will walk and talk differently. You will go forward knowing that you are forgiven. Knowing that you start fresh. God's mercies are new every morning. (Lamentations 3:22-23) Great is His faithfulness.

11 February I was at a fast food restaurant one day and as I was leaving I saw a friend in the drive-thru lane. Running back inside, I made it just in time to pay for her lunch anonymously. I had felt prompted by God to do something nice that day and I obeyed. It's great to be blessed, but greater to be a blessing.

Today's song, "I Give Myself Away" ~ William McDowell. This song says that I give myself away so God can use me. How warm your heart gets when you show love for someone. Kindness. Selfless gestures. Caring. Compassion. It's that action that conveys to another that they are important. They matter. Somebody cares. It makes you think more about what you can do to impact a life today. What can you do with excellence that makes God look good? (And not what just makes you look good.) Let yourself be used of God with a humble heart. Romans 12:3 says, "For I say, through the grace given unto me, to every man that is among you, not to think of himself more highly than he ought to think; but to think soberly, according as God hath dealt to every man the measure of faith." You have to remember that just because you do something nice that you are not 'all that and a bag of chips' important. You are an instrument to be utilized for good works. Colossians 3:23 (MSG) says, "...don't just do the minimum that will get you by. Do your best. Work from the heart for your real Master, for God, confident that you'll get paid in full when you come into your inheritance. Keep in mind always that the ultimate Master you're serving is Christ." So, do these things as unto the Lord. Do them with a whole and pure heart. It's that attitude of giving that you need to embrace. It's that attitude of selflessness and love. When you feel in your heart that you need to do something to help some one, do it. Do not hesitate. There is a reason that God places that person on your heart. God will not ask you to do a thing that you cannot do. James 4:17 (CEB) says, "It is a sin when someone knows the right thing to do and doesn't do it." This is enough for you to see how important it is for you to do those good deeds. When God finds you in a position to give, that is the time to act. He can use you through a chicken sandwich or a listening ear. Whatever it is, you give yourself away. It doesn't matter if it's known that you did it or not. So go, do something good today! Be a blessing and you will be blessed!

12 February I went out to start the old truck one morning and it wouldn't turn over. I kept trying. Suddenly I heard a commotion from under the hood. A kitten had crawled inside and was scrambling to escape. I found there were actually three kitties in there and they ran out in three directions. They all got out okay. Only one with minor injuries. So, once the engine was clear, the truck started and I got on my way.

Today the song is, "You Are Everything" ~ Kutless. This song talks of God being the strength in my weakness, my refuge and everything I need. The kittens sought refuge that morning in the truck, but it was not a safe haven. It could have easily been a death trap. Thankfully, they averted calamity. You have to choose wisely when you seek refuge. Psalm 46:1 says, "God is our refuge and strength, a very present help in trouble." If you are hurting today or afraid or need rest, choose God. If you are weak or sick or spent, choose God. If you are helpless, hopeless, or apathetic, choose God. He is there ready to assist. He will guide you. He will comfort you. He will strengthen you. Stuff will happen in life and it will cause a commotion, attempt to hinder your progress, even stop you. That's when you take a look at what's settled in your heart and mind and stir it up. What shouldn't be there needs to get out. If it's a bad attitude, a grudge, a hurt, a betrayal, or a disappointment, you can overcome it by taking refuge in God. Turn it over to Him. He will get you going again. He is everything you need.

13 February I was in labor with my first son. It was a long night. Though I was getting a dose of inducement drugs, the contractions were still minimal. My husband was right by my side. I held his hand through the rail of the hospital bed, looked at him and said, "I don't think I want to do this." He reminded me that I was already committed. There was only room to go forward in this endeavor. The baby was born just after midnight. My husband slept on the floor that night. He stayed right there with me and our new 'bundle of joy'!

Today's song, "Your Love Never Fails" ~ Jesus Culture. This song reminds me that there may be pain in the night but joy will come in the morning. If you ever get around a bunch of moms telling their birthing stories it can get to be a contest of sorts. One wild story after the other. When you're pregnant you don't want to get into the middle of that circle, especially if it's your first baby. It can be pretty dramatic! You may recall the pain, but it is ultimately eclipsed by the joy of the newborn. So in life there will be pain. There will be hurt. But it doesn't have to linger. You go through the pain. Then you can see the victory on the other side of it. Psalm 30:5b says, "Weeping may endure for a night, but joy comes in the morning." In The Message translation, "The nights of crying your eyes out give way to days of laughter." So, there is a light at the end of the tunnel. That cloud has a silver lining. It will all come out in the wash. So many times we hear these adages. They are true – With God. Psalm 18:32 says, "It is God that girds me with strength, and makes my way perfect." God gives you the power to get through the dark of night. Your horrible times. Your painful times. Your disparaging times. He brings you to the light of the morning that is joy. Nehemiah 8:10 says, "Do not sorrow, for the joy of the Lord is your strength." He is still your strength. The joy that comes in the morning will bring you into a new day. A new perspective. A new attitude. A new vision. A new direction. In pain? Take your time, stay committed. God will bring you through. Know someone in pain today? Remind them that God is their strength. Though they may labor in pain, they do not labor in vain. God has great joy for them on the other side of it. They are birthing something amazing and in time, those 'babies' grow up to be mighty 'men' of God!

14 February Today's song is, "Jesus In Disguise" ~ Brandon Heath. I looked at this song today and thought about what I could possibly see. There have been other days for this tune and I easily discerned what God wanted me to write about. Really, I thought I had exhausted the song. "What else could there be, God?" I asked. Today was hard. He urged me to look deeper. The lyrics in this song are a reflection of how I have been writing. Each day I seek God. Yield to Him for what He would have me say and only today have I seen the part of the song that says to speak the word my lips have never known because my heart told me. My heart is my spirit. God's Spirit, the Holy Spirit, speaks to my spirit. That is what I write. I don't want to get all spooky, but sometimes it's hard to explain. Supernatural? I believe so. Mystical? Not so much. Crazy? No. How I submit myself to God is manifest in the writing. It's a great exercise in staying open to the presence and urging of the Lord. Psalm 119:13-16 (MSG) says, "I'll transfer to my lips all the counsel that comes from your mouth; I delight far more in what you tell me about living than in gathering a pile of riches. I ponder every morsel of wisdom from you, I attentively watch how you've done it. I relish everything you've told me of life, I won't forget a word of it." The words of my mouth should be what God is telling me. His wisdom. His guidance. His example in Jesus. Pressing in brings the thoughts, the words, the sentences, the stories, the verses – all of it.
If you feel like your heart has not been open to God, stop and pray right now. Ask Him to open it to what He has to say about your situation, your relationships, and your life. It will be far better than anything you could dream up on your own. His hand will be on it and you will be blessed. Relish all He says and don't forget a word of it.

15 February Driving through the automated car wash struck terror in the heart of my son. Everything would be sunny and happy, and then suddenly water was pelting the outside of the car. Visibility limited. Then suds! Oh the suds! Everywhere! Visibility zero! Then the tears, the crying. "It's okay" I say. "We're safe" I assure. "It's a car wash" I affirm. Then the huge tentacles slapping the outside of the car like a giant octopus. And then the deafening sound of the blowers shaking the windows and obliterating the water drops, creating the appearance of entering warp speed. Then the quiet as we exited. Only faint sobbing was audible from the back seat. It took awhile before he saw that his anticipated 'impending doom' was only a process to eliminating the dirt that had plagued the outside of our vehicle. Eventually, as he grew, car washes became great adventures and they weren't so scary anymore.

Today's song is, "Your Love Never Fails" ~ Newsboys. This song assures that when the oceans rage, you don't have to be afraid. Things can be terrifying when you don't understand. You can fear the unknown. You think – What is happening? You don't know if you can stop it. You don't know if you'll live through it. You can't see what's ahead. You don't know what's causing it. So, what do you do when you find yourself in that situation? Realize that you can rest safely in the arms of God. You do not have to be afraid. Proverbs 1:33 (NIRV) says, "But those who listen to me will live in safety. They will not worry. They won't be afraid of getting hurt." If you listen to your feelings, they will lead you astray. They are fickle. You must listen to God. His word. His assurance. His affirmation that everything will be okay. Then you can know you are safe. You may not know all the details of what is happening in your life, but you can be assured that God knows the end from the beginning. He has a great plan for you. So you don't have to be afraid. He just wants to restore you to Him. Putting you in a position for your life to become spotless. Stuff may be happening on the outside, but know that God has you protected inside where the storm cannot destroy you. So listen to God today and trust Him. Let your life be a great adventure, it won't be so scary anymore!

16 February We found a great place to stay on vacation. The lodge had a walking trail behind it so the four of us decided to go. It was getting dark so we brought flashlights. Our youngest was about three years old, so he rode on daddy's shoulders, and instead of shining it on the path, he put the flashlight in his mouth. His whole face lit up! Literally! We had a great time. It was unforgettable!

The song for today is, "You Are Everything" ~ Kutless. This song reminds me that when life is a mountain that I can't climb, Jesus will carry me. When the terrain is rough and your footing is unsure, you can depend on Jesus in your life to carry you. Atop His shoulders, which bore the weight of the world, the sins of the world, your perspective will be so much better. You have to let Him be a part of your life. Let Him help. Reach out to Him and He will pick you up. So many times you think you can do it all on your own. You think you're strong enough. You think you're mature enough. You think you're independent enough. But you are *not* enough. You are just a mere mortal. 1Peter 5:10 (NIRV) says, "God always gives you all the grace you need. So you will only have to suffer for a little while. Then God himself will build you up again. He will make you strong and steady. And he has chosen you to share in his eternal glory because you belong to Christ." He will establish, strengthen, and settle you. The joy of the Lord is your strength today. He is enough. He is more than enough. One of His names is 'El Shaddai' which means 'the God who is more than enough.' Should there be any question at all today, affirm El Shaddai as your God and Jesus as Lord. You will never fall short. You will be carried through all the stuff life has to throw at you. Jesus, the light of the world, will direct your path and make your way clear. Burdens will be lifted, your face will light up, and your great life will be unforgettable.

17 February When we built our house, I wanted an oval window on the wall in our bedroom. It was a splurge in the budget and so we decided not to get it. While I was out of town, my husband called and said there was a change and we had enough to add the window. Wonderful! It's a beautiful oval window on the east end of the house. He called me in this morning to look at the sunrise. It was picture perfect! I thought, "May we never take for granted the beauty of the sunrise and may we always welcome each new day." Even now as I look out on the horizon, I appreciate the gorgeous view of this golden sunrise.

Today's song is, "Lift Me Up" ~ The Afters. This song talks about seeing the dawn breaking and feeling overtaken with God's love. Starting each day with God should be as consistent as each morning beginning with a sunrise. It's magnificent! Taking time to feel His love in the midst of anything that might try to plague your day is necessary to center yourself. It gets you a better perspective. It calms you. It reminds you that God loves you. He thinks you are significant. He believes you can do what He has called you to do. When you feel like something's impossible, He proclaims, "It is possible!" Matthew 19:26 says, "But Jesus beheld them, and said unto them, 'With men this is impossible; but with God all things are possible.'" I also like The Message which says, "Jesus looked hard at them and said, 'No chance at all if you think you can pull it off yourself. Every chance in the world if you trust God to do it.'" I love that! You have every chance in the world if you trust God! He will do it! The fretting can stop. The worry, the fear, the doubt, the wondering. Can God? God can! Of course He can. Some one said to let go and let God. It doesn't mean give up and quit. It means to accept His help. Don't be selfish or prideful. Stop trying to do it on your own. Let His love overwhelm you today. Let the sunrise be a reminder to you that He wants to be a part of your life and He wants you to have every chance in the world to succeed. With Him each day can be magnificent!

18 February

With caller ID, you can see who it is before you answer the phone. Screening my calls has become habitual. I decide who I want to speak with or who I have time to speak with. I can let people leave messages. If I don't answer then I think, "If it's important, they will call back." Sometimes they do. The thing is, when I call and someone doesn't answer it gets frustrating. Why don't they want to talk with me? I am a likeable person, am I not? They are too busy for me? Loveable me? I know it's usually not that personal. I hear you saying, "Calm down, it's no big deal." It's just not always as important to the other person as it is to me that they answer. So, I will keep trying...

Today's song is, "I Am A Friend Of God" ~ Israel Houghton. This song asks who am I that God is mindful of me and that He would hear my call? Yes, God has caller ID. He knows when you're calling and you are important to Him. He hears you and He answers. Psalm 118:5 says, "I called upon the Lord in distress: the Lord answered me, and set me in a large place." So, you call upon Him and not only will He hear and answer, but He will also put you in a good place, a large place, which is freedom. Things in your life may be tying you up. Binding you. Hindering you. Keeping you captive. True freedom comes from turning to God. John 8:32 says, "And you will know the Truth, and the Truth will set you free." That Truth is Jesus. He is the key that will unlock the door. You are on His mind today. Being a friend means that you communicate. You fellowship. You spend time together. That's what friendship with God includes. It enhances your life. He enhances your life. Jeremiah 33:3 (MSG) says, "Call to me and I will answer you. I'll tell you marvelous and wondrous things that you could never figure out on your own." Why not tap into your source today? You won't have to leave a message with God. There is so much more He wants to tell you. So you have to answer when He calls too. You'll know when it's Him. Just don't hang up. You're important. He will never regret His call to you. He's never too busy to talk.

19 February Years ago, we were at a crossroad in our life and we had some serious decisions to make about our future. My husband and I talked and prayed. One thing I knew, no matter what, that we would be okay because we would be together. When I made the decision to spend the rest of my life with him, it was settled. There is no other option for us. We are committed and there has never been a question about it

The song for today is, "Right Beside You" ~ Building 429. This song assures that when the world is on your back and you think that you won't last, when you're lonely and confused, He will be right beside you. Sticking with a person through 'thick and thin' is admirable, but unfortunately it can be unusual. Pledges must mean something. A covenant is a promise to keep. There is a particular bond between a husband and wife that cannot be duplicated in a mere friendship. It cannot be reproduced with same sexes. It is different than a parent and a child. There really is nothing like it except the relationship that Jesus has with the church. Ephesians 5:23-25 (MSG) describes it this comparison. "Wives, understand and support your husbands in ways that show your support for Christ. The husband provides leadership to his wife the way Christ does to his church, not by domineering but by cherishing. So just as the church submits to Christ as he exercises such leadership, wives should likewise submit to their husbands. Husbands, go all out in your love for your wives, exactly as Christ did for the church—a love marked by giving, not getting." Marriage is not 'give and take' it is 'give'. Receiving is a benefit, not a goal. There is a purposeful design in marriage that God has established. The key is committing, staying, respecting, and loving one another. There is a fit between husband and wife that makes a strong union. And, whether you are or are not married, you must still establish a relationship with God. He loved you first. So much He gave His Son for you. He should be the basis for all your relationships. He will be present when you need Him, right beside you. Recommit to your husband or wife today if you are married. Be the person who attracted them in the first place. If you aren't married and you wish to be, draw closer to God, let Him establish you. Don't get in a hurry. Then when you make that commitment, there should be no question.

20 February I got a notice from my phone… "Battery low, please charge." Really? I thought I just charged it. Where has the energy gone? It wouldn't work without power. My husband says to charge it every night. I admit, I forget. I think it will work enough the next day before I have to hook it up to the charger. Wrong again. So I apologized. I am striving to be more diligent in keeping it connected.

The song today, "All Things Possible" ~ Mark Schultz. This song encourages me to hold on; there is strength in knowing I belong to God, who makes all things possible. When your spiritual battery is low, you need to charge it up. That strength comes from the Lord. You have to know that with Him all things are possible. Then you will have the ability and the fortitude to do what He has called you to do. You just have to be connected. Daily. Matthew 19:26 says, "But Jesus looked at them and said, With men this is impossible, but all things are possible with God." (This verse is also in Mark and Luke!) What a great guard against defeat! Knowing that something is possible keeps you looking forward. It's hope. It gives you power today. You can continue to look at the situation from different perspectives, stay in prayer, seek help and come to the conclusion when you know that it's possible. If you've messed up, or you've neglected to include God, just apologize. He forgives. He remains with you. He continues to help as long as you are willing to receive His help. Just stay hooked up and God will see you through what you're going through today.

21 February There's a movie where the little guy stands up to his nemesis against whom he seemingly has no chance of survival when several large men step in behind that guy to assist in his defense only to result in the swift departure of the opposition! In other words, the big guys stand up with the little guy and the enemy flees! I love that scene!

Today's song, "Whom Shall I Fear" ~ Chris Tomlin. This song assures me that the One who reigns forever is my friend. The God of angel armies is always by my side. Snow is now gently falling as I sit to write today. It reminds me of the power of unity. One snowflake by itself is insignificant, but what an impact it makes when they band together in the hundreds of millions! A force to be reckoned with! Just so is the result of banding together with God – A force to be reckoned with! God, for you, is power. Is confidence. Is victory. Is success on so many levels. When the enemy comes for you, you can boldly confront him, knowing that God's angel armies are on your side. They are the 'big guys' behind you. Then, look! The enemy runs away! Romans 8:31-33 (MSG) says, "So, what do you think? With God on our side like this, how can we lose? If God didn't hesitate to put everything on the line for us, embracing our condition and exposing himself to the worst by sending his own Son, is there anything else he wouldn't gladly and freely do for us? And who would dare tangle with God by messing with one of God's chosen? Who would dare even to point a finger? The One who died for us—who was raised to life for us!—is in the presence of God at this very moment sticking up for us." Security. When you are a friend of God, they can't touch you. As long as you stay under His umbrella, you are okay. That means obedience to His Word. That means doing what you know to do. That means repenting when you've messed up and believing that God forgives you. Walk in a manner pleasing to Him, be fruitful and increase in knowledge. (Colossians 1:10) Then He has you covered. Know who is on your side today, and know whose side you are on. God's side assures confidence, boldness, power, and strength. So, stand up straight, hold your head high, and confront whatever the world wants to throw at you because when you choose the winning side, nothing can stop you.

22 February After a half foot of snowfall, my husband and son trekked out to the store. My son came back in the house a few minutes after they left. "We're stuck." he said. After some pushing and shoveling they were on their way. Awhile later they arrived home. "We're stuck again." Process repeated, my husband navigated back into the garage. Victory! Adventure is great. Safe and warm at home is great. Eating popcorn and watching a movie is also great.

The song today is, "Only The World" ~ Mandisa. This song reminds me that the best is still yet to come. Even when my days here are done there will be so much more than 'only the world' for me. Sometimes it snows. Sometimes there's a storm. Sometimes it's really hot. The weather changes daily where we live. People still go to work. People still do things. Even if travel is difficult, it doesn't stop everything. You can get upset about it or deal with it. That's what the world is like. It's only the world. The state of your eternity does not hinge on a cloudy day or a sunny day. It comes from a decision you make in your heart. Impervious to the elements. Safe from the effects of the stuff of life. Having a bad day, or a weird day, or a dumb day should not sway your decision to follow the Lord. You are bigger than that. You are better, stronger, and more mature than to be taken aback by a setback. Some one said that you should always let a set back be a set up for a come back! Ephesians 4:14-15 is a reminder to grow up, don't let things or people move you from your relationship with Christ, saying "that we should no longer be children, tossed to and fro and carried about with every wind of doctrine, by the trickery of men, in the cunning craftiness of deceitful plotting, but, speaking the truth in love, may grow up in all things into Him who is the head—Christ—" So be firm and steadfast in your decision today to follow the Lord. Be decided. Be strong in it. Grow up as needed to steady yourself so you can thrive. If you feel stuck, seek help. You may need a little push. You may need to shovel some of the junk out that has accumulated in your life. If it happened before, it could happen again. Be of good cheer! You can have victory today. Remember, it's only the world and I can assure you that the best is yet to come!!

23 February I am the baby of the family. The four of us span 19 years. My brother has inspired me with his organizational skills. He keeps records. He numbers things. He knows what happened on a certain day 2 years ago and has it written down in a book in his shirt pocket. My sister has inspired me to write. She wrote poems before I did. If she's reading this right now, she's probably proof reading it too. My other sister has inspired me as a florist. Her creativity and skill, outstanding. More recently, she has dramatically changed her life. In ways she is a different person. She made a decision to do something about her situation and has gone through a laborious and amazing transformation. It is inspiring. All of my siblings have had an impact on my life for good. I am grateful for each one of them.

The song for today is, "Who You Are" ~ Unspoken. This song tells me that it's never too late, so bad, or so much that you can't change who you are. There is a lot of talk about 'reinventing yourself'. A reinvention comes from an idea, a situation, or a need in your life. It's taking a look at who you are or what you have become and thinking "I can have more, be more, do more." It's looking at your situation and thinking, "Things could be better, I could be better." It's not a time to cry in your cereal. It's a time to make a decision. It's time to resolve to make changes. It could be a health issue. Have you talked to people who are battling diseases? Are you experiencing some atrophy? What choices are you making regarding your health? It could be a relationship issue. Know people who aren't getting along? Not talking to one another? Bad influences? What choices have you made in your relationships? Maybe it's financial. Know folks who barely have enough to buy food? Ones who spend but don't save? They think money buys happiness? What financial choices have you made? There are so many areas of life that can be changed. So pick something you need to change. Get creative. It's not too late. Decide. Then follow through. Get help if you need it. You will have control in that area. It will influence other areas of your life. Eventually, it will influence other people. My son posed this question, "Don't give up now, 'cause if you did, how many people did you just influence to give up as well?" Be tenacious. Things can be different. You can be different.

24 February Our field trip to the zoo. How many times had we been there before? I don't know. A lot. This time we strolled through the ape house gazing at the primates through thick Plexiglas. Kind of sad, I thought, that the monkeys were just trying to live their life while droves of school children and chaperones stared at them. A few boys drew near the glass to get a closer look. A large ape approached and slammed into the transparent wall! BAM! That got our attention. The boys jumped back a bit, surprised by the sudden outburst. The question arose, who was really watching whom? I just thanked God that the Plexiglas held up.

The song today is, "Shine" ~ Newsboys. This song invites you to shine and make others wonder what you've got. Make them wish that they weren't on the outside looking bored. The school kids may have been bored watching the swinging and preening monkeys, but they caught a glimpse of excitement when one slammed into the glass. It became a trip to remember. This song makes me think of the mischievous students I had in school. They'd smile and you'd wonder what they're up to. They had a zest for life. They were creative. I would encourage them to use their 'powers' for good and not evil. In other words, don't let your enthusiasm for life get you into trouble! Enthusiasm for life in Christ can and should get people's attention. That is the 'powers for good' part. You know the saving grace of the Lord? Then shine. Don't look like you've been baptized in lemon juice. Proverbs 15:13 (MSG) says, "A cheerful heart brings a smile to your face; a sad heart makes it hard to get through the day." Are you getting attention for the right reasons? Are you acting like you have hope today? Are you being cheerful? Are you looking on the bright side? Do people think, "I wonder what she has? Or what he has?" And do they want it too? Being positive in a negative world shouldn't be a rare occasion to you. With God on the inside of you, you can draw others by your countenance. By your outlook. By your example. You are influencing them daily. Don't take it lightly. You can decide to have a good day or a great day. It's up to you. Slamming into the wall can be counterproductive. So make the best of each situation and play nice. Then, you will be remembered for all the right reasons.

25 February Many years ago my pastor's wife asked me to be a part of a surprise for my pastor's birthday. My part was to find a way to delay him from starting the service on time to give her a chance to let the congregation in on the secret. Though extremely nervous, I acted the part of distraught staff member who just *had* to speak with him before worship. The plan worked and later I had to confess that the problem was false and it was all a ruse. I love my pastor and his wife. We laughed about it, but I don't ever want to do that again.

Today's song is, "The Heart Of Worship" ~ Matt Redman. This song says that God searches much deeper, through how things appear. He looks into my heart. I can be a convincing actress. However, if you know that, you may doubt me. I do not relish in deception. If it's for a play, okay. If it's for a surprise, a good surprise, okay too. But not for manipulation or fraud. That's not me. To not doubt me, you must know my heart. 1 Samuel 16:7b (MSG) says, "God judges persons differently than humans do. Men and women look at the face; God looks into the heart." God knows your heart. He sees what others do not. He sees deeper than just the surface of your life. But also know that your outer person is a reflection of what's on the inside. Zig Ziglar said, "You cannot consistently perform in a manner which is inconsistent with the way you see yourself." So, you can only act a part for a certain amount of time. Soon, the truth about you will come out. Matthew 12:34b says, "For out of the abundance of the heart the mouth speaks." Often times, you tell on yourself. So, it's important to know who you are today. Who you are in Christ. Who is the real you? Know that God sees the 'you' deep down. He sees what you are going through but He also sees the answer. So, don't be afraid to open up to Him today. Admit where you've missed it, but also see your worth in His eyes. You are important. You are significant. Life is not a play. Don't be acting. God knows you. He loves you. He wants to show you the way, the way through, the way out, and then the way to the next part of your journey today. Don't be nervous, God is on your side. You will find that He will speak to your heart because He truly knows – you won't surprise Him.

26 February One Easter when the boys were little, the youngest about three, we announced to them to meet us on the front porch for the egg hunt! Our oldest was on the porch, basket in hand, ready. The younger came through the door, toy rifle in hand, declaring, "I'm ready for the hunt!" We had a good laugh, and then gave him a basket to carry his spoil.

Today's song is, "Already There" ~ Casting Crowns. This song explains that when I'm lost in mystery, my future is a memory to God, because He is already there. My son was clear, but clearly mistaken about the event called "egg hunt". Sometimes you can misunderstand what is happening in your life. You clearly think it's one thing when it's actually all together something else. The great thing is that God knows what's going on. Isaiah 46:10 says that He knows the end from the beginning. He has a plan. You must choose, though, to walk in it. Jeremiah 29:11 (MSG) says, "I know what I'm doing. I have it all planned out—plans to take care of you, not abandon you, plans to give you the future you hope for." It's that destiny and outcome He speaks of that is filled with hope for you. He's already seen your future and it is bright! You may have to make some adjustments. You may have to add a new skill, method, or technique. You may have to increase your prayer and Bible study time. You may need to read more. Most of all, you may need to hunt for God. That won't be hard because He said, "If you seek me, you will find me." (Deuteronomy 4:29) The time that you invest to seek Him will be greatly rewarded. If what you face today is a mystery, go to the One who has already been there, seen the outcome, and wants the best for you in it. You will eventually find exactly (egg-actly) what you were searching for.

27 February I was baptized in Marvin Earl's pond. I had been baptized as a child, but I felt that this was an important part of my journey. To be fully immersed. So we went out to the pond that day. It was an amazing experience. Baptism is an outward symbol of an inward change. I truly felt buried with Christ as my pastor lowered me into the water. Then that glorious feeling of resurrection as I was lifted out of the water refreshed and strengthened! Though I had become a Christian years before, I felt like this was an appropriate time and place. I always felt welcome in Fayette, Missouri. I went to college and church there and lived there when we were first married. It was a home away from home. So many of those people are still our friends. Who would have thought, looking back, we would be where we are now. I thank God for that time in our lives and the day I got baptized in Marvin Earl's pond.

Today's song, "Already There" ~ Casting Crowns. This song says that one day I'll stand before God, look back on the life I've lived, and enjoy the view seeing how all the pieces fit. You don't always know how the events of the day will lead to the tomorrows you will have. How great it is to have perspective. I am in awe of how God brought me to a place where I would solidify the relationship with my husband, be mentored by great men and women of God, and make friends that would last a lifetime. When I look back only this far, I can see the tapestry that has been created that is my life. My journey. How great will it be to stand before the Lord and look back at the path that I have walked, the lives that I have touched, the legacy that I have left. Like a giant puzzle that He and I have been putting together so many years. All the while, God has seen the end result. He saw the picture on the box. I am excited for all things to fall together, fulfilling His plan for me. So, you don't have to worry if you can't see where some piece might fit, He will guide it to the right spot. It will fit perfectly. Romans 8:28 says, "And we know that all things work together for good to those who love God, to those who are the called according to *His* purpose." He will work it all together for your good! So, I tell you now, be fully immersed in what God has for you today, you will be thankful for the result!

28 February We turned over the first shovel-full of dirt, stood together and prayed. We buried a spent firework named "Red Devil" symbolic of the defeat of any evil in our lives. There we built our house. When the stud walls went up, I printed scriptures and we fastened them into the walls of almost every room before they put in the insulation and installed the sheet rock. The structure sits on a million pounds of rock. Literally. Our house is built on the Rock. The Word of God is in the walls. There are several verses posted around the house that have been there since we moved in. Matthew 7:24 says, "Therefore whoever hears these sayings of Mine, and does them, I will liken him to a wise man who built his house on the rock." Today marks the groundbreaking for our home. Though everything is not perfect, today's song is just right, "Jesus Be The Center" ~ Israel Houghton. This song invites Jesus to be the center of our lives from beginning to end. Keeping Jesus at the center is not always easy, but it's always right. It's always the best. Bathing your home in prayer and the scripture is critical to the abundant life God wants you to have. Today, simply focus on God. Let Jesus be the center of your life and the life of your family. Put aside pettiness, disagreements, pride, and grudges. Be the family God intended you to be. Matthew 7:25 says, "and the rain descended, the floods came, and the winds blew and beat on that house; and it did not fall, for it was founded on the rock." The storms will come. But you can stand. Be grounded. Be focused. Bury the enemy. Claim your victory and declare that your house is built on the Rock!

29 February It was fun to play 'Hide n Seek' when the boys were little. They could hide in great places like under the couch cushions and in the kitchen cabinets. Golly, a seven year old that's creative can get his two year old brother to hide just about anywhere. And it was fun looking for them. Thankfully, they were found every time (unlike that Easter egg one year that got lost inside a chair). Funny.

The song today is "My Redeemer Lives" ~ Nicole C. Mullins. This song declares that I know my Redeemer lives. There are days when you may feel like you are playing 'Hide n Seek' with God. Maybe things are going rough and you think, "God, where are you? Come out; come out where ever you are!" He is quiet for awhile. So you can pout or you can search. Pouting yields poor results. Searching, however, is quite fruitful! If you feel like God has left your life today, look around. He's not far. He's waiting for you to come and find Him. Don't leave Him there by Himself. You don't want to be without Him. What you find will be a great reward! And you may discover that you are the one who needed to be found.

1 March I was blessed to borrow my son's sports car, vowing to take good care of it. It was fun driving down the highway smiling and enjoying the music. Suddenly a bird approached from the right. Tragically, it collided with the windshield of the car. I glanced in the rear-view window and saw only a cloud of feathers. At first I was startled! Then I was thankful that nothing bad happened to me or the car. Though unfortunate for the bird, I was quite relieved. God had protected me. It was a long time before my son let me drive his car again though.

The song for today is, "Whom Shall I Fear" ~ Chris Tomlin. This song says that nothing formed against me shall stand. In the Bible it comes to light that God has put up a hedge of protection around Job. He was an upright man who respected God. Picture it as a fence, not to keep him in but to keep what was evil out. Job's hedge though, was compromised by fear. The story goes on and things get bad for Job before they get better, but they do get better. He gets double for his trouble! It's a great book to study. Job.

In reference to today's lyrics, Isaiah 54:13-17 paints a fairly complete picture in The Message, "All your children will have God for their teacher—what a mentor for your children! You'll be built solid, grounded in righteousness, far from any trouble—nothing to fear! Far from terror—it won't even come close! If anyone attacks you, don't for a moment suppose that I sent them, and if any should attack, nothing will come of it. I create the blacksmith who fires up his forge and makes a weapon designed to kill. I also create the   destroyer—but no weapon that can hurt you has ever been forged. Any accuser who takes you to court will be dismissed as a liar. This is what God's servants can expect. I'll see to it that everything works out for the best." You really don't have to be afraid today. Imagine the enemy trying to stop you, but he just hits the windshield and disintegrates. He is unable to stand up to your authority in the Lord. Be encouraged today. Be hopeful. Understand that things will work out no matter how it may look. Just keep on driving, smile, and enjoy the music... The sweet sound of you receiving double for your trouble too!

2 March "Carry me, Mommy!" How many times did I hear that when the boys were little? We'd be walking and those little arms would reach up. Who could resist that cute face? That earnest request? And when Mommy was tired, Daddy always had the strength to hoist a toddler onto his shoulders. Now, grown up, they drive places on their own, but sometimes I miss those carrying days.

The song today is, "Carry Me" ~ Josh Wilson. These lyrics speak to me today saying that the only way I will ever make it out is if God carries me. Some days are those 'I'm tired of walking' days. You want someone to carry you. They can do the work. They can clean up the mess. They can organize the – whatever it is. Just carry for awhile. Psalm 28:9 (MSG) says, "God is all strength for His people, ample refuge for His chosen leader; save your people and bless your heritage. Care for them; carry them like a good shepherd." Jesus is the Good Shepherd. He will carry you. He's there especially when you need Him most. But you must let Him carry you. Don't be squirmy or impatient. In due season, you will reach your destination. When you get there, you'll know you are in the right place, with the right people, to do what God has called you to do. Don't be hesitant to take a ride. Reach up to the Lord. Ride on His shoulders awhile. He's always strong enough to carry you. When you look to Him, and ask of Him, He can't resist your earnest request and of course, your cute face!

3 March One October my friends and I went through one of those goofy 'haunted' attractions. Mostly they turned off the lights and people screamed and grabbed at you. We held hands and inched down the passageways. Even though there were times when I was really scared, I knew that I would get out all right. After all, it was just a bunch of kids trying to frighten another bunch of kids. Regardless, I didn't go back the following year.

The song today is "Already There" ~ Casting Crowns. This song admits to the Lord that from where I'm standing, it's hard for me to see where this is going and where He is leading me. When you can't see where you're going, you can find a 'hand' to hold. That is the Lord. You can put your hand in His and He will lead you through. How do you do that? Find out what He has to say – read the Bible. Find out what He wants you to do – pray. Find people to come along. See who is with you. Who will be an encouragement? Who will be a friend? You should stay away from those who just want to frighten you. Frighten you with their bad attitude, their bitterness, their hurt, their negativity. When it's dark and you can't see, turn on a light. John 8:12 says, "Then Jesus spoke to them again, saying, 'I am the light of the world. He who follows Me shall not walk in darkness, but have the light of life.'" There's your light. He can show you the way and you don't have to be afraid. If you feel left alone, in the dark, and you don't know where to go next, seek God. I heard my pastor say that when you can't see His hand trust His heart. So, no matter what, you can find Him today when you look. All those goofy specters will flee. You will get out all right and you don't have to go back. Ever.

4 March When I rap the can of pre-made biscuits on the counter, the tube pops open. The dough expands immediately. There would be no way to get them back in the container. So, I place them on the pan and bake them in the oven. Several minutes later, they come out beautifully browned and delicious! I especially like those hot biscuits with butter and jelly!

Today's song, "I Won't Go Back" ~ William McDowell. This song declares that I can't and won't go back to the way it used to be before God's presence came and changed me. Like the biscuits, once a change - God's presence - occurs in your life, your world is opened. There is no going back to how it was. You have expanded and now face your potential. Though heat may be involved - tough times - you can know that you would come out much better than before. God did change your life. Things have progressed during this time. Life gets more amazing daily. Are there challenges? You bet. Are there setbacks? Yep. Are there times when you will feel like quitting? Sure. But, because of God in your life, you can face the challenges. You can overcome the setbacks. You can keep going whether you feel like it or not. Remember the change you have experienced in God. 2 Corinthians 5:17 says, "Therefore, if anyone *is* in Christ, *he is* a new creation; old things have passed away; behold, all things have become new." You don't have to go back. You can't go back. Like the biscuits, you can't get back in the can. You have expanded. You are different. It's time to reach up to your full potential! There may be heat, but you will truly come out better. Keep your eyes on the Lord. Stay in His presence. You are a new creation, so live renewed today.

5 March One day, I was really sick and alone at home. All my cats seemed to take turns watching over me. When I fell asleep, one was at my side. When I woke up, another was there. I moved to the couch and a third came to lie on my lap. Later, the fourth took a nap with me. It was comforting. They were right there with me the whole day. My husband said, "I think they know you don't feel well." It was nice to have that company when I felt bad.

Today's song, "Light Up The Sky" ~ The Afters. This song admits that I can't deny that God is right here with me. There is an undeniable presence of God in your life when you seek to be with Him. He knows what you're going through today. He will be right there with you. He can comfort you in times of grief, sorrow, illness, and tragedy. He will also be with you in triumph, promotion, and joy! He's a 'no matter what' God. In Hebrews 13:5b-6 (MSG) it says, "Since God assured us, 'I'll never let you down, never walk off and leave you,' we can boldly quote, 'God is there, ready to help; I'm fearless no matter what. Who or what can get to me?'" He will be with us no matter what. He is ready to help. Nothing and no one can get to you with God on your side. He will light up the sky for you today and show you that He is with you. Feel His presence today. It's comforting and it's nice.

6 March Children's choir. As they take the stage there's always some fidgeting. When they begin to sing, standing in rows, hands poised, there is at least that one child (you've seen that tyke) doing a jig or shouting lyrics or waving to Mommy and Daddy. That kid steals the show. When they're little, it's cute because they don't know any better. Not so cute when they've grown.

Today's song is, "Steal My Show" ~ TobyMac. This song says that if God wants to steal my show, I'll sit back and I will watch. I have had the opportunity recently to observe, on a couple of occasions, people blatantly showing disrespect and disregard for those in authority. They were adults. I was sickened. Not the kind of 'steal the show' that was cute at age 5. I'm thinking, "They should know better." Romans 13:7b (CEB) says, "Show respect to those you should respect. And show honor to those you should honor." and verse 14 (ERV) says, "But be like the Lord Jesus Christ, so that when people see what you do, they will see Christ. Don't think about how to satisfy the desires of your sinful self." If anyone steals the show, it should be the Lord. He deserves the honor and the respect. When people walk away from you, who do they see? Have they seen the goodness of God? Are they better because they were with you? Were you respectful? Were you an encouragement? Earlier in Romans 13 it talks about how God has placed people in authority. You may not like them, but you are called to respect their office. God can bless your obedience in the matter. Spiritual Authority by Watchman Nee shows just how important that respect for authority is. Protocol. Manners. Consideration. Respect. There are spiritual implications to the manner in which you treat those in authority. And, how you follow is how you will lead. You must be under authority to be in authority. It's important to be accountable. It's important to bring others along. Help. Teach. Show. Be an influence for their blessings as well as your own. Today, honor some one in authority. Say, "Thank you." Send a note. Give a gift. Donate your time. Praise them to others. Do it out of a Godly heart. And remember to praise God for who He is and all He's done. You can sing a song of praise to Him. Then let Him steal your show. Sit back and watch what He will do on your behalf – Watch Him Go!

7 March "King of the Mountain" is a children's game. The goal is to stay on top of a hill or 'mountain.' Players attempt to knock the current King off the top and take their place, and then they become the new 'King of the Mountain'. The best way to get to the top is to push.

The song for today is, "Standing" ~ William McDowell. This song proclaims that by standing on God's promises, we will see the impossible. Our mountaintop today is – God's promises. When you are standing on what God has said in a situation, you are on top. God says that you are the head and not the tail...above and not beneath. (Deuteronomy 28:13) He says that you are more than a conqueror. (Romans 8:37) And He says that you can do all things through Christ which strengthens you. (Philippians 4:13) There are verses in the Bible specific to your situation. 'Standing' means to proclaim and be assured of the result. Proclaim God's word on the matter and believe in the intended outcome. Then you will see what you at first thought, or others thought, was impossible, come to pass! But it's not going to just happen. It's not, "Whatever will be, will be." Or "If it's God's will, it will happen." You still have to work. You still have to pray. You still have to believe. And yes, you still have to push. Matthew 11:12b (AMP) includes these words, "share in the heavenly kingdom is sought with most ardent zeal and intense exertion." Our high school cheerleaders used to chant, "You've got to fight to win!" Exactly. The Kingdom of God is not occupied by wimps. Your stance will produce miracles, because you stand strong in Him. You push against the forces of darkness, the enemy, the devil, all hell to obtain God's best. You are victorious because He is King of your life.

I believe you will see the impossible. You will reach the unreachable. You will be in the place you dreamed. God's plan for you realized. Stand on His promises. Stand on top.

8 March There was a burger place we went to when the boys were little and they gave each child a crown. What fun to wear a paper crown. It was really fun when they tried to get Mommy and Daddy to wear the crowns too! I think maybe my head was too big for that adjustable adornment. Crowns. What a great way to let the kids know they are significant.

Today's song is, "Gold" ~ Britt Nicole. This song encourages you to not let anybody tell you that you're not loved or that you're not enough. We've got to let children know their significance. They are important. They are enough. "Less than" is only used in math problems and can never define them. I was blessed to see my friend's grand daughter the other day, all of 2 years old. She was announcing, "I am beautiful!" Her confidence was encouraging. And of course, we know she is adorable! You should have the confidence to be yourself. To use what God has given you and make it great! To not make excuses or lay blame on others who may have told you that you'll never make it. That you're mediocre. That what you want is impossible. That you are too much of something or too little of another. It's time to shake off what others have said to you, about you, and over you and start declaring and decreeing what God has said about you! You are a new creature in Christ! (II Corinthians 5:17) You are complete in Him! (Colossians 2:10) You are forgiven! (Ephesians 1:7) You have peace with God! (Romans 5:1) And Philippians 1:6 (MSG) says, "There has never been the slightest doubt in my mind that the God who started this great work in you would keep at it and bring it to a flourishing finish on the very day Christ Jesus appears." Yes! Flourishing! A life that is blooming, expanding, going strong, in full swing, in top form, lush, luxuriant, prosperous, rich, robust, successful, thriving, mushrooming, doing well! (Thanks, Thesaurus) WOW! How about that? You are enough today! Don't ever let yourself think otherwise. Listen to God. He believes in you even when no one else does. He knows your potential and He's working to see it come to pass. Proclaim with confidence, "I am beautiful!" Then, stand tall today and wear your crown!

9 March I saw a dime on the ground one day. It was so dirty. I thought it was a penny. Then I looked more closely it was worth 10 times what I originally thought! Some people walk right by money that is on the ground. They don't have time to pick it up. I do. It's money. Pick up a dime 10 times and you have a dollar. Repeat 10 times and you have 10 dollars. It adds. You just have to stop and pick it up. Just a dime? It's the beginning of wealth.

Today's song, "Kings & Queens"~ Audio Adrenaline. This song says that boys become kings and girls will be queens when they're wrapped in God's majesty. When we love, we love even the least of them. Honor. Respect. Love. It is our opportunity to show it to all. At first glance, a person may seem different than they really are. The object is not to look at them with your own eyes, but through the eyes of God. It changes your perspective. I have had the opportunity to meet celebrities, poor villagers, wealthy business owners, and bums. They are all just people. They have dreams, needs, desires, a longing for relationships, and they have history. There may be some darkness in their lives, but take a closer look and they are worth far more to God than opinions, stereotypes, and circumstances. Matthew 25:40 (MSG) says, "Then the King will say, 'I'm telling the solemn truth: Whenever you did one of these things to someone overlooked or ignored, that was me—you did it to me.'" How you treat others is how you are treating the Lord. Some people just need a friend. Some one to listen. Some one to encourage them. Some one to affirm their value. You are some one.

Romans 12:1-2a (MSG) says, "So here's what I want you to do, God helping you: Take your everyday, ordinary life—your sleeping, eating, going-to-work, and walking-around life—and place it before God as an offering. Embracing what God does for you is the best thing you can do for him. Don't become so well-adjusted to your culture that you fit into it without even thinking. Instead, fix your attention on God. You'll be changed from the inside out." What you do matters today. Who you reach. Who you help. Who you offer Jesus to. Make it count. One person at a time. It adds. You just have to stop and pick them up with a kind word, a smile, a conversation. It's the beginning of true wealth in their lives.

10 March When we were in youth ministry, we scheduled a night at the water slide. Problem. I hadn't been for a long time and my husband had never been on one. Solution. We went a week early so we could get used to the slide. Why? Slight fear. Somewhat terror. There was hesitation when we got to the top and saw the rushing water and the ominous looking 'tube of doom'. We summoned up all our courage and literally took the plunge. We conquered that slide! Returned to the top and slid again and again. Soon we were pros. The key is that we overcame our fears and were able to lead the youth in a night of fun the following week at the water slide.

Today's song, "Courageous" ~ Casting Crowns. This song reminds us that we were made to be courageous and lead the way. Someone said that courage is not the absence of fear. Courage is feeling the fear and doing it anyway. You can't let fear paralyze you. You can overcome it with courage. Isaiah 41:9b-10 (MSG) says, "I've picked you. I haven't dropped you. Don't panic. I'm with you. There's no need to fear for I'm your God. I'll give you strength. I'll help you. I'll hold you steady; keep a firm grip on you." God has given you His assurance. He will be with you and hang on to you. You may feel like you have entered the 'tube of doom', but He will pull you through! You may get a little wet but, take a breath and rejoice because you will see that you made it! Then you will be ready to go again. Your courage will overcome your fear. Step out and the fear will dissipate. Joshua 1:9 (MSG) says, "Haven't I commanded you? Strength! Courage! Don't be timid; don't get discouraged. God, your God, is with you every step you take." That's it! Rise up to the challenge you have been given. Do not vacillate. Decide. Stay firm in your decision. How? Look at verses 7-8 in Joshua 1. It says, "Give it everything you have, heart and soul. Make sure you carry out The Revelation that Moses commanded you, every bit of it. Don't get off track, either left or right, so as to make sure you get to where you're going. And don't for a minute let this Book of The Revelation be out of mind. Ponder and meditate on it day and night, making sure you practice everything written in it. Then you'll get where you're going; then you'll succeed."Be of good courage today. Conquer your fears. God will be there with you.

11 March When we went to Maui for the first time there was an opportunity to go whale watching. We took the tour. Out on the water we scanned the horizon for activity. Occasionally we would see a fin break the surface, or a water spout erupt. There was a time when the whales came close to the boat. They are huge creatures. Amazing. I was in awe of the majesty in which they glided through the water. They were bigger than I had ever dreamed. I was overwhelmed by the sight of them. It was a great experience.

Today the song is "Nothing Is Impossible" ~ Planetshakers. Luke 1 :37 tells me that nothing is impossible. Philippians 4:13 says that I can do anything. Is there something that lies before you today that is bigger than you imagined? Larger than you dreamed? Seemingly impossible? You have an opportunity, but you're not sure you want to take it? Maybe it's scary. Maybe you are uneasy about it. Maybe it worries you. Take a breath and remember that God has called you to greatness. He wants you to succeed. He has a great plan for you. (Jeremiah 29:11) Take it a step at a time. Look at the daunting task in workable segments. Discern the pieces that can be controlled. Do what you know to do and ask God to help you with the rest. It's not impossible. It may take more work than you thought. It may be more complicated. But the best things are not always the easy things. You will have to pay a price for doing what God has called you to do. You may feel overwhelmed. However, remember that the benefits far out weigh any cost. Stick with it. Keep looking for something to break the surface. Something will stand out. Then you will know you are headed in the right direction. What you see will be magnificent and amazing.

12 March I was talking to a friend about his knee replacement surgery. After having several friends and relatives go through that particular procedure, I have seen the difference between those who did their therapy diligently and those who did not. The key is to do those exercises required after surgery in order to get full function restored. Then you can be as good as or better than new!

Today the song is, "The Hurt & The Healer" ~ MercyMe. This song talks about how you are still alive, even though a part of you may have died. When you have an injury it can change so much of your life. There is pain. There are tears. You may want to give up. Or give in. It could stop your work, your productivity, your advancement. It can blur your focus. It can distract you. This may be a set back, but you are getting ready for your come back! Philippians 3:13-14 (KJV) says, "Brethren, I count not myself to have apprehended: but this one thing I do, forgetting those things which are behind, and reaching forth unto those things which are before, I press toward the mark for the prize of the high calling of God in Christ Jesus." What ever has happened, happened. Now is the time to not ask, "God, why me?" Now is the time to ask, "God, what now?" He is not teaching you a lesson by causing you heartache and pain. God loves you and wants the best for you. But we live in a broken world. Bad things happen. People can be reckless, selfish, and ignorant. The key to the situation is how you deal with it. How will you deal with it today? You may have been hurt physically, emotionally, financially…whatever the hurt may be, God is the healer. He can restore you, make you as good as, no, better than you were! Trust. Obey. Stay. God will see to it that you are healed of your hurt. Then, what a fantastic opportunity you will have to help others who are heading into or going through what you have overcome! Your test will become a testimony. God will take what the devil meant for evil in your life and turn it around for your good. Romans 12:21 (KJV) says, "Be not overcome of evil, but overcome evil with good." It's your choice today to nurse your wounds or to allow them to be healed by God. Be diligent about your recovery. Stay focused. Check out what God's word has to say about your situation. Then stand on that word and begin to take the steps you need to be restored.

13 March It was a great day at our business workshop. Several others and I were set to be recognized for qualifying for our promotions. The event was punctuated with a "high-five" tunnel of leaders. My husband was on his way to the event, though running a bit late, and as this was kind of a big deal for me, I hoped that he would make it in time to see me there. Believing that he just might arrive before it was over, I waited to be the last person through. It was exciting. It was electrifying. Definitely a power moment! But I didn't see him anywhere. Then as I got to the end of the congratulatory tunnel of those wonderful women, I saw him. He stood at the end of the tunnel, arms outstretched to receive me, hug me, and kiss me. I thought he missed that important moment, but he was already there. WOW! I will never forget it!

Today's song is, "Already There" ~ Casting Crowns. It talks about how God is already in your future. He knows what it looks like. He knows how everything will turn out. When you have big moments in your life, you want to celebrate. You want to share them with the ones you love. It's important. It's special. It's those power moments you cherish. You can go through a tunnel of encouragement or pain, one of advancement or one of anguish. Either way, God is already there at the beginning believing in you; at the middle, encouraging you; and at the end waiting for you, ready to rejoice with you! So, go forward even if you don't see Him right now. He will be there, arms outstretched, ready to receive you. The important moments won't be lost; you will enjoy your promotion and what a great celebration it will be!

14 March Years ago we took a group horseback riding. It was a trail ride. Those horses are trained to follow the one in front of them - no matter what. They are conditioned to handle inexperienced riders. That's me. It was scary. We went up big hills and down steep grades. My horse followed. We went through the woods and across a shallow creek. He still followed. When the passage was narrow, he squeezed through, not minding that my leg was pinned between him and the tree. Ow! As we rounded the last corner of the trip, he and all the other horses spotted the barn. They took out running full speed! No amount of tugs on the reins would even slow them down. That barn was their sweet reward! However, getting off that valiant steed was my sweet reward!

Today the song is, "You Lead" ~ Jamie Grace. This song talks about how if God leads, I will follow. The world may try to push or pull me, but God's love doesn't fail. Going your own way in life can get you lost in the woods. God wants you to follow Him. Joshua 14:9 says, "So Moses swore on that day, saying, 'Surely the land where your foot has trodden shall be your inheritance and your children's forever, because you have wholly followed the Lord my God.'" There are benefits to following God. Your inheritance is from God. He has so much for you. But you cannot stray. You cannot let the world push you around. You can't let them yank on your reins and try to get you to go in another direction. You can't mind a few bumps and scrapes. There may be hills and valleys, but you can continue. Keep following. You can make it through. When your destination is in sight, you can race on. Complete all that God has called you to and you will enjoy your sweet reward!

15 March I helped in the nursery one Sunday morning in the toddlers' class. My favorite job is to hold the ones that are crying. They need extra attention. They want a lap to be on or arms to cradle them. That morning I had one on each knee and another begging to be picked up. I had them take turns for a few minutes, but I finally got them calm and off they went to play with the toys. Just that bit of tender loving care and they were all better.

Today's song is "Healing Begins" ~ Tenth Avenue North. This song talks about where the healing begins. It starts when you come to a place of brokenness. That's where the dark parts of your life meet the light of Jesus. You get on the path to restoration. Healing is progressive. Are there instant manifestations? Yes. But, for the most part, it is a process. The important part is to get started. Psalm 23:3 (KJV) says, "He restoreth my soul: he leadeth me in the paths of righteousness for his name's sake." God will restore you. He will bring you to a place of completeness. It may be one day at a time, one month at a time, or one year at a time. He will do it. When you surrender, lift up your arms to Him, sit on His lap, allow yourself to be calmed by Him and His Word; you will be 'all better'. Your extra attention does not need to come from people. Let the Lord be your strength. Your healer. Your restorer. What ever you have lost, how ever you have been injured, what ever has plagued your body, soul, or spirit, God has the answer, He has the healing balm you need. Rest in Him today. His tender loving care will help you to run off and play again. You will be able to rejoice and enjoy your restoration.

16 March We went to a fish dinner at a church in the city. It was quite popular. We were told upon our arrival that it would be a two hour wait. What? Two hours? I was ready to go elsewhere. However, we drove an hour to get there and my husband reminded me we were there for the experience. So we stayed and it was fun. The food was good. Our sons and their friends hung in there and had a good time too. I'm glad we waited.

Today's song is "One Thing Remains" ~ Jesus Culture. I'm focusing on the part that talks about how God's love never fails or gives up. He never leaves you. Even when you feel like giving up on God, He doesn't give up on you. He believes that you are worth the wait. You are worth it especially when you're having a day of conflict, a day of doubt, or just a dumb day. He is patient with you. Romans 15:5 (KJV) says, "Now the God of patience and consolation grant you to be like minded one toward another according to Christ Jesus:" In The Message version it says that He is dependably steady. You don't have to worry if God is having an "off" day. He is steady. You can depend on that. He will be right there, ready for you. He is ready for your love, your devotion, your gratitude, your willingness, your obedience, your faithfulness. He is ready to give to you His blessing, His favor, and His power. Today, don't make God wait any longer. The spiritual dinner He has prepared for you is like a buffet of amazing options. Psalm 34:8 says, "Open your mouth and taste, open your eyes and see—how good God is. Blessed are you who run to him." Time to turn your life over to Him. It will be fun; it will be good, and you will be so glad.

17 March I went to my first Trivia Night. It was more fun than I thought it would be. We had a great team. 100 questions! Sometimes we were absolutely sure of our answers. Other times not so much. Then there were times we questioned each other. Which was right? My guess? His guess? So we picked. Many were right. Others wrong. We laughed. We cheered. We clapped. It was great. We came in 2nd place.

The song today is "All Things Possible" ~ Mark Shultz. This song talks about how God is strong, mighty, faithful, and able. You can put your hope in Him. It would have been great to get every question right at the Trivia Night. Normally that just doesn't happen. But with God, He's got every answer you need. He lacks nothing. Psalm 23:1 (CEB) says, "The Lord is my shepherd. I lack nothing." So, if He is your Shepherd and He lacks nothing, that's how you can lack nothing. How great is that? Very great! Not that we should have prayed, "God, give us the answers to this game." But, "God, help us remember all we have been taught." (Yes, kids, history is important. You will use it someday.) In life there are opportunities daily to make choices. Decisions are necessary. God can guide you in the right way. He will lead you in the path you should take. Don't think anything is too little for God or too big for Him either. He knows the amount of hairs on your head (even if the number fluctuates.) And His arm is not too short. In Genesis 18:14 God refers to Himself and says, "Is any thing too hard for the Lord?" This was when He promised Sarah a baby – and it happened! Whatever your question is today, ask it and be assured that God will help you with the answer. Don't doubt what He says. Don't argue. Don't hesitate. Don't guess. Soon you'll be laughing and cheering and rejoicing because you will have the right answers and that will put you in the lead! And that, my friend, is nothing trivial.

18 March Magic shows generally frustrate me because I want to know how they do it. Slight of hand, misdirection, special mechanisms, contortionists, mirrors, smoke, all meant to distract you from what's happening and make you think someone is really being sawed in half. Or really disappearing. Or really being replaced by a tiger. And how did he know my card? How did he know my number? You are thinking, "That's what magic is, illusion." The whole heart of it is that you don't know the tricks. But it still frustrates me. Yes, it was the 10 of diamonds. How did you do that??

Today's song is, "Born Again" ~ Newsboys. It talks about giving the best of yourself to the Lord. Taking a stand with Him after a life of being deceived. Lots of things in life can deceive you. It can be easy to make assumptions, draw conclusions, think you've got it right and then later find that you were mistaken. Maybe you only heard one side of the story. Maybe some details were left out or erroneous. Maybe you saw what you wanted to see and not what was really there. Maybe you gave somebody the benefit of the doubt, but you would have been more right to doubt them. People are fallible. Some are cunning, some are selfish, some are deceived themselves, some are dishonest, some are very lost. However, in the midst of all the falseness you can find what is true. Find your truth in the Lord. Galatians 6:7a says, " Do not be deceived *and* deluded *and* misled…" (AMP) In John 14:6 "Jesus said to him, I am the Way and the Truth and the Life; no one comes to the Father except by (through) Me" (AMP) That's the way. Through Jesus. The One who died for you. He was blameless and took the blame upon himself. He was crucified a horrible death and rose again. Rose again. That is the key. He has redeemed you from the curse which is sickness, poverty, and eternal death. Realizing that and accepting His offer for you, to come into your heart, will restore you. It will help you to see the deceit that has derailed you. He will give you a new start. A new birth, to be 'born again' if you will. Ask God today to reveal to you what has been deception in your life. Ask Him to show you what's really going on. Your eyes will be opened and you can make the choice to accept the truth. Then walk in it. Reach out to Him and give Him your best.

19 March "Surprise!!!" We shouted as the birthday girl came down the stairs into the room. Her sister had planned it all. She arranged for the people, the presents, and the sweets! It was great anticipating the arrival of the guest of honor. We had all been nervous and excited. Then in a phrase that we hoped we wouldn't hear, she announced, "I knew it!" (Rule #1 even if you aren't surprised, act like it for the sake of those who planned it.) The party went on and it was great fun. Somehow we doubted whether she really knew about it or if we caught her off guard.

Today's song is, "Already There" ~ Casting Crowns. It tells about how the Lord can see from where He's standing, all that He imagined, all that He designed coming together as he planned for you from the very beginning of your life. What is going on in your life is no surprise to God. Have you sought His plan? Have you accepted His invitation to live the life He has for you? If you feel like you're off track, go back to the last thing He told you to do. It was that overwhelming prompt to...Could be-talk to that person. Could be-help at the church, or the shelter, or the nursing home. Could be-reconcile with your child. Could be-care for your parent. Could be-teach others. Could be-give to the needy. Could be-anything. You are probably thinking of it. So, go back to that thing and do it. That's a great starting point. Psalm 40:17 (AMP) says, "[As for me] I am poor and needy, yet the Lord takes thought *and* plans for me. You are my Help and my Deliverer. O my God, do not tarry!" No matter where you are today, God still has that plan for you. It's still deep in your heart. He put it there. Even if you've ignored it or fought it, it remains. He's not going to take it from you. He wants to help you with it. His grand design includes you and the part you play is important. Don't ever diminish your own importance. Don't ever take for granted what your life means to others. The Dream Giver by Bruce Wilkerson talks about how comfort is the biggest enemy of your dream. Dreams help others. Comfort helps you. You need to step out of your comfort zone today. It is the thing that has kept you from doing that last thing God asked of you. Don't feel like you have to know where all this is going. God knows, He planned it. Just keep taking steps and enter into all He has for you. You'll enjoy God's presence and your rewards will be so sweet!

20 March I heard it illustrated so well. An egg, a carrot, and a tea bag. Put each into hot water and here are the results: The egg gets hard. The carrot gets soft. The tea bag makes tea. Both the egg and carrot are affected by the water and heat. However, the tea bag affects the water. So when tough times come, the heat is turned up, which will you be most like? The egg which gets hard? The carrot which gets soft? OR the tea bag which changes the water?

Today the song is, "Only The World" ~ Mandisa. This song declares that there is no reason for giving in, because there is so much more to life than what's going on in the world. Are you in a place today where you have allowed your circumstances to determine the direction of your life? Have you bowed to your environment? Have you settled for "whatever will be"? Or have you decided that you will pursue, no matter what? Pursue your dream. Pursue your goals. Pursue your faith. Pursue your destiny. Pursue. It means to chase after, cultivate, persevere, persist. It's more than just taking a look or merely stepping out. Pursuing is assertive, nearly aggressive. Going after it. It involves a passion. What's your passion today? If your answer to that question is true, then that is what you are actively pursuing. If not, then you are only taking a look. You're a carrot. Have you been hurt by people who have stood in your way? Naysayers? Upset about the obstacles or not reaching your goals in the time you thought you would? Bitter, hardened? You're an egg. Or have you developed a resolve? No matter how much or how long it takes that you will fulfill your destiny? You jump over, go around, and break through any obstacle? You push on? Then you're the tea bag. You will change your world, your environment, your circumstances to become what you were destined to be. Today is the day to affect your world. Remember to be yourself. Pursue. Don't back off. It's what you were made for and it fits you to a "T".

21 March I got this fluffy blanket for Christmas. It's like a super soft stuffed animal, without the animal parts. It's so cuddly. I like to put it over me when I sit on the couch. It's warm and snuggly and nice. Like a big hug. It's just the best blanket ever! I know, you want one just like it, don't you? Well, this one's mine. If you ever come by my house, I might share. It's a great blanket!

Today's song is, "My Hope Is In You" ~ Aaron Shust. The chorus talks about how your hope is in God all through the day. You don't have to be upset by the storms of life or the dry times of life. You can have God's peace. The peace that goes beyond what you can understand. Philippians 4:6-7 (MSG) says, "Don't fret or worry. Instead of worrying, pray. Let petitions and praises shape your worries into prayers, letting God know your concerns. Before you know it, a sense of God's wholeness, everything coming together for good, will come and settle you down. It's wonderful what happens when Christ displaces worry at the center of your life." His peace surpasses what you can possibly comprehend. God's peace is what can get you through the biggest storms. Hope in Him, what He has promised, and knowing that He loves you makes all the difference. It helps you sleep at night. It gives you drive in the daytime. It prods you when you're stalled out. It lifts you when you are down. You don't have to worry today. Frankly, you don't have the time or energy to waste on it. There are people depending on you. God is depending on you. Feeling the pressure? Turn to God. That's where the peace is. That's where the calm is. That's where the answers are. When everything in your world is chaotic, falling apart, ripping at the seams, God is there. God. Go back and re-read Philippians 4:6-7. He will settle you. It's like a blanket wrapped around you. It's warmth. It's like a spiritual hug. Within His peace you will gain new strength. You will have hope. When you have that hope, then you can share it with others. They need it today. They need God today too. They need that peace that only God can bring. And His peace is better than the best blanket ever.

22 March "Tell me about your drawing." I said to my son as he worked on a crayon masterpiece. He was just a little guy and he explained all the squiggles and lines. "And what's that mean?" I inquire. "It doesn't mean anything. It just is." He replies. I have saved a lot of art work from both my sons over the years. They are great mementos, especially to me – Mom. But even if I had a gallery full of their work, it would never take the place of the relationships I have with each of them. I love them. You can't put that on a piece of paper.

This morning's song is "Don't Have Love" ~ Holly Starr. This is a song pointing out that you can have all the material things in life and be popular, but it doesn't mean anything if you don't have love. What is it if you can fill up a house or a garage or a gallery? The stuff of this life is just that, stuff. God wants you to be blessed, yes. It's okay to have stuff, just don't let the stuff have you. When it's your motivation, you have the wrong motivators. Be motivated by love. Love for God. Love for your family. Love for your friends. Love for the people in your church. Love for your neighbors. Love for the rich and the poor. Love for the lost. In Mark 6:34 it says, "And Jesus, when He came out, saw a great multitude and was moved with compassion for them, because they were like sheep not having a shepherd. So He began to teach them many things." He was moved with compassion. In The Message, it says that His heart was broken. This is the love He had for the people. I know that in ministry, you are there for the people. Helping them make it through. Helping them succeed in life. It's not about 'me, me, me'. What you can do for me, what you can give me. That's selfishness and it leads to emptiness, loneliness and destitution. Picture the character, Ebenezer Scrooge from Charles Dickens' A Christmas Carol. There it is. You do not want to become him, unless you see the end of the story where he turns his heart to others. Only God can truly give you the grace to step outside of yourself and look to those who are in your life. Your love for them can help change their circumstances. Your love for them can change your own life Things and money can pass from your hands, but love never fails. The masterpiece that is your life deserves the colorful addition of all the relationships and love you can embrace. And that cannot be put on paper.

23 March There's a certain part of our church foyer that I accidentally got locked into one day. It was after hours and I was helping my husband with some things. The doors shut and there I stood. No keys. I could go outside, but that wouldn't be helpful. Lobby and hallway both locked. Then I saw it, the elevator. I could go down, then work my way back through a passage to where my husband was in the front lobby. It took awhile, but I made it. I guess I could have called him on his cell phone, but that would have been too easy, now wouldn't it?

Today's song is, "Mighty to Save" ~ Hillsong United. This talks about how our God can move mountains. He is so mighty. So often we feel trapped by circumstances or by decisions we ourselves have made. I locked myself in that foyer. I didn't plan ahead. I didn't have a key. I didn't think it through. I made it difficult for myself when the solution could have been quite easy. Has that ever happened to you? When it happens, it's important to stop, take a breath, settle yourself and see what is really happening. Your obstacle may very well become a bridge. What's stopping you may be deceiving you. What is in your way may be easily movable. Check your perspective. Search for the key that will unlock the trap you find yourself in. It could be the trap of fear, procrastination, laziness, carelessness, apathy, complacency, bitterness, or selfishness. Identify the trap and use the key. You find the keys in God's word. It says to fear not. It says to get up quickly. If you don't work, you don't eat. Be careful and full of care. Let the zeal of God consume you. Let bitterness be put away from you. And remember, God loves a cheerful giver! It's all in there! When you hide God's word in your heart, you will always have the keys. If you are staring at a mountain today, you may think, "No key will help here, I need some dynamite! God's power is "dunamas" (the root of 'dynamite'). Tap into His dunamas today through prayer, faith, belief, and trust in His ability to move the mountain when you declare it. Matthew 17:20b (MSG) confirms that, "The simple truth is that if you had a mere kernel of faith, a poppy seed, say, you would tell this mountain, 'Move!' and it would move. There is nothing you wouldn't be able to tackle." Other versions use a 'mustard seed' as their example, but bottom line is that it doesn't take much faith, but it takes faith. Believe it.

24 March I was only 21 when my father retired. He was 65. For three years he sat, his health declined. It is painful for me to recall. At age 68 he suffered a fatal heart attack. There are so many things he missed of our lives. He died way too young. I just can't help but think that there could have been more to my father's life if he had made more goals, kept busy, and had purpose instead of quitting when he retired.

Today's song is, "My Life Is In You" ~ Joseph Garlington. This song declares that my life, strength, and hope is in the Lord. The biggest thing on my mind today is hope. Hope in the future. That is what will give you power in the present. The will to go forward. The challenge to meet new goals. The excitement that comes from having purpose. Finishing one stage of your life or accomplishing one big goal is not an end, it is only a step. When you get there, you take another. Then another. There is no advantage to 'resting on your laurels'. There is much left to win. Much left to achieve. Many more to touch, impact, and influence. Bumping along in life is unguided and uncomfortable and unproductive. Your course needs to be set. If there has to be a detour, keep going. If there is a delay, keep at it. There is so much more in you than you ever could imagine! Our pastor's wife reminded us that we each have something important inside of us that we need to share. Who do you still need to share with? Who is waiting for you to fulfill your purpose? Who wants to see you succeed so that they will be encouraged to succeed themselves? Retirement should only be a change of pace. Not a cessation of pace. Keep going. Keep growing. Keep learning. Keep moving. Keep stepping. It doesn't matter what age you are, if you have completed what you started, then it's time to start some thing new. If you haven't finished what you started, what are you waiting for? Perfect circumstances won't come. You must make them. Go for it. Do not become complacent. Do not sit. You will become weak. It can kill you, spiritually and physically. Your race isn't over – you are still breathing! Muster up all you have and make the rest of your life count for even more. You deserve it and so do the people that only you can help by how you live your life now.

25 March   A big blizzard hit in our area. Big here, at least. The thing about a snow storm is getting out afterwards. For us the toughest part is getting out of our driveway. It's over 200 feet of uncooperative gravel. It was slow going, got a bit stuck, but made it out. Years ago there was a similar snow and a friend of mine couldn't believe I was getting out in the stuff. She lived in an apartment complex and could see the mounded snow from her ground level unit. What she couldn't see is that just beyond the mounds all the streets were completely clear!

Today's song, "Who You Are"~ Unspoken. This song talks about change. Changing who you are. Every day when your feet hit the floor, you have to get up and get out there. It won't be easy, but it will be worth it. The journey to changing who you are is toughest at the beginning. It's hard to start. Why? Fear. Lack of confidence. Doubt. By the way, none of that is from God. Just like the snow, the toughest part is getting out of the driveway. If you want to be great, you must start. Start new habits. Start better discipline. Start doing what you know to do. But mostly, be brave. Trust. Be confident. Have faith. You need to realize that when you start something new or start something again, it won't be easy. You may get stuck. The road may be uncooperative. You may need help. But friend, when your feet hit the floor (which means you must get out of bed!) you be strong. You be what you were destined to be – successful. Success is multifaceted. Include faith, family, and your career. Your success will come one step at a time. You won't just wake up one day and be there. It won't be easy, but you better believe beyond a shadow of a doubt that it will be worth it. What do you need to change today? What do you need to learn? What do you need to add to your life; and what do you need to subtract? You may need a shovel to get all the junk out of the way so you can get on your way. It's time. Philippians 1:6 says, "being confident of this very thing, that He who has begun a good work in you will complete *it* until the day of Jesus Christ." Nurture that vision that God has given you. Feed it. Work at it. Remember, it's toughest at the beginning, but once you get going, keep going, and you will see your destination. You'll find out that what you thought was impassible was only an obstacle to the clear path ahead. You'll make it. You'll make it!

26 March Vacation time when I was growing up usually meant going to see relatives. We lived in Missouri and most of them were in Pennsylvania. We drove. About 2 weeks before the trip, my mother was packing. I remember the suitcase lying open on my parents' bed. Everything was packed so neatly. Each day something else was added until the day we left. I don't even remember what kind of bag I had, just that big brown suitcase lying out on their bed.

Today's song is, "Who You Are" ~ Unspoken. Today I am reflecting on the bridge of the song that talks about coming back from wherever you've been and going to the foot of the cross, back to Jesus. We all spend time packing the baggage of our lives. You tuck in a hurt here, a disappointment there, fold up a mistake along with the consequences and stick it in a corner. You lay a wound and a betrayal on the top. You carry it around with you and believe that if the case is closed, no one will see it. Yet it is there, weighing you down. Slowing you. Taxing your energy. Sapping your strength. Sometimes you pick up some one else's bag. You think it's your duty. But you really can't carry it for them. They have to carry it themselves. The destination must be the foot of the cross. That is the best place to take all that baggage. Return it to Jesus. I Peter 5:7(AMP) says, "Casting the whole of your care [all your anxieties, all your worries, all your concerns, once and for all] on Him, for He cares for you affectionately *and* cares about you watchfully." Time to stop carrying all that on your own shoulders. You are not a superman or superwoman. It's not for you to try to handle yourself. Give it up. Go to Jesus. Leave it with Him. He will take it on. He will restore to you your strength, your energy, your focus. The weight will be lifted. You can continue unhampered by the stuff of this life and start fresh. And when you leave that suitcase full of hurts and concerns, do not go back and pick it up. 2 Corinthians 5:17 says, "Therefore, if anyone is in Christ, he is a new creation; old things have passed away; behold, all things have become new." Yes! The old is passed away. It's a new day!

27 March When the boys were little, we went to an Easter Egg hunt at a park. They had multitudes of plastic, candy-filled eggs in the grass all over the field. There were ribbons around the perimeter to keep everyone out until the whistle blew. At the sound, all the children, baskets and bags in tow ran excitedly into the area and begin gathering their bounty! Parents watched, helped, and cheered them on. My guys did great and we went home with lots of goodies!

Today the song is, "Redeemed" ~ Big Daddy Weave. The chorus talks about how I am redeemed and been set free. When Jesus went to the cross, He paid a price we couldn't pay. He redeemed us from the curse of sickness, poverty, and eternal death. Galatians 3:13 (MSG) says, "Christ redeemed us from that self-defeating, cursed life by absorbing it completely into himself. Do you remember the Scripture that says, 'Cursed is everyone who hangs on a tree'? That is what happened when Jesus was nailed to the cross: He became a curse, and at the same time dissolved the curse." So, when you accept what Jesus did, accept Him into your life, you are redeemed. You have been set free. It's like you have been behind the ribbon and you saying "Yes" to the Lord is the sound that allows you to come in. Come in to the family of God. Come into a life that is redeemed from poverty – you don't have to be poor. Come into a life that is redeemed from sickness – you can be healthy. Come into a life that is redeemed from eternal damnation – you will go to Heaven and have eternal life. What a great time to celebrate! Run on in! Be excited and you will be able to pick up all the benefits, the bounty that your life in Christ includes!

This is also a great time to share with others how great God is to have sent His Son to die for all of us. It's an opportunity for them to make a decision to accept His gift for them. Also, time to celebrate His resurrection!

28 March My youngest played on the High School Varsity soccer team. He is an excellent player. I absolutely loved going to the games. I am a soccer mom. I'd ask him, "Can you hear me yelling when you're out on the field?" He'd say, "Yes, Mom." I would often get hoarse from screaming and shouting words of encouragement. The moms cheered incessantly. Even though I didn't know all the plays, I was right in there hollering with the rest. Especially when we scored, and even more when we won! Now that he has graduated, I miss going to see him play, but I still know my son is great. He's definitely a winner.

Today's song is, "Rez Power" ~ Israel And New Breed. This is a celebration of the resurrection of Jesus Christ. It inspires you to clap your hands and shout to God. Shout about the triumph of Christ over death! Get excited! Our savior rose from the dead! He lives in Heaven and sits at the right hand of God! Ephesians 1:19b-20 (NIV) says, "That power is the same as the mighty strength he exerted when he raised Christ from the dead and seated him at his right hand in the heavenly realms." That's amazing! You should be shouting and telling of His greatness. Have you been solemn and silent for too long? It may be time to alert yourself that an exciting thing has happened. Christ rose from the dead. It was miraculous. It was phenomenal. It was extraordinary. Don't let this week pass you by and find that you have not shared with someone about how Christ died for them and rose again. The same spirit that raised Christ dwells in you when you have accepted Him into your life! Romans 8:11 tells of it and that He will bring life to you! Are you lively today? Are you attracting people today? Attracting, not attacking? I'm not talking about you being a crazy soccer mom type about Jesus. I'm also not talking about the fan who sits under the bleachers, unnoticed. You can be cheerful. You can be lively. You can celebrate. The joy of God in you attracts people. You lift Jesus up and people are drawn to you. Be a magnet. Be an influence. Be an answer. You have so much in you; I know it makes you want to shout! So, declare today – Jesus is Lord and God raised Him from the dead. Celebrate! God is great! Realize that you are a winner!

29 March Summer camp. I loved summer camp. That is where I learned to do a back dive. Standing on the board, looking at the water, I was petrified and hesitant. I don't remember how long it took before I turned around, put my hands above my head and finally gave it a try. Splash! I know the first one was sloppy. But, I kept at it, my confidence grew, and soon I was doing great for a 12 year old novice!

The song today is, "Walk On The Water"~ Britt Nicole. The song questions what you're waiting for. Pondering what you have to lose by trying. Your insecurities may be holding you back, but you shouldn't be afraid. You were made for more than where you are today. You have potential. What if? What if you could do that thing you're dreaming? What if there was enough money, resources, and time? You can't lose by trying. Even if you fail, you will find out something new. Then try again. Matthew 14:29-32 (MSG) tells this story, "He *(Jesus)* said, 'Come ahead.' Jumping out of the boat, Peter walked on the water to Jesus. But when he looked down at the waves churning beneath his feet, he lost his nerve and started to sink. He cried, 'Master, save me!' Jesus didn't hesitate. He reached down and grabbed his hand. Then he said, 'Faint-heart, what got into you?' The two of them climbed into the boat, and the wind died down." So if you are nervous today or hesitant, step out and dive in. If you falter, Jesus will be there to help. You just have to call to him. He will grab your hand and lead you. You may think, "What got into me?" You may wonder why you waited. You can get into the boat, staying close to the Lord. The wind will calm and your confidence will grow. Soon you will be doing great!

30 March I gave a gift to a friend. She said, "You didn't have to do that!" That's what makes it a gift. If I had to do that, it would be an obligation. I gave because of my love for her as a friend and because I thought of her and I believed that it was something she needed. She thanked me repeatedly. It made me happy because I saw her using it the very next week. It's a joy to give gifts, especially when the recipient appreciates it.

Today's song is, "How Many Kings" ~ Downhere. This song poses the question, asking how many kings have done what our King – God – has done for us? Who else has given their son for us? No one, only God. He offered His Son, Jesus, to pay for our sins. Jesus was His only, unique son. There has never been someone like Him. God gave His best for us. Jesus went to the cross. They didn't take His life from Him. He laid it down. He had a choice. He did it for us. For you. In John 10:15-18 Jesus says, "As the Father knows Me, even so I know the Father; and I lay down My life for the sheep. And other sheep I have which are not of this fold; them also I must bring, and they will hear My voice; and there will be one flock *and* one shepherd. Therefore My Father loves Me, because I lay down My life that I may take it again. No one takes it from Me, but I lay it down of Myself. I have power to lay it down, and I have power to take it again. This command I have received from My Father." You are one of His sheep. God thought of you and believed that you needed salvation. It was an amazing gift, Jesus' life for yours. The key is to accept the gift and thank God for it. Thank Him for the gift of Jesus. The forgiveness. The redemption. The bridging of the gap between you and God. Re-peatedly thank Him. He paid a big price for it. It pleases Him when you use that gift and choose to live your life in Christ, faith-ful, thankful, and fruitful. It was His joy to give that to you. John 3:16 says, "For God so loved the world that He gave His only be-gotten Son, that whoever believes in Him should not perish but have everlasting life." He loved so much, He gave. Don't take that for granted today. Pause and reflect on His gift. Then share it with some one who may not realize that the gift is theirs to re-ceive as well.

31 March We were on our way to church on Sunday and I told my son that I felt sorry for people who had to work that day. That was how I saw it-for a couple seconds. Then I realized, we were all going to work at the church. But it is different because we are serving. All four of us had different responsibilities to assist the people and help in the ministry. "It doesn't seem like work." I told him. It's the people who don't get to go to church because they work on Sunday that I am concerned for. I wonder how they see it.

Today's song is, "Give Me Your Eyes" ~ Brandon Heath. This song is asking the Lord to give me His perspective, His eyes, so I can see all that I have been missing. You can complain about your situation or you can look again and see what else could be there. God can help you see what you are missing. Sometimes you miss it because of fear. Sometimes it's apathy. Sometimes it's selfishness. Sometimes you just jump to a conclusion that isn't even right. But you are missing something when you are stressed, angry, frustrated, or upset. You have to change your perspective. There really are other ways to look at things. Just ask a camera operator. It's amazing. You often can see what you want to see. Your positioning has a lot to do with it. How are you looking at your situation today? Glass half empty? Glass half full? Glass with potential? Cool drink? Consider the blessing hidden in your challenge. Realize that your promotion is held by your giant today. Slaying that giant problem brings you to the next level! Stop and take a look again. What have you missed? Ask God to show it to you. Calm down. Breathe. Take in what He has for you in the situation. Always remember that your outlook determines your outcome.

1 April I was about seven and I had a bicycle with training wheels. Early in the morning I rode that thing up and down the sidewalk in front of our house and down the block from stop sign to stop sign. The neighbors must have cringed because those little wheels squeaked horribly! It was a long time before I had my daddy remove those trainers. But he was right there with me; hand on my back, steadying me as I learned how to ride. I rode miles after that, but I always remember my daddy being there when I really needed him. I'm sure he still kept an eye on me even when I wasn't looking.

Today the song is, "Need You Now" ~ Plumb. This song is a cry to God, affirming that I need Him. It says that no matter how many times I have cried, I know I still need Him. It's never bad to need God. You always need Him. Even when you don't think you do, you do. Just like I needed those training wheels to keep me up. To help me balance. To build my confidence. And I needed my dad there to steady me and help me. If you ever get to a point where you think you don't need God, then you are lost. You may think you know where you are going, but you have abandoned the one who can guide you. Matthew 19:26 (MSG) says, "Jesus looked hard at them and said, 'No chance at all if you think you can pull it off yourself. Every chance in the world if you trust God to do it.'" You can be confident in the ability of God to assist you. He will help. However, you must admit that you need the help. You must ask. You must receive it. God is there whether you acknowledge Him or not. He is still watching over you. But He is a gentleman. He will not act until asked. He will not invade your life until He's invited. So ask today. Lean on Him. He cares for you as a good father cares for his children. He has your back today. He will steady you. You will be riding far, but never forget how much you really need Him.

2 April I've been taught to say daily affirmations. Reminding myself who I am encourages me and strengthens me. It keeps me focused. It lifts me and builds me. Even more so I need to say daily – who God is. My focus on Him will encourage me. He will strengthen me, lift me, and build me so much better than all I can say about myself.

Today's song is, "I Am" ~ Eddie James. This song lists all the 'I am's' that God is. Especially, saying that He is your future, so you can leave your past behind. He is also relief to your stress. I first heard this song two days ago, delivered by an amazing vocalist at our church. I heard it in my heart this morning and was reminded how powerful both the song and God are! My focus on God, my reminder of how amazing, how great, how awesome He is makes all the difference in my life! That can make all the difference in your life as well. Getting caught up in the cares of everyday existence can cloud your judgment, skew your attitude, and discourage you in your dreams. Getting caught up in God can give you clarity, wisdom, direction, purpose, and drive. Matthew 6:33 says, "But seek first the kingdom of God and His righteousness, and all these things shall be added to you." Once you get your priorities correct, the other concerns, opportunities, and needs will come into place. Do what's best and there will be room for the rest. Do the rest and there's no place left for the best. You can have it whichever way you choose. Be mindful of God today. He holds your future, you just need to go and get it. No need to stress. No need to feel powerless. You are in control. You choose. You decide. It's free will – God's gift. He gives the plan, but you work it out. So, take a look at all God is today. Remind yourself. It's the very best affirmation.

3 April The first several mornings after we moved into our new home out here, fog rested in the fields and surrounded the house. It was unusual, curious, I thought. It was a gentle presence. You could see some of the trees, but barely see the road. It was still and quiet in the early morning as the sun rose. My youngest, having just turned 10, came into the kitchen one day and glanced out the window. "It's the glory cloud, Mom!" he exclaimed. "I guess it is!" I replied. I looked at it differently from then on, realizing how blessed we really were and are. It is God's presence in our lives. Now, I look forward to those foggy mornings out here on the farm.

Today's song is, "After All" ~ David Crowder Band. Part of this song talks about how Heaven and Earth are filled with God's glory. Isaiah 6:3 says, "Holy, holy, holy *is* the Lord of hosts; the whole earth *is* full of His glory!" Whether it was the glory cloud of God or just some low lying haze, my perspective was enlarged that day with a simple acknowledgement of the Lord's presence. There's an acronym for the favor of God. F.O.G. What a great reminder of His existence in your life. To have Him there. To have His favor. To have His grace. To have all you need for every situation. His Glory. Where ever you go, what ever you encounter, you can have God. Include Him today. Feel His presence in your life. Know that He is there in the stillness and the quietness of each morning. He obscures your distractions and He shows you the way. Rest in Him and let Him surround you. You will begin to look at things differently and know just how blessed you really are.

4 April We have in our house the culmination of items from both of our families. There are a lot of memories connected to the items we have inherited. I have recently started to evaluate their actual vs. perceived value. Trinkets or treasures? Maybe we could put some of it on a shelf. Maybe we could take some of it to the road show for antiques. Maybe we could take some of it to the ditch. Whether we keep the things or not, we can recall the moments, the people, and the relationships. That's all more important anyway.

Today the song is "I Won't Go Back" ~ William McDowell. This song declares that I am not going back to the way I used to be, before I experienced God's presence in my life. The "good ole days" were not really as you remember. They also cannot be duplicated. In growing, you have gained more wisdom, knowledge, experience, and character. There's something that comes with growing up, but there is so much more that comes with experiencing God in your life. God changes you. He transforms you. (Romans 12:1-2) He makes more of you. That renewal, the new birth, gives you that second chance that you have been hoping for. In John 21, the story is told of Peter following the death of Jesus. He went back to what he had done prior to following the Lord. He returned to his past profession for he had no hope in the future. After fishing all night, the Lord came to him and in verse 5 (MSG) it says, "Jesus spoke to them: 'Good morning! Did you catch anything for breakfast?' They answered, 'No.'" They had caught nothing. That is what is in your past for you – Nothing. It's not the same since you left it. Now when Jesus stepped back in, Peter and his cohorts cast again and drew in nets full of fish! God wants to be involved in your future. He doesn't want you to return to your past. Might there be a challenge? Yes. Might it be hard at times? Yes. Might it be out of your comfort zone? Yes. Memories are memories. It is time to move on. Time to let go of the past hurts, trials, anger, mistakes and reach forward by reaching up to God. Make room in your life for new experiences, new moments. Some of those memories need to be shelved. Some reevaluated. And others, just throw them in the ditch! You deserve better. You deserve more. You deserve a life to be celebrated and not just tolerated. You deserve all God has for you.

5 April When my eldest son was a very little boy he received a pair of penny loafers, handed down from a friend whose son had out grown them. My little guy would put them on and go out to the front porch and do a dance. He said they were his dancin' shoes. He was so excited. He loved those shoes. They were for celebrating anything, everything, and nothing at all. It was a pair of pure fun for him.

Today's song is, "Something Beautiful" ~ Needtobreathe. This song brings out a yearning to be consumed by the fire of God. It expresses a desire to be touched by something beautiful. There is an excitement that comes with knowing God. When you relinquish yourself to His plan for your life, abundant joy can overtake you. I'm not talking about some wacky response you should have, but you can be dancin' on the inside. You can smile. You can be joyful. You can be kind, loving, helpful...with God; evidence will follow in your life. Galatians 5:22-23 (MSG) says, "But what happens when we live God's way? He brings gifts into our lives, much the same way that fruit appears in an orchard— things like affection for others, exuberance about life, serenity. We develop a willingness to stick with things, a sense of compassion in the heart, and a conviction that a basic holiness permeates things and people. We find ourselves involved in loyal commitments, not needing to force our way in life, able to marshal and direct our energies wisely." It really is exciting. So, if you feel depressed today, not having met a goal, things not going quite right, feeling like you want to give up, renew your relationship with God. Be thankful. Be hopeful. Celebrate what you have instead of moping about what you've lost. Be touched by the beautiful presence of the Lord. Then, go get your dancin' shoes on, get out there, dance, be powered by your zeal for God, and from now on may all your shoes be dancin' shoes.

6 April We were talking about a children's show this morning. It aired on television when I was a child. At the end of the program, the host held up a mirror and said a poem. Then she would look into the camera and say, "I see Jimmy, and Tommy, and Janey, and….." I would shout at the TV and wave so she could see me. But she never did. She never said, "I see Starr." Sad, right? Thankfully, I didn't get my self worth from whether Miss Lois saw me or not. It would have been great though, to be a part of the show.

Today the song is, "Steal My Show" ~ Toby Mac. In this song, the artist is at a concert performing and invites the Lord to take center stage. He yields to God to be the focus and the people receive what He has for them. It's not just a concert, it's a God encounter. God wants to be a part of your "show" today. I can picture sometimes Him waving to you and saying, "See me!" You see the other parts of your life…Your job. Your boat. Your yard. Your hobby. Your buddies. Your car. Your portfolio. But do you see God today? God wants you to notice Him. He wants to be a part of all of your life. He's not just a convenient Sunday acquaintance; He yearns to be your Father. The Lord wants relationship. He wants you. He chose you. He pointed you out. You are important, you are special. There is no one else who is uniquely gifted to do what God has created you to accomplish. Others may not see, but God has noticed you. Time to notice Him. Thank Him for what He has done in your life and stop blaming Him when things don't go your way. God can work through those bad situations, but He does not cause them. He is only in control of what we let him control. Sometimes people say, "It's all good." It's not all good. We live in a broken world. But God can turn the bad around. He can restore, replace, and renew. Be excited today. Let God in. Give Him center stage and He will be with you the whole way, good times and bad. You'll see how great it is for Him to be a part of your show.

7 April That day was a "Wow" day. My husband had the privilege to speak to the congregation of our church about marriage. We've worked at our marriage all these years and it's a really great one. One impacting moment was when he pointed to me, sitting in the seats, and said, "She's my best friend." Our relationship is paramount, second only to our relationship with God. That's what makes it stand strong. We are blessed because we give God and each other our best.

"Courageous" is the song today ~ Casting Crowns. This is a call to men especially to be courageous and to take back the fight for their families and to love their wives and children. I feel like there's an urgency to strengthen family relationships. Strong families make strong churches. Strong churches make strong communities. Strong communities make a strong country. Moral fiber should not be disintegrated, it should be fortified. Weapon restriction and laws will not reform the lawless. Family stability will. Security of relationships will. Value of life will. Family strength will send the enemy of God into a tail-spin. The men have a key role. You, as a man, must be courageous for your family. You, as a woman, must be supportive and encouraging for your courageous man, which also takes courage. John 16:33 (MSG) says, "I've told you all this so that trusting me, you will be unshakable and assured, deeply at peace. In this godless world you will continue to experience difficulties. But take heart! I've conquered the world." He has conquered the world already, so don't let them take your life or your family! Stand up. Stand firm. Stand strong. Be courageous. You will be victorious.

8 April From the time my boys were born until now, there is a part of them that needs me. Why? Because I'm Mom. Whether it was to rock them to sleep or bandage a boo-boo or create a Valentine box or make a party costume, pack lunches, shop for clothes, bake cookies, organize birthday parties, shuttle them wherever, go to games, wash their uniforms, cook breakfast, lunch, supper, give them money, permission, advice, correction, or just be there to talk, listen, share, cheer, encourage, and pray for them, they need me. But as much as they need me, I need them too. They have added to my life in so many ways. I could never regret having them, loving them, and raising them. Both my husband and I are proud of who they have become. We are excited to see what the future holds for them.

Today's song, "I Love You Lord" ~ Petra. This is a worship song. In it God sees that I love and worship Him. I pray that what He hears when I worship gives Him joy and pleases Him. God has added so much to my life; I can't help but thank Him. I can't help but take the time to worship. To be still and know that He is God. (Psalm 46:10) This is actually the first worship song I ever sang aside from any church hymns. It was at a concert in a park. It was a time when I really felt the Spirit of God. I believe He was pleased at that moment when I took the time to surrender to Him. I needed Him. He desired that fellowship with me too. Today, take the time to worship the Lord. Say thank you for all that He is and all that He's done in your life. The sweet things, the good things, all He has provided for you and all the times He protected you. He loves you. Make Him proud of who you are becoming. He will be excited for your future, especially because He has already seen it, and it is good. It's just your job to step into it. God will never regret what He has done for you, what He has given you, and what He has placed in your heart to do. Your gifts and calling are irrevocable. (Romans 11:29) So turn to Him. Give Him your all today. Just simply say, "I love you, Lord".

9 April We have indoor/outdoor cats. They roam the farm at night and come back to sleep inside all day. Sometimes they stay out. Sometimes there's one that doesn't come home for a few days. For seven years, they have always eventually returned. There's food here. There's care here. They are connected here. They are our cats. All of them, and we love them.

Today's song is "One Thing Remains" ~ Jesus Culture. This song reassures that God's love never fails, gives up, and never runs out on you. God is always there. His love is strong. His love is present. His love is eternal. You can always depend on Him. You may not understand how or why He works in the ways He does, but know that He is there. You can trust Him. You can rest in Him. You can seek Him and you will find Him. You can connect with Him. He cares for you. He cares for all that's going on in your life. He's there for the brightest of days and for the darkest of nights. Matthew 28:20b says, "'I am with you always, *even* to the end of the age.' Amen." If you have walked away from God, maybe you are mad or disappointed; it's time to come back. He yearns to be your companion. He wants you close. He wants to bless you. I Corinthians 13:4-8a (MSG) says, "Love never gives up. Love cares more for others than for self. Love doesn't want what it doesn't have. Love doesn't strut, Doesn't have a swelled head, Doesn't force itself on others, Isn't always 'me first,' Doesn't fly off the handle, Doesn't keep score of the sins of others, Doesn't revel when others grovel, Takes pleasure in the flowering of truth, Puts up with anything, Trusts God always, Always looks for the best, Never looks back, But keeps going to the end. Love never dies." Go back over that list. That's God, His love for you and His love through you. You can depend on it today. Work on strengthening each aspect of love in your life. Don't feel bad if you have fallen short in any or many areas. You are a work in progress! Be mindful of His love today, it never fails or gives up. Ever.

10 April I almost made it into my meeting that morning before the storm caught up with me. I had driven through the rain, but when I reached my destination, the ground was still dry. As I fetched my briefcase from the back seat a raindrop landed on my shoulder. "Here it comes!" I thought. More drops followed in rapid succession. So, I hurried. An umbrella was in the trunk. Retrieving it quickly, I hoisted it above my head and it sheltered me a bit, however the rain was driving – I still got wet.

Today's song is, "Word Of God Speak" ~ MercyMe. This song is entreating God to speak. Pouring down like the rain. To show through His Word that He is present. To show His majesty. To show His holiness. Sometimes God wants to speak to you in a still, small voice. (I Kings 19:12) Other times, He brings it like a thunderstorm. (Exodus 9:23) He knows what you need and when you need it. The key is in His Word – the Bible. Don't wait for a booming voice to overwhelm you, telling you what to do or where to go. What God has to say to you is written in His book. His letters. The accounts of the works of God and the life of His people and His Son. Instruction, direction, revelation, encouragement, wisdom are all found within its pages. To really hear His Word, you must be familiar with His Word. All He has to say about you is there. You may feel like you are on your own, but God will catch up with you. He will show you, dropping a little at first into your heart. Then get ready because, "Here it comes!" God will pour out blessings, wisdom, and direction, everything you need. So listen to Him today. It may be the still, small voice, or it may be the thunderstorm that you need to hear. Seek Him in the scriptures and soon you will be soaked with God's presence and His love.

11 April There was a show we used to watch that had a character who often said, "Look what I can do!" He would desire all the attention. He was a child. He wanted the focus to be on him. We though it was silly.

Today's song is, "Show Me Your Glory" ~ Third Day. This song expresses my desire to see God's glory. I want to see your face, God. I want to be in your presence. I just can't go on without you...It's a yearning for the environment that only God can create. How much of your life is focused on what you can do? What you can do is limited. When you focus on God however, your potential is limitless. Your mindset today is critical. Focusing on the negative will grow it in your life. But, focusing on God will increase His presence in your life. Long to see His face. Long to be in His presence. Long to experience His glory. This brings you to a place where you can receive from Him. Don't let it be all about you. Let it be all about God. Matthew 6:33 says, "But seek first the kingdom of God and His righteousness, and all these things shall be added to you." Putting God first opens the channel for all the things of this life. Set aside your silliness, direct your focus to the Lord. Seek all that He is and all that He has. His face. His glory. His presence. It will affect you. Change you. Cause you to increase. So then you will say, "Look what God can do!"

12 April We built our house on a deer path. The deer still come by and leave their mark. They have destroyed several trees and dined on the tender leaves of plants in our yard. It's still their territory; we just decided to put our home right in the middle of their spot. They were here first and I suppose they will still be here for years to come.

Today the song is, "You Reign" ~ MercyMe. Even before the world was created, God was. Now, He is. He will always be. He reigns and He deserves the glory. You are in His territory today-a part of His Kingdom, if you have built your house on Him. The Rock. Matthew 7:24-27 (MSG) says, "These words I speak to you are not incidental additions to your life, homeowner improvements to your standard of living. They are foundational words, words to build a life on. If you work these words into your life, you are like a smart carpenter who built his house on solid rock. Rain poured down, the river flooded, a tornado hit—but nothing moved that house. It was fixed to the rock. But if you just use my words in Bible studies and don't work them into your life, you are like a stupid carpenter who built his house on the sandy beach. When a storm rolled in and the waves came up, it collapsed like a house of cards." Realize that He does reign today. The key is if you will let Him. He has a path for you. Trust in Him. Proverbs 3:5-6 (MSG) says, "Trust God from the bottom of your heart; don't try to figure out everything on your own. Listen for God's voice in everything you do, everywhere you go; he's the one who will keep you on track." He was here before you and He will be here forever. Declare that He reigns in your life today. Release your burdens and lean on Him. Be the smart carpenter and build on the Rock.

13 April When my husband embraces me, I feel safe. I feel secure. It's comforting. It's empowering. There is actually a 'bonding' chemical released when people hug called oxytocin. So it's like medicine. I always feel better when I get a hug from my sweetheart. It reassures me. It helps me refocus and refresh. It's a few moments when it seems like we are the only two people in the world and all the stuff of life is suspended in time, waiting for us to return.

Today's song is "Revelation" ~ Third Day. This song entreats God to give me a revelation and show me what I should do. It declares that when I try to do things on my own, I find myself clueless. It includes the confession that I am nothing without God. You probably have some one special in your life. Someone to look to for direction, companionship, compassion, and love. You feel like you can do anything when they are on your team. You are strong because of them. That's how I feel about my husband. But anything I can do on my own, or even with him, pales in comparison to everything that God and I can do together. Jeremiah 33:3 (NIV) says, "Call to me and I will answer you and tell you great and unsearchable things you do not know." God will show you what you need to know. When He is with you, you can feel safe, secure, refreshed, comforted, refocused, and reassured. He will strengthen you even more than any person could and you can enjoy His presence. Nehemiah 8:10b says, "...for the joy of the Lord is your strength." So look to God today for your spiritual 'hug'. Be enveloped in His embrace. Take a few moments and be wrapped up in Him with all the stuff of life placed on hold. The stuff will still be there when you return, but you will be different. You will be better. You will have direction and you will never find yourself without a clue.

14 April We spoke with our financial planner regarding some land adjacent to our property that was part of the family farm. My husband expressed the dream to one day own the land between our house and the creek at the edge of the farm. The planner replied, "You already own it." It's part of our inheritance. Sometimes we have more than we realize.

Today's song is, "You Are I Am" ~ MercyMe. This song talks about how God can conquer giants and shut lions' mouths. Through all my feelings of doubt in myself, He lives in me. God is the "I am". I heard a message recently that reminded me – I have an inheritance with God and I need to claim it. He has so much for me. He can do so much for me.

The challenge that lies before you is in fully grasping His magnificence and abilities. There are amazing benefits to knowing God and accepting His Son, Jesus. His death and resurrection opened the door to your inheritance. It's powerful, but you must claim it. You can have a relationship with God today because of Jesus. He made a covenant with God and because you believe in Him, you can benefit from it. You are an heir of salvation! You have more than you realize. Shake off your inadequacies today – those feelings you are not good enough – Jesus was good enough! And pay attention, God doesn't want a performance from you. He wants to fulfill His promises for you. He can because He is 'I am'. He makes you more than a conqueror.

15 April We took a pod to the top of the Gateway Arch in St. Louis, Missouri. There were several of us on a school field trip. As a chaperone, I had to be brave. The Arch is 630 feet high! Wow. So we looked out the windows to the ground below, but we could also see the city streets, the park, the courthouse, the river, the stadium, and so much more. I went up with the first group and stayed until the last of our students had seen all they wanted. I was surprised at how much we could see from such a height. It's quite a different perspective.

Today the song is, "Already There" ~ Casting Crowns. From where God can see, He sees all that He designed and imagined. When He breathed life into me, all of the chaos of the world began to come together just like a great masterpiece. It's a plan that's picture perfect. God certainly has a different perspective on our lives than we do. Have you ever felt so close to a situation that you just couldn't figure the outcome? It's because you can't get a proper perspective. You are only seeing it from your point of view, which is limited. You can ask some one to help, finding what their observations are, but still limited. Or you can go to God and ask. He has unlimited perspective. He can see the big picture. He has the box top that goes with the puzzle which is your life. Psalm 25:4 (NIV) says, "Show me your ways, Lord, teach me your paths." He can and will show you. Throughout the Bible it says, "tell me", "show me", "teach me", "make me". God will do it for you. He will tell, but you must hear. He will show, but you must see. He will teach, but you must receive. He will make, but you must be pliable. You cannot learn from someone who does not know. You can not be shown by someone who has not seen. You can not be led by someone who has never been where you want to go. Seek qualified mentors today, but mainly seek God. He has the master plan for you. He can right the chaos in your life and make it picture perfect.

16 April At 5 years old, my youngest enjoyed his birthday at the campground. We tent-camp. His prized possession was a cowboy toy that talked. The cowboy had a pull string and was a featured character in a movie that told a story about toys. Though my son initially fell asleep on top of the picnic table, we moved him to the tent for the remainder of the night. At sunrise the silence of the campground was broken with the toy's exclamation, "There's a snake in my boot!" That cowboy toy went a lot of places with us, but I will never forget that camping trip.

About the movie. The cowboy toy was nabbed away from the little boy to whom it belonged. It was repaired and the inscription on the bottom of its foot – the name of the boy – was covered. Though the evidence of who the cowboy belonged to was gone, he knew he still belonged to the boy, Andy. Eventually the cowboy was returned to his rightful owner.

Today the song is, "Lord, I Give You My Heart" ~ Hillsong United. This song reminds you to honor God with all your heart. Give Him your heart and soul, live for Him. Give Him praise and adore Him. Ask Him to have His will be done in your life. No matter how far you have strayed today, or maybe you thought you've erased the evidence of where you really belong, you still belong there. You may have been hurt, misunderstood, falsely accused, or overlooked. You still belong with the one who calls you His own. The Lord wants you. He chose you. He knew you from the beginning. It's time to return. Go back into the arms of God. You belong. Let God's will be done in your life. If you have children or grandchildren, or someone young you care for, remind them that no matter how far they stray, they are loved. They belong in the family of God. They can come back. Let them come back. Pray for them. They may be struggling today. Take time to intercede, pray for them. Stand in the gap and help bridge their lives with the life that God has for them. Don't ever lose sight of how precious they are. Break the silence in your life today. Exclaim the goodness of God. Share it. Live it. Rejoice in it. You can make your journey unforgettable.

17 April I write today amidst the din of a hotel lobby. People enter and leave. Hostesses assist breakfast customers. The television broadcasts the daily news. Two men converse in a language unknown to me. Dishes clank. Radio plays. Refrigerator runs. There is a lot of activity, yet I sit quietly composing as I do daily. How, in all this distraction can I be calm, concentrated, and focused? Because this is a time God has given me. Today, I choose to not let the stuff of life keep me from what He has for me, and for you.

Today's song is, "You Are God Alone" ~ William McDowell. This song reminds us that God has been on His throne since before time began. He is eternal. The presence of God in your life as your source, your motivation, your guide, your help, your comfort, strength, joy, peace, patience, love, and your inspiration is more precious than gold. I Peter 1:7 (MSG) says, " I know how great this makes you feel, even though you have to put up with every kind of aggravation in the meantime. Pure gold put in the fire comes out of it *proved* pure; genuine faith put through this suffering comes out *proved* genuine. When Jesus wraps this all up, it's your faith, not your gold that God will have on display as evidence of his victory." It's your faith that matters. Your faith in God. Your faith in all that He has in store for you. He is holding on to it until you are ready to receive it. When you are distracted, you can miss it. When you have to put up with aggravation, delay, and heartache, you can be assured of your faith. Hebrews 11:1-2 (MSG) says, "The fundamental fact of existence is that this trust in God, this faith, is the firm foundation under everything that makes life worth living. It's our handle on what we can't see. The act of faith is what distinguished our ancestors, set them above the crowd." So, do you see God today on the throne of your life? Are you able to focus on Him, strengthen your faith and see what He has for you? It's good. Putting up with and working through the difficulties that you are facing is helping to prove that your faith is genuine. Don't give up or give in. Press on, press in. Be still for a moment or longer. Focus. Believe. Enjoy His presence as you would welcome the warmth of the sun on a spring day. Turn your face toward Heaven, breath gently and feel God. He is for you today. Don't ever, ever doubt it.

18 April At our high school football games we would direct a chant to the opposing fans, "We've got spirit, yes we do! We've got spirit how 'bout you??" The volley of cheering would continue until both sides were yelling, "We've got more! We've got more!" I enjoyed being a fan and it was even better when our team was winning! Go Pirates!

Today's song is, "Our God" ~ Chris Tomlin. This song proclaims that our God is stronger, greater, and higher than any. He is awesome and powerful. That's our God. This week I was reminded that people do not want to board a sinking ship. They want to be involved with a team that is winning! How exciting it is to be a part of the family of God. Winners like no others. Our God is the greatest. Why? His love. His character. His power. His sacrifice of His only Son. His choice to give us free will to accept Jesus. As a Christian, you should know beyond a shadow of a doubt that you have the best. You have promises and an inheritance. You have grace and favor. You have power and authority in Christ. You need to believe the best and believe you have the best. Even if it's by faith. You have the best spouse, the best kids, the best family, the best pastor, the best church, the best job, the best friends, the best relationships, and the best future. When you believe that you have the best, you can stop struggling. I'm not saying stop setting goals or reaching for all God has for you. I'm saying, you have the best available. Partake. Don't second guess. Stay on the team where God has placed you. Win there. Psalm 23:1-3 (MSG) says, "God, my shepherd! I don't need a thing. You have bedded me down in lush meadows, you find me quiet pools to drink from. True to your word, you let me catch my breath and send me in the right direction." Focus on what you have today. Focus on the best that is to come. God will direct you. He will lead you. He's the best. And remember, you've got Spirit, yes you do!

19 April My cousin from Pennsylvania welcomed us when we visited years ago. It was the January that my mother passed away. He shared with us a gift that he often gave to his friends. It was a round wooden disc the size of a half-dollar. On it was the word, "Tuit". He said, "You know how you've wanted to do something special or significant but can't muster the motivation? You decide that you will work on that when you get around to it. Well, here's 'a round Tuit'. Now you can proceed!"

Today the song is, "Lift Me Up" ~ The Afters. This song tells you that God lifts you when you are weak. His arms are there to catch you, so you can let go and surrender to Him. You try on your own strength over and over again. You fall short. Again and again. So you stop. 'Not worth it', you think. 'Too hard', you whine. 'Never will happen', you lament. 'Maybe later', you sigh. Stop it. Pretend that I am right now handing you one of my cousin Bob's round 'Tuit's'. So now that you have one, you can get around to doing what God has called you to. No more excuses, whining, lamenting, or sighing. Yes, you are weak, but He is strong! 2 Corinthians 12:9-10 (MSG) says, "My grace is enough; it's all you need. My strength comes into its own in your weakness. Once I heard that, I was glad to let it happen. I quit focusing on the handicap and began appreciating the gift. It was a case of Christ's strength moving in on my weakness. Now I take limitations in stride, and with good cheer, these limitations that cut me down to size— abuse, accidents, opposition, bad breaks. I just let Christ take over! And so the weaker I get, the stronger I become." You have limitations today. But focus on your gifts. Focus on what you and God can accomplish together! Let go and surrender to Him. He will catch you when you fall. He will bring you back up again. Surrender completely. He will make you strong. It's time you got a round Tuit.

20 April I guess I was about 8 when my mom launched a huge surprise party for my birthday. The girls all hid in the basement and I ventured down to fetch something Mother had told me to get. Surprise! What a great occasion! How did she get so many friends to come to the party? I remember getting lots of presents, lots of dolls. We took a group picture on the front porch-so many little girls. It was a beautiful April day, one I will never forget.

Another birthday is on the horizon. The mark of yet another year of life. Time to reflect on what has changed, what is the same, what I have learned, how I have grown, what I have experienced, lost, and gained. It's time to regroup. Time to look forward. Relish in the past accomplishments, yes, but focus on the future. I am sure it will be a happy birthday.

Today the song is, "Jesus The Same" ~ Israel & New Breed. He is the same yesterday, today, and forever. James 1:17 says, "Every good gift and every perfect gift is from above, and comes down from the Father of lights, with whom there is no variation or shadow of turning." No variation. God is consistent. You can count on Him. Always. His stability fuels your ability to change. His word is a constant guide. His ways are a steady standard. His character is dependable. James 1:16-17 (MSG) says, "So, my very dear friends, don't get thrown off course. Every desirable and beneficial gift comes out of heaven. The gifts are rivers of light cascading down from the Father of Light. There is nothing deceitful in God, nothing two-faced, nothing fickle." So stay on course today. Keep moving forward. Year after year improve. Grow. Change. Keep your eyes and heart fixed on Him. That will keep your path straight. Just like plowing a field, you focus on a stationary object. Because focusing on something that is changing or moving (like a cow) will cause you to go off course and your rows will all be crooked. God is there, ever present in your life. Consistent. Reliable. Faithful. Strive likewise to be consistent, reliable, and faithful. Your harvest will be huge and you will look forward to each new year with great anticipation. Who knows, you might just get a fantastic surprise!

21 April There is a launch roller coaster at a local amusement park. I like roller coasters, but this one goes backwards too! So, I was afraid to go on it. I wanted to be brave, but I just couldn't even think about going. My son was a great encouragement as I recall. Okay, basically he called me a "chicken". But he reassured me that it was no big deal. After all, so many people had been on it and survived! Finally, my courage rose to a level for me to get in line for this adventure. I trusted that it would be fun. Guess what. It was fun! I wish I would have taken the ride much sooner! Next time I won't freeze up when I get the opportunity to try something new, even if it's scary to me at first.

Today the song is, "When I Am Afraid" ~ Clay Crosse. This song talks about how I will trust God when I am afraid. He is a fortress and a shelter for me. I can rest in him and renew my courage. He is faithful and true to His promises. Trust in the Lord. Where is your trust level today? Are you walking by what you see? Or are you walking by faith? Proverbs 3:5 says, "Trust in the Lord with all your heart, and lean not on your own understanding;" Fear is contrary to trust. The Bible says, "Fear not." Isaiah 41:10 (MSG) says, "Don't panic. I'm with you. There's no need to fear for I'm your God. I'll give you strength. I'll help you. I'll hold you steady; keep a firm grip on you." Don't react to what it looks like today; respond to what God has to say about it. When you feel launched out to who-knows-where or you feel like you are going backwards, trust in Him. He will hold you steady and give you peace in the situation. Philippians 4:6-7 (MSG) says, "Don't fret or worry. Instead of worrying, pray. Let petitions and praises shape your worries into prayers, letting God know your concerns. Before you know it, a sense of God's wholeness, everything coming together for good, will come and settle you down. It's wonderful what happens when Christ displaces worry at the center of your life." It's the peace that goes way beyond what you can comprehend! In the midst of chaos, you can have that calmness. You are immune to the whirlwind. That's God's peace. The best way to ensure the peace of God is to soak yourself in scripture. Know God by knowing His Word. It becomes your foundation and gives you the stability you need. So face your fears today. Tell them to back off, because your God is bigger!

22 April I have a couple of good friends who each had loved ones die recently. The loss is never easy, no matter how much you think you're ready for it. For me, it is an opportunity to reflect on my own losses and how I have come through them. I always pray that I can be an encouragement to others during these times. It is reassuring when I find that the person who has passed knew the Lord. Why? Because they are in heaven! The earthly body is like a glove that falls away while the spirit goes to God. 2 Corinthians 5:8 says, "We are confident, yes, well pleased rather to be absent from the body and to be present with the Lord." So, for those who die in the Lord, we who believe in Christ as Savior will see them again upon our own arrival into eternity.

Today's song is "Mighty To Save" ~ Hillsong United. This song reminds us that Jesus rose and conquered the grave. That's what sets Him apart from the other spiritual leaders in the world. He rose from the dead! He ascended into Heaven! He sits at the Father's right hand! He destroyed the finality of death for us as believers. 1 Thessalonians 4:14 (MSG) says, "And regarding the question, friends, that has come up about what happens to those already dead and buried, we don't want you in the dark any longer. First off, you must not carry on over them like people who have nothing to look forward to, as if the grave were the last word. Since Jesus died and broke loose from the grave, God will most certainly bring back to life those who died in Jesus." I get excited when I think about seeing my mom again. About seeing all those who have gone before me. Honestly, it's not about the good people and the nice people. It's not about the famous or the heroes. It's about those who surrendered to the Lord and said something like, "Jesus, come into my heart. I believe you died for me and you rose again. Forgive me for my mistakes. Make me new." John 3:16 says, "For God so loved the world that He gave His only begotten Son, that whoever believes in Him should not perish but have everlasting life." Today, remember those who have gone before you. Make sure your place is secure in eternity. Share this good news with some one who you think may not know. Being saved from eternal death is like being pregnant. You are, or you are not. You aren't "kind of". There aren't earned levels. There is God's grace for you to accept. Now is the time. How exciting it is when you know you have life eternal with the Lord!

23 April College days were fun. I decided to apply for membership in a campus club. However, I was initially rejected. Later, I found out that someone had reservations about me joining because I was "squirrel-ly" in high school. First of all, I didn't even know what that meant. Second of all, I wasn't going to let that get me down. At the next opportunity, a friend campaigned for me, assuring the members that I would be a great asset. Result – Accepted! Being liked and being part of a group is fulfilling. It's fulfilling when it adds to your life. The relationships can last a lifetime.

I was reluctant to accept this song today. 'More whimsical than inspirational', I thought. 'Not spiritual enough', I thought. 'Not substantial enough', I thought. 'Must be something to learn here', I concluded.

Today's song is "Love You Like A Love Song" ~ Salena Gomez. A love song is positive, inspiring, and idealistic. It's an emotional embrace. This song declares a love like that. There was a time when some one thought of me as too whimsical, not spiritual enough, not substantial. But then I was given a second chance. I was offered the opportunity for a relationship, one that would last for the rest of my life. Relationships with friends and family can be positive, inspiring, and idealistic. You can be excited about great relationships. You can love them like a love song. You feel good when they are around. You relax. You enjoy their presence. Now think of your relationship with God. That is fulfilling. That is amazing. That is motivating. It's so much more than any connection you can have with people today. Immerse yourself in God's presence. Feel His embrace. It is like no other. It's knowing that you belong in the family of God. If you feel lost, turn around. God is there waiting for you. Stressed? He's there. Hopeless? There. Discouraged, depressed, disillusioned? God is there – to be your Father, and Christ is there to be your friend. (Psalm 68:5, Proverbs 18:24) You aren't alone. You're never alone when you have God in your life. You are a part of a group in eternity. You are – Accepted!

24 April When we go to the beach, we like to take some cheese curls snacks. They aren't for us to eat; they are to feed the seagulls. It only takes one throw and you have a crowd of gulls hovering, swooping, and catching the curls. Even when the boys were little, we would let them stand on the sand and toss the treats to the birds. There was a lot of laughter. It was so much fun! Before we knew it, all the cheese curls were gone. Then so were the seagulls.

Today the song is, "The Stand" ~ Michael W. Smith. This song talks about surrendering yourself to the Lord. Be in awe of Him who gave all. Sometimes you just want to keep things to yourself. You want to say, "Mine" and yet when you do that, then that is all you will have. When you give it to God, dedicate it, surrender, then He can do so much more with it. A bag of cheese curls can feed two little boys who already had lunch or feed 50 hungry seagulls; and in the process create laughter, memories, and stories to tell. Giving them up and not keeping them resulted in more. Exodus 4:2-4 (KJV) says, "And the Lord said unto him (Moses), What is that in thine hand? And he said, A rod. And he said, Cast it on the ground. And he cast it on the ground, and it became a serpent; and Moses fled from before it. And the Lord said unto Moses, Put forth thine hand, and take it by the tail. And he put forth his hand, and caught it, and it became a rod in his hand." After Moses surrendered his walking stick to God and His instruction, it was changed. Moses now held the rod of authority. When you follow Moses throughout Exodus, you see that what Moses gave to God became more. What is in your hand today? What do you have that you can surrender to God? Say, "Use this, Lord....Use me." It may be something others think of as insignificant, like a walking stick or a bag of snacks, but to you it is important or special. You have held it tightly and said, "It's mine". Relinquish it and God will make more of it. It will still be yours, but it will be changed. God wants to work through you. "Through" means that it keeps going. Keeps helping. Keeps giving. Keeps making a difference. It does not mean that it stops with you. You want to be used of God to help others. When you lay it down, whatever it may be, then pick it up, it will bring joy to your life. Take time now to give it to God. Make the most of the opportunity because before you know it, it will be gone.

25 April We have some friends that just adopted a son. How amazing that is. He was chosen. He belongs in their family now. I can see just by being around them that they love him a lot! They love him deeply. It's a great opportunity and a great responsibility. They are already great parents and I am certain that there are tremendous days ahead for all of them.

Today's song is, "Kings & Queens" ~ Audio Adrenaline. This song reminds us that every child dreams of belonging and being loved. God will not let them be defeated. It declares that we will love "the least of these." Matthew 25:40 (CEB) says, "Then the king will reply to them, 'I assure you that when you have done it for one of the least of these brothers and sisters of mine, you have done it for me.'" Sometimes the people or things that seem 'least' on the outside, turn out to be real game changers. That little boy has turned my friends' lives upside-down, in a good way. Things are incredibly different for them. What is it in your life that could be a 'game-changer' today? You maybe haven't noticed it before. You may have overlooked it. Some one else may have walked away from it, but you saw. It's a key, a key to your future. What is it that can make all the difference? Who is it that can make all the difference? God is sending people your way every day. Have you noticed? Have you been a help to them? Have you ever considered that the "chance meeting" was actually not by chance at all? God has a design for your life, a floor-plan if you will. He knows how every part fits together. It's an intricate design. It's complex. Take a look. How have you been building your life? How much of your life plan is complete? What parts are you still deciding on? What has not arrived quite yet? What did you forget to request? Is your foundation firm? Is your life secure and protected? Do you have room for others? Make sure you have a place for even the 'least' in your home, your group, your life. Love them. They have a need to belong, just like you. Don't be moved by stereotypes, statuses, backgrounds, appearance, giftedness, or skills. Love them for who they are. Leave the rest to God. He will not let them be defeated. They are not losers. We can all be adopted into the family of God. We are chosen, loved, and we belong. You are accepted when you accept Jesus in your heart. Know that. Embrace that. Then, go out and turn your world upside-down!

26 April I was introducing myself to several groups of people at a church youth event when I met my husband. Part of my job was to make everyone feel welcomed. I liked meeting new people, especially cute boys. I was 16. A bunch of us went to a burger place afterwards. I am forever grateful to my friend who got that cute boy's name and address. It was the beginning of an amazing relationship that has made a difference in my life on so many levels.

Today the song is, "Hello, My Name Is" ~ Matthew West. This song names the many lies that the enemy tries to tell you about who you are. But you are no longer defined by what is in your past because you've been saved, changed, and set free. Your name is "Child of the one true King." Today is my birthday. I am looking at who I am, who I am becoming, how far I have come and how far I have to go. Though I have already lived many years, there are so many more to enjoy. I am not yet middle-aged, for after all, what is the middle of eternity? The life you have is because of the choices you have made. You may be able to look back on the crossroads in years past and see what has led to where you are now. It's great if you like it. But if you don't, you can change it. You can change your location by changing your choices. If you are struggling today, you may be listening to lies of who you were. With God though, you are a new person. 2 Corinthians 5:17 says, "Therefore, if anyone *is* in Christ, *he is* a new creation; old things have passed away; behold, all things have become new." Shed the labels of the past and see yourself for who God sees you. Your relationship with God is like no other. Treat it that way. Don't ever take it for granted. You deserve to have a fulfilled and abundant life. Take hold of all that is yours in Christ and say, "Hello" to the you that is victorious, the you that is free, the you that is confident, the you that is courageous, the you that is wise, and the you that is simply amazing! You are a child of the one true King!

27 April I've met children with confidence and I've met ones with attitude. Confidence in this sense is positive. Attitude, offputting. Several days ago, I met a young man with confidence who shook my hand, looked me in the eye, and spoke politely. He offered conversation at lunch among adults without demanding to be the center of attention as is the tendency of so many children. I could tell he had been taught by his parents. He was given a good example. He was secure in his family and with others. I believe he will be a success as an adult as well, because of positive influences and the reality of God in his life. What a difference that makes!

Today the song is, "My Redeemer Lives" ~ Nicole Mullins. This song reflects the payment for my sins that Jesus made by giving His life. He rose from the dead and there is life in me because of Him. You may have grown up going to church. You may have never been to church. Though church does not a Christian make, going to church is where you grow, develop, and can continue to be transformed. Your relationship with Christ is paramount, but you are not an island. Other people in your life can make all the difference. Great Bible teaching can make all the difference. A good example can make all the difference. Think about that when you decide to go to church. Philippians 1:6 says, "Being confident of this very thing, that He who has begun a good work in you will complete *it* until the day of Jesus Christ;" You can be confident of His work in you. You can also be confident because of His work in you. I really like The Message version of this verse which says, "There has never been the slightest doubt in my mind that the God who started this great work in you would keep at it and bring it to a flourishing finish on the very day Christ Jesus appears." Be thankful for that ongoing work! Remember that when you have a rough day or a tough day. Remember that when people let you down and maybe you didn't handle it well. Remember it when you had a bad attitude or wanted to be the center of attention when it wasn't your place to be so. He's working on you! It's going to be a great life and a great finish – a flourishing finish! So, be mindful that your Redeemer lives today. He is not in the grave. He has risen! Then go out, look life in the eye, shake hands with it, and be polite. Your confidence will attract others and your confidence because of Christ will make all the difference.

28 April Fluffy, the short-haired cat, likes to be mischievous. He gets up where he shouldn't. He can't settle himself. He's very energetic. He scratches the furniture. I corrected him the other day. "NO" I said. "Get down!" I exclaimed as I nudged him. A few minutes later he still wanted to sit in my lap. He was unscathed by my harshness. He knows I won't hurt him. He knows he belongs here and he's loved. Will he stop his nonsense? Probably not. He's a cat. He thinks he owns the place.

Today the song is, "Love You With My Life" ~ Steven Curtis Chapman. This song talks about the question of when I say, "I love you Lord" what does it mean? It's one thing to say it and another thing to show Him that this love is true. The way to do it is to love with your life. Listen, obey, and live your love for the Lord. Love is a choice you make. It's not a feeling. Feelings are fleeting. Love is committing. When I got married I promised to love my husband in all situations. This love is forever. There is no other option for me, for us. We say, "I love you" a lot. But we also show our love. When you love God, you can't just say you love Him, you need to show Him. Show Him by your deeds. By your attitude. By your serving and giving to others. By dedicating your life to be the person God meant for you to be. Love Him with your life. Circumstances can cause you to falter in your love for God. They can cause you to question. They can cause you to want to quit. They can hurt you. They can make you think, "What's the use?" But I earnestly advise you…do not let circumstances determine your love for the Lord. You may think He has turned His back, but He is working in the background until you are ready for all He has for you. Be committed. This love is forever. God showed you His love when He sent Jesus. John 3:16 says, "For God so loved the world that He gave His only begotten Son, that whoever believes in Him should not perish but have everlasting life." He loved you so much – He gave. Time to reciprocate. Dedicate your life, your family, your portfolio, your job, your stuff to God. Show Him that you love Him too. This will enable the tide to turn in your favor. Do not lose heart. If things are tough, you feel nudged out of what you thought should be yours, remember where you belong. Remember who loves you. Be unscathed. Untouched. Unharmed. Settle yourself and crawl into the lap of God. He cares for you. He loves you. So love Him with your life.

29 April My husband told me that there's one thing I can never cross off my 'to-do' list as finished. It's the laundry. It's always there. I can put the last load in and there it is, something else to wash. Laundry will forever be in process. Fortunately, our household has evolved and everyone now does their own wash. But the principle still holds. I cannot ignore it. It grows. I cannot out run it. I cannot work ahead. It can be overwhelming at times. However, when I make head way and really feel like it's under control, it can be satisfying. (Until I walk into the next room and see the dirty socks on the floor.) Laundry is like love. It is eternal, it never ends. (I Corinthians 13:8) So, I love laundry.

Today's song is, "One Thing Remains" ~ Jesus Culture. This song reminds me that God's love never fails, gives up, or runs out. It both satisfies me and overwhelms me. You may love laundry. But, God's love is greater! You can always count on God to love you, no matter what. He doesn't base His love on what you've done. He doesn't base it on your past, your heritage, your finances, your neighborhood, your education, or even your emotional stability. He loves you. Period. Deuteronomy 23:5b says, "but the Lord your God turned the curse into a blessing for you, because the Lord your God loves you." He can take what's messed up, stained, and dirty in your life and turn it to blessings! 1 John 1:9 says, "If we confess our sins, He is faithful and just to forgive us *our* sins and to cleanse us from all unrighteousness." He is a pro at cleaning. You can place your sins before God and His forgiveness is there. You can be spotless before God. Each day remember to look to Him, confess, and you will be clean again. His love is overwhelming especially when you don't feel you deserve it. His love is satisfying when you realize it's always there.

30 April Tenacity. It means to be diligent, courageous, gutsy, persistent, stubborn, determined, firm, inflexible, resolved, and steadfast. When you are tenacious you have backbone, spunk, moxie, chutzpah, true grit. It's that dogged determination that, like a bull dog, will not let go. It's that part of you that will never, ever give up.

Today's song is, "Will Not Be Moved" ~ Natalie Grant. This song declares that though I stumble or fall down, I will not be moved from the solid rock of Jesus, upon which I stand. Even through mistakes and heartache, I won't be moved. I will stand firm. What does it take to move you today? What will shake you to the core? What will move you from your stand? Whatever it is indicates your strength – your tenacity. It's time to stop being moved by your feelings, opinions, hurts, fears, doubts, and others lack of encouragement. Time to pull up your boot straps, put your big boy or big girl pants on and get to it. Get to what God has for you to do. That thing you know you have backed away from. You've avoided. You've stepped away. You hoped that some one else would do it. That some one else would rescue you. Time to stand up. Stand firm. Stand strong. Find your tenacity again. Read that first paragraph once more. Say it aloud. That's you. It is! Matthew 7 talks about building your house on the Rock. Build your life on the Rock which is Christ. You will stand firm when others sink. You will stand strong when others are blown away. You will be victorious when others have given up. Do not be moved today. Be the one with moxie, chutzpah and true grit! You can do it!

1 May I had started working out – exercising. My son was coaching me and I couldn't even manage 1 sit-up. So I gave up and I went out for ice cream. NO I didn't. I tried again. It wasn't too many days and I could do some sit-ups. I did 87 of them in one session! Going from zero to 87 seemed impossible. I didn't think I could. I'd say, "I can't" My friend would reply, "Well, can't never could!" Another would have said that 'I can't' stands for I Certainly Am Not Trying. A movie character once said, essentially, that there is no 'try', only 'do'. I could talk about it when I was doing it, but now I am silent on the matter. Why? I am not currently working out. Time for me to overcome my obstacles and 'do' it again. NO more trying.

Today's song is, "We Will Overcome" ~ Desperation Band. This song affirms that we will overcome the trials and challenges of life because of Jesus' life sacrifice and because of the Word of God that is a part of our testimonial. There are so many things you have to overcome in your life. I am sure you have your own list. It may be a really short list, or it may be super long. Either way, the obstacles you face are not impossible to defeat. You can conquer them. Proverbs 6:6-11 (MSG) says, "You lazy fool, look at an ant. Watch it closely; let it teach you a thing or two. Nobody has to tell it what to do. All summer it stores up food; at harvest it stockpiles provisions. So how long are you going to laze around doing nothing? How long before you get out of bed? A nap here, a nap there, a day off here, a day off there, sit back, take it easy—do you know what comes next? Just this: You can look forward to a dirt-poor life, poverty your permanent house guest!" That may sound harsh, but it's Bible. It does no good to live a life of laziness. Today's choice to sit idly by will lead to an idle future. Then it will lead to poverty. Poverty occurs not only in money, but in health, relationships, family, education, and skills. Just so, riches occur in all those areas. So you can overcome today, no matter what life has thrown at you. Sit up! You can do it. You can repeat it. You can hang in there and you will see great results. It's time to work it out.

2 May We have a wooden chair that was a part of my parents' bedroom set. I'm not sure how old it is. It was in disrepair. It was put in a corner in the basement. I didn't want to get rid of it, but it wasn't usable in that condition. So, a while back, I brought it upstairs. I gave it a fresh coat of paint and recovered the seat. It looks great! Now it's right inside our back door where we all pass it several times a day and are able to use it. I'm really glad I took the time to restore that old chair. It's now both functional and beautiful!

Today's song is, "Mighty To Save" ~ Hillsong United. This song requests that God take me as I am with all my failures and my fears and restore my life as I surrender and follow Him. Restoration. God wants to restore to you all you have lost. He wants you to have better. It's your job to surrender to Him. Let yourself be changed by Him. In 1 Samuel 30, David returns home to a devastating situation. His city is burned and his family has been kidnapped. His friends turn on him. He had a choice. He chose to go from destruction to restoration. In verse 6, he strengthened/encouraged himself. In verse 8, he asked God's help and his expectations were lifted – he could see the possibility of victory. In verse 24, David shows favor and honor to all the men who worked/fought with him by sharing the spoil with all because of the result that was in verse 19, "And nothing of theirs was lacking, either small or great, sons or daughters, spoil or anything which they had taken from them; David recovered all." You may feel like you're stuck in a corner. You may feel unusable, unworthy, in disrepair, but God. God is a restorer. You may need a recovery. You may need a new coat of God's love, forgiveness, understanding, grace, mercy, and favor. Encourage yourself. Get ready for what God wants to do in your life. He can do a new thing, a beautiful thing in you. Your life will be a testimony of God's goodness. If you are waiting for your breakthrough, God's probably waiting for you to get ready. He's waiting for you to be strong enough for all He has for you. So, get strong today. Your best days are ahead!

3 May There's a difference between knowing how to juggle and being a juggler. My son knows how to juggle and he is a juggler. To him it is not just a skill or a gift. It is a passion. It is a lifestyle. It is consuming. It's becoming a quest, a career, a future. It is more than a simple 3-ball cascade. I am inspired when I see his dedication. I marvel at his achievement as a juggler. I have become an encourager and promoter for him. It makes me proud to see him do so much more with something he first learned at age 10. Now he excels and he often draws a crowd. It's not just what he does that makes him a juggler, it's who he is.

Today's song is, "Mighty To Save" ~ Hillsong United. Here's a part to this song that is in my heart today. The part about shining your light and letting the whole world see, singing for the glory of Christ, who is risen. Christian witnessing is openly sharing the good news about Christ and His offer of redemption. Being a Christian witness is openly living the life that Christ intended and exemplified in the Bible. Shining the light of the Lord is more than something you do; it's who you should be. Matthew 5:16 says, "Let your light so shine before men, that they may see your good works and glorify your Father in heaven." and in The Message verses 14-16 says, "Here's another way to put it: You're here to be light, bringing out the God-colors in the world. God is not a secret to be kept. We're going public with this, as public as a city on a hill. If I make you light-bearers, you don't think I'm going to hide you under a bucket, do you? I'm putting you on a light stand. Now that I've put you there on a hilltop, on a light stand—shine! Keep open house; be generous with your lives. By opening up to others, you'll prompt people to open up with God, this generous Father in heaven." There are so many opportunities to show the love of Christ, wherever you go. Your witness made a difference in people's lives. That's what it's all about. Know that today, people are watching. People are listening. Is your conversation uplifting? Are you pleasant? Are others glad to see you? How are you being a witness of the love of Christ? How are you letting your light shine? What good works are you doing? Your Christian witness, make it a passion. Make it a quest. Make it a lifestyle. Be dedicated. Be generous. Be excellent. Draw a crowd.

4 May We used to play 'Follow the Leader' when I was a kid. As leader, I'd go up on the sidewalk and everyone in line would too. I'd go around the tree and they would too. I'd go under the clothesline, they'd follow. Jump off the curb. Skip to the stop sign. Hop around to the back gate. It was more fun when there were more of us. If it was only me I'd be just out there goofing around.

Today's song, "Me Without You" ~ Toby Mac. This song conveys a message...Take a look. I am different because of the Lord. I was hooked from the beginning. There is no leader without followers. You are different because of the leaders in your life. The leader's significance as a leader is contingent on your response. Just so, when you are a leader, observe the response of those who follow you. This will let you know if your leadership is effective. To be a great leader, you must first be a great follower. Who are you following today? Is that person solid, reliable, and honest? Do they follow someone? Who is it? Observe your leadership heritage. Now decide what your leadership legacy will be. How will those who follow you be better or different? When you have decided, walk in it. Work in it. You have the ability to affect the lives of others. In Matthew 4:19 Jesus says, "Then He said to them, 'Follow Me, and I will make you fishers of men.'" Know who you are following and know why. Have an idea of the path. Have an idea of the destination. Then dedicate yourself to follow but also dedicate yourself to lead others. You are part of a bigger plan. Part of a lineage of leaders. In Christ you have a place to go and you have a responsibility and a privilege to lead others to His saving grace. Don't be out there by yourself. You don't want to live your life just goofing around.

5 May About 12 years ago, my chiropractor told me that the knee trouble that I was having was a degenerative condition. He thought he could help me, but basically said that it would get worse as time went on. It was painful and annoying. That week I had the opportunity to go for prayer at our church. The pastor's wife prayed for my knee. God healed me. The pain left and I do not have knee trouble even today. I am thankful for God's healing hand upon my life.

Today's song is, "Healing Hand Of God" ~ Jeremy Camp. This song talks about seeing how the healing hand of God reaches out and mends broken hearts. I am thankful that God not only heals bodies, but also broken hearts. It's hard to go forward when you are battling disease, but it's nearly impossible to continue when your heart, your will, is broken. You lose sight of the future. You lose hope. You lose the reason to fight for your promises. God is able and He is willing. Your job is to believe. Don't vacillate. James 1:6 says, "But let him ask in faith, with no doubting, for he who doubts is like a wave of the sea driven and tossed by the wind." Be all in today. Believe your guts out for all that God has for you. Don't believe the lies that God wants to hold back or that He's forgotten you. Don't believe that poverty, destitution, illness, and lack are your 'cross' to bear. Jesus already bore those things for you. 3 John 1:2 says, "Beloved, I pray that you may prosper in all things and be in health, just as your soul prospers." Yes! God wants you to prosper! Be healthy! Succeed! Joshua 1:8 gives the key to your success... "This Book of the Law shall not depart from your mouth, but you shall meditate in it day and night, that you may observe to do according to all that is written in it. For then you will make your way prosperous, and then you will have good success." That's it. He's there waiting to make it happen for you. In the meantime, soak yourself in the Bible, the Scriptures. Therein lays your promise. Your hope. Your future. Your strength. Your ability to handle the process that will get you to your victory! Once you know what God has to say about your situation, speak the answer. Do what you know to do and God will change things. Things do not have to get worse. You will see His healing hand upon your life!

6 May I played softball in the summer of my freshman year of high school. Mediocre at best, I played outfield. Finally, a ball came right to me and I caught it! I jumped up and down, celebrating my accomplishment! Then I realized that my team mates were yelling, "Throw it in! Throw it in!" I didn't know there was still a runner heading into home plate. Sadly, it's the only play I remember of that season.

Today the song is, "Forever Reign" ~ Hillsong. This song talks about how God is good even when I feel there's nothing good in me. Sometimes when you have a great victory, you can still feel painfully inadequate. It's humbling. It can stick with you. You can let it occupy your thoughts, your time, your life. When that happens, you stall. You stop. That is exactly what your enemy, the devil, wants to cause. How is it that when God gives you a win that it can be taken from you for the notion that you are somehow less? Humility is healthy. Self abasement is not. You need to feel a sense of accomplishment when you have truly achieved something. Ephesians 6:10-12 (MSG) says, "And that about wraps it up. God is strong, and he wants you strong. So take everything the Master has set out for you, well-made weapons of the best materials. And put them to use so you will be able to stand up to everything the Devil throws your way. This is no afternoon athletic contest that we'll walk away from and forget about in a couple of hours. This is for keeps, a life-or-death fight to the finish against the Devil and all his angels." The devil does want to destroy you. He wants you to discount your own strength. He wants you to waver and give up. But God has a different opinion of you! Psalm 18:32 says, "It is God who arms me with strength, and makes my way perfect." and The Message phrases it, "...God who armed me, then aimed me in the right direction". God wants to make you strong today. He wants to direct your path. So, shake off the lies of the devil who wants to tell you that you are less. Accept the truth of God that you are more. Celebrate your wins. Though you may not be perfect in all your endeavors, God is perfect. He is good. That's what you need to remember!

7 May I enjoyed my seven years as a school principal. On one particular occasion a student was suspected of cheating. It was thought that he was writing answers from a check key into his workbook, then blacking them out. When asked about the blotches in his book he claimed they were merely doodles. Thinking the answers may have been written in red ink (the only pen available at the scoring station) I got an idea. I applied correction fluid to the blotches in the student workbook. Though he tried to hide it, his secret was revealed! As if by magic, the red ink – which is not susceptible to being 'whited out'- suddenly appeared. There on the pages were the answers, clearly written!

Today the song is, "I Cannot Hide From You" ~ Clay Crosse. This song talks about how God knows everything about me, seeing every corner of my soul, all my thoughts, my steps, my words before I speak, where I've been and where I will go. He knows me well, all my stories, all my life. I can't hide from Him. You don't always get what you expect, but you get what you inspect when it comes to being a leader. So checking on things is what we did at the school. Having a good working relationship with the students was important. Having standards of honesty, integrity, and scholarship was also important. Standards. God still has them. He has requirements and there are consequences. He asks you to choose, and then you either reap the benefits or pay the price. Without standards, there is no excellence. Without expectations, there is mediocrity. Jeremiah 4:6 talks about setting the standard, "Set up the standard toward Zion. Take refuge! Do not delay! For I will bring disaster from the north, and great destruction." In this case it is a physical symbol, like a flag, that indicates a central rallying point for battle. It's a sign of resolve. It's a sign of strength. It's a sign of a special cause or of sovereignty. It is set firm in its place so it will not move. God knows all about you today. He's got a handle on who you are. He sees the hidden things in your life. But, He grants you the choice to select your standard. What will you allow in your life? What will you overlook? What will you support? What will you deny? What will you stand for? Make the choice. Set the standard of your life today. Make it excellent. When things get bad, your standard will stand firm. It will be your rallying point for victory over all that would come to destroy you. And by God's grace, you will not be moved.

8 May We went on a trip one weekend with some of the leaders from our church's youth ministry. One of the ladies in our room brought black shoes, about 5 pairs of black shoes! She explained – there were flats, heels, high heels, low heels, closed toes, and open toes. I laughed, thinking how absurd to have so many black shoes! However, I look in my closet today (all these years later) and I have about 18 pairs of black shoes! I know!

Today the song is, "Who You Are" ~ Unspoken. The part of the song I'm hearing today is about letting ashes fall where they will and return to Jesus, the foot of the cross, to His feet. When I think about feet it reminds me of a person's "walk" – their life. The feet of Jesus represent the life He lived. They represent where He walked and how He walked. His feet got Him where He wanted to go. His feet led Him out on the water. His feet took Him on the path of His ministry. His feet. Isaiah 52:7 (MSG) says, "How beautiful on the mountains are the feet of the messenger bringing good news. Breaking the news that all's well, proclaiming good times, announcing salvation, telling Zion, 'Your God reigns!'" Beautiful feet. You can stand on your own two feet, meaning that you are independent. You can drag your feet, postponing what you need to do. You can be swept off your feet, overwhelmed by someone who shows charm or enthusiasm. You can also sit at the feet of a mentor, leader, or teacher to learn from their wisdom. Where your feet tread is significant in Genesis 13:17, Deuteronomy 11:24, and Joshua 1:3, God makes the promise, "Every place that the sole of your foot will tread upon I have given you." This is a part of possessing your inheritance. Claiming what is yours by the location of your feet! Where are you walking today? What is your life like? Is it going on a path others would like to follow? Are you wandering on your own? Procrastinating? Enthralled by a personality? Or are you camped out at the feet of Jesus to learn, grow, and rest in Him? Let the junk of life fall away and seek His presence. Go to His feet. In His presence is fullness of joy. (Psalm 16:11) You will be bringing good news. So be ready for all occasions, events, and conditions. You can take His promise to all your walks of life. No matter what shoes you have on, or how many pairs you have, be assured that it's the feet of Jesus that paved the path for you, bled for you, and rose to walk again for you. His beautiful feet.

9 May My parents were married for just shy of 45 years. My husband's parents married nearly 61 years. Both separated only by death. They were committed. Examples. They showed us that you can stay together when you work at it. They took their vows seriously. So do we. Now, not long before we are 30 years married, there is no person that I would rather be with than my husband. Ever.

Today's song is, "I Won't Last A Day Without You" ~ Carpenters. (A hit single in 1974) This song professes that when I can't get over the rainbow and when my small dreams won't come true, even though I can take the madness the world gives to me, I won't last a day without you. This is an assurance that God has His hand in today's offering, because I'm thinking, "Where did that song come from?" I definitely have not heard it lately, but God has something to show both you and me today with it. How many days have you tried to make it on your own without God? How many more days will you attempt something great without letting Him have His hand in it? Even more so than a wife committed to a husband should be that covenant with God to abide in Him. Without God, you can do nothing significant. That is why you need Him to escape the ordinary and move into the extraordinary in your life. You believe things are fine, but they can always get better. You can do more, reach more, have more, affect more, lead more, give more, and experience more by taking that time each day to spend time with the Lord. He wants a lasting, consistent relationship. A life-long love affair. The yearning for His presence each day. The strength you get from fellowship with Him. The power to overcome obstacles, trials, and madness of the world comes from remaining faithful to Him. That sentence simply put…The power comes. You can't afford a day without Him. You need the power in your life. You need to stay long enough for results to happen. Don't quit on God. Build a relationship with Him. It is progressive. Don't think that things in your life will be instantaneous. Greatness takes time. A step at a time. It's an accumulation. Expect tomorrow to be better than today. Just keep working at it. Others will be inspired by your example! Then be assured that even when this life ends, you won't be separated from God.

10 May We rented jet skis in Gulf Shores. I rode with my oldest son. I was a bit apprehensive in the open water, but he did a good job driving. There was one really scary moment for me when we almost dumped, but my son recovered the vehicle and off we went! It was a beautiful day and the waves were maneuverable. I had a much better experience when I relaxed and trusted him to manage the jet ski. I trusted him with my life that day. We ended up having a lot of fun.

Today's song, "I Give Myself Away" ~ William McDowell. The part of the song speaks today where it declares that I am standing here, placing my life in your hands, Lord. I want so much to see your desires for me. I'm giving myself to you so you can use me.

Your life is in God's hands when you trust Him. It's not in His hands just because you say it is. And it's not something when things go wrong you say, "Well, my life is in God's hands" blaming Him for your wrong decisions. You must trust Him. Then your will lines up with His. His desires for your life will be revealed. When you give yourself to Him, you never lose; you always end up with more. The waves of life may wash upon you. Things may get scary at times. You may have some mishaps. But you will recover. Trust Him! Trust Him with your life! Proverbs 3:5-6 (MSG) says, "Trust God from the bottom of your heart; don't try to figure out everything on your own. Listen for God's voice in everything you do, everywhere you go; He's the one who will keep you on track." So relax today, trust God. He will bring to pass all that He has promised. You will enjoy life so much more. You will have so much more. In the process you will end up having a lot of fun!

11 May We have a cyclamen plant that sits by our sink in the kitchen. It has pink blooms. Usually when you get one of those, they bloom once, and then it's pretty much just a foliage plant. Sometimes you may get it to bloom again. However, we have had it now for about 3 years and it has bloomed constantly that entire time! Miraculous! Right now it's going through the second time of all the leaves dying away, but there are still about 5 flowers on it.

Today's song is, "Hurt & The Healer" ~ MercyMe. This song talks about how I am alive even though part of me has died. God takes my heart, bringing it back to life. There are times when part of you has died. It may be the loss of a person, a relationship, your health, your finances, your dream, or your confidence. Loss happens. It's a part of life. When you experience loss, your heart hurts. You feel emptiness or a wound. God is the one who can heal it. He can heal it faster than therapy. He can heal it more completely than medication! When are broken, God can fix it! Psalm 34:18 (MSG) says, "If your heart is broken, you'll find God right there; if you're kicked in the gut, he'll help you catch your breath." Others may think you will just have seasons and you can't bloom and thrive all the time, but God can make your seasons more productive. He will hold you up when you are weak, if you lean on Him. Don't give up. Help is right here waiting for you. You can bloom where you are planted. You can live again. You can experience the miraculous!

12 May I thought I saw one of my cats on the side of the highway this morning. Not alive. However it was time to get to church and I had to make a decision. Pets are important, but the people who were coming to be ministered to at the church are more important. My role each week is to serve. I volunteer. So, I committed the situation to prayer and kept heading for church. I knew the song for today and my question...was I willing to do what I was about to tell you? Surrender. I prayed. I confessed. I believe that what is important to me is important to God. That's because what is important to God is important to me too. My confession? That my cat would be there waiting for me when I got home. Alive. And that he would be the first one I would see. When I returned several hours later and entered the kitchen I was greeted by a very much alive and well "George" – incidentally the first one I saw. Then as if to say, "We're all okay." All of our cats filtered in and gathered around my feet. Well, I couldn't help but rejoice, celebrate and of course, give them all treats!

Today's song is, "I Surrender All" ~ Judson W. Van DeVenter (1896) "All to Jesus I surrender; all to Him I freely give; I will ever love and trust Him, In His presence daily live." This is a powerful song. The composer accepted Christ as Savior when he was 17 but made a full commitment to Christ about 24 years later. There's a difference between making a decision acknowledging Jesus as Lord and actually making Him Lord of your life. Submitting completely to His will. Luke 14:33 (NIV) says, "In the same way, those of you who do not give up everything you have cannot be my disciples." So, are you willing to trust God today? With all things, little and big? Do you find yourself doubting? Doubt saps your strength. Doubt is frustrating. Doubt will rob you from what God has for you. Could my cat situation have turned out differently? Yes. But it didn't. What are you saying today? Are you believing God for the best but still declaring that it won't happen? How's that working for you? Keep the words of your mouth lined up with God's word. Even if you are still in the convincing stage, convince yourself. Shake off doubt. Shake off fear. Shake off negative thoughts. As you surrender each and every part of your life to the Lord, you will find more fulfillment, more joy, love, and peace. You will find yourself fully alive. That's worth celebrating.

13 May My parents were 42 and 44 when I was born. Well seasoned by my siblings, my Mother and Daddy guided me well. I was later thankful for being raised with the values of my peers' grandparents. Education was important, as was social protocol, etiquette, honor, and responsibility. Sometimes it was a little embarrassing when the men my dad bowled with asked me if I liked coming to the alley with my 'grandpa'. I didn't like going to the amusement park with my parents because they were worn out in the early afternoon. However, they were my parents. I now have a better perspective. I am happy to have been their daughter.

Today the song is, "I'm Not Ashamed" ~ Ricardo Sanchez. This song affirms that I'm not afraid or ashamed of worshiping the Lord. There's a lot of different ways I can worship and I will not hold anything back. Sometimes it doesn't make sense that kids would be embarrassed around their parents. Maybe because they aren't in the loop of the latest trends. Maybe because they expect something other than what the son or daughter thinks is reasonable or rational. Maybe because they haven't taught honor. Maybe the children are being influenced by their peers. Do you ever feel embarrassed that you love God? Do you ever think that if you pray over your food or thank God openly that people will think badly of you? Do you fear persecution? 2 Timothy 3:12-13 (MSG) says, "Anyone who wants to live all out for Christ is in for a lot of trouble; there's no getting around it. Unscrupulous con men will continue to exploit the faith. They're as deceived as the people they lead astray. As long as they are out there, things can only get worse." Persecution will come. Are you strong enough to stand? When you are thankful for what Jesus has done for you, knowing that He gave His life in an excruciating, torturous death so that we may live life eternal, then persecution is bearable. The world hates the things of God. 1 John 3:13 (MSG) says, "So don't be surprised, friends, when the world hates you. This has been going on a long time." Do not be ashamed of God in your life. Eternal life is much more valuable than the approval of people. Honor God today. Give Him your attention, your admiration, your devotion. Do not be ashamed; be happy that you are His child.

14 May My goal is to consistently write this book, 1 page a day for an entire year. I sincerely don't believe that it was my idea. I believe that it was God's idea. My gifts and skills have been handed over to Him and daily He gives me a song. Additionally, an illustration comes. Someone asked me if it was hard to write every day. I have to be honest, no. This has been easy. It flows. The words just seem to be there. But, I do have to sit and write it. I do have to spend time praying. I do have to do some research. I do have to get still before God and listen. From day 1 this project has been dedicated to God. My aim is to yield each day to what it is to be for me and for you. Uplifting, challenging, thought provoking, and igniting. I want to help you in your spiritual walk, but I have found that my own walk has grown so much more steady, sound, and focused in the process.

Today the song is, "I Give Myself Away" ~ William McDowell. In this song, I offer my heart and my life as a living sacrifice. I place my dreams and plans in God's hands. What is your dream today? Is it bigger than you alone can achieve? Does it make you queasy because it's so big? Does it make you cry tears of joy when you think about reaching it? Creating a clear picture of your dream is great. Including God is paramount. But let's think a bit differently...Get still before God and listen. Don't try to think, "What shall I do?" Listen for instruction, direction, and inspiration. This is a listening with your heart, your spirit. That still small voice that speaks. That thought that comes into your head. The thought you know didn't come from anything you already knew. Jeremiah 33:3 (MSG) says, "Call to me and I will answer you. I'll tell you marvelous and wondrous things that you could never figure out on your own." The King James Version says, "... things, which you do not know." It's not spooky. It's not clairvoyance. It's not telepathy. It's God's supernatural ability. It can only happen when you yield yourself to Him. You give yourself away, so He can use you. He creates the dream in your heart. You may have your own ideas today, but what is God's idea for you? He can truly take you from good to great. From emptiness to fulfillment. From defeat to victory. Submit to God's will for you. Dream. Then do. Let each day be uplifting, challenging, thought provoking, and igniting. My prayer for you is that your God-given dreams all come true!

15 May We have 35 windows in our house. There is a lot of light that comes in each morning. I love the spring and summer months because the house is bright very early. It's easier to wake up and get going. There's not a lot of 'sleeping in' around here. When we have moderate weather, it's great to open windows and let in the fresh air. Gentle breezes cool the house and it's very pleasant. I am so thankful for our windows.

Today the song is, "Good Morning" ~ Mandisa. This song declares that it's a good morning! Waking up to a brand new day, I can step out because God gives me strength. It's just what I need – Hope for today is rising. God's mercy is new, it's a good morning! There's so much opportunity in each new day. You have a chance today to make of it what you wish. You decide to spend your day or to invest it. What are your plans? What are your goals? What are your dreams? Today you get another shot at success. Another time to get it right. Another opportunity to seize your destiny. If you feel like you have had it rough, take another perspective...In the sad, sad Book of Lamentations in the Bible, this song of wailing mourns the devastation in Jerusalem. However, in the 3rd chapter, Jeremiah realizes that he has hope, and in verses 19-24 (MSG) it says, "I'll never forget the trouble, the utter lostness, the taste of ashes, the poison I've swallowed. I remember it all—oh, how well I remember—the feeling of hitting the bottom. But there's one other thing I remember, and remembering, I keep a grip on hope: God's loyal love couldn't have run out, his merciful love couldn't have dried up. They're created new every morning. How great your faithfulness! I'm sticking with God (I say it over and over). He's all I've got left." When you think you're done, you're not. When you think it's over, it's not. When you think you have nothing left, you have God. His mercy. His grace. They can abound in you. You may be remembering the sadness, the sorrow, the failure of your life, but the other thing to remember and keep remembering is that God's love never runs out! So it *is* a good morning! Tell yourself if you haven't noticed yet. Stick with God. He is faithful. Don't sleep in. Let the fresh air cool you today. Create a pleasant atmosphere. Let as much light in as possible. John 8:12 says, "Then Jesus spoke to them again, saying, 'I am the light of the world. He who follows Me shall not walk in darkness, but have the light of life.'"

144

16 May I asked my son one day as we were going home from church, "What did you learn about today?" His response, as usual, was "Jesus." "What else?" I inquired. "God" He added. Though he wasn't articulating it, I knew that there was so much more being poured into him and his brother week after week about God, His Son, His character, and His love for us. Our boys have grown up in a Godly, teaching environment. I see now more than ever how valuable that has been.

Today's song is, "Whom Shall I Fear" ~ Chris Tomlin. This song talks about knowing who goes before me, who stands behind me, and who is always by my side. It's God. He's the God of Angel Armies. Here's what Zechariah 8 (MSG) tells about the God of Angel Armies...He cares. He's involved. He lives where you are. Nothing is too much for Him. He will bring you home (where you belong). He will stick with you. He will do right by you. He is taking your side. He will get you what you need. He will save you. He will bless you.

It also tells you in the same chapter...Get a grip on things and hold tight. You've come through a hard time, but things will get better. Become a 'good news' person. Don't be afraid. Be tuned in to what God is doing. Tell the truth. Do right by one another. Don't take unfair advantage of others. Don't lie about things. Live a simple and honest life. Love peace. And see that lots of people will want to go along with you because they want the blessings of God-They have heard that God is with you. Take another look and study out that chapter. It includes promises and instruction. It outlines a personal relationship with God. The one He wants to have with you.

Get to know God a little better today. Study His character. To know Him is to love Him, right? When you know His character, you won't blame Him for things that weren't His doing. You know better. Your relationship will make you stronger. You will realize that He is for you. Not against you. (Romans 8:31) Create for yourself a Godly environment. It's incredibly valuable.

17 May We got up really early one morning to hold a garage sale at our house. I mean, before the sun came up we were outside shlepping stuff onto the driveway. Going through my "treasures" those last several days in preparation, I found myself having to let go. It's stuff. We relived the memories, kept some things back, but in the end did pretty good at releasing many, many items. After the sale, we will donate the remainder to a local charity. So, our treasures can become someone else's treasures. It's the recycle of life.

Today the song is from way back when…. "We Bring The Sacrifice Of Praise" ~ Kirk Dearman. This song proclaims that we bring sacrifices of thanksgiving, praise, and joy to the Lord, especially in the House of God. Sometimes it is a sacrifice to praise God. You don't feel like it. You're tired or defeated or discouraged or disgruntled. You had a bad day, week, month, or year. Or maybe you need a stronger "why" in your life. But you must realize that your praise is just the thing to turn it around. Psalm 27:6 (MSG) says, "God holds me head and shoulders above all who try to pull me down. I'm headed for His place to offer anthems that will raise the roof! Already I'm singing God-songs; I'm making music to God." It's praise. It's singing, even shouting about God's goodness, about His kindness and His mercy. It can take you out of the mullygrubs and propel you into joy. God will raise you up above the defeatist attitude of the world. But, you will have to let go. Let go of the emotions that are holding you. Let go of all that is cluttering your life. Take a closer look at what you treasure. Is it really treasure or just another trinket? Release what's not of true value. Then sacrifice your praise to God. Thank Him for all He has done in your life. Don't focus on what has been lost. Focus on what is left. Look to what He has for your future. (Jeremiah 29:11) It's a good future. Something you can truly treasure.

18 May My son got into a nest of hornets one day while mowing a lawn for a friend. It was horrible. He was stung repeatedly. There were welts on his legs and he was in a lot of pain. We used some baking soda paste on him and remedied the situation. The pain subsided and before too long he was better.

Today the song is, "Christ Has Risen" ~ Matt Maher. This song decrees that Christ has risen from the dead. Wake up. Death has no sting or hell any victory. The sting of death can be harsh if you don't have the Lord in your life. Hell wins out when some one neglects the call of God. 1 Corinthians 15:55-58 (MSG) gives us this, "Death swallowed by triumphant Life! Who got the last word, oh, Death? Oh, Death, who's afraid of you now? It was sin that made death so frightening and law-code guilt that gave sin its leverage, its destructive power. But now in a single victorious stroke of Life, all three—sin, guilt, death—are gone, the gift of our Master, Jesus Christ. Thank God! With all this going for us, my dear, dear friends, stand your ground. And don't hold back. Throw yourselves into the work of the Master, confident that nothing you do for him is a waste of time or effort." Nothing should hold you back today. Even when things are horrible, God can be the balm of healing that comes to you and restores you. Then go at it. Work like it all depends on you; believe like it all depends on God. You are victorious through Christ today, nothing less. So, hold your head high, walk with confidence, and show the goodness of God to others. Nothing you do for Him is a waste. All your situations will be remedied. Before long you will be even better than you are now!

19 May At 5 years old, he stood in front of the entire student body and recited Psalm 1. Recently, this student, now a grown man, wrote a speech and included a bit about my influence in his life. It honored me. Delivering the piece with eloquence, he has won more than one award already and I am certain he will continue to achieve. I'd like to say that winning was due to the amazing subject matter (as I smile), but the truth is that I have been just a small thread in the fiber of this young man's life – privileged to spend time with him and his family, blessed to know him and watch him grow up. I may have been mentioned in his speech, but it's not about me at all. That speech means so much more, and it's about him. It's hard to not be too proud when someone you have had an occasion to mentor excels. For me it has been a valuable seed. Both of my sons have been mentored by this man. That benefit is priceless. I believe that this is one of those life-long relationships for both of our families.

Today's song, "Jesus Lover Of My Soul" ~ Kari Jobe. This song is a reminder that it's not about me, it's all about the Lord. It's for His glory. I surrender to how He wants things, His will, not insisting on my own way. So many times we draw attention to ourselves for what we have done, said, or given. But God really deserves the glory for those things. Your focus should be on Him. Your focus should be on His will, His plan. If you aren't sure of the plan of God today for your life, seek the God of the plan. Know Him better. Build a life long relationship. Allow Him to be an intricate part of all you do. It's not about you today. 1 Corinthians 13:4-5 (MSG) says, "Love never gives up. Love cares more for others than for self. Love doesn't want what it doesn't have. Love doesn't strut, doesn't have a swelled head, doesn't force itself on others, isn't always "me first," So, it's really about love. Do you love God enough to put others first? Do you love Him enough to not insist on your own way? Do you love Him enough to not brag about what you have done? Do you love Him enough to not covet what you don't have? What is your love level? Your level of surrender to God will reveal it. Your ability to step aside and let God be God will ignite it. Your decision to give Him the glory and the praise will be the seed that will reap valuable benefits in your life. Invest in your relationship with God today. It's priceless and it's about Him.

20 May My son left for a mission trip to New York City this morning. He left the familiarity of home. For a week, he will dedicate fully to the work set before him to impact the lives of people in need. He will see new things. Experience new things. Think new things. Learn new things. Do new things. And I believe in the end, he will be new. One cannot help but be changed when changing the life of another. God has sent him to do a good thing. The entire group will be giving of themselves on this trip. It's going to be great to hear the stories when they return.

Today's song is, "Steal My Show" ~ Toby Mac. This song reminds you that every day you can choose to give all to God – Your heart, life, friends, family, dreams, and career. You can grow weary when you stay in the land of familiar. You can get stuck in the routine. You can be mired in the rut of common. Or you can give your life to God and live in the land of dreams, creativity, and new possibilities. You can invite God to lead you. He can show off on your behalf and you can accomplish more than anyone could believe. So step out today. Do something new. Do something different. Learn something new. Have a new experience. Grow. Change. Become. Give. It will be great to hear the stories you will tell.

This scripture passage makes it clear – Be changed, and then tell others. 2 Corinthians 5:17-20 (MSG)says, "Now we look inside, and what we see is that anyone united with the Messiah gets a fresh start, is created new. The old life is gone; a new life burgeons! Look at it! All this comes from the God who settled the relationship between us and him, and then called us to settle our relationships with each other. God put the world square with himself through the Messiah, giving the world a fresh start by offering forgiveness of sins. God has given us the task of telling everyone what he is doing. We're Christ's representatives. God uses us to persuade men and women to drop their differences and enter into God's work of making things right between them. We're speaking for Christ himself now: Become friends with God; he's already a friend with you." This is a great mission.

21 May Devastation lies in the aftermath of a tornado. Houses leveled, people, pets, and possessions lost. Heartache and pain permeate the site of horrendous tragedy. It makes me cry to think of it. But stories emerge of triumph over circumstances. Thankfulness of what is left. Hope in the atmosphere of despair. Resilience, resolution, and strength in spite of the current situation. Like the phoenix, rising from the ashes of what was, reborn to life anew.

Today's song is, "Rise Up" ~ Matt Maher. This song encourages you to rise up when life has you down and look up when you're searching and find nothing. So many times you find yourself looking for answers and coming up empty-handed. You think, "I should know this." or "God, where are you?" You feel lost or abandoned. You feel forgotten. Frustrated. Depressed. Devastated. Things weren't supposed to be this way. But they are. Your choice has to be to rise up. Rise up. Proverbs 24:16 (MSG) says, "No matter how many times you trip them up, God-loyal people don't stay down long; Soon they're up on their feet, while the wicked end up flat on their faces." And the New King James Version puts it this way, "For a righteous *man* may fall seven times and rise again, but the wicked shall fall by calamity." Has calamity knocked you down today? Get up. Dust yourself off. Pick up the pieces or find new ones. Shake off the hurt, the sorrow, the dismay and put on – like a coat – the garment of praise, replacing that spirit of heaviness.

Isaiah 61:1-7 (MSG) encompasses the attitude of the righteous when tragedy occurs. It talks of rebuilding in the wake of tragedy. This is the message of hope for all that have experienced a heart wrenching catastrophe. Look up. Rise up. No matter what you have gone through, God is there to help you reassemble the pieces. You are not Humpty-Dumpty, you can be put back together again. No matter the loss, God's love is here and now. He will get you back on your feet. You will stand stronger than ever, not because of what happened, but because of your choices in the aftermath and because of who you became in spite of it.

22 May We have a set of weights in our garage. No one really uses them. They are outdated, I guess. Definitely heavy. They are basically gathering dust bunnies on them. We tried to sell them, but no buyer emerged and we didn't give them away. So there they sit. Taking up space. Waiting to trip me. Mocking me. And making me feel guilty. The fate of the weights? I know not. We shall see. For now their home is here.

Today's song is, "Forgiven" ~ Sanctus Real. This song reminds you that you are forgiven. You no longer have to carry the weight of who you've been. Oh the drama of things not dealt with. The feeling of what could have been. The dismay of what has transpired that was less than fruitful. The condemnation of past mistakes. You can let it all weigh you down, or you can throw off that encumbrance and be free of it by the forgiveness of God. Hebrews 12:1 says, "Therefore we also, since we are surrounded by so great a cloud of witnesses, let us lay aside every weight, and the sin which so easily ensnares *us,* and let us run with endurance the race that is set before us." People are watching. Set aside those things which have held you back. Run your race with zest! Run to win! Hebrews 12:1-3 (MSG) says it mightily, "Do you see what this means—all these pioneers who blazed the way, all these veterans cheering us on? It means we'd better get on with it. Strip down, start running—and never quit! No extra spiritual fat, no parasitic sins. Keep your eyes on *Jesus*, who both began and finished this race we're in. Study how he did it. Because he never lost sight of where he was headed—that exhilarating finish in and with God—he could put up with anything along the way: Cross, shame, whatever. And now he's *there*, in the place of honor, right alongside God. When you find yourselves flagging in your faith, go over that story again, item by item, that long litany of hostility he plowed through. *That* will shoot adrenaline into your souls!" If this doesn't excite you, check your pulse! The weights of sin and the past have to go! They are not benefiting you. They want to trip you up. They take up space, mock you, and make you feel guilty. Romans 8:1 says, "*There is* therefore now no condemnation to those who are in Christ Jesus, who do not walk according to the flesh, but according to the Spirit." Strengthen your spiritual walk today. Don't let your past hinder you. Get in shape. You're forgiven.

23 May The 3am feedings. Signaled by his crying, I would get up with my son to comfort him and rock him gently. He stared into my eyes. It was a quiet time. It was a bonding time. I didn't talk to him because it wasn't play time. It was rest time. He would eat and soon drift back to sleep. There's nothing like it.

Today the song is again, "Forgiven" ~ Sanctus Real. This part is the focus today; the song says that you are a treasure in Christ's arms. Sometimes you know you need something and you get frantic, crying out to the Lord. Then He comes and settles you. He takes you in His arms to rock you gently. He wants you to know that it's going to be all right. Isaiah 66:13 says, "As one whom his mother comforts, so I will comfort you; and you shall be comforted in Jerusalem." His comfort is like no other. His quiet presence calms you. His strong embrace keeps you safe. Psalm 46:10a says, "Be still, and know that I *am* God." It's rest time. Time to listen. Time to reflect. Time to breathe. Time to relax. You may think you are too busy to take time for God today. You cannot afford to *not* take time for Him today. Settle. Quiet. Calm. Just stop, even if for a few moments to praise Him, thank Him, and enjoy what He has for you. There's nothing like it.

24 May A bridge collapsed somewhere in Washington state. Cars went into the water. Thankfully, no one was seriously hurt. Miraculously, no one died. Years ago I had a great fear of crossing bridges. Mainly, I thought of a collapse and was terrified of going into the water, possibly becoming trapped in my car. I found that facing my fear, praying, and crossing helped me to overcome the phobia. Tragedy could happen (because we live in a broken world), but I cannot live my life worried about it.

Today the song is, "Whom Shall I Fear?" ~ Chris Tomlin. The part that I hear today says that God holds the whole world in His hands. He is faithful and I can hold on to His promises, confident that nothing formed against me will stand. Someone said that fear is False Evidence Appearing Real. Some one else said that danger is real, but fear is a choice. God said, "Fear not." Isaiah 41:9-10 (MSG) says, "I pulled you in from all over the world, called you in from every dark corner of the earth, telling you, 'You're my servant, serving on my side. I've picked you. I haven't dropped you.' Don't panic. I'm with you. There's no need to fear for I'm your God. I'll give you strength. I'll help you. I'll hold you steady; keep a firm grip on you." With the whole world in His hands, God surely has an excellent resource pool. I can imagine Him saying, "Hang on, I've got this." You can be confident in His ability and His willingness to be a help to you. He wants to strengthen you today so you can face your fears. Don't let them paralyze you. Take a deep breath and go forward. Even if you fall, He will pick you up. In water rescue one of the difficulties for the rescuer is when the victim panics and struggles. They can actually drown their deliverer because of their unwillingness to relax, trust, and believe that they will be saved. Today, if you are afraid, remember God. You can't spend your life in worry and fear. He will help you. He can rescue, deliver, and save you. But you must relax, trust, and believe. No weapon formed against you will stand. There is no need to fear when He is your God.

25 May A while back, a friend told me that they will soon have another child in the family. They were thrilled! At just over a month into the pregnancy, she told me the doctor detected the heartbeat of the baby. That is so astonishing. When I looked at documentation of fetal development, I saw that at conception, the genetic make up of the child is complete, and even around 12 weeks, the baby is already making its own movements. It fascinates me. Even in the very beginning of life, things are incredibly intricate.

Today's song is, "I Cannot Hide From You" ~ Clay Crosse. This song reminds me that before I took my first breath, He knew me. He knows my secrets, my thoughts, everything about me. God watched as I was formed. People couldn't see, but He could. He knows all the stories of my life. He said in Jeremiah 1:5 (MSG), "Before I shaped you in the womb, I knew all about you. Before you saw the light of day, I had holy plans for you: A prophet to the nations—that's what I had in mind for you." He knows you today. He knows all the intricate workings of your life. Where you've been. Where you're going. All of it. From the beginning, He knew you, because He was the one who formed you there in the womb. He made you and will continue to make you. This life journey is fascinating.

Psalm 37:23 says, "The steps of a *good* man are ordered by the Lord, and He delights in his way." God has ordered your steps. He planned it from the very first moment. He wants your life to be a delight. He wants your life to be fruitful. He wants your life to be astonishing. He's got big plans. Jeremiah 29:11 (CEB) says, "I know the plans I have in mind for you, declares the Lord; they are plans for peace, not disaster, to give you a future filled with hope." Those are great plans! So today, know that God knows what you're up to. He's happy with your great decisions. He wants to help you with your not-so-great decisions. You cannot hide from Him. You are complete in Him. And your future will be incredible.

26 May I met a woman at the grocery store. She helped me find some bread that was on sale. As she and I cruised down subsequent aisles, I passed her again. We happened to end up in the same check out lane and chatted a bit more. Surprisingly we had parked next to each other out on the lot. We talked some more about getting snacks for the kids and how we loved catching a great sale. We wished each other a great weekend and parted ways. "She was so nice", I thought. This chance encounter brightened my day and now I am telling the story. You don't have to know someone to have a pleasant conversation. She may have been hurting. She may have been in a bad situation. I don't know. I had a chance to be nice. I hope I brightened her day. Maybe she told her friends the story too.

Today the song is, "Need You Now (How Many Times) ~ Plumb. This song reminds me that every one has a story to tell and every one has a wound that needs to be healed. And that I need God. He gives me strength to keep going. Everyday, God is sending people your way to help you or for you to help. You have your story, they have theirs. You don't have to tell your story to receive encouragement from someone. God knows. He knows what you need and when you need it. Don't take for granted those bread-sale friends He sends your way. God will give you a nudge-an inkling that prompts you to reach out by smiling, talking, or being helpful. You never really know how much it means to someone when you turn your attention from yourself to them. Matthew 25:37b-40 (CEB) says it this way, 'Lord, when did we see you hungry and feed you, or thirsty and give you a drink? When did we see you as a stranger and welcome you, or naked and give you clothes to wear? When did we see you sick or in prison and visit you? 'Then the king will reply to them, 'I assure you that when you have done it for one of the least of these brothers and sisters of mine, you have done it for me.'" What is in your hand to use for another's benefit today? Time to be more mindful of others. Develop generosity. Nurture selflessness. Thrive on giving. Excel in hospitality. Smile more. Every one has a story. Will you be the good part of the story? Every one has a wound that needs healing. Will you offer a balm of restoration? The solution? They need God. You can make a big difference. Brighten someone's day today. Give them a good story to tell.

27 May It was fun yelling along with the cheerleaders at our high school football games. I never did know much about football, but I knew all the words to the chants we screamed during those 4 quarters. If we were winning, the cheers went up. If we were losing, the cheers went up all the more. It was an exciting time. No matter the outcome, we still went for pizza afterwards.

Today's song is, "Make it Loud" ~ Martha Munizzi. This song is powerful. It beckons to make your praise big, and make it loud. The people celebrate all around the world that no other God can save, heal, deliver, or set you free like our God! There are times to be still and there are times to shout. Ecclesiastes 3 tells about the times to be silent and times to speak, times to weep and times to laugh. So don't forget about those loud times of cheering. Be excited for who God is in your life and all that He's done. The energy that comes from praising God is refreshing. It can pull you out of a losing trend and get you on the path of victory. You don't have to know all about God to praise Him. You just need to know Him. Then you can be a voice. A leader cheering others on. Attracting people to God. Being loud, being bold. But not being noisy or obnoxious. You praise Him when you're winning and still praise Him even if you are losing. Because, no matter the outcome, He's still your God. He's still good. Daniel chapter 3 is an amazing story; verses 17-18 (MSG) say, "Shadrach, Meshach, and Abednego answered King Nebuchadnezzar, 'Your threat means nothing to us. If you throw us in the fire, the God we serve can rescue us from your roaring furnace and anything else you might cook up, O king. But even if he doesn't, it wouldn't make a bit of difference, O king. We still wouldn't serve your gods or worship the gold statue you set up.'" No matter the outcome, they chose God from the beginning. They didn't say, "We'll love and worship God if He delivers us." They were decided and nothing was going to change their minds. Is your mind made up today? Remember that no matter your outcome, God is still a good and awesome God. He still loves you. He still has a great plan for your life. Even in the midst of setbacks, confusion, or transition, He has not left you. So, make it big and make it loud today. Make your praise be heard around the world. There is no other God like our God!

28 May We played "tag" when I was a child. There was the person who was "it" and there were the runners and always a base where you were safe from being tagged. The goal was to escape "it" and reach the base – safety!

Today's song is, "Need You Now (How Many Times) ~ Plumb. This song beseeches God, asking how many times have you heard me cry out, wanting Him to take this situation away. He gives me strength to keep breathing and I need Him now. It's a song of yearning. A song of desperation. A song of humility. It's that song of searching for answers as you lay on the floor crying out. It's a song of brokenness before God. That epiphany that you can no longer strive on your own, but depend on God to wrap His arms around you and rescue you. You have probably been in this place before, but you find yourself again despairing and reaching for what and who gives you the strength to continue. The "its" of life will try to chase you. They want to tag you, bring you down, and stop you. But today is the day to leave those deterrents behind. Escape the cares and the worries and run to God. He is your home base. He is your safety. Psalm 46:1 (MSG) says, "God is a safe place to hide, ready to help when we need him." God is ready for you. He is waiting with open arms. He wants to help. But you must run to Him. Not away. Get to the base. There is room for you there. He will give you the strength to breathe, relax, and be calm again. You'll always be safe with God.

29 May When my son first learned to walk I would stand across the room with arms outstretched saying, "Come to Mommy!" He would toddle along and fall into my embrace. Later it was a full out run to me. When he got there, I would swoop him up and we would celebrate. "Yay! You did a great job!" He'd smile a big smile and run off only to come back again with even more gusto. I loved those moments.

Today the song is, "Forever Reign" ~ Hillsong. This part of the song is what I heard today…that I'm running into God's arms. Nothing compares to His embrace and His love will always be enough. He is the light of the world and will reign forever. I've always wanted to be the best mom. I wanted my sons to know I would be there for them. I wanted to make things great and fun and exciting. But I'm not perfect. I've fallen short. And I love them from the bottom of my heart. However, God is the best, He's infallible. Run to Him. He will be there for you. He will swoop you up when you get there. He will celebrate with you. He loves you. It's okay if you don't know what to do today. God knows. He's already been there. You may be learning how to walk well in this life. Sometimes you fall. Just get up and go again. Soon you will be at an all out run. Matthew 25:21 says, "His lord said to him, 'Well *done,* good and faithful servant; you were faithful over a few things, I will make you ruler over many things. Enter into the joy of your lord.'" It's great to celebrate when you do well. Doing well is pleasing to the Lord. It leads to joy. So today, put away sorrow and regret. Do well. Ecclesiastes 9:10a says, "Whatever your hand finds to do, do *it* with your might;" Go run. Run to God. Get up. Get up from your slumber. Stand up. Stand up for what you know is right. Get going. Get going on the mission and plan God has for you. Then you will hear Him say, "Yay! You did a great job!"

30 May One night we came home from a youth band rehearsal and thought, "Nobody was there tonight." Then we thought again, several people were there, just not everyone. We were looking at who was missing instead of who was there. Our conversation quickly turned. We realized that we were counting wrong.

Today the song is, "10,000 Reasons (Bless the Lord)" ~ Matt Redman. This song is about worshiping the Lord. Sing and worship Him. Keep singing because of His goodness. There are 10,000 reasons your heart can find to worship Him. How many times have you looked at a situation and thought it was hopeless? Or impossible? Or impractical? Illogical? Futile? Unreasonable? You jumped to a negative conclusion, only to give up before you ever tried? You talked yourself out of it? You worried your way into retreat? When that happens, you need to shake it off. It's wrong perspective. Why? Because of God. He is the God of possibilities. With Him it is possible. Matthew 19:26 says, "But Jesus looked at *them* and said to them, 'With men this is impossible, but with God all things are possible.'" There is a way. God can make a way where there seems to be no way. He can make streams in the desert. (Isaiah 35:6) But how are you looking at it today? Is the glass half empty? Or is it half full? How exactly do you see things? Do you see it how God sees it? Or do you see it how some negative, hurt, offended friend sees it? Are you focusing on what you don't have today? Or are you looking at what you do have? Your perspective will lead you to your future. A poor perspective leads to struggle and stagnation. A great perspective leads to growth and fulfillment. Now stop and look to God. Worship. Thank Him. Praise Him. It could be a prayer. It could be a song. It could even be a dance. Worship Him for who He is and for what He's done. He is provider, healer, deliverer, redeemer, victor, shelter...Really there are thousands of reasons to worship Him. That worship will create an intimacy with God. A strong relationship. A growing relationship. A thriving relationship. It helps you to look on the "bright side" of life. It helps you count right. So take a look at your glass today. Your life. What do you see? That is the key to your destiny. If you don't like it, change it. Turn the conversation around. Remember God's goodness. He's counting right, and He's counting on you.

31 May My husband and I are a team. Today we jumped the old truck so we could go into town to get some plants for the yard. We fixed breakfast and lunch together. Shopped for groceries, relaxed, watched a movie, and soon we will plant a tree near our porch. We don't have every day like this one, but I certainly enjoy the ones we do have to spend with each other. We also have occasion to collaborate on more serious matters like finances, raising our sons, projects, and life decisions. It's a great team. A winning team. We do very well together.

Today's song is, "I Will Follow" ~ Chris Tomlin. This song says that where you go, stay or move that I will follow you. Ruth 1:16 says, "Entreat me not to leave you, *or to* turn back from following after you; For wherever you go, I will go; And wherever you lodge, I will lodge; Your people *shall be* my people, And your God, my God." Naomi was dedicated to her mother-in-law, Ruth. She wanted to be with her. She had a relationship that was special. It was the key to her future. Who are you in relationship with today? Who is on your team? Who do you want to be with? Who will you follow? I made a decision a long time ago who I wanted to be with. We made vows. We were serious. We meant it. For life. That is the kind of relationships you want in your life. Ones that stick. Ones that say, "No matter what, I'm with you." The ones where you both seek God for your future. You have the same goals and the same dreams, because you dreamed them together. God has His hand on you and you are traveling the same path. He wants that for you today. Not only with another person, but with Him. God desires the relationship with you that doesn't waver if things don't go like you thought they should have. He desires a consistent, everlasting, enduring, expecting relationship. Do you? Step toward God today. Engage Him in your projects. Get His help with your endeavors. Seek His face. He'll get you that jump start you need. He will keep you going. He will lead you. He will be there for the little things and for the serious things to. You make a great team. A winning team. With God on your side, nobody can triumph against you. (Romans 8:31) Evaluate your relationships today. Are you true to your promises? God is. Spend time with Him. You and He will do very well together.

1 June One day I was planting a shrub. As I dug the hole, it refilled with rocks. Again as I dug, more rocks and dirt fell into the hollow. It took several attempts to clear the space so that the plant could be placed and secured in its new home. I am excited to see it grow there in the months to come, and anxious to see it flourish and bloom in our beautiful garden.

Today the song was a challenge in that I only knew the melody. I did not know the words or the artist. I did not really know what the song was about. But I knew it was the song for today. I also knew what the illustration would be today-about planting the shrub. So I kept at it. The easy thing to do would have been to just get still and let another song come to my heart. God would give me another if I gave up, right? But I just would not give up! It took help from my son and a friend to track it down....it's "New Soul" ~ Yael Naim. The song talks about being a new soul in a strange world, hoping to learn. Feeling both joy and fear and making mistakes along the way. Knowing that you have a mandate, knowing that you are destined to succeed will keep you going even when it looks like it's not going to work, even when you think you have made every mistake possible. It can be really disheartening when you make attempts and fail. You make headway and somebody or something happens and your project gets filled with rocks. But you have to keep going in spite of the obstacles. In spite of the setbacks. In spite of what you don't know at the beginning. That's something God is good at...He takes you step by step. He knows the end from the beginning (Isaiah 46:10) and Psalm 119:105-107 (MSG) says, "By your words I can see where I'm going; they throw a beam of light on my dark path. I've committed myself and I'll never turn back from living by your righteous order. Everything's falling apart on me, God; put me together again with your Word." So you have made mistakes, you have fallen short. But you are learning, growing, changing, and making progress day by day. Keep at it. What isn't clear today may be crystallized tomorrow. There is a specific place for you, a place for you to be secure, to grow, to flourish, and to bloom. You may feel sometimes like you are in a strange world, but God has a special plan for you. Soon you will be right at home. And you can look forward to a happy ending.

2 June Severe storms hit our area a while back. My brother's house was in line with the tornado. Some big trees were uprooted in his yard, but he, his wife, and their house are okay. There was devastation a block over and many houses on the surrounding streets looked horrible. When he told us his story, how the big trees in his yard all missed the house when they fell and how he got his vehicle into the garage before the storm only to later find a huge limb where it had been parked earlier, I thought, "God protected you!" I believe in those moments, God's grace in his life was bigger than the storm around him. I am thankful for that.

Today's song is, "God Is So Good" ~ Velna A. Ledin. Simply stated, this song says that God is so good. He's so good to me. Even in the midst of the storm, God is good. Even when there is loss, God is good. Even when you don't understand, God is good. Even when things are scary or uncomfortable or inconvenient or down right painful, God is still good. You can trust Him. Are there bad things in this world? Yes. We live in a broken world. A world that chooses things over relationship. They choose self over others. They choose what feels good instead of what's right. They choose convenience over responsibility. Remember, it is the devil that comes to steal, kill, and destroy. John 10:10 (MSG) says, "A thief is only there to steal and kill and destroy. I came so they can have real and eternal life, more and better life than they ever dreamed of." The Lord is the one who wants to give you more. More than you ever dreamed. Insurance companies may call weather tragedies an "Act of God." but that's not how God operates. Satan is the prince and power of the air (Ephesians 2:2) God loves you. He wants the best for you. When things happen, He's there. Let Him help you pick up the pieces. He's throwing you a life preserver, put it on. Don't get mad at Him. He's not the one who pushed you in the water. He wants you to be saved. Trust God today. He will direct you. He will turn your questions into a quest. He will show you your purpose. His grace will be sufficient for you. His angels will watch over you. He is bigger than any storm you face. God is so good.

3 June I thought I slept late this morning, but it was still quite early when I arose. I trudged outside with my sleepy head and swollen eyes. Groggy from my slumber, I sat quietly for a few moments. The air was crisp and the sun shone brightly. A new day, I sighed. Then I decided to spend some time in worship. Worship God for who He is. Thank Him. Enjoy His presence and the gift of this new day. The sleepiness fell away. I became alert, tuned in to God and what He has for me. A new day, I smiled. "This is the day the Lord has made; I will rejoice and be glad in it". (Psalm 118:24)

Today's song is, "Worn" ~ Tenth Avenue North. This song exclaims that being so worn out, you should reach to God, because a song can rise from a broken life. When you feel like there's no hope, you wither. You lose purpose, drive, and excitement. You give up. When you are on the edge of the precipice, it's time to look up! Reach up! God is your strength. HE is your redemption. He will renew your zeal. Awaken today to His promise for your life! He wants to bless you. But He needs you to ask. He needs you to seek. He needs you to knock. Matthew 7:7-8 says, "Ask, and it will be given to you; seek, and you will find; knock, and it will be opened to you. For everyone who asks receives, and he who seeks finds, and to him who knocks it will be opened" He is waiting for you, your request, your faith, your trust. "And Jabez called on the God of Israel saying, 'Oh, that You would bless me indeed, and enlarge my territory, that Your hand would be with me, and that You would keep me from evil, that I may not cause pain!' So God granted him what he requested." (1 Chronicles 4:10) Ask. It's okay. God wants to bless you. It's His pleasure. Philippians 2:12-13 (MSG) says, "What I'm getting at, friends, is that you should simply keep on doing what you've done from the beginning. When I was living among you, you lived in responsive obedience. Now that I'm separated from you, keep it up. Better yet, redouble your efforts. Be energetic in your life of salvation, reverent and sensitive before God. That energy is *God's* energy, an energy deep within you, God himself willing and working at what will give him the most pleasure." Let God work in you; pull you out of defeat and into victory. Give you energy. Sleepiness will fall away and you will be alert, rejoicing in each new day.

4 June I have some friends who, at first glance, might appear to be an unlikely couple. Seemingly so different from one another, they are really great as husband and wife. They adore each other. They take care of one another. They love each other. They follow their goals and dreams together. They love God and they love people. Just a great pair. My friends.

Today's song is, "Amazing Grace" to the music from "House Of The Rising Sun". John Newton -1779 (Amazing Grace). This is a great pairing of Christian Hymn with traditional folk song. Its message is that forgiveness and redemption are possible in spite of your sin. Your soul can be delivered from despair by God's great mercy. Sometimes you get stuck in the familiar. How you think things are supposed to be. What you've known or grown up with, should be how it is. But you have to know that God can work in new ways. He can be tech-savvy. He can still be creative in today's world. He is not outdated. New pairings can reach more people. New kinds of musical arrangements, new looks, new designs, different methods, can all be used by God. It may surprise you. It may make you feel uncomfortable. (Many people despise change.) Growth can be uncomfortable and sometimes downright painful. But if you aren't growing, you're dying. Isaiah 43:19 says, "Behold, I will do a new thing, now it shall spring forth; shall you not know it? I will even make a road in the wilderness and rivers in the desert." That's something uncommon, a road in the wilderness. That's something unusual, rivers in the desert. That's how God works. He takes the unlikely and uses it for His glory. Maybe you seem "unlikely" today. He can use you. You can reach people in a way that no one else can. Be open to new things. Do not disregard the effectiveness of something different. It may be a way to reach people that nothing else can. Avail yourself to God's power in and through you – You and God make a great pair.

5 June We boarded the plane. The flight crew began to speak to the passengers seated in the emergency aisle, explaining their responsibilities in case of an event where they would need to act. It was then necessary to get the verbal agreement of the passengers to these expectations. When pointed to for a response, one woman said, "What?" She had not been paying attention. With that, the attendant directed her to move so that someone who would heed instructions could replace her in this vital position. Visibly miffed, she moved to another seat and grumbled as she went. Continuing to complain, she and her bad attitude were soon removed from the plane, protesting all the way. The crew members weren't messing around with the safety of the passengers and would not tolerate her belligerence.Thankfully, the rest of the flight was without incident and we enjoyed our trip.

Today the song is, "Whom Shall I Fear" ~ Chris Tomlin. This song speaks of knowing who goes before you and knowing who stands behind you. And God is always by your side. When you travel through life, you need to be aware. You need to know who is in front of you, behind you, and beside you. That doesn't just apply when you are flying in an airplane. Think about who you surround yourself with...are they paying attention? Are they responsible? What is their attitude? Is it good or bad? Do they protest when something doesn't go their way? Do they grumble and complain? Look at yourself; are you the one who is ready in the emergency aisle to handle events that need action? Or are you the one who must be removed because of your criticism? Now, take a look at your relationship with God. Joshua 1:5 says, "No man shall *be able to* stand before you all the days of your life; as I was with Moses, *so* I will be with you. I will not leave you nor forsake you." When God's love and grace surround you, you know you are in good company. He's got your back. God always wants the best for you. He's paying attention. Whenever things get rough or temptation is great, God has a way of escape. A safe passage. He is a very present help in time of need. (Psalm 46:1) So position yourself today in an advantageous spot. One where you can be surrounded by people of excellence and God, who is excellent. Then be excellent yourself. Don't be afraid of turbulence and have faith so you can enjoy a great trip and a safe landing.

165

6 June My mother-in-law enjoyed putting puzzles together. She would sit at the kitchen table, gaze at the picture on the box, and assemble the pieces. It was pretty amazing, sometimes she would stare at all that was on the table for awhile and select a piece and put it right where it went. At 93, she was a puzzle pro.

Today's song is, "Already There" ~ Casting Crowns. This song says that to God my future is a memory because He is already there. He stands at the end of my life, waiting for the day I arrive to the other side. Then I will see how all the pieces fit together. God has the whole picture of your life already. He sees what it's supposed to be. He's got a plan and a path for you. If you veer off the path or stray from the plan, He can recalculate. He can help you get back on track. Proverbs 3:6 (MSG) says, "Listen for God's voice in everything you do, everywhere you go; He's the one who will keep you on track." You may not understand the direction you are moving, even when you are listening to God. You are seeking Him, but things don't always make sense. Sometimes it's like looking at a painting by Georges Pierre Seurat up close; it's just a lot of colored dots. However, perspective changes when you step back and take a look...you will see an amazing picture. You may just be up too close today. Time to step back. This may be just one dot in the grand scheme of things. Your life is made up of many pieces. Alone they may seem unusual or insignificant, but joined with the other elements that make up your life experience; they can create a magnificent picture! Keep in mind that God already sees that picture and He's the one who can direct you in placing that next piece. He's a pro. You know that in the end, that will be amazing. Don't be discouraged today; you are moving into position to receive from God all that is your future. Be willing and obedient. You will enjoy the best the land has to offer. (Isaiah 1:19)

7 June My husband, son, and I camped in tents at the state park over night. It was relaxing and fun. We built fires, cooked our food, and spent time together. The weather was perfect. But there were bugs and we slept horribly. Wait, I said it was "relaxing and fun"! My husband said that it was such a nice trip that the memory of not sleeping well had already virtually disappeared. The excellent experience far outweighed any hardship. One of my favorite times was gazing into the clear night sky and seeing all those stars. It was magnificent!

Today the song is, "Who Am I" ~ Casting Crowns. This song declares that I belong to God. It's not because of who I am, it's because of what He has done, and it's not for what I have done, but who He is. He knows my name. He feels my hurt. He catches me when I fall. He tells me who I am. He calms the storm in me. You will have times when you fall and when you hurt. The key is getting back up again. Life's experiences are far too full for you to waste energy on what is less than perfect. Focusing on the wounds will not enable you to heal. Focus on what's good and amazing and wonderful. Warren Adams Bacon of Florida State University said recently, in part, "Magic and wonder abound in the world around us if we view the world through the eyes of a child..." There is a sense of awe and wonderment that you must strive to keep in your life. It's an untainted optimism that believes the best in people and situations. It's valuing what is really important, things like God, family, church, friendships, and making a difference in the lives of others. Matthew 18:3 says, "And said, 'Verily I say unto you, except ye be converted, and become as little children, ye shall not enter into the kingdom of heaven.'" There is something to be said for child-like faith. Children don't often doubt. They believe. They believe in possibilities. They believe in results over and above what they could ask. They believe in miracles. It's time to return to God as that child, filled with wonder. He knows you, all about you, all you are going through. Time to trust again. Believe again. Expect again. Enjoy again. Stop focusing on what's wrong and see what's right. Don't worry about the bugs, look up and you will see the stars.

8 June A canary sits in his cage. He swings. He eats. He drinks. He sings. He sleeps. He stays. The robin pulls a worm from the ground in my back yard. She hops. She eats. She drinks. She sleeps. And she flies up to the trees. The canary is wonderful, but remains confined. The robin is also wonderful, but unfettered, she's free.

Today's song is, "I Am Free" ~ Jamie Page. This song says that I am free and no one can take that away from me. Ever since Jesus paid the price – He gave His life as a sacrifice. You may have a wonderful life, but are you confined? Are you living life in the perimeter of familiar, comfortable, and safe? Day to day you repeat routine. You do what you do because that's what you do. Or, do you live life unfettered? Free? Have you lived some adventure lately? When was the last time you did something for the first time? Have you been waiting for the right time, or are you choosing to make time? It's time to seek the Lord. In Christ you are a new creation. 2 Corinthians 5:17 says, "Therefore if any man be in Christ, he is a new creature: old things are passed away; behold, all things are become new." Because of the Lord, you are free. Your spiritual freedom belongs to you. The world can't take it away. No matter what happens, you own it. Christ paid for it, because freedom does not come without a sacrifice. That was His gift to you. Accept it. Renew your relationship with Christ. Then, try something new. Stop putting off what you know you should have done long ago. Follow what the Lord has been showing you to do. Reach out to someone. Help someone. Walk in what you have been called to do. You can sing. You can hop. You can fly. You are free.

9 June As we drove through the state park a few nights ago, we traveled a winding road, took a few turns, and ended up at the campground. My husband was driving and he knows the park far better than I. It seemed like such a long road to me and a bit confusing at times. I wanted to say, "Are we there yet?" just like the kids used to ask. When we arrived, I was so glad I trusted him to get us there. It was a beautiful spot, the campsite where we stayed that night.

Today the song is, "Already There" ~ Casting Crowns. This song again is on my heart today. The part at the beginning – the song says that from where I'm standing, it is hard for me to see where this is all going, Lord. You don't always know where everything is going to end up in life, but God does. You may not have it all figured out, but God does. You may not be sure what's coming, but God does. You may feel like you're just on some winding road. Some long winding road. You may be confused, impatient, or frustrated. Now is the time to trust God. Proverbs 3:5 (MSG) says, "Trust God from the bottom of your heart; don't try to figure out everything on your own. Listen for God's voice in everything you do, everywhere you go; he's the one who will keep you on track." This is one of my favorite verses. You can spend so much time and energy on trying to figure things out that you miss the opportunity to do something great. God will keep you on the road, just listen to Him. His wisdom, His direction. You find that out by spending more time searching the Bible. You find that out by spending more time in prayer. Your steps will become clearer as you go forward. Your path will be sure. Your destiny will be evident as you continue to do all that God has called you to do. You will be glad that you trusted Him. Your destination will be beautiful.

10 June One of the funniest things I have seen on vacation was a woman who was returning to her hotel room. We exchanged greetings and I noticed that she was sporting a lapel button that said, "Lose weight now! Ask me how!" and cradled in her arms was an entire box full of doughnuts! Well, I thought it was funny. Somehow, I didn't trust her for her weight loss promotion. Those crispy sweet pastries made me doubt that she could do what that button on her blouse promised.

Today's song is, "Whom Shall I Fear" ~ Chris Tomlin. The bridge is what I'm looking at today; it says that I am holding on to God's promises, because He is faithful. Parents sometimes remark, "Do as I say, not as I do." to their children. But it's important to be a great role model for them. I have heard that children don't learn what is taught, they learn what is caught. They see the example and imitate it. Children learn whether to trust their parents or not. They see the character of their parents. When we left our boys with a sitter, they learned that we were coming back for them. They became more stable because they were assured that Mom and Dad would return. Today, take a look at how you see God. He is Father. Galatians 4:6-7 (MSG) says, "You can tell for sure that you are now fully adopted as his own children because God sent the Spirit of his Son into our lives crying out, 'Papa! Father!' Doesn't that privilege of intimate conversation with God make it plain that you are not a slave, but a child? And if you are a child, you're also an heir, with complete access to the inheritance." You can trust what He says today, Romans 4:20-21 says about Abraham that, "He did not waver at the promise of God through unbelief, but was strengthened in faith, giving glory to God, and being fully convinced that what He had promised He was also able to perform" Abraham was convinced that God would do what He said He would do. Be convinced that what He promised you, He will do. You don't have to doubt. You don't have to wonder. You can trust. Have faith, because God is faithful. Be full of faith, because God will keep His promise. If it seems God has left and won't be coming back for you, be assured that He is still there. Count on Him. It will stabilize you. It will establish you. See His character. Follow His example. And know that in spite of all the doughnut-toting nutritionists out there, God has a solid, stable plan for you – one you can trust.

11 June There are lots of products available to help increase your energy level. It might be a protein bar or a shake, a tablet or a powder. Some claim to energize you for several hours. Some will increase your strength. Some will keep you awake. You can buy those things, or you could take care of yourself by getting sleep, exercising, and eating energy boosting foods. Your attitude makes a big difference too. I think I'd rather have a long term restoration than just a quick fix.

Today the song is, "Revive Us Again" ~ Big Daddy Weave. (Originally written by William Paton Mackay in the 1800's) This song reminds me that the glory belongs to God and it is He who will revive me. There are times when you will feel weak. You feel like you can't go on. Or you just aren't at 100%. You may want to give up. You may want to do something that is just a temporary solution. It's like trying to tape together something that should be nailed. It works for awhile, but doesn't hold up in the long run. God wants to be your restorer. He wants to be your reviver, today. He can uphold you. Psalm 28:7 says, "The Lord *is* my strength and my shield; my heart trusted in Him, and I am helped; therefore my heart greatly rejoices, and with my song I will praise Him." He is your strength. He is your shield, protecting you. Trust Him. You will be helped. Then remember to thank Him. Give Him the honor and the glory. Quick fixes never last. They lack stability. They lack longevity. They lack substance. The short cut you take today will hurt you later. My pastor said, "What you compromise to gain, you will eventually lose." That attitude of compromise or short cuts will end up in regrets. So, take the time to seek God on the matter at hand. Let Him show you the best way. The way that will last a lifetime. His strength, His energy will keep you going when others have left the race.

12 June At our house, when it's about to rain, the wind will pick up. We don't have any large trees to stop the breeze, so when it blows in, it throws just about anything loose out into the yard. Sometimes things end up at the neighbor's house. The rain falls, drenching everything. But in the rain is life for the plants. It's a refreshing. After the rain, the air is crisp and the wind is still. The storm has passed. It's calm. It smells sweet. The sun shines again.

Today the song is, "Open Up The Sky" ~ Deluge. This song expresses the yearning for the presence of the Lord. That the sky would open up and blessings like rain would fall. You can say simply, "God, bless me" or you can yearn for His presence and His blessing. Like a deer pants for the water. You can be complacent about God, or you can be desperate for Him, wanting the sky to open up and for His presence to fall like rain. Blowing in, throwing all the loose stuff of your life out of the way. The obstacles. The hindrances. The setbacks. The annoyances. Away, out of your yard. So nothing can hold it back. Don't let anything stop the drenching of His blessing. Because in the Lord's presence there is life. Job 33:4 says, "The Spirit of God made me what I am, the breath of God Almighty gave me life!" You can have the life of God in you. His Spirit. He will refresh you. He will calm you. Become serious and bold about seeking the Lord. Look for the outpouring of His blessing. Desire to be pleasing to Him. Spend time to worship Him and your life will be sweet.

13 June Friday nights were roller-skating nights back when I was in middle school. We weren't old enough to drive, so our parents would drop us off for the evening. Friends would meet up and roll around the rink for a couple of hours. You could skate by yourself or make a big chain with your buddies. If a girl liked a boy she could safely hold hands on the "couples skate". If a kid didn't know how to skate, he could hold the rail and inch himself around, or he could catch the hand of a friend to stay steady. I remember the music, the food, the old theater seats in the 'gallery', and of course, the famous sparkling mirrored ball!

Today the song is, "You Hold My World" ~ Israel Houghton. This song says that, God holds my world in His hands. I'm amazed at His love, and that He loves me. There was trust involved in catching the hand of someone at the roller rink. You believed that they wouldn't bring you down. They wouldn't cause you to trip or stumble. They would help you stay on your feet when you were wobbly. They helped you get better. They helped you feel better. Like someone was on your side, rooting for you and lifting you up. Your relationship with God is like that. He loves you and you can trust in Him. Psalm 4:5 says to put your trust in the Lord. He wants the best for you. Jeremiah 29:11 tells of His plan for you for a good future. You may feel wobbly or unsure today, so look to God when you need to be steadied. He will hold your hand, with you every turn you take. Even if you feel like you are just inching along, He is there to help. In no way does He want to trip you up, cause you harm, or teach you a lesson by evil means. He wants you to get better, stronger, faster, and more skilled. So, get up on your feet and know that you have an advocate. He's rooting for you. He's excited about your success. Excited to see you sparkle. He has your world in His hands.

14 June In a tent in the woods. There were raccoons, deer, turtles, turkeys and all sort of other birds and bugs. Plants of many kinds. The stars shone. The crickets chirped. The campfire crackled. The air smelled of sweet blooms. Tree leaves rustled in the wind. How could anyone ever deny the incredible hand of God amidst all He has created? The beauty and magnificence of nature brought me even closer to my heavenly Father. So relaxing. So refreshing.

Today the song is, "You Hold My World" ~ Israel Houghton. A different part of the song today I hear, that I am not afraid because my world is safe in God's hands. With God in your life, you don't have to be afraid. His hands are gentle hands. His hands are loving hands. His hands are open hands, reaching hands, tender hands. They are also strong hands, just hands, creative hands. Genesis 1:1 (MSG) says, "First this: God created the Heavens and Earth—all you see, all you don't see." When you look at all He as created today, let yourself be overwhelmed with His awesome, breathtaking, impressive, magnificent, mind-blowing excellence! Psalm 8:9 says, "O Lord, our Lord, How excellent *is* Your name in all the earth!" Look at the intricacies of nature. The plants, the animals. How they know what to do. The plant emerges from a tiny seed. The duck flies south for the winter. Parents protect their young. Animals forage and hunt. Trees reach for the sunlight. Flowers bloom in season. God planned it all. He arranged, organized, and initiated it – all. So what ever you may fear today, fear not. Matthew 6:34 says, "Therefore do not worry about tomorrow, for tomorrow will worry about its own things. Sufficient for the day *is* its own trouble." Don't worry; put it in God's hands. He can obviously handle it. He is incredible. And enjoy your life. There is more good than bad. Focus on the good. Philippians 4:8 (MSG) reminds you... "Summing it all up, friends, I'd say you'll do best by filling your minds and meditating on things true, noble, reputable, authentic, compelling, gracious—the best, not the worst; the beautiful, not the ugly; things to praise, not things to curse." So dwell on those positive things today. Dwell on God's goodness, and with your world in His hands, you can be relaxed and refreshed.

15 June Flash! Crack! The lightning followed by thunder at about 5am. I sat up immediately, startled from my sleep, and got out of bed. It was as if, in that moment, I was completely awake. As I looked out the front door, I saw another flash of brilliant lightning on the horizon. The air was calm and I could see that it had started to rain. The storm passed quickly and dawn was approaching. It was a new day.

Today the song is, "Moving Forward" ~ Israel Houghton. This song reminds me that God brought me to the moment that I found freedom in Him. He heals me and makes all things new. When you ask Jesus into your life, there is a quickening that happens on the inside. A moment of change. A time of renewing. You are different. There will be other times of your life where you experience a new direction or a shift. It's one of those "ah ha" moments. You make up your mind. You decide. You are not going back to how it was. You are determined to go forward. Philippians 3:12-16 (MSG) says, "I'm not saying that I have this all together, that I have it made. But I am well on my way, reaching out for Christ, who has so wondrously reached out for me. Friends, don't get me wrong: By no means do I count myself an expert in all of this, but I've got my eye on the goal, where God is beckoning us onward—to Jesus. I'm off and running and I'm not turning back. So let's keep focused on that goal, those of us who want everything God has for us. If any of you have something else in mind, something less than total commitment, God will clear your blurred vision—you'll see it yet! Now that we're on the right track, let's stay on it."

Strive to progress in your health, knowledge, service, skill, and commitment. There is an energy that you experience. A supercharge. Your dream is reborn. Your quest is resumed. You stop waiting, rehearsing, planning and you start going, doing, and being. God has His hand on you in a big way and things begin to happen for you. You are more alive than you have ever been. More alert. More astute. More aware. More ready for all God has for you. He has been waiting for you to be ready. So today, shake off the dust of procrastination, solitude, and complacency. Get up. There's a brilliance that you deserve to experience each new day. You can meet the dawn completely awake and completely ready.

16 June There was that last coffee cup that I wanted to get off the high shelf. I reached with all my might. But my arm was too short. Then I had an idea. I went to the utensil drawer and extracted the pasta spoon. It was like my personal claw. Reaching again, I eased the cup toward the edge and retrieved it safely. Thank you, Pasta Spoon! You know, when I really want something, I can find a way to get it.

Today's song is, "I Will Not Be Moved" ~ Natalie Grant. This song declares that though I stumble, and though I fall down, though I make mistakes and face heartache, I will not be moved, because I stand on Christ – the solid rock. Just because you make a mistake, it doesn't mean you are a mistake. Just because you fail, you are not a failure. Being knocked down doesn't mean you're knocked out. Things happen. If the road was perfect, you'd never know how good you really have it. If plans don't work out, figure out what you have to do to make it work. If people don't come through, figure out what you have to do to make it through. Time to stop waiting for someone to rescue you. Jim Rohn said, "What if that guy doesn't show up?" Your hope has to be built on the Rock – Jesus. Because you see, the rain falls on everyone's house. But your foundation is the key to whether you'll stand or crumble. The Lord can extend your reach. He can help you accomplish what you can't do on your own. Numbers 11:23 (NIV) says, "The Lord answered Moses, 'Is the Lord's arm too short? Now you will see whether or not what I say will come true for you.'" God was asking Moses if he thought God wouldn't take care of him. Then He assured him with a kind of "Watch and see" And God came through. His arm was not too short at all. So take a look today at what you may think you can never reach. You can't, at least not on your own. You can give up or get help. The choice is yours. But with God all things are possible! (Matthew 19:26) Expand your thinking. Dream bigger. Look higher. Reach farther. You can do it. God is waiting to assist you.

17 June Our pastor gave us some homework a couple weeks ago. He said to memorize your "Top 10" verses from the Bible. They would be your life verses. Not just random ones, but ones that have particular meaning in your life. One of the verses that I memorized long ago, my main life verse is Proverbs 3:5-6, "Trust in the Lord with all your heart and lean not on your own understanding. In all your ways, acknowledge Him and He shall direct your paths." The key word for me is 'Trust' but more importantly, 'Trust in the Lord'. Remember the old hymn that said, "Oh, for grace to trust Him more"? I have had occasion to sing it many times over the years. Trust.

Today the song is, "Trust God" ~ Rick Muchow. This song is based on The Message version of Proverbs 3:5-6, "Trust God from the bottom of your heart; don't try to figure out everything on your own. Listen for God's voice in everything you do, everywhere you go; he's the one who will keep you on track." It goes on to say commit to God what you do. Then your plans will succeed. Another of my life verses is Psalm 37:5, "Commit your way to the Lord, Trust also in Him, And He shall bring *it* to pass." Trust God. He will do it. Be fully convinced that what He promises, He'll perform. (Romans 4:21) There's something about trusting. You know that everything will be okay. In spite of how it looks today, it will work out. It may take a day, a week, a month, a year, or longer, but in the end you win if you will continue to trust the Lord. The way to trust some one is to know them. Have a relationship with them. Know their character. When you know, you don't have to wonder if they are going to do something that will sabotage your life. So get to know God. When you know Him, you know His character and you know He will only do that which will lead to your success. But you have to follow. It's like when you're on a tour and your guide says to follow. Then you decide to explore on your own. Then wonder, "Why am I so lost? Where am I?" And you blame the guide. See what I'm saying? Follow Him. Stay with Him. Being lost is not fun. It is not productive. And don't blame the Lord when you were the one who walked away from Him. Trust God. He knows where He's going and He knows where to take you. Stick with it. Don't quit. You will see that everything will be okay.

18 June Of all our cats, one is especially energetic. He is lean and active. Storms scare him. He disappears for several days only to return, often with some kind of injury from a scrape with some other animal. He usually paces in the house. He'll be up on my desk when I am working, run in and out of my office, and chase toys, pens, or other objects all over the living room to the kitchen and then down the stairs. It's difficult for him to settle himself. Then when he does calm down, he's practically unconscious. He's Fluffy, the short-haired cat. Gotta love him.

Today the song is, "I Will Not Be Moved" ~ Natalie Grant. Here again this song talks about standing on Christ, the solid rock. Because of that, I will not be moved. When your life is built on the solid rock, which is Christ, you can settle yourself. Matthew 7:24-25 (MSG) says, "These words I speak to you are not incidental additions to your life, homeowner improvements to your standard of living. They are foundational words, words to build a life on. If you work these words into your life, you are like a smart carpenter who built his house on solid rock. Rain poured down, the river flooded, a tornado hit—but nothing moved that house. It was fixed to the rock." Storms come, but they do not have to scare you. You can be stable in rough times. Calm in the face of hardship, because of the Lord. Philippians 4:6-7 (MSG) says, "Don't fret or worry. Instead of worrying, pray. Let petitions and praises shape your worries into prayers, letting God know your concerns. Before you know it, a sense of God's wholeness, everything coming together for good, will come and settle you down. It's wonderful what happens when Christ displaces worry at the center of your life." This is another of my life verses. Simply put, "Don't worry about anything, pray about everything." The peace of God will come. If you have walked away from God, it's time to return. Even with the wounds you've sustained out in the world, you have a place with Him. Stop your pacing. Stop your wandering. Stop your playing around. Stop your antics. That will get you nowhere. You are on sinking sand when you choose those things. Seek God. Find calm and rest. Take a breath. Focus. He loves you, and He is working all things together for your good.

19 June There's a leader I know that is the epitome of confidence. Granted, I know a lot of leaders who are confident, bold, strong, and amazing, but the woman that comes to mind today has always stood out to me. When she enters a room, she has a presence that speaks volumes. Leadership. Example. Work. Grace. Class. Humility. Joy. Strength. Tenacity. Wisdom. Her life has affected thousands. A woman among women. Such a success and still easy to talk to. She has inspired others to reach for their dreams by living the example of reaching her own. She's an encourager, a giver, a mentor, an achiever, and a Godly believer. She is truly a Proverbs 31 woman.

Today's song is, "You Are I Am" ~ MercyMe. This song acknowledges God as the one who conquers giants, calls out kings, shuts the mouths of lions, and tells the dead to breathe. Romans 8:31 says, "What then shall we say to these things? If God *is* for us, who *can be* against us?" There's a confidence in knowing God. Knowing that He is the champion. He's the one who defeats the enemies in your life. He is the source of your strength today. The source of your joy, your boldness, your tenacity, your wisdom. There's nothing like going into a room, knowing that God is on your side. You can put your head up, face whatever life has dealt you, and know that you can be successful. Things don't defeat you. Circumstances don't stop you. Obstacles don't detain you. So rise up today, acknowledge God and His greatness. Draw on His presence in your life. The presence that speaks volumes and affects people's lives. Be inspired today. God is for you.

20 June Praise and worship. It's a time of adoring God for who He is and what He's done. It's a time to enter into His presence. Often we sing. We raise our hands. We give voice to what we feel in our hearts. It's a time to get lost in God. It's an expression of love. We are here for Him.

Today the song is, "Here For You" ~ Matt Redman. This song declares to God that our hearts are open to Him in worship. Nothing is hidden and He is our desire. He is the one worthy of our praise. We are here for Him. Hebrews 13:16 (MSG) says, "Make sure you don't take things for granted and go slack in working for the common good; share what you have with others. God takes particular pleasure in acts of worship—a different kind of "sacrifice"—that take place in kitchen and workplace and on the streets." Hebrews 11:6 says, "It's impossible to please God apart from faith. And why? Because anyone who wants to approach God must believe both that he exists *and* that he cares enough to respond to those who seek him." Today, just take some time and worship God. Whether it's in your house, office, car, outside, wherever. Just do it. He's waiting for you. You need Him whether you think you do or not. Really, you do. Let it be your desire today to please Him. Drop pettiness, hurts, and strife. Sacrifice. Surrender. Relinquish yourself and be filled with His Spirit. It's like a breath of fresh air. A light spring rain. A cool breeze. Bask in His presence even if for just a few moments. It will make a big difference in how your day goes. Why? Because your perspective changes and you have a better focus. When you put God first, the rest of the stuff of life falls into place. Matthew 6:33 says, "But seek first the kingdom of God and His righteousness, and all these things shall be added to you." Don't make it hard. Don't wait for it. Pull yourself aside, just like you'd take an important call, and have yourself a moment with God. He is here for you. And you are here for Him.

21 June My oldest son is a strategist. He was always good at games like Othello and Stratego and especially paintball. They are thinking games – you have to plan ahead, knowing your next moves before it's time. He pays attention to people, to things, places, and events. It's hard to surprise him. He's calculating and purposeful and pretty much always prepared for action. He's creative and has some amazing insights, ideas, and concepts. (I'd say that even if I wasn't his mom.)

Today the song is, "Blink" ~ Revive. This song reminds me to count every moment and every day before they slip away, before the colors fade. I don't want to miss a single second! Time passes in a blink and a flash. You need to look at what you are doing with your life. How many times have you not paid attention to what is going on around you? How fast does opportunity pass you by? You look and say, "When did that happen?" You missed it. Doris Day used to sing, "Que Sera, Sera (Whatever Will Be, Will Be)" Has that been you lately? Did you just think that if it happens that it is God's will? Well, you were mistaken. When you operate like that, you are like a ship without a sail. The wind will toss you all over the place. Instead, pay attention. Seek God daily for direction. Do things on purpose, don't just let them happen. Think about it, if you leave the baking mix in the pantry, a cake will never happen. You must do the work. You must look at the directions. Use the right ingredients. You must turn up the heat. Put in the time. Then it will happen. Believe it and do it. Here's the key, James 1:6 (MSG) says, "If you don't know what you're doing, pray to the Father. He loves to help. You'll get his help, and won't be condescended to when you ask for it. Ask boldly, believingly, without a second thought. People who 'worry their prayers' are like wind-whipped waves. Don't think you're going to get anything from the Master that way, adrift at sea, keeping all your options open." So today, seek your purpose, see your purpose, and live on purpose. It will be gone before you know it. It happens in a blink.

22 June I loved it when my boys were babies. I thought, "This is the best time." Then toddler stage, discovery and development. That was the best. But then I think about them starting school. Such a great time. Then, though their experiences vastly different, high school was the most fun. Now, as adults, finding their calling, growing, continuing to seek God, these really are the best times. Honestly, it just gets better and better. Every stage has been 'the best'.

Again today, the song is "Blink" ~ Revive. This part today, says that there's no stopping time. It passes even when I hold on tight. When I look back it seems like it all went by so fast. Transition happens. You can't stop it. You move through it, but you choose how. Do you dread change? Do you focus on the 'terrible two's' of life? That time when you just know things will be awful? They don't have to be terrible. You can go into what others think will be bad with a good attitude and make the best of it. Learn from it. Transition through it and you will look back and say, "That wasn't so bad, what was everyone worried about?" Get into an attitude of trust. Trust God for the next step. His word will guide you through. If you're not sure today, do an overload of scripture and helpful books and resources that you can read or listen to. A theme will emerge. A direction will be evident. God will speak to your spirit and you will know what the next step is. Psalm 119:105-112 (MSG) gives this advice, "By your words I can see where I'm going; they throw a beam of light on my dark path. I've committed myself and I'll never turn back from living by your righteous order. Everything's falling apart on me, God; put me together again with your Word. Festoon me with your finest sayings, God; teach me your holy rules. My life is as close as my own hands, but I don't forget what you have revealed. The wicked do their best to throw me off track, but I don't swerve an inch from your course. I inherited your book on living; it's mine forever— what a gift! And how happy it makes me! I concentrate on doing exactly what you say—I always have and always will." Commitment through the transition is the key, following what God says every step of the way. Stay on track. Time will pass, but you choose how you will pass through. Pray your transition will be smooth. Look at it and say, "This is the best time."

23 June I saw a church with a black iron fence and large heavy gate around the perimeter of the property. As we drove by I sarcastically thought, "Visitors Welcome". By no means did that fence say, "Welcome! Come on in!" I really have no idea what that particular church or congregation is like. I only know by what I saw that day. I wondered how they would attract new people to attend their services.

Today's song is, "Christ Is Risen" ~ Matt Maher. This song exclaims that Christ is risen and we are one with Him again. When this tune came up in my heart today, the words were different than the actual lyrics, or perhaps I failed to find the correct song. The words I thought were, "You are welcome in this place, you are welcome in this place" How do you make people feel welcome? Are you open? Do you smile? Pay attention? Listen? Ask interesting questions? A hand shake? A hug? What makes people want to be a part of your conversation, your circle, your life? Proverbs 18:24a says, "A man *who has* friends must himself be friendly..." You create an atmosphere around yourself that is either off-putting, like a fence, or welcoming, like an open door. You choose. You also have the choice to welcome Christ into your life today. Is He a part of your conversation, your circle, your life? Do you see that He is risen and wants to be with you? Welcome Him. Be open. Listen. Pay attention. You may have a fence up today. Are you hurt? Are you bitter? Are you offended? Are you skeptical? Are you afraid? These are all barriers that can affect the response you receive. Time to tear down the fences and open the doors to your heart. You will attract what God has for you and you will like what you see.

24 June Nik Wallenda made history by walking a high wire across the Grand Canyon. Without a net or a tether, he succeeded in what was thought impossible. During the walk, he prayed aloud, quoting scripture, talking to God, and praising Him. He commented that his visual perspective was off because of an optical illusion created by the canyon walls and the swaying stabilizers on the wire, but his spiritual perspective was spot-on. High above the river and canyon floor, Nik knew that God was even higher. His confidence was in the Lord. It was a walk of faith and trust, a result of vision, plans, preparation, skill, and fulfillment of destiny. He was born for this. It was amazing.

Today's song is, "No One Higher" ~ Martha Munizzi. This song says that there is no one higher than our God. No one. Whatever the preparation, skill, gifts, or talents you possess, it is nothing without God. 1 Chronicles 29:11-13 (MSG) says, "To you, O God, belong the greatness and the might, the glory, the victory, the majesty, the splendor; Yes! Everything in heaven, everything on earth; the kingdom all yours! You've raised yourself high over all. Riches and glory come from you, you're ruler over all; you hold strength and power in the palm of your hand to build up and strengthen all. And here we are, O God, our God, giving thanks to you, praising your splendid Name." God must be higher than your dreams today. He must be higher than your goals. He must be higher than what you think you should be or do. When you exalt Him above all else, then your perspective will be correct. Your priorities will be right and you will walk in your destiny. (Matthew 6:33) You will still have to work for each step as Nik did. But your footing will be sure. You can walk in confidence, knowing that God is on your side, right there with you. What you thought was impossible, you will achieve. Discover what you were truly born to do and who you were born to be. Walk in it. It will be amazing.

25 June I was talking to a friend about an unrealized business goal. Actually I had postponed pursuit of it in order to take care of other things pressing in my life. My thought was that she would be disappointed in and even reject me because of it. What she said next was seared in my memory from that day. She said, "Starr, we love you no matter what you choose to do." I realized that I thought acceptance and love was contingent upon my achievements. However, this group of associates did not operate on that principle. They didn't like me for what I had done; they liked me for who I was. It shifted my perspective and helped me see that I am more than a position and an achievement.

Today the song is, "Who Am I" ~ Casting Crowns. In this song it asks essentially, who am I, that God would see my sin and still love me, watch me rise, call to me, and calm me in the storms of my life? I am His. So you have blown it. Messed up. Made a wrong choice. Over reacted, under thought, or jumped to a conclusion. Welcome to the human race. Things don't always go quite like you planned. People don't respond how you think they ought. You make choices. Take wrong turns. Go off on tangents. There are so many variables. You must see that in spite of flaws, God made you amazing. He formed you in your mother's womb. You are unique. Look at your fingertips. There is no one just like you. God sees your faults, your mistakes, your choices, your unrealized goals and loves you anyway. Deuteronomy 23:5b says, "But the Lord your God turned the curse into a blessing for you, because the Lord your God loves you." God has the power to turn things around in your life because He loves you. Don't feel like you've missed too much, waited too long, messed up too many times. God is redemptive. Jesus paid your way. There is another chance for you. So let God calm you in the storms you are facing. Let Him love you because of you. Achievements are great. You should be growing. But God's love does not depend on that. He loves you. Period. Remember to love Him back. Embrace all He can be to you and for you. Shift your perspective today; you are more than a position or an achievement. You are a child of God. His love for you is unconditional.

26 June I remember the years we directed youth camp. It was a time when we worked really hard to create the environment where young people would be open to God. Our prayer was that they had a real encounter. We prayed that their lives would be changed. Not just for that week in the summer, but for the rest of their days. We saw so many decisions not only to receive Christ, but to serve Him. Many of those youth are in ministry today because they said "Yes" to what God had for them.

Today the song is, "Who Am I" ~ Casting Crowns. This song reminds me that I am temporary, like a flower. Here today, gone tomorrow. Like an ocean wave or a vapor. When I read these verses, camp again came to mind. They paint a great picture of what we envisioned for those young people. James 4:7-10 (MSG) says, "So let God work his will in you. Yell a loud *no* to the Devil and watch him scamper. Say a quiet *yes* to God and he'll be there in no time. Quit dabbling in sin. Purify your inner life. Quit playing the field. Hit bottom, and cry your eyes out. The fun and games are over. Get serious, really serious. Get down on your knees before the Master; it's the only way you'll get on your feet." The scripture goes on to talk about how you need to look to God, not judge others, and that you cannot know exactly what tomorrow will bring – your life is like a vapor. Youth is fleeting and making a decision when you are young to follow God is magnificent. But, what if you are past your teens? Think you're too old for a change? Well, you aren't. You may not know about tomorrow, but here you are today. Take just a moment. Look to God. Let Him know you'd like to stop playing games now. You'd like to get serious. Surrender, cry your eyes out. Clean up your act, purify yourself. Make a new commitment. That's how you will get on your feet. Yell "No!" to the devil and say "Yes!" to God.

27 June On part of our tour in Israel we were able to go into a cavern (part of an ancient water system) equipped with stairs down and through the rock. We eventually came out on the other side. A couple of tourists became fearful, refused to descend the stairs, and chose to go around, meeting us later. I must admit I was somewhat anxious myself as we went through, but very grateful that I stayed the course. Though walking the path was strenuous as we ascended the steps and ramp that led out, I could say that, "I did it". We had an amazing trip and I am so glad that I did not miss any of it.

Today's song is, "Worn" ~ Tenth Avenue North. The person in this song seeks redemption, wanting to know the struggle ends and God can mend a frail and torn heart. You have to remember that when you are going through something, it's just that – You are going through it. The trials and struggles in your life are not a camping ground. They are a path. It may be scary at times. It may make you anxious. But you can make it. Even if you feel like avoiding the challenge, take it. Be strong and courageous. Joshua 1:9 says, "Have I not commanded you? Be strong and of good courage; do not be afraid, nor be dismayed, for the Lord your God *is* with you wherever you go." Psalm 23:4 says, "Yea, though I walk through the valley of the shadow of death, I will fear no evil; For You *are* with me; Your rod and Your staff, they comfort me." You walk through the valley. Through it. It doesn't say that you pitch a tent and camp there. The valley is for going through. Have you pitched a tent where you are today? Have you set up residence? Do you want to just stay there and mope? God can mend your broken heart. The struggle is temporary. You can move forward and move out of the valley today. Or have you been avoiding a situation because you are afraid? You want skip it? You want to ignore it? Chances are it's not going away. It's time to deal with it. Ask God. He will give you a plan and a strategy. Steps on the way down and steps on the way back up. How to go through. How to succeed. How to triumph. You can look to Him today for the strength and courage. He will be with you. And when you come out on the other side, you can say, "With God's help, I did it!"

28 June My husband and I had just eaten a great dinner and went for a stroll down Main Street with another couple. Though quite full, we headed to the ice cream parlor. Wow. They had so many flavors. Then the candies! Their showcase was full of chocolates and nuts and chocolate covered nuts, then fudges and caramels and taffies, oh my! I settled on a double-decker drumstick. Soooo good. I do enjoy ice cream.

Today the song is, "Every Good Thing" ~ The Afters.   This song proclaims that God is the reason for every good thing. Every heartbeat, every day, everything that lasts, second chances, and laughs. Life is sweet. Focusing on the positive today can help melt away the negative, like a double-decker ice cream on a warm, sunny day. God is good. James 1:17 says, "Every good gift and every perfect gift is from above, and comes down from the Father of lights, with whom there is no variation or shadow of turning." Then Psalm 34:8 says, "Oh, taste and see that the Lord *is* good; blessed *is* the man *who* trusts in Him!" When you get a taste, have an experience with God, you will know He is good. You will want to share your story. You can get excited about how good He is. Just like I want to tell you about that amazing ice cream, you want to tell others about all the good things God has done in your life. When you focus on the good, your perspective changes and you see things in a better light. You smile more. You say nicer things. You are more patient, more kind, more loving. People will be drawn to you because of the goodness of God in you. It shows by your countenance, your words, and your actions. So today, look on the bright side. See that God is the reason for every good thing. Trust Him. Take time to enjoy your life, your family, and your friends. And if you get a chance, have an ice cream cone – and make it a double-decker!

29 June When we moved to the small town where my husband grew up, the street name was our name. We built on the family farm. People knew my in-laws, aunts, uncles, and cousins. Purchasing some items at a local store, my husband wrote out a check to pay and said, "Do you need some identification?" The merchant looked at it and said, "No, your name is good here."

Today's song is, "Because Of Who You Are" ~ Vicki Yohe. This song explains that I worship God because of who He is. I give Him glory and praise. We experienced favor in the small community because of who we were. Our name made the difference, even when they didn't know us well. Don't feel like you know God well today? That's okay. You can still experience His presence. You can still worship and praise Him. Maybe you don't know all He's done for you, but you can love Him for who He is. Creator, healer, redeemer, sustainer, comforter, shelter, defender, strength, Father. He is mighty and awesome. Deuteronomy 10:17 says, "For the Lord your God *is* God of gods and Lord of lords, the great God, mighty and awesome, who shows no partiality nor takes a bribe." There are so many names of God. They describe His character. That would be a good study to do sometime. You can really see all He is. If you only see God for what He does, He will be like a genie to you, or a robot. You will bring your list of wants to Him. It would be like some one you don't know coming up to you and saying, "Give me your wallet, give me your clothes, give me your food." That sounds less like a loving relationship and more like a mugging. God wants a relationship with you. Don't mug him. Spend time with Him because of who He is. Not for what you can get from Him. If I had that kind of relationship with my husband, it would be unhealthy. That is not good. Seek that healthy relationship with God today. Praise and worship Him for who He is. Know His character. Know His name. His name is good here.

30 June When I return from a meeting, a church service, a project, or appointment at night, it's tough for me to go right to bed. I am restless and I need to wind down. Often I will have a warm cup of tea with honey. It relaxes me so I can go off to bed without tossing and turning. Then I have a good night's sleep.

Today's song is, "Restless" ~ Audrey Assad. This song says that I am restless until I rest in God. I want Him to hold me close and speak to me in a still small voice. Then let the small voice rise to a shout and a cry. This is such a gentle, soothing song. It speaks of solace and the melody itself lends to the feeling of rest as well. Some days are hectic. You get busy with people, projects, meetings, appointments and you can forget to take the time to rest in God. Isaiah 30:15, 16, & 18 (MSG) says, "God, the Master, The Holy of Israel, has this solemn counsel: 'Your salvation requires you to turn back to me and stop your silly efforts to save yourselves. Your strength will come from settling down in complete dependence on me—The very thing you've been unwilling to do. You've said, 'Nothing doing! We'll rush off on horseback!' You'll rush off, all right! Just not far enough! You've said, 'We'll ride off on fast horses!' Do you think your pursuers ride old nags? But God's not finished. He's waiting around to be gracious to you. He's gathering strength to show mercy to you. God takes the time to do everything right—everything. Those who wait around for him are the *blessed* ones." It's so important to wait on God. That's where blessing comes from. Get quiet. Get by yourself. Find a spot where you won't be disturbed and pray. Then listen. Know that He is God. There is none like Him. Don't rush off trying to do it all yourself. God is not finished with you. If you are having trouble sleeping, take time to settle. You will be restless until you rest in Him. Proverbs 3:24 says, "When you lie down, you will not be afraid; Yes, you will lie down and your sleep will be sweet." Take a moment now and several throughout the day to be quiet. Turn off the music and the noise. Step away from the din of the crowd. Step away from the activity and just shut down. He will speak in that still small voice. Then that voice will rise to a shout and a cry. You will know God is speaking to you and you will know His plan for your life. His assurance. His peace. His wisdom and His direction. No more tossing and turning, and I've got a feeling that for you, tonight's going to be a good night.

1 July For many years we have entered a float in the Independence Day parade here locally. It's an outreach for our church. We want our participation to make an impact in the community. Some years, the subject of the float has been very patriotic, sometimes historical, other times musical. But it's always memorable. One year we made our float into a celebration. People were dancing, clapping, smiling, and having a great time when they saw and experienced our presentation. It was great to show people that Godly believers can really have a lot of fun following the Lord.

Today the song is, "Dance" ~ BJ Putnam. This is a song of celebration, urging everyone to dance the dance of freedom, shout for joy, and praise God. Make some noise! There are times to be quiet and reflective, but there are also times to get loud. Psalm 47:1 says, "Oh, clap your hands, all you peoples! Shout to God with the voice of triumph!" Then in Joshua 6 the walls of Jericho came down with a shout. Psalm 150:4-6 says, "Praise Him with the timbrel and dance; Praise Him with stringed instruments and flutes! Praise Him with loud cymbals; Praise Him with clashing cymbals! Let everything that has breath praise the Lord. Praise the Lord!" So, dancing, singing, and shouting can be acts of praise to God. They are strong expressions of joy and thanks for Him. You may think, "My faith is private." My pastor clarified that it is not private, it is personal and it is to be shared. So loosen up a bit. Try a new expression of your love for God. Let your response to His goodness be exuberant and full of passion. Show your enthusiasm. Impact others, make God memorable to them. Show people that Godly believers can have a lot of fun following the Lord!

2 July When I think about our country, I think about the sacrifice of our military forces that have kept us free thus far. They train, they fight, they get wounded, and they die. The ones that return are forever changed. Whether supported or denied, they know that what they do is noble and heroic. They are committed to a cause. It humbles me to see this dedication, discipline, and strength. It makes me proud to be an American.

Today the song is, "God With Us" ~ MercyMe. This song is talking to God saying that you show us love that we could never afford. The offering of ourselves that we bring to you is small compared to what Christ gave on Calvary. We are free, released from the chains that bound us. When you see dedication and commitment it's got to make you proud. You see someone who will do 'whatever it takes' and you appreciate them. Our military has secured our physical freedom and our Savior has purchased our spiritual freedom. Christ paid the ultimate price. Philippians 2:5-8 (MSG) it says, "Think of yourselves the way Christ Jesus thought of himself. He had equal status with God but didn't think so much of himself that he had to cling to the advantages of that status no matter what. Not at all. When the time came, he set aside the privileges of deity and took on the status of a slave, became *human*! Having become human, he stayed human. It was an incredibly humbling process. He didn't claim special privileges. Instead, he lived a selfless, obedient life and then died a selfless, obedient death—and the worst kind of death at that—a crucifixion." He paid a high price. He didn't owe you that. You didn't deserve that. He did it because of His love for you. You were the cause of Christ's commitment. Whether you accept it or deny it is your choice, nevertheless, He died for you. Any sacrifice you make pales in comparison, yet make it anyway. Put God first. Adjust priorities. Have you made the right things important? Where your treasure lies shows your heart condition. Matthew 6:21 (MSG) says, "The place where your treasure is, is the place you will most want to be, and end up being." What have you set at the foot of the cross today? What have you given to God? Focus on the giving today, not the getting. Appreciate all Christ did for your spiritual freedom and remember the sacrifice of our military for our physical freedom. Never, ever take it for granted.

3 July I remember putting a puzzle together with friends. We all wanted to be the one to complete it. Fewer and fewer pieces remained until finally only one spot was vacant. What? There were no more! After a momentary gasp, one smirking young lady pulled the last piece from her chair and claimed victory. Pretty slick, I thought, but we needed what she had to finish the task.

Today the song is, "Strangely Dim" ~ Francesca Battistelli. This song tells about all the plans I have and not yet realized, but when I focus on God my doubts grow strangely dim. Working on a project, task, or goal – if it's a big one – takes a team to make it successful. Each person holds a piece or pieces to completing the big picture. Every piece is important, for without any one of them, the goal falls short. You have dreams. You have plans. You have goals. When you make them big and when you make them clear, you will need others to come along to help. You may doubt that it will all come together. You may wonder why you got yourself into it in the first place. You may get flustered. But God. God focus can mute your doubts. Looking to Him will provide the answers you need. He will show you the resources. He will lead you to the optimal situation to obtain amazing results. God will direct you to all those who have the parts to your masterpiece. Like a giant puzzle, know that it will come together. Even if someone is sitting on their potential, pray they give it up, knowing that this cause is worthy and what they have to offer will be key in the victory. So, look to God today in all of your endeavors. He's got the plan. He needs you to help finish the task. Stop gasping at what is missing, locate the missing pieces, add them in, and claim your victory!

4 July Patriotism. We were raised to respect and love our country and its symbols. We stand and take our hats off during the Pledge of Allegiance and National Anthem. We put our hands on our hearts. We sing the Star Spangled Banner. We tear up when we see the color guard and we remember and thank our veterans for their service. Today I reflect on that sense of pride that I was taught and now feel for myself. We've taught our sons as well. I am a patriot.

Today's song is "Boogie Woogie Bugle Boy" ~ The Andrews Sisters. This song is about a musician, drafted into the army. In the service, he plays his style of bugle. The bugler was put in a place that was unfamiliar, maybe uncomfortable, but definitely not his style. However, he made it work. He did what he needed to do in serving our country. It didn't matter that he liked to play boogie woogie, he could still play there in his new situation. He was a part of something bigger than himself. You are a part of something bigger than yourself. You can choose to say, "No, man, that's not my style. I'm not doing it." or you can be a part, do what you need to do to serve. God needs you and the people need you. How many more can you impact today by just working with the situation you are in? You may not agree with every aspect, nevertheless, you are a part of it. It could be your family activities and goals. It could be your workplace. It could be your church or a charity organization. Whatever it is today, be committed wholeheartedly. Ecclesiastes 9:10a says, "Whatever your hand finds to do, do *it* with your might." When the going gets tough do you get going (away)? Nowhere to be found? Or are you all in today? There to contribute. There to finish a job that was started. There to support your leader, boss, family. Today, make a new promise to be fully committed. Do things with all your might. Do not accept halfway anything. Then teach your children or young relatives, students or neighbors to do the same. Be an influencer for right and for what pleases God. Then you will be proud of your achievements, your associations, your workplace, your family, your church, your life. Especially remember veterans and thank them for their service. Your respect will make an impact.

5 July When I am working on a project, putting something together, I am focused on how the thing looks. My husband concentrates on whether it is secure and stable. I want it to be pretty and he wants it to stay together. I have found that no matter how good it looks, if it falls apart then it's not really worth much. So here's a salute to my husband who offers the structure and stability in my life that still allows me to make things look beautiful!

Today's song is, "We Won't Be Shaken" ~ Building 429. This song affirms that whatever will come our way, fire, rain, or the uncertainty of tomorrow, we won't be shaken. We will rise and sing, trust in God, and we won't be moved. Stability is crucial to coping with all life can throw at you. Your stability is contingent upon your foundation. Your core values. Your priorities. The parts of your life that are optional, convenient, or preference versus what is nonnegotiable, inalienable, and unchangeable. What things could you either take or leave? What is just a part of who you are and what you do? That is a key to being grounded. Does your life appear to be stable, but lack the strong foundation and conviction that it needs to stand in the face of adversity? Matthew 7:26 says, "But everyone who hears these sayings of Mine, and does not do them, will be like a foolish man who built his house on the sand: and the rain descended, the floods came, and the winds blew and beat on that house; and it fell. And great was its fall." Without a firm foundation – Christ – you will fall apart. Strength comes from seeking, listening to, and doing what God has said. This is the Rock upon which your foundation should be built. You can trust Him today. So when the storms of life come, you will stand. You will not be shaken. You will not fall apart. You will not be moved. And your life will be beautiful!

6 July I was having a hard time walking. My knee was very sore so I had my chiropractor check it out. He told me I had a degenerative joint. His assessment was that it would not get better. My pastor's wife prayed for me at church the following week. God healed me. I also had chronic low back pain. My doctor told me it was arthritis. He showed me on the x-rays. During church that night, my pastor was telling a story about visiting with his family. One relative told him that he would get arthritis in his finger and Pastor said that he would not accept that. In that moment of merely telling the story, my back pain – which was intense-vanished. God healed me. It has been several years since both of these instances. The pain has not returned and I believe it never will.

Today the song is, "Our God (Is Greater)" ~ Chris Tomlin. This song says that our God is greater, stronger, and higher than any. He is Healer and awesome in power. My personal experience with the healing power of God is proof to me that He is Healer. You can never convince me otherwise. The prophetic words in Isaiah tell about Jesus in 53:5, "But He *was* wounded for our transgressions, *He was* bruised for our iniquities; The chastisement for our peace *was* upon Him, And by His stripes we are healed." The price Jesus Christ paid bought your healing. Proverbs 3:7-8 (MSG) says, "Run to God! Run from evil! Your body will glow with health; your very bones will vibrate with life!" By making the choice to run to God, you position yourself for health. 3 John 1:2 says, "Beloved, I pray that you may prosper in all things and be in health, just as your soul prospers." John saw the validity of praying for prosperity and health in alignment with the condition of your soul. Today, if you are struggling with your health or know someone who is, be encouraged that God wants you to be healthy. However, He can't override your choices. You decide to walk in wisdom or foolishness. You treat your body like a temple or a trash can. You decide. You have options. You have opportunities. So, take care of yourself. Ask God for wisdom in the matter of eating, activity, and rest. Do some research if you have to. Then do what you need to do and God will come along side. He can restore. He wants to restore. Be open to Him. I pray then that your body will glow with health and your very bones will vibrate with life!

7 July My pastor is a great teacher, a great leader, and a great mentor. A mentor is someone who will lead and guide you. Some one who will help you grow, encourage you to step out of your comfort zone, and to be others-minded. A mentor is not someone who will always tell you what you want to hear. He will not accept excuses for poor performance or bad behavior. He will not let you slide by nor tolerate tardiness, laziness, or mediocrity. A mentor cares enough to refuse that you stay the same. A good mentor is valuable. A great mentor is golden.

Today's song is "I Give Myself Away" ~ William McDowell. This song is surrender to God that here I am, and here I stand. My life is in your hands and I want to see your desires show in me. I give myself away so you can use me, God. A great pastor is a great mentor. He gives a lot to be dedicated to the people to whom he is called to serve. He gives himself away so God can use him. He helps the people grow. He helps the people see that they are more than what they are, see, and have right now. God's desires show in him because he has surrendered his life. You may not be a local pastor, but you do have a calling to give yourself away so God can use you. You grow to a point where you desire the things of God. His will. His way. When you serve others, you fulfill an assignment to "Go into all the world..." Mark 16:15 says, "And He said to them, 'Go into all the world and preach the gospel to every creature.'" The Good News of Christ is told when you serve. You help. You give aid. You reach outside of yourself and do good to others. You do it and it's not contingent on their ability to reciprocate. In turn, you receive a blessing, but often it comes by another route. It's usually something unexpected. Harvest on seed, sown unselfishly.

Today, remember your pastor and your mentors. Pray for them. Take time to write them a "Thank You" note. Include a gift. Honor them any chance you get. Realize that they give their lives for service to you-to help you grow and fulfill God's plan and destiny for your life. They give themselves away, placing their lives in God's hands. They want the best for you. Offer the best you have to them, their presence in your life can be golden.

8 July When my eldest son was small, I wanted to keep him occupied for a few minutes while I prepared supper. I gave him a cookie sheet and a bag of chicken nuggets, and then showed him how to put the nuggets out on the sheet one at a time, asking him to repeat the process for all of them. He promptly took the bag, inverted it and dumped all the nuggets out at once. "Done!" he exclaimed.

Today's song is, "Oh How I Love Jesus" ~ Frederick Whitfield. "Oh, how I love Jesus, because He first loved me!" We sang this song as children and occasionally as adults. It is so simple yet so profound. How many times have you looked at a situation and seen it as complicated, intricate, or complex and found later that the solution was incredibly elementary? Simple? Easy? Like dumping all the nuggets on the tray at once? You find yourself so conditioned to think that answers must be excavated from all the clutter of facts, figures, and details that the obvious is cloaked, hidden beyond your perception. It may be time to take a step back. Think. There may be a simpler way. The answer may be so close that you cannot see it. Perhaps you have been treating your faith in the same way. You want to search all of the intricacies of belief, religion, scripture, doctrine, and tradition. By doing so, you might have missed the simple fact that Jesus loves you. Then make the simple decision to love Him back. Luke 17:18b (MSG) says, "Mark this: Unless you accept God's kingdom in the simplicity of a child, you'll never get in." Don't make things complicated today. Realize the simple fact that you are loved by God and He simply wants you to love Him back. All the rules, guidelines, regulations, and rituals are secondary. They are not a requirement for your salvation. You can figure that out another day. Today, respond, love, and follow. Mark 1:17 says, "Then Jesus said to them, 'Follow Me, and I will make you become fishers of men.'" He is the one who will make you become what you are called to become-one step at a time as you follow. So take a first step today, or merely take another step. Step closer to God. Don't just occupy yourself with busyness, make what you do count. It doesn't have to be difficult. It can be as simple as nuggets on a tray.

9 July It was vacation time. I got in my bumper boat anticipating a fantastically fun few minutes on the water. The boats were equipped with squirt guns that my sons mercilessly shot me with repeatedly. Unfortunately, my sunscreen was dripping into my eyes, causing a horrible burning sensation. I began to shout, "Stop squirting me!" This excited them all the more. Things seemed to get worse as the round continued. I struggled to get them to stop, but it fueled their enthusiasm. They were having a great time. I, however, was beside myself thinking, "Don't they care? I'm hurting here!" When the ride was over, they were laughing. I was crying. I was so wrapped up in what was happening with me that I missed how much my children enjoyed those crazy bumper boats.

Today the song is, "The Heart Of Worship" ~ Matt Redman. This song resolves that I'm coming back to the heart of worship and it's all about Jesus. I'm sorry for what I've made it because it's really all about Him. Have you ever been so involved with yourself, what you want, your needs, your desires, your pain that you totally missed what was really going on? You struggled to get attention? You ached to get noticed? You wanted it to be all about you? What have you missed seeing because you had your eyes on yourself? When you get wrapped up in 'you', you can't appreciate or enjoy others. It's all based on where your love lies. I Corinthians 13:4-7 (MSG) gives you a checklist, "Love never gives up. Love cares more for others than for self. Love doesn't want what it doesn't have. Love doesn't strut, Doesn't have a swelled head, Doesn't force itself on others, Isn't always 'me first,' Doesn't fly off the handle, Doesn't keep score of the sins of others, Doesn't revel when others grovel, Takes pleasure in the flowering of truth, Puts up with anything, Trusts God always, Always looks for the best, Never looks back, But keeps going to the end." What a great attitude to have. You can apply that to how you treat others and you can also apply it to how you treat God. You worship. You appreciate what He has done for you. Panicking about the situation you are in will not make things better. A lot of times it makes it worse. God notices your pain, your struggle, your tears. Don't miss the enjoyable moments. The fun. The blessings in life. Just focus on God. Focus on the good in your life. It may be a bit bumpy at times, but you will be okay.

10 July We took children on many field trips the 7 years I was a school principal. Many times it was critical that each student had a "buddy" and they were told to never go anywhere by themselves. The buddy system worked well. We didn't lose a single child on any of those outings.

Today's song is, "Right Beside You" ~ Building 429. This song is assurance from one friend to another that even when the walls are closing in, you want to give up and you feel like you've lost everything, I'll be right beside you. It's so good to have friends that will be with you, watch out for you, have fun with you, go on adventures with you, and even take care of you. You were made for fellowship, being with others. There is so much you can contribute to and so much you can glean from friends. You can have close friends, work friends, long time friends, acquaintances, and best friends. The best friends are the ones who stick with you no matter what. They are the ones who know your faults and love you anyway. They don't leave when things get tough. Proverbs 17:17 (MSG) says, "Friends love through all kinds of weather, and families stick together in all kinds of trouble." Friendship is an important bond. You choose your friends. Choose wisely. Proverbs 12:26 says, "The righteous should choose his friends carefully, for the way of the wicked leads them astray." If you have the wrong friends, they can influence you in wrong choices. Good friends can keep you from getting lost; and if you do manage to get lost, they can help you find your way back. Today, check your friendships. Are your friends people who you truly want to be like? Are they good or bad? Do they add to your life or just take away? Proverbs 27:17 (MSG) says, "You use steel to sharpen steel, and one friend sharpens another." You and your friends should be making each other better. Make sure you have "buddies" that will never let you have to tackle life alone. There was a Girl Scout song that said, "Make new friends, but keep the old. One is silver and the other is gold." The friendships that last a lifetime are like pure gold. Realize that your true friends are just that, precious, to be treasured, rare, and valuable.

11 July The fields were planted with soybeans awhile back. They are coming up quite nicely now and we anticipate a great harvest this season with ample rainfall and moderate temperatures. It just may be a bumper crop! I was thinking about the seeds. After a cursory study I found out a few things…Though a seed in the ground is not visible and may be thought to be dead, it is very much alive. When there is a delay in the germination of the seed it may be due to awaiting the optimal conditions for survival, or to avoid catastrophe that would wipe out all the plants at once. But here is the big thing… "This true dormancy or innate dormancy is therefore caused by conditions within the seed that prevent germination. Thus dormancy is a state of the seed, not of the environment" (wikipedia.org/wiki/seeds) To germinate, the seed must be viable, overcome what is preventing germination, and be in the right environment.

Today's song is, "It's Not Over" ~ Ricardo Sanchez. This is a song of encouragement. This part I am hearing today….That it's darkest just before dawn. This could be your hardest season so far. It hurts, but it won't be long because you are close to your victory. Help is on the way. You are the seed today. Within you lies everything you need to produce all that God has in store for you. You lack nothing. Psalm 23:1 (AMP) says, "The Lord is my Shepherd [to feed, guide, and shield me], I shall not lack." You may be in a state of dormancy, where it looks dark, maybe even hopeless. You may feel buried in the stress, problems, and overwhelming feelings of it all. You may be hesitating because you want to avoid catastrophe. But you are close to your victory. Stay alive. Stay viable. Stay hopeful. God is here to help you. Just look up to Him. He is your strength today. You must place yourself in the right environment so that you can grow. Create that environment through praise and thanksgiving. Here is the big thing…what has stalled you – is you. The dormancy lies within the seed, not the environment. Don't blame the economy, the government, the church, your family, your job, or your friends for what's going on. Don't let those factors stop you from thriving today. It's not over! You are very much alive and you can break through and break out of all that you have allowed to hold you back. You are closer than you think. Awaken yourself, get going, and get growing. You just may have a bumper crop!

12 July The hike. That day we decided to go for a "walk". My husband's research told us of a moderately easy trail that would take approximately 40 minutes to circle the lake. I thought, "This, I can do". So we set out and at what we guessed to be the halfway point, we discovered a trail sign which revealed that this path would actually take about 2 hours and 40 minutes to complete! With our camp out of sight we decided to forage on.

Today's song, now so clear why God picked it… "I Won't Go Back" ~ William McDowell. The chorus says that I won't go back, can't go back, to the way it used to be before God's presence came and changed me. There is a point when you simply cannot go back.

Things I learned on the hike: 1. It's easy to begin, but it may become unpleasant when you find that the journey may be longer than you anticipated. 2. Consistency is a key to reaching your goal. Keep going, rest when your can, don't give up. Philippians 3:14 says, "I press toward the goal for the prize of the upward call of God in Christ Jesus." Press on! 3. Whining does you no good. 4. Two are better than one. Ecclesiastes 4:9-10 says, "Two *are* better than one, Because they have a good reward for their labor. For if they fall, one will lift up his companion. But woe to him *who is* alone when he falls, for *he has* no one to help him up." We helped each other when the terrain got especially rough, and encouraged one another to keep going, then to finish. 5. Large steps taken with confidence get you farther than small hesitant ones. 6. Take the high road when you can-you're less likely to fall in the water. 7. The path isn't always clear at first. Follow your leader. Watch your step. The path will soon become evident. 8. Short cuts are not usually a good idea. 9. When you are focused on the goal, don't forget to stop now and then to enjoy the view. 10. It is sweet to reach your destination! Once we completed the trail, there was a 118 step stairway up to the road. With feet and legs aching, I ascended the final 100 slowly. Then with great effort reached the top and my husband, who was waiting for me with a hug, a kiss, and a "We did it!" (Not bad for 2 novices!)

So, take a look at your goals today. The trip may be tougher than you thought. There will be hills and valleys, obstacles, and detours. But keep going. Jesus has blazed the trail for your journey and it will be so sweet to reach your destination!

13 July I have a friend who has known me since we were young children. I'll just tell you that it's a lot of years. We grew up together. We lived 3 houses away from each other in the neighborhood. We spent a lot of time together. Even though our paths eventually parted, we are still friends. Every reunion over these decades has been a combination of memories and updates. We always seem to pick up right where we left off the last time we saw each other. It's just a special friend-bond that we have. Though we have changed in many ways, our friendship has remained the same.

Today's song is, "Jesus The Same" ~ Israel & New Breed. This song reminds me that Jesus is the same yesterday, today, and forever. His name is greater than any other. There's a confidence that comes when you know that some one or something will be consistent. It's a comfort you can have in the reliability or dependability of a relationship. You don't have to be guessing, "Are we still friends?" You know you are. No matter how far apart you are or how much time has passed, there are some friends you have that you can just get back together with and none of those lapses matter. That's the way your relationship with Jesus can and should be. You can rely on Him to be the same. His word is still true after all these years. Even if you have walked away from Him. He still wants that bond with you. He still loves you. None of the lapses matter. You may change, but He hasn't. His memories of you are good, regardless what you've done in the past. Psalm 103:12 says, "As far as the east is from the west, *So* far has He removed our transgressions from us." You are forgiven – when you ask. And you seek Him. And He doesn't remember any of those transgressions. So, if you have a great relationship with Jesus, tell some one else about it. If you have drifted away from Him today, it's time for a reunion. It will be like old times, when you were close. If you have never had a relationship with Jesus, time to build one. Ask Him to be a part of your life. Ask for forgiveness for all the wrong and mistakes. Turn over a new leaf. You won't have to guess, "Are you my Savior?" You know He is.

14 July As a floral designer and manager I had the occasion to talk to many a bride about her wedding flowers. Often she would say something like, "I really want my bouquet to be different." As she described her dream, I knew that it was the same as the last three brides, just another size or color. So, she still thought she was being different but it was really more of the same. Nevertheless, she was happy, because it was hers.

Today's song is, "Moving Forward" ~ Israel Houghton. This song declares that I am not going back, I'm moving ahead. I'm moving forward. Moving forward does not mean more of the same. The same habits. The same routines. The same people. The same path. Moving forward must include something different. Something truly different. Something better. Something greater. Something bigger. Do you feel like you have re-invented yourself lately? Have you truly changed, or is it just the same 'you' in a different shirt? The same 'you' in a different car, or job, or church, or home? Take a closer look. Pinpoint the change. Have you changed for the better? Why have you changed? Why are you different? Check your motivation. Some people are motivated by politics, race, pride, or finances. Others are motivated by morality, benevolence, and spirituality. What drives you? Have you stretched to be a leader? Or are you just a part of the pack? Pulling forward with dreams and ideals worth emulating? Or hanging out with negative, minimal thinkers? Your choices will determine your outcome. Don't get caught up in the drama, distractions, and difficulties life will throw at you. Create your own amazing life. God's plan for me is not the same as anyone else's. Neither is yours. Take a close look. See what you see. Evaluate and adjust. Philippians 3:12-14 (MSG) says, "I'm not saying that I have this all together, that I have it made. But I am well on my way, reaching out for Christ, who has so wondrously reached out for me. Friends, don't get me wrong: By no means do I count myself an expert in all of this, but I've got my eye on the goal, where God is beckoning us onward—to Jesus. I'm off and running, and I'm not turning back." God has created you for greatness in spite of daily events. Just believe it, grow into it, and choose to move forward. Then, own the life that is yours.

15 July There was a rip in my bed sheet. I decided to fix it with a patch. So I ironed on a big swatch of adhesive patch material to both sides. Then I patted myself on the back, "Good as new." I thought. Returning the sheet to the bed, I took pride in my handiwork. After a good night's sleep I found that my efforts were in vain, because the sheet tore away from the patch making the problem worse. Solution? Throw that sheet away and replace it with a new one. That was much better!

Today's song is "Moving Forward" ~ Israel Houghton. This part of the song has stood out to me today, that my past is over and all things are made new since I surrendered my life to Christ. I'm moving forward. Have you ever tried to make a change but been unwilling to fully commit to it? You wanted to make do or get by with somewhat of a change but hesitant to discard what's not working and start over? It turns into more work than you thought. It isn't the same as brand new. With furniture it can be trendy and chic, but with your life mission, goals, dreams, or destiny, it can be disaster. You need the wisdom to start completely over when it's time. Time for a new project, time for a new job, time for a new group of friends. That wisdom comes from God. James 1:5 says, "If any of you lacks wisdom, let him ask of God, who gives to all liberally and without reproach, and it will be given to him." When your past is over, move on. New things await you. Go forward. Don't just put a new patch on the old trying to fool yourself into thinking it will work. Start again. Let God show you. In Matthew 9:17 it says, "Nor do they put new wine into old wineskins, or else the wineskins break, the wine is spilled, and the wineskins are ruined. But they put new wine into new wineskins, and both are preserved." The inside and the outside will be new for you. It's a total make over. Is it time? Are you ready? Are you willing? Surrender to the Lord, then your efforts will not be in vain. Soon you will be as good as new. You'll be a much better you.

16 July I struggled this morning with the song God gave me again. How odd that I seemed to be stuck on this song for yet a 3rd day. I asked, "God, what have I missed that you want to show me?" His prodding in my spirit made me look again. Today the song is, "Moving Forward" ~ Israel Houghton. Here is the part...that Christ is risen with all power in His hands and I have been given a second chance.

How often have you looked at something and thought you saw everything, and then find later that you had missed an important part? You see things your way, but that's really not the only way? You think your perspective must be right. You think that you have been thorough, observant, detailed, accurate, complete, and comprehensive, yet you seemed to have missed something. Have you have settled for your assessment and have decided that everyone else's opinion pales in comparison? That's called 'narrow-minded', or 'bull-headed', or 'selfish', or 'prideful'. When you become shut off to considering alternatives for your plan, your project, your direction, or your methods, you have limited yourself to the small box that is 'you alone'. You have rejected the infinite scope that comes from including others and more importantly, including God. Philippians 3:13 says, "Brethren, I do not count myself to have apprehended; but one thing *I do,* forgetting those things which are behind and reaching forward to those things which are ahead..." Don't think you know it all. Humility says, "I don't know everything." James 4:6 (MSG) says, "It's common knowledge that 'God goes against the willful proud; God gives grace to the willing humble.'" Be willing today to hear another view point. Be willing to learn something new. Be willing to admit you have room to grow. Be willing to work things out. Be willing to try again. You may find something you never saw before, something you missed. Thank God for showing you new things and pray that He will continue to bring people into your life that will increase your scope, and help you grow. That's moving forward.

Footnote: Being teachable does not mean to accept all opinions. Seek God and His word on matters in the Scriptures - that surpasses the thoughts of anyone else.

17 July I never realized how selfish I was until I got married. After living on my own for awhile, I had a routine. There was an expectation that what I left in the freezer – ice cream sandwiches – would still be there a couple days later when I went back for them. However, sharing became a startling reality. Alas, my frozen treats were gone...the culprit was the man God had given me! So here we are many years later and I still don't like to share desserts, but I plan for all of us and am willing to give mine up if we happen to be a bit short. At least I'm honest and God is still working on me. Besides, sharing always feels better than keeping it all for myself.

Today the song is, "I Give Myself Away" ~ William McDowell. This song reminds me that my life is not my own. I belong to God. So I give myself away so He can use me. When you reach the point where you can selflessly give, you have attained a greater level of maturity. When you have been gifted, are skilled, or blessed it's great to share. Share when you are needed. Share when someone is hurting. Share when you want them to know you care. Share when you can help, really help. Not a hand out, a hand up. James 4:17 (MSG) says, "In fact, if you know the right thing to do and don't do it, that, for you, *is* evil." Do the right thing. When God is prompting you, you should act. Don't hesitate or make excuses, give. Be willing to be a part of something bigger than yourself. Give of your own free will. It's much better to offer yourself, gifts, skills, etc. than to have someone demand it and take it. John 10:18a says, "No one takes it (my life) from Me, but I lay it down of Myself. I have power to lay it down, and I have power to take it again." Even Jesus gave his life. They did not take it from Him. He gave it in payment of our sins. He made a sacrifice. There will be sacrifices involved in giving, give anyway. Sacrifices in sharing, share anyway. Sacrifices in being used of God, be used of God anyway. And sacrifices in serving, but serve anyway. Mark 10:45 says, "For even the Son of Man did not come to be served, but to serve, and to give His life a ransom for many." Today, be alert. God wants to use you, but you must give yourself away. You probably won't realize how much it will mean to those involved. Many times it will mean much more than you think. It may not be easy, but sharing always feels better than keeping it all for yourself.

18 July I got to hold a friend's seven week old baby today. He was adorable. He fell asleep in my arms. I actually held him long enough to feed him when he woke up. Then he did what babies do, doo-doo. So, I'm a fair-weather friend because I handed him off to his grandma. It was time for a change!

Today's song is, "Our God" ~ Chris Tomlin. This song reminds me of the miracle at the wedding, Jesus' first miracle of turning water into wine. Then tells of Him healing the blind. There is no one like Jesus, no one like God. A miracle happens without natural explanation and is credited to the supernatural – God. Have you felt like you needed a miracle in your life? You knew something had to change. You didn't know anything you or anyone you know could do to make it happen. Yet, somehow it happened. The circumstances changed, or the people changed, or the weather, the system, or the whole scheme of things became different. Without natural explanation, you realize that it must have been God. Romans 8:28 says, "And we know that all things work together for good to those who love God, to those who are the called according to *His* purpose." He will work it out. The criteria? Love God and be focused on what God wants. Some translations say that God causes all things to work together...note: God does not cause all things. He causes them to work together. He can take your mess and turn it around. He can cause that miracle in your life that you need. It's time for you to be transformed. Jesus is the change agent. Romans 12:2 (MSG) says "Don't become so well-adjusted to your culture that you fit into it without even thinking. Instead, fix your attention on God. You'll be changed from the inside out. Readily recognize what he wants from you, and quickly respond to it. Unlike the culture around you, always dragging you down to its level of immaturity, God brings the best out of you, develops well-formed maturity in you." So take a look at yourself today. Look at your life. It may be time for a radical make-over or maybe just a bit of a tweak. Either way, when you do what you do – if it stinks, you definitely need a change. Let God do a miracle in you. Transform you. Make you, your life, your situation different. God is no fair-weather friend. He will be with you every step of the way.

19 July Skinned knees were pretty common for my boys when they were little. I learned soon enough that my response when they fell would influence how they handled the injury. Minor as it was, drama on my part would only make it worse. If I said, "You'll be okay." They believed me. I'm their mom. And they were okay. The knees healed. Running resumed! Both boys became active in sports through the years. Many times those minor injuries became trophies for how hard or well they played. When they got hurt, they began to tell me, "Mom, I'm okay." I believed them, they're my sons.

Today's song is, "I Will Lift My Eyes" ~ Bebo Norman. This song reminds me where to look when I am hurting, need strength, in fear, doubt, or unrest. I will lift my eyes to God. There are so many things you can decide to do when you are hurting. Get angry. Get withdrawn. Get working. Get around people. Get alone. Get to church. Get to a bar. Get loud. Get quiet. But here's what God wants you to do. Look up and get up. When a guy falls in a soccer game everyone waits for him to get up. Then they cheer. They cheer because he got up! Not because he fell. No one of any value is celebrating your defeat today. The people who care do not rejoice in your hurt. They want to see you get up! Psalm 121:1-5 says, "I will lift up my eyes to the hills—from whence comes my help? My help *comes* from the Lord, Who made heaven and earth. He will not allow your foot to be moved; He who He who keeps you will not slumber. Behold, He who keeps Israel shall neither slumber nor sleep. The Lord *is* your keeper; The Lord *is* your shade at your right hand." He is your keeper today. On that you can rely. He will keep you today. He will help you today. He's always on guard. He won't leave his post. He won't run away from you, so run to Him. He believes you when you tell Him you're hurting, believe Him when He says, "You'll be okay."

If you know someone who is hurting today, share this with them. Share your own personal victories. Let them know that they will be okay. It may take time to heal, but soon they'll be up running again. Then the very same hurt that they have come through will become a testimony of the goodness of God in the midst of trial, struggle, pain, and loss. It is a trophy to their victory over the attempts of the enemy to get the best of them.

20 July People say that "The apple doesn't fall far from the tree." I see that in our sons. They are a great combination of my husband and me. Each has different attributes, yet you could tell that they are most certainly ours. Some one said the other night that my oldest and I looked just alike. I said, "Not so much since I shaved my beard and he still has his." Ha Ha. (Of course I do not, nor have I ever had a beard) From sense of humor, their good looks, kindness, creativity, to musicianship, it's all in the family! I love my guys! They are the apples of my eye!

Today's song is, "You Lead" ~ Jamie Grace. This song declares that if God leads, I'll follow. God's hands hold my tomorrow. By His grace, He knows the way and will guide me tenderly in it. Taking the lead in life is fruitful if some one follows in your foot-steps, taking on your attributes, character, values, and traits. Usually it's your children. Not only do they have a genetic bent toward what's all about you, they grow up in an environment heavily influenced by you. Proverbs 22:6 says, "Train up a child in the way he should go, And when he is old he will not depart from it." The 'way he should go' in that verse refers to his natural bent. His tendency. His gifts and abilities. It also says 'train'. That means that you must give children guidance, direction, instruc-tion, correction, information. Do not leave them to themselves. They need to be trained. Proverbs 29:15 says, "The rod and re-buke give wisdom, But a child left *to himself* brings shame to his mother." and in The Message it says, "Wise discipline imparts wisdom; spoiled adolescents embarrass their parents." Be proac-tive in the care for your children. Be involved. Build relationships with them. Build trust with them. Just remember to be their par-ent. Then, how great to be the apple that doesn't fall from the tree that is God? Taking on the character, attributes of a loving, caring, awesome God? Following God is a sure path. One that will be complimentary to your natural bent. One that flows with your gifts and talents. God will lead you to a place that has been specif-ically designed with you in mind...your destiny. Sometimes you will be guided, directed, and instructed. Other times you will be corrected and redirected. God will train you; He will not spoil you. So follow Him. Choose not to be like a weed today – out of control, but choose to be a strong apple tree – bearing much fruit. After all, you are the apple of God's eye! (Zechariah 2:8)

21 July Every once in awhile I got to be recess monitor when I was the Christian school principal. The younger children loved to be pushed on the swings. They held on tight and went higher each time. They would pump their little legs to help as I pushed them. Scary as it could be, sometimes they would take a leap off the swing and land on the smooth gravel below. Then, jumping back on, would say, "Let's go again!" I liked recess and swing time.

Today's song is, "Lift Me Up" ~ The Afters. This song reminds me of my reliance on God. He lifts me up when I am weak, wrapping His arms around me. His love catches me, so I'm letting go. There's trust involved in putting yourself in a swing and letting someone push you. There's courage involved in hanging on as you go higher. There's boldness involved in taking a leap off. There's satisfaction in landing well. There's excitement in committing to go again. Life swings to and fro. You have a chance to get on and ride. Sitting on the bench pales in comparison to the great fun and adventure you can embark upon. Two things that help make you a success: 1. Get someone to push you. 2. Help by working yourself. God has a plan for your life – wisdom and direction. His urging, by the Holy Spirit will guide you. That's a push. Also, it's critical to have a coach, a mentor, an example, a model-when you want to go to a new level. That's a push. When you get yourself to church, read and study the scriptures, and hang around people of faith, that's a pump. Reading, listening, seeking great teaching, that's a pump. Keeping calm in chaos, that's a pump. Staying positive in the midst of defeat, that's a pump. These things will help you go higher, be stronger, do more, accomplish much, and have the courage to keep going. Keep leaping. Keep landing on your feet. And keep getting back on. God will be there every step of the way. But you have to let Him. Don't be the kid who says, "Leave me alone, I will do it myself!" There is no one to catch that kid. He will be face down in the gravel, crying. Be the one who says, "Help me, God!" God will lift you, catch you and wrap His arms around you. Then you will be the one flying and laughing, standing strong and always getting back up.

22 July "Up, Up!" When I had toddlers, I heard that a lot. They knew how to walk, but wanted to be carried. Tired of going it on foot, they wanted a better view and a rest from all the work of those baby steps. I loved toting them around when they needed it. Well, until they got too big for carrying!

Today the song is, "Rooftops" ~ Jesus Culture. This is a song of surrender telling God that I am standing here with wide open arms to Him. How great is it that when you need a better perspective and a rest from all your labor, God is there to pick you up? When you stand with your arms wide open to Him, He has the opportunity to give you a lift. It's surrender to Him. It's a "Help me, God." It's an "I need you, God." Psalm 53:1a says, "The fool has said in his heart, '*There is* no God.'" In other words, you are a fool if you think that you don't need God. If you have gotten too big for God, it's time to evaluate yourself. Romans 12:3 says, "For I say, through the grace given to me, to everyone who is among you, not to think *of himself* more highly than he ought to think, but to think soberly, as God has dealt to each one a measure of faith." Don't be so conceited to think that you are 'all that'. It's unbecoming. It shuts people out. It's foolish thinking. Realize that you really can't make it on your own. Check your humility. Check your teach-ability and your openness. Don't be full of yourself, but instead empty yourself to be filled with the power and presence of the Lord. Without God, you can do nothing of significance. But with Him all things are possible. Mark 10:27 (MSG) says, "Jesus was blunt: 'No chance at all if you think you can pull it off by yourself. Every chance in the world if you let God do it.'" You still need to do your part, but let God lift you, carry you, and walk beside you. You have to reach for Him and know that He will always be there. So today, talk to God. Turn and say, "Up, Up!"

23 July I have a lot of well-made, heirloom quality baskets. But I don't just have them on display, I use them every day. They are in my bathroom, kitchen, and living room. They are strong and useful. Some one said, "Don't put all your eggs in one basket." I can tell you though; one of these baskets could take it. I think everyone should have a good strong basket. I really like my baskets.

Today's song is, "My Life Is In You" ~ Hillsong. This is a worship chorus that we sang several years back. It's about declaring that my life, hope, and strength are in the Lord. God is like your strong basket. He can take it, His capacity is infinity. You can confidently place all of your life, hope, and strength in Him. He won't break on you. Psalm 71:5 says, "For You are my hope, O Lord GOD; *You are* my trust from my youth." And Exodus 15:2 says, "The Lord *is* my strength and song, And He has become my salvation; He *is* my God, and I will praise Him; My father's God, and I will exalt Him." Then Psalm 27:14 says, "Wait on the Lord; Be of good courage, And He shall strengthen your heart; Wait, I say, on the Lord!" And in Proverbs 22:4 it says, "By humility *and* the fear of the Lord *are* riches and honor and life." So you see, He is your hope today. He will strengthen your heart. And when you respect Him you will have riches, honor, and life. It's about surrendering to Him. Saying, "I give it all to you, God." Your capacity increases. You can do more, have more, be more. His basket is big enough and strong enough to hold all of your concerns, your hurts, your failures, and your regrets. It is also big enough and strong enough to hold all of your dreams, your goals, your hopes, your desires, your successes, your victories, your wealth, your health, your feelings, and your life. Today put something else in the basket which is God. What have you not placed in that basket? What have you been trying to hold on to yourself? You can only carry so much. When you put it all in the basket, your hands are free to do what God has uniquely called you to do. Don't ever put God on the shelf. Don't just go to church on Sunday and not think about Him all week. Don't think, "Maybe someday, I will give my life to the Lord." You are not promised tomorrow. Decide today to fill that basket with all you have so it can be used and multiplied. In return, you will have a full life, lots of strength, and great hope. And you will never be a basket case.

24 July Someone once said that when you get to the end of your rope, tie a knot and hang on. There can be rough days and there are awful days. There are times when you just want to give up. Be done. Throw in the towel. Those are the days when you have to muster all the strength you have, little as it may be, and turn your heart to the Lord. Tell Him you need a miracle, and then hold on.

Today the song is, "I Need A Miracle" ~ Third Day. This song reminds me that everyone at some time in their life needs a miracle, because they can't make it on their own. People can say all the "good" things, the cliché's, the standard words of encouragement, but when you are really hurting, they can seemingly fall on deaf ears. You are spent. You are worn. You are in shock. You are angry. You are numb. It just hurts. "But God." That's all you have to remember. He absolutely knows what you are going through. Your pain. Your agony. Your despair. He sees your tears and He hears your cries and He's there. Psalm 18:6 says, "In my distress I called upon the Lord, and cried out to my God; He heard my voice from His temple, and my cry came before Him, *even* to His ears." If you are hurting or know someone who is today, offer your prayers. Your miracle or theirs may not be packaged how you expect. It may not come when you think it should. Be sure of this though, that it will be there right on time. Just how God planned. Your job is to receive it. Open your hands just long enough to catch what He has for you. Psalm 34:17 (MSG) says, "Is anyone crying for help? God is listening, ready to rescue you." And Psalm 61:2, this is the prayer, saying, "From the end of the earth I will cry to You, when my heart is overwhelmed; Lead me to the rock that is higher than I." The Rock is Jesus. He is your salvation today. He is the healer of the broken-hearted. (Psalm 34:18) He makes a way where there seems to be no way. (Isaiah 43:16). He is your rescue, your comfort, your victory. There's no one like Him. You will make it, just hold on. Help is on the way.

25 July We got engaged on Thanksgiving Eve. The ring, beautiful. After 20 years of marriage, we got the diamond reset into a different, thicker band that shows off the stone even better. The ring is still beautiful. It is precious to me. Precious not only for what it is, but mainly because of what it stands for: Promise, Commitment, Fidelity, Love, Eternity, Relationship, Happiness, Companionship, God's will. All of that is my marriage to my amazing husband. That's what this ring means to me.

Today the song is, "Right Beside You" ~ Building 429. This song reminds us that we are precious, more than priceless. We are loved by God, we are His children. Sometimes you can take for granted people and relationships, but you can also underestimate the value of your own life. Maybe you think you're not good enough, or important enough, or smart enough, brave enough, strong enough, creative enough, or beautiful enough. When is enough, enough? When you feel that way, your perspective is off. Is there room for improvement? Always. You have to know that in God's eyes, you are precious. You are priceless. You may "remake" yourself or get remade through a conversion or transformation due to your redeeming experience with God, but whatever state you are in today, you are still quite valuable. You are one of a kind. No one else can do exactly what you can. Your particular set of experience, skills, knowledge, and abilities are unique. That also makes you uniquely qualified for God's plan for your life. Don't discount your worth. Don't say you're not enough. Isaiah 43:3-4 (MSG) says, "Because I am God, your personal God, The Holy of Israel, your Savior. I paid a huge price for you: all of Egypt, with rich Cush and Seba thrown in! That's how much you mean to me! That's how much I love you! I'd sell off the whole world to get you back, trade the creation just for you." You mean so much to Him. He paid a high price for you. He wants a relationship with you. One of Promise, Commitment, Fidelity, Love, Eternity, Happiness, and Companionship. Seek His will and He will be right beside you. All the way, every day, through every thing with every one. He wants you to have a fascinating and fulfilled life. Don't question your value today or any day. It's more than priceless.

26 July The cabins at church youth camp each housed about 24 teens. There was a "counselor's room" in the corner of the building. It was a room for the leaders with its own door to the outside, as well as a way into the main cabin. We never used those rooms because we didn't want the counselors to be separate from the campers. They couldn't be some elite, untouchables. They needed to connect with the teens. The time they had together was important for relationship, fellowship, devotions, and just talking. Also, while in the main cabin, they could watch over the campers, making sure they were safe and were faithful to the rules. Special bonding takes place at camp. Kids remember their cabin leaders for years. Camp can be a place of great transformation for young people. After camp, their lives are never the same.

Today's song is, "You Are I Am" ~ Mercy Me. This part of the song today speaks, saying that since the veil is torn, I live with the Spirit in me. It's the same Spirit that raised Christ from the dead. Before Christ died for you, there was a separation between you and God. Even then, God knew of you. He knew you needed a Savior. He had a plan. Separation was not a good thing. It blocked God's fellowship with you. It hindered a relationship with you. There was no devotion, not even talking. But when the veil was torn, separation ended. The door was open and you were able to accept the price Christ paid for you. Jesus was able to join your hand to God's again. So, His Spirit can dwell in you. It's supernatural. It's miraculous. There is nothing like it. Romans 8:11b (MSG) says, "With his Spirit living in you, your body will be as alive as Christ's!" He will quicken you. You've known people who just don't seem to care, have no drive, they are lazy or lethargic, negative, grumpy souls. They need that quickening and that transformation that only God can give. They need to walk the bridge from separation to relationship with God. If that's you, then do it. Walk to God. Accept Christ. Enjoy the special bond you can have as a redeemed believer. If you know some one who needs to take that walk, remind them that the veil is torn. There is no longer separation. God is not an elite untouchable. He is an awesome Father. Make that connection today. Your life will never be the same.

27 July In the theater company we always had a dress rehearsal the night before a big performance. We had the costumes, make up, scenes, lighting, everything just like it would be in the show. If there was a problem or a mistake, we could fix it at the rehearsal. Then we could perform a flawless production the following evening.

Today's song is, "One Life To Love" ~ 33 Miles. This song talks about how life is a one shot deal. I have to admit that I hesitated to write today when I found out what the song was. I didn't want any confusion about how God is the God of a second chance. You need to know- that chance is within this lifetime. Someone once said that life is not a dress-rehearsal. You can have a "do-over" in a season, but when your life ends, you have already made the choice. Joshua said in Joshua 24:15 (MSG), "If you decide that it's a bad thing to worship God, then choose a god you'd rather serve—and do it today. Choose one of the gods your ancestors worshiped from the country beyond The River, or one of the gods of the Amorites, on whose land you're now living. As for me and my family, we'll worship God." It's up to you how you live this life and who you will worship. When a day is done, you have spent, invested, or wasted that day. Mindlessly bumping along, waiting for Friday, the weekend, vacation, or even retirement is opportunity lost. Have you ever had some one close to you die? You would give just about anything for one more day, or even one more moment with them. You regret not doing or saying what you should have. You wonder how it could have been different. It's time to stop letting time pass without making the most of it. Living life to the fullest. Building relationships. Spending time with friends and family. Working. Playing. Enjoying. Devoting yourself to God's plan for you. The abundant life. The joyful life. The fulfilled life. So, maybe you've wasted some days, weeks, months, or even years. Start today. From this day forward, purpose in your heart to make the most of each day. To touch lives for the better. To be helpful, loving, giving, caring, and enthusiastic about life. Realize that this isn't a practice session. It's real. It's important. Don't waste another moment.

28 July There's a cartoon where a woman is attempting to squeeze through a window that is too small and she soon finds herself stuck. Unable to go forward or back, she has to rely on her cohort to attempt to free her. Pushing and pulling, he finally gets her out. She is then able to help conquer the enemy using her amazing ninja skills.

Today the song is, "You Lead" ~ Jamie Grace. This part of the song today says that the world may push and may pull, but God's love never fails. I will follow His lead. He knows the way and He will gently guide me. Sometimes you may feel like the woman in the cartoon. Stuck. You attempted to do a task, a project, or an activity that really wasn't "your size". It wasn't a fit. It maybe was too soon. Or you waited too long. You can't really go forward, and you know you can't go back. So you need some help getting free. The world may push and pull you, but God will enable your release. His hand can guide you out when your progress has been impeded. Then He will show you what to do and where to go next by the gentle leading of His Holy Spirit. First, you need to stop struggling. Get quiet. Listen. Tell God you need Him. Listen again. A thought will come. Then another. Don't dismiss them. Write them down. Pray. Listen some more. You will begin to know what to do. Then do that. God will guide you in steps. He's not going to go too fast for you to keep up. He leads gently. The people who have stood in your way before, said bad things about you, stopped you at every turn, He will work on your behalf to change them or move them out of your path and continue to lead you. Isaiah 41:11-13 (MSG) puts it this way, "Count on it: Everyone who had it in for you will end up out in the cold—real losers. Those who worked against you will end up empty-handed— nothing to show for their lives. When you go out looking for your old adversaries you won't find them—Not a trace of your old enemies, not even a memory. That's right. Because I, your God, I have a firm grip on you and I'm not letting go. I'm telling you, 'Don't panic. I'm right here to help you.'" What a great promise! You can shake off discouragement today. You can drop your feelings of inadequacy. You can discard sadness, regret, and shame. Take God's hand. He will lead. You can get up, go up, and achieve what He has for you. You can get 'un-stuck' today.

29 July Girls especially around age 11 or 12 are fascinating. They are beginning to step out of childhood and are starting to dip their feet into adulthood. As preteens they vacillate between the two worlds. Independent, confident, and responsible in one moment and clutching the security of their favorite stuffed bear in the next. Tears come easily most times. They can be brash, sullen, and annoying. They can also be sweet, tender, and sensitive. And they can be all of that in the same hour. It's a dramatic time of transition and growth. Discovery. Exploration. Identity. Some call these the 'formative years'. But I think it's a rite of passage, a journey for parents and child to transverse in expectation of a glorious outcome. In other words, once you get through it, things will be better. My advice to parents at this time-enjoy the journey. Marvel and affirm how God made your child unique and amazing.

Today the song again is, "You Lead" ~ Jamie Grace. This part of the song tells about how I know what you have for me is more than I can see. Sometimes when I wake up, I don't want to get out of bed, but I trust God to lead me. It's progressive, one step at a time. It's also perpetual. Asking Him to lead you on Monday will take you through Monday. What about the rest of the week? So continue to allow God to lead you on and on. Day after day. As you grow in God, there will be transition. You may feel confident and independent now, but you felt insecure yesterday. You may think you are ready to take on the world but somehow manage to stay in bed a bit longer so you don't have to take on the world quite so early. In God you will experience discovery – of God's character and His love for you. He has a plan and a purpose for your life. (Jeremiah 29:11) In God you will be able to explore – your gifts and calling. (Romans 11:29) In God you will find your identity –your true self. God made you to be victorious, a winner, more than a conqueror. (Romans 8:37) Maybe there's some drama right now, but know that once you get through it, things will be better. You can have expectation of a glorious outcome! Your journey will be the rite of passage – you will experience all God has for you and you will see that you are unique and amazing. So enjoy your journey today.

30 July While driving back home from a business meeting, I noticed the sign on the highway that said, "Keokuk 81" That's Iowa. North. The problem was, I was in Louisiana, Missouri headed for St. Peters, 58 miles South – or so I thought. Just one wrong turn sent me on the way to a whole new place. Thankfully I discerned my error, took the next exit and headed in the right direction. Lesson? You may think you know where you're going, but if you are wrong you can always find a place to turn around.

Today's song is, "Me Without You" ~ Toby Mac. This song ponders and answers the question of, "Where would I be without God?" I was incomplete until He rescued me. Finding God can take you in a new direction. It happens when you repent. You may see that word "repent" and think of some crazy radical pointing his finger and yelling at you in a condemning or condescending manner. But "repent" means simply to change your mind, turn around, and go in a new direction. It's that time when you realize that you have made mistakes. You have blown it. You have misjudged, mis-stepped, or messed up. You thought you knew where you were going but now see the error in your ways. So you decide to get headed in the right direction – the way that leads to your home in Christ. The place of peace. The place of victory. The place of courage. The place of abundance. The place where you will reach your full potential. Matthew 4:19-20 says, "Then He said to them, 'Follow Me, and I will make you fishers of men.' They immediately left *their* nets and followed Him." He said that if you follow, He will 'make you'. The Lord will make you into who you need to be today. Don't worry about how much you do or do not know, what you have or have not done. Matthew 4:20 (MSG) says it this way, "They didn't ask questions, but simply dropped their nets and followed." There wasn't a debate, a committee meeting, or a trial period. They just followed Him. You make the choices. You choose to follow or not. To grow or not. To change or not. To succeed or not. You cannot blame others, circumstances, geography, or the climate. It's not according to your age, your race, your education, economics, or family as to whether or not you can follow Christ. Just as a wrong turn can send you to a whole new place, a right turn or a turnaround can take you to the best place you can be.

31 July In <u>The Wizard of Oz,</u> Dorothy finds herself inside the house when the tornado hits. She is taken up in the whirlwind, seeing all kinds of things in the funnel including a cow and Miss Gulch on her bicycle. When the house lands, she is in a whole new world with new people, experiencing new adventures, and searching for what's 'over the rainbow'. She has friends and foes there. She finds advocates and obstacles. She gets carried away by monkeys, overcomes treachery, and melts a witch! Eventually she realizes that all she ever wanted was in her power all along. Her heart's desire was in her own back yard.

Today the song is, "Every Good Thing" ~ The Afters. This song confesses that I tend to be busier than I should be and I tend to think that time will wait for me. I don't want to take for granted this beautiful life God has given me. Sometimes life is like a whirlwind. Opportunities are coming to you and passing you by. Events, meetings, gatherings, parties, weddings, funerals, christenings, showers, out to dinner, out to the ball game. You go to soccer and ballet and baseball and band rehearsal and shopping, exercising, eating, visiting, traveling, working, and playing. Are you exhausted from just reading that? Too much. Too much. You can have a full life, but don't get so caught up in it that your head is spinning, you don't know where you'll land, or you feel like there's a house on you. So, take a breath. Take one step at a time. Learn to enjoy your journey. There may be obstacles. There may be monkeys. There may be some witches. There may be danger along the way, but you are an overcomer. You were designed to win over the storms of life. Check your desires today. The more time you spend with God, the more they will line up with His will for your life. God has given you a beautiful life so don't ever take it for granted. Then, as Psalm 37:4 says, "Delight yourself also in the Lord, and He shall give you the desires of your heart." Not only will He give you the desires – His desires become your desires, but also He will give you the desires – Grant that you would have those things. You don't have to go far to get them. Just go to God. He's not somewhere over the rainbow, He's right there in your own back yard. That's the place to be because, after all, there is no place like home.

1 August It seems like, at one time or another, we all have the occasion when illness of some sort creeps in. Maybe there's a "bug" going around. Maybe something you ate was bad. Maybe an injury has you down. It may be minor, but it also may be serious. Some people say, "Well, you should have taken better care of yourself." Possibly. Others may think that it's some punishment for sin in your life. Perhaps, but not at God's hand. Why? Because God is the healer. "Jehovah Rapha", God who heals, is one of God's names. Someone else may just blame it on the devil. It's true, the devil does want to destroy you and discredit God. However, your response in the matter is the key and it can change your outcome.

Today's song, "You Are I Am" ~ Mercy Me. Part of the bridge in this song says that Christ lives in me. Galatians 2:20 (MSG) says, "I identified myself completely with him. Indeed, I have been crucified with Christ. My ego is no longer central. It is no longer important that I appear righteous before you or have your good opinion, and I am no longer driven to impress God. Christ lives in me. The life you see me living is not 'mine,' but it is lived by faith in the Son of God, who loved me and gave himself for me. I am not going to go back on that." This life in Christ gives you access to divine health. So when you are experiencing illness of any sort, respond in prayer and action. I Peter 2:24 His wounds became your healing. So pray 1 Peter 2:24. Then in 3 John 1:2 it says that He wants you to be in health. Pray 3 John 1:2. And in Mark 1:34a it says, "Then He healed many who were sick with various diseases…" If Jesus did it for them, He will do it for you. So, after you have prayed, act. Do what you know to do. See a physician or a nutritionist, read information, change habits of eating, exercising, or rest. Find a believer to agree with you in prayer. Resist doubt and fear. Speak positively. You may not always know why you are in the condition that you are in, but you can ask God, "What now? What should I do next to regain my health? What should I say? Who should I speak with? Where should I go?" Listen to the still small voice of God that will direct you. Proclaim healing. Be strengthened by God's word, the Bible, by finding more verses that will encourage you. Ones you can stand firmly upon, not wavering. It will be your faith that will sustain you. His design for you is to be healthy.

2 August An old lady sat amidst stacks of newspapers, magazines, junk mail, books, papers, and an array of other items. Her house had become a dingy den for all her possessions. With barely room to walk or sit, her guest marveled at the enormous collection. She asked the senior, "How did this house get so cluttered?" The old lady replied, "I don't know, it just happened so gradually."

Today the song is, "Slow Fade" ~ Casting Crowns. This song explains that there is a continuous pull of compromise and sin in life. It starts with choices you make as you give yourself away, bit by bit. The excess in the old lady's home accumulated with daily deliveries of junk mail, weekly deliveries of the paper, and monthly deliveries of magazines. Items were taken in, but nothing discarded. Piles grew over time. She created her own prison of sorts. Caught in a confinement of her own design, it was created by her repeated choices. So it is with sin in your life. It starts with one delivery accepted...a thought of deception, maybe a little lie or indiscretion. And if, by your own choice, it continues, then day after day more lies, more indiscretions until you are merely a shadow of your former self. What you are doing or thinking may not seem like a big deal, but compromise leads to further corruption. Soon the 'piles' are higher than you expected and if you don't rid yourself of the issues past, you will have a very limited and dingy future. Take a look at the decisions you have made that have led you onto a path that frankly is not going in the best direction. You have ignited the fuse that may lead to your destruction. Wake up. Stomp out that fuse and decide now to get rid of the junk in your life. Hebrews 12:1 says, "Therefore we also, since we are surrounded by so great a cloud of witnesses, let us lay aside every weight, and the sin which so easily ensnares *us,* and let us run with endurance the race that is set before us." The sin will easily ensnare you. Lay it aside and run the race, your race, your path. It is God's plan for your life, to have abundance in every area. Also read Romans 6:22-23 (MSG). Life of sin = death. Life with God = life. You choose. The initial step...1 John 1:9 says, "If we confess our sins, He is faithful and just to forgive us *our* sins and to cleanse us from all unrighteousness." God is the ultimate pro in helping you de-clutter your life.

3 August Standing in line for the water slide is exciting and scary at the same time. A giant tube with rushing streams that descends, twisting and turning into a final landing – the plunge into the pool that waits so far below… It's good if you have one of those inflated 'O'rafts, but even better if you have the '8'raft so a friend can go with you. It's great to have someone to laugh, scream, and get dunked with. Then, they can help you carry the raft back up the stairs because you know you are going again!

Today's song is, "Right Beside You"~ Building 429. This song reminds me that when the walls are closing in, and I think I'd rather sink than swim, with nothing left to lose, I have a friend that will be with me, beside me. Great friends cannot be found on every corner. They are developed over time, through circumstances and events. Great friends show up when no one else does. They dare to go down the big slides with you even if they are scared themselves. They will laugh with you, cry with you, and sometimes scream with you. They will visit in the hospital, stop by for coffee and cheesecake, comfort you when are hurting, and listen to your problems, challenges, and dreams. They can help carry the load when you have to get back up and get going. They pray for you, give you hugs, and sometimes just sit quietly. You are better because of them. They are better because of you. It's because you are great friends.

Think about who your friends are today. Are they great friends? Are you a great friend? The best way to have one is to be one. Proverbs 18:24a says, "A man *who has* friends must himself be friendly" Look at yourself and check your 'friendship meter' is it registering on 'awesome' or 'awful' today? Ask God to show you how you can be a better friend. How you can pour into someone's life. Some one who needs to know that they are important to you. Matthew 6:33 says, "But seek first the kingdom of God and His righteousness, and all these things shall be added to you." Great friends may not be your friends forever, but they will be a blessing through out your life. Some are there for a reason, some for a season, and others for a lifetime. In every case, you are better because of them, and they are better because of you.

4 August When I was younger, a child, I did not like my first name. People thought my parents were hippies. Not so. They also liked to sing "Twinkle, Twinkle Little Star". Making fun of my name was funny to them. Kids thought they were clever or creative. Again, not so. Now that I am an adult, working with people every day, I like my name. It's memorable. It's unique. It suits me.

Today's song is, "I Want To Be In The Light" ~ DC Talk. This song declares that I want to be in the light, which is Christ, and I want to shine like the stars. Being in the light of Christ is not like being in the 'lime-light'. It's not a popularity contest. It's a life that seeks the Lord in each day. It's one where you seek to reach the potential that He has created in you. Your time to shine is what can make God look good. When you are excellent in what you do, it is a testimony to Him working in your life. Did you do it? Yes. Did you build it? Yes. But by the grace of God, you did. When you shine, shine because of the Lord. When you were young, you thought as a child and acted like one too. Now that you are grown, your life should be unique and memorable, not like anyone else. Don't compare. Don't be upset about what you've been called to do. The Lord picked it out for you. Just like my parents picked my name. So shine today. Step into what you are uniquely created for. It's yours. It suits you. Be a star.

5 August My parents were married on August 5th. So says their marriage certificate. They eloped. I remember when they celebrated their 40th Anniversary. There was a big party. Their friends were there. I helped with some of the food preparation. There was a lot of food. It was a great party. I think that I got my inspiration to have great parties by watching my parents. Nice, but not extravagant. Fun, but not crazy and out of control. We always want others to feel welcome in our home and we love to have a reason to celebrate!

Today's song is, "Sing" ~ Josh Wilson. This song invites us to sing because God is with us, He came to save us, and He will never leave us. It's important to take the time and make the effort to celebrate. God is with us. What a great reason! He saved us! An even better reason! He will never leave us! That's a party waiting to happen! Where would you be without God today? Or are you without God? They call that, 'lost'. God doesn't want anybody lost. Find someone today to talk to about this. Your life is so important that Christ died for you. You've got to have that reason to celebrate. God has abundance for you and He wants you to share it with others. Make them welcome in your home. Take the time and make the effort to feed others, physically and spiritually. You have a lot to offer. You can make a difference. Then celebrate your blessings, your accomplishments, your friendships, your anniversaries, but mostly, your relationship with God. It will be a great party!

6 August Being with a group of associates this week, I have been reminded of what unconditional love looks like. In the enormous crowd of people, barriers that you may expect in a business setting disappear. Size, shape, age, and race are of no consideration. Those who may not get a second look in other settings are treated like royalty. Most highly valued is the servant's heart. God is honored and people are important. I am extremely grateful for this chance to experience an example of how God sees me.

Today the song is, "Jesus, Friend of Sinners" ~ Casting Crowns. This song reminds me to see Jesus in response to others, to be moved with the same compassion as He was. That my heart should be broken for the same things that break His heart. He was the friend to sinners. So, what does it hurt to be kind and compassionate? It doesn't. You might think you will be taken advantage of. Maybe you will, but why not take that chance? You may find something you never knew. You might find someone you never knew. If you can just stop looking at the surface of that guy you met or that lady you've known for quite awhile; take a deeper look at who they really are. Look through the eyes of compassion instead of judgment and you will see something far different than you expected. Seeing the good in others will help develop the good in you. Remember, you are not perfect today, so do your best to not place that expectation on others. Your perspective is a key. You may not know by merely observing, what someone is about, so take the time to listen to their story. See why God has made them. Then know that they are important and so are you.

7 August Each day is full of potential, but today was a day that had potential of everything going wrong. The list of today's events is long, but let me just say this, we have an amazing God that will take us through every circumstance, every event, everything in our lives and bring us out on the other side. I firmly believe that my family and I are well and safe because we serve God.

Today's song is, "You Are My Everything" ~ Byron Cage. The song talks about how God is everything to me. He's the air I breathe and the song I sing. The key is perspective. How do you look at things in life that occur? Do you see the bad, the impossible, the horrible, and the unthinkable? Or do you see the benefits, the blessings, the good, and the amazing possibilities? When God is everything to you, there is a great chance you will see things from a better perspective. Looking positively at what comes to pass will enable you to be encouraged in a discouraging world. It helps you see that all is not lost. That in every bad situation, something good can come from it. When you are in the middle of the storm it's hard to see a good outcome, but trust in the Lord. (Proverbs 3:5-6) Don't depend on your own understanding. When you acknowledge Him, knowing He's your everything, He will direct you. When the clouds clear, the sun will come out and you will see that His goodness will prevail in spite of circumstances! So, look on the 'bright side' today. Things may be tough, but you can make it. There is something good in all that's happening, just look harder. See that God wants to move on your behalf. He is faithful. Make Him everything.

8 August I saw a shiny rock in the store one day, gold in color with flecks that sparkled. It was beautiful, but it was not gold as I suspected. It was pyrite. They call it 'fool's gold'. It's quite common. Not very valuable. Nice to look at and priced cheap. I set it back down on the shelf. My heart is set on the real thing. This girl likes genuine gold!

Today the song is, "Gold" ~ Britt Nicole. This song is a reminder of the value you have as a child of God. You are worth more than gold. There really is no substitute for authentic and valuable gold. Imitations yes, but never the same. That's you. You are rare and valuable. There is no one like you. Your appearance may be flawed, but deep down is what matters. Your character, your spirit, your love for God and others is what shines as gold. You aren't cheap, you are the real thing. The people in your life are also like gold. They are rare and valuable. It's important to treat them that way. Take the time to appreciate them. Look at them in a good light. See what they have to offer. See who they really are. Value them. Do not take them for granted. There is more to them than what meets the eye. Today, make a call, write a note, or personally tell someone how valuable they are to you. Tell them what you really appreciate about them. Be genuine. Be specific. Be caring. Connect with them while you have a chance. Share your heart. It's worth more than gold.

9 August It was so fun to teach our boys to swim. With floaties on their little arms, splish splashing away, they would paddle and kick just to reach our outstretched arms. When they arrived, they would get a big hug and a "Great Job! Now let's do it again!" over and over, back and forth, until they got better and better. The best thing was being there to catch them when they would start to go under and help them make it across. It was our joy as parents to be there for them.

Today the song is, "If We've Ever Needed You" ~ Casting Crowns. This song is a plea to God that we need Him. We are desperately reaching out for His hand. Sometimes you are in a 'sink or swim' situation and you really need a hand. That is when you can reach out for God and He will hear your cry and rescue you. Psalm 34:17 says, "The righteous cry out and the Lord hears them; He delivers them from all their troubles." God's arms are there waiting to catch you when you start to go under. Here's the key though, you must reach for Him. Realize you need Him, whatever the situation. Pride says, "I can do it all on my own." That's a great way to sink! It's foolishness. Today, if your situation looks like it won't end well, reach out. Call out. God will hear you and deliver you. You will have to do a bit of paddling and maybe even some kicking, but extend your hand and your heart to the one who can truly save you. It's His joy to be there for you.

10 August My son showed me a feature on my camera to-day that brings into focus only certain parts of the photo. That way I can bring more attention to what's important in that picture. It's really quite a remarkable way to enhance the objects I have captured with the lens.

Today the song is, "Strangely Dim" ~ Francesca Battistelli. This song reminds me that when I fix my eyes on all that God is, then every doubt I feel in my heart grows strangely dim. My worries fade and fall to the ground, because when I seek His face and focus on Him, all that's around me fades. It's all about focus. Where are you looking today? What is the most important thing about your life right now? Hint: the most important thing is what is getting the most attention from you. Where do your investments lie? Time, money, energy, thoughts, passion are all going into ____. You fill in the blank. Matthew 6:21 says, "For where your treasure is, there your heart will be also." What is your heart condition? Is your focus in a healthy place? One that is fruitful for you? One that brings you a great return? One that helps others? One that is long lasting? When you focus on God, praising Him, thanking Him, then the things of this world: the chaos, the drama, the hardships, they all fade away. Some one recently said that when you deal calmly with the tough circumstances that come about in your life, it is an indicator that you are spiritually mature. So fixing your eyes on God in the midst of the storms of life shows that maturity. It puts the emphasis on what is right about your situation. You don't have to doubt or be worried when your face is turned to His face. So today, hone in on God. You'll see that there's more good in your life than bad. There's hope in the desert places. There's calm for your storms. His way is healthy. It is fruitful and long lasting, one that helps others and brings you great return. It brings to mind the hymn, "Turn Your Eyes Upon Jesus" Here are the lyrics, "*Turn your eyes upon Jesus*, Look full in His wonderful face, And the things of earth will grow strangely dim, In the light of His glory and grace." Focus on Him and all that stuff that has been getting your attention, holding you back, will indeed grow strangely dim – in light of His Glory and Grace.

11 August College classes were challenging, but I usually got 'A's and some 'B's. Except for Greek class. Wow, was it hard. It was the only course in my four years that I came close to failing. However, for me, failing was not an option. My scholarships depended on my grades. That language, it was tough to understand. Why? Because it was all Greek to me! Though I struggled, I kept at it and managed to get a 'C' by the end of the class. I must admit that it has been helpful in Bible study throughout the years, when I remember what I learned. Of course, I can also read the names of fraternities and sororities. (Not always quite as impressive.) But, I am glad I took Greek.

Today the song is, "One Thing Remains" ~ Jesus Culture. This song reminds me that God's love never fails or gives up. It never runs out on me. Have you been in some situations where failing is not an option? You tried, but it didn't seem to be working? When you want to give up, try one more time. Then another. Then another. Do it until. Until it works. Until you get it. Until it comes through. Until you get a "yes". Until. The fuel for your trying must be God's love. You tap into it with thankfulness. Psalm 138:1-3 (MSG) puts it this way, "Thank you! Everything in me says 'Thank you!' Angels listen as I sing my thanks. I kneel in worship facing your holy temple and say it again: 'Thank you!' Thank you for your love, thank you for your faithfulness; most holy is your name, most holy is your Word. The moment I called out, you stepped in; you made my life large with strength." God loves you so much that He will step in when you call out. His love will make your life large with strength! That is exciting! He won't give up on you. He won't fail you. He won't run out on you. He will stick with you until you pass the test of circumstances, difficulties, trials, and temptations. You may not understand everything. You may struggle. You may find it difficult, but nothing is too hard for God. Jeremiah 32:17 says, "Ah, Lord God! Behold, You have made the heavens and the earth by Your great power and outstretched arm. There is nothing too hard for You." So take heart today, God is in your corner. Seek His love and His presence and you will pass this test and those to follow with impressive results!

12 August Today is my youngest son's birthday. He's a joy in our lives. His bright personality attracts others. I love to hear him laugh. When He smiles, it makes my day. There are so many things that make him wonderful, but now I'm gushing. I'm such a mom. There is so much love that I have for both my sons, it overwhelms me sometimes.

Today's song is, "Your Love Is Amazing" ~ Phillips, Craig & Dean. This song celebrates God's love. It makes me sing. His love is amazing, unchanging, a firm foundation, and a mystery. He lifts me, surrounds me, and carries me with His love. Joy rises up inside of me when I see His goodness. God gives you something special when you become a parent. More than the child you have is the capacity to love incredibly. When you first meet that little cherub, you immediately feel it. It's the opportunity to get a picture of how God loves us. His love truly is amazing. It's consistent no matter how far you stray, what mistakes you make, or if you come in after curfew. He loves you. There's a great picture of His love in Ephesians 2:4 (MSG) "It wasn't so long ago that you were mired in that old stagnant life of sin. You let the world, which doesn't know the first thing about living, tell you how to live. You filled your lungs with polluted unbelief, and then exhaled disobedience. We all did it, all of us doing what we felt like doing, when we felt like doing it, all of us in the same boat. It's a wonder God didn't lose his temper and do away with the whole lot of us. Instead, immense in mercy and with an incredible love, he embraced us. He took our sin-dead lives and made us alive in Christ. He did all this on his own, with no help from us! Then he picked us up and set us down in highest heaven in company with Jesus, our Messiah." God can make you alive in Christ. He loves you enough to save you. Save you mainly from yourself, this broken world, and Satan. His love can overwhelm you. It can leave you speechless. It can bathe you in exuberant joy. It will make you want to sing.

13 August As a little girl, I sometimes fell asleep in our basement after listening to music or eating snacks late in the evening. The next morning I would wake up in my bedroom, snug in bed. I would think, "How did I get here?" I found out that my daddy had carried me there. He didn't leave me down on the couch, but got me to "my place", a sweet powder blue room with white furniture. I loved my dad.

Today's song is, "Sing" ~ Josh Wilson. This song says that every bit of history and every single breath we breathe has led us here. It has brought us to our knees. God is with us to save us and never leave us. Have you ever looked around at your life and said, "How did I get here?" You may be in a place where that question is concerning. Or you may be in a place where that question is a relief. In either case, the steps you take each day determine where you will end up. Each decision. Each action or inaction. Each choice. Every meeting. Every meal. Every time you move or stay still. Every call. Every note. Every conversation. Every prayer. They all add up to who you are today. That's how you got here. There's a poem called 'Footprints in the Sand' by Mary Stevenson. It talks about a dream the author had, recalling scenes of her life at which there were footprints in the sand. During the easy times, two sets of prints (Jesus walking with her). During the trying times, only one set. Feeling the Lord had left her during the hardships, she asked why, as she saw only one set of footprints in the sand. He said that He did not leave, but instead that is when He carried her. Your decisions and choices may take you to a point which is unbearable to you alone, that is when the Lord will pick you up. He won't leave you. Allow Him to carry you today to the place where you truly belong. "Your place." Then when you look around at your life, you will not have to wonder how you got there.

14 August It was one of those times when being confronted took me off guard. As my colleague proceeded to tell me how I felt and what I had done that had upset her, I was dumbfounded. Speechless. In my politeness, I failed to make clear what really happened, how I really felt, and what I had already done about the situation. She continued to talk. When I walked away from that conversation, I assumed defeat. It's a horrible, hopeless feeling. Much later, being prepared, I went into a similar situation thinking clearly, talking honestly, and conveying the truth with confidence. That's when victory became mine. However, it is not always about wins and losses; it's about clarity and understanding. It's about working through what comes your way.

Today the song is, "God's Not Dead" ~ Newsboys. This song reminds me of the revival in my life when I look to God, because He is not dead. He is surely alive, living on the inside of me and roaring like a lion! Your confidence will be strong because God and you have a relationship. He strengthens you. His word helps to stabilize you. When you are solid in your faith, you will not be easily shaken. You won't waver. You will be an over-comer. When confrontation comes, and it will, you will be able to stand. It's not a license to be obnoxious, thinking that you can bully people because 'God is on your side' but it's that calmness and grace under pressure. It's your maturity in faith that enables you to deal with what happens. Charles Swindoll said, "I am convinced that life is 10% what happens to me and 90% of how I react to it." So how are you reacting today? Are you dumbfounded by the events in your life? Or are you prepared? Have you readied yourself with information and inspiration from God? He is alive. He is the roaring lion. Think of the lion, it is both strong and gentle at the same time. It's his majesty, power, leadership, boldness, bravery, and courage that make him "King of the Jungle" What a great picture of the Lord. Tap into all that God is today. He will give you that confidence to work through what comes and to walk away victorious.

15 August Traffic. I seriously didn't think we left early enough to make it on time. That was okay though, we were on our way. Then it started raining. I started praying. "Please God, just let us make it there before it starts" My husband called the theater. There was a delay because of a power outage. Yes! We would make it before the performance started! We arrived to a dark lobby and joined the rest of the ticket holders waiting for a word on the status of the show...cancelled. We planned to drive home in the morning so we would have to get our tickets refunded. Then we realized that we could stay a little longer and go to the 3pm show the next day. Bonus: every ticket holder received a voucher for food in their cafe!

Today the song is, "You Are" ~ Colton Dixon. This song declares that if I had no voice, and if I had no tongue, then I would still dance for the Lord, like the rising sun. When my circumstances leave me with empty hands, then I know God will provide for me. Life holds drama. If not, things would be pretty boring. Sometimes it looks like there are too many obstacles. Time ticks by. Rain falls. Things cancel. But God. He will provide. He will make a way where there seems to be no way. (Isaiah 43:16) He will bring you through your situation and bring you out on the other side. Many times with a bonus added! The key is, don't "freak out" in the middle of everything. Stay calm, so you can think clearly, you can pray, and you can be open to the possibilities that God has for you. You may have plans, but He has something new. Something better for you! Isaiah 43:19 says, "Behold, I will do a new thing, now it shall spring forth; Shall you not know it? I will even make a road in the wilderness *and* rivers in the desert." When God has His hand in it, things you thought were not possible – are possible. Philippians 4:4 says, "Rejoice in the Lord always. Again I will say, rejoice!" So don't give up today. Don't give in. Don't freak out. Even if you are speechless, you can still dance.

16 August I've tried moving large pieces of furniture on my own. It's often a recipe for disaster or at least minor injury. My shoeless feet get crunched (yes, my loving husband told me about wearing shoes), sometimes my fingers get smashed, and usually my back gets wrenched. It's foolish to attempt this by myself. So I call for some assistance and there you go…It's so much better, easier, and safer when you have help!

Today's song is, "Strong Enough" ~ Matthew West. This song confesses that I know I'm not strong enough to be all that I am supposed to be. I give up trying to do it on my own. God's mercy will cover me and I ask Him to be strong enough for both of us. By yourself, you are not strong enough to handle all that life throws at you. You are only one person. God's plan for you is bigger than just you. And the devil's plan for you is to wear you out so you cannot fight any longer alone. That's where you must get to the point of giving up trying to do it on your own. Batman had Robin. Burt had Ernie. Abbott had Costello. But you, you have God. Romans 8:31 says, "What then shall we say to these things? If God *is* for us, who *can be* against us?" God is strong enough for both of you. Isaiah 40:31 (MSG) says, "But those who wait upon God get fresh strength. They spread their wings and soar like eagles, they run and don't get tired, they walk and don't lag behind." Now there's a plan for victory! So stop trying to do everything by yourself today. It's foolish to continue all on your own, and it can be quite painful. One of my very good friends likes to say, "There's no heroes in the Hall of Pain" When you can get God's assistance, why not? It's so much better, easier, and safer to have Him on your side, helping you. No telling what mountains you can move when the two of you work together!

17 August I don't know if it's my personality type, my genetic make up, or my environment that gives me a tendency to be emotional at times. It's that urge to be reactive instead of responsive. It's being an easy crier. It's being passionate about a cause, an issue, or an injustice. It's being taken in by the cuteness of a lost kitten at the back door. It's feeling responsible if everyone is not happy. It's absorbing feelings. It's loving others. It's caring. It's that desire to fill a need or right a wrong. Sometimes irrational, sometimes over-zealous, sometimes funny, or weird, or immature. That's who I am. God gave me unique characteristics to fulfill the plan He has for me. My life will touch those who no one else can. My heart will hurt for them. My hands reach out to them. My voice comfort them. Not because of who I am, but because of who my God is. That's me. I love my life.

Today the song is, "Every Good Thing" ~ The Afters. This song reminds me that there will be days that give me more than I can take, but I know that God can change my heartache into beauty. I never want to forget or take for granted my beautiful life and the moments in it. God is the reason for every good thing. For every heartbeat, breath, laugh, what lasts, and each second chance. Life is sweet. There are too many things going on, too many voices in your head, too many times that you can miss what's going on for all the distractions. No matter what others say when they try to discourage you, be yourself. There is a place for your uniqueness. There is a place for what God has created in you. There is a place for your emotion or your stoicism. There is a place for your gifts, talents, skills, interests, and abilities. There is a place for your humor, your creativity, your ingenuity, and your inventiveness. God has created a beautiful life for you. Beauty is in the eye of the beholder and the beholder is God. Check out His perspective. Mary Kay Ash said, "God didn't have time to make a nobody, only a somebody. I believe that each of us has God-given talents within us waiting to be brought to fruition." Don't take any day for granted. See what you can get from each day to make yourself and others better, happier, stronger, and more faithful. Make the most of the moments you have been given. Don't let others take the wind out of your sails. Pursue your dreams. Be yourself. Be who God intended you to be. Love your life.

18 August It was the only year among many there was enough snow to run the snow mobile. The guy driving was a part of my future husband's family. I was confident that he knew what he was doing so I rode along through the fields and over the snow. I later found out that 'the guy' was kind of a daredevil and no one could believe that I took a ride with him. It was fun though, and thankfully, no one got hurt that day.

Today the song is, "From The Inside Out" ~ Hillsong. This song expresses a desire for God to consume me from the inside out. In my heart and my soul I give God control of my life. It's important to have trust, but you need to know in what and whom you place your trust. You trust a chair when you sit down. You trust the little white lines on the highway to keep people in their lanes. You trust your nutritionist when he tells you the best course of eating. You trust your mentors. You trust your spouse. But do any of those things ever let you down? Fail? Leave? Yes. However, God does not. Numbers 23:19 says, "God *is* not a man, that He should lie, nor a son of man, that He should repent. Has He said, and will He not do? Or has He spoken, and will He not make it good?" God will stay true to His Word. He will not leave you. He will not lie to you. He will not let you down. Others may not believe that you trust God. But go anyway. Go with God. He will sustain you. He will protect you. He will take you on a journey that will be fun and rewarding. So trust Him today. Give Him your life, your heart, your soul. He's there, not to be blamed for the wrecks, but to pick you up from them and help you go again. He can only control what you give Him. Not like a puppeteer, but like a driver – guiding and directing, taking you on the path you need to go so you will enjoy the process and the success. Ephesians 3:20-21 says, "Now to Him who is able to do exceedingly abundantly above all that we ask or think, according to the power that works in us, to Him *be* glory in the church by Christ Jesus to all generations, forever and ever. Amen." Trust God.

19 August I was looking at my son's birth certificate. It says right there that I am his mother. I realize that no matter what, I will always be his mom. I will always love him. I will always care for him. I will always want the best for him. Always.

Today's song is, "Forever" ~ Chris Tomlin. This song reminds me that God is forever faithful, strong, and with us. When you have a relationship with God, you can call Him "Father" Galatians 4:6 says, "And because you are sons, God has sent forth the Spirit of His Son into your hearts, crying out, 'Abba, Father!'" As a parent, He will always love you. He will always care for you. He will always want the best for you. He is faithful and strong, you can depend on Him. Even when you don't understand everything that's going on, know that God is working, behind the scenes to pull it all together for you. Romans 8:28 says that God causes all things to work together for your good. God does not cause all things, He causes the things to work together for your good when you love Him and you are going about His purpose for your life.

He will be with you. Deuteronomy 31:6 says, "Be strong. Take courage. Don't be intimidated. Don't give them a second thought because God, your God, is striding ahead of you. He's right there with you. He won't let you down; he won't leave you." Then it is your job to go about letting others know of the goodness of the Lord. Again, He will be there by your side. Matthew 28:18-20 (MSG) says, "Jesus, undeterred, went right ahead and gave his charge: 'God authorized and commanded me to commission you: Go out and train everyone you meet, far and near, in this way of life, marking them by baptism in the threefold name: Father, Son, and Holy Spirit. Then instruct them in the practice of all I have commanded you. I'll be with you as you do this, day after day after day, right up to the end of the age.'"

If you feel abandoned today, God is still there. If you feel betrayed today, God is still faithful. If you feel weak today, God is still strong. Whatever you need today, God is. He always has been and He always will be. Always and forever.

20 August We decided to go to the corn maze at the farm down the road. We had a map and there were check points to find all throughout the path. My concern was getting out when we were ready. I found that if I could look up over the stalks, I could see the barn – our destination. So I knew when we were headed in the right direction. It was confusing at times. I felt lost sometimes. In the end, I completed my mission of finding all the check points and making it safely back to the barn. So did the rest of the family! We celebrated with a cool bottle of 'pop'.

Today the song is, "I Still Believe" ~ Jeremy Camp. This song expresses a desire to take the scattered words and empty thoughts that come from my heart, that feeling of being torn – not knowing where to start, and feeling God's grace wash away my pain. It confirms that I believe in God's faithfulness, His truth, and His word. Ever feel like you are in a maze and you aren't sure where to head because you don't know if you will end up in the right place? You feel scattered, alone, afraid, lost, confused? That's the time to get out your map. It's the map that guides you, the Bible. God's word is true and He is faithful. It may look like you are at a dead end today. You may wonder, "Should I go left or right?" The best thing is to look to God. Like that barn at the corn maze, He will show you your destination. When you keep your eyes on Him, you will know that you are headed in the right direction. Jeremiah 42:3 says, "(Pray) that the Lord your God may show us the way in which we should walk and the thing we should do." Seek God to show you the path, the decisions, the choices that are right and good for you. If you are confused or fearful, let His grace wash you like rain. Calming you. Comforting you. Directing you. You will make it out. You will complete your mission in life. Acts 16:31 says, "So they said, 'Believe on the Lord Jesus Christ, and you will be saved, you and your household.'" This is the promise that you can bring your family with you. Then, you will be able to celebrate!

21 August "I know just how you feel." She said. But she had no idea what I was going through. She wanted to understand. That was just impossible. No one could know exactly. I felt like a failure and as I got off the phone, I simply cried. It was a tough time. Tough decisions. Reality. Heartbreak. Sadness. Loss. My best strategy was to hang on. And that I have done. Sometimes, barely. Often times, tightly. Because of this, I have become stronger. I have become better. I have sought God and He has always been there for me.

Today's song is, "God Is Still God" ~ Heather Williams. This song admits that we've all been lost and hurt at times. Those are times when our hope is spent and our faith doesn't seem to work. But nothing lasts forever. The only thing that matters is that God is still God and He holds it together! So, hang on. Things can be tough for you sometimes. It may be due to your own decision, but perhaps it was out of your hands. However, it still affected you. Your life. Your future. Your dreams and goals. Here's the thing, God really does know what you are going through. Jesus, while on this earth, experienced it all. Hebrews 4:14-16 (MSG) puts it this way, "Now that we know what we have—Jesus, this great High Priest with ready access to God—let's not let it slip through our fingers. We don't have a priest who is out of touch with our reality. He's been through weakness and testing, experienced it all—all but the sin. So let's walk right up to him and get what he is so ready to give. Take the mercy, accept the help." That's what you need to hear, right? He wants to help you through today. He wants to bring you to a larger place. A high place. An abundant place. He has help, grace, and mercy for you. He has an answer to your problem. He has a solution to your situation. He has a great finish for your circumstances. He has deliverance for your drama! Don't give up. Get up. Do what you know to do. Be your best. Be tenacious. Strong. Wise. You have so much amazing-ness to experience, time to be about it! Be encouraged today that God is still God. He still loves you and He is still here for you. Then don't just hang on, CLIMB. You can do it.

22 August As we walked the beach early one morning, the sun rose and the horizon was beautiful with orange and blue hues. The waves washed up on our feet. You could hear the gulls out over the water looking for breakfast. One of the magnificent things about those ocean waves is that they just keep coming in. Rain, shine, morning, noon, or night, the rhythmic repetition, washing the beach, smoothing the rocks and shells, carrying various items in to shore and back out again. It was an amazing place, so relaxing and calming.

Today's song is, "My Heart" ~ Jermaine Rodriguez. This song reminds me of God's love. I know that just one moment with Him and my pain is gone. That's when I know that I can go on. Sometimes I feel far away from God, I seek His face, call out His name, and I realize that I'm lost without His love. I need Him. There are times you feel God's love washing over you like the waves of the ocean. It could be a song, a place, a moment. You call out His name, He responds. He responds because He loves you. He returns over and over to smooth the rough places in your life. To calm you. To comfort you. To bring peace in your life. Even when you are far from God, you just reach out. He is there. Rain, shine, morning, noon, or night. Today take some time just to appreciate all God has made for you to enjoy. All the sunrises, all the sunsets, the oceans, the mountains, the sun, the sky, the birds, your family, your friends, and much, much more. Be still for awhile. Psalm 46:10a says, "Be still, and know that I *am* God;" He is bigger than any challenge, any problem, any giant in your life today. God is magnificent.

23 August My reading glasses were broken. I needed them. They only had one arm, but I could still balance them enough to make due. Solution? Go buy a brand new pair! Of course, it's so much better to have what I need, what works, and what has all the parts to be complete! Vision, it's a wonderful thing!

Today the song is, "Hello, My Name Is" ~ Matthew West. This song reminds me to not listen to the lies that I am less, a failure, defeated, or lost. My true name is "Child of the one true King" I have been changed and made brand new by accepting Christ and I can leave the wreckage of my past behind. 2 Corinthians 5:17 says, "Therefore, if anyone *is* in Christ, *he is* a new creation; old things have passed away; behold, all things have become new." In Christ, you are more. You are brand new. You are a child of God with all the rights, privileges, and benefits that come with it! It's time to decide not just who you are, but more importantly, whose you are. You no longer need to be lost in regret, indecision, stress, panic, disease, loneliness, or despair. You no longer need to "make due" or "take the hand you've been dealt". Rise up! Start fresh with a new attitude, perspective, and life from God. He's what you need. He's what works. He is what you need to be complete today. Your vision should be clear. Your destiny defined. Your path lies before you, but you must walk it. Don't walk alone today. Go with God and He will show you. Psalm 119:105 says, "Your word *is* a lamp to my feet and a light to my path." His word. The Bible. So find some scriptures that you can use today to address your situation. His promises. His declarations. His peace. Whatever you need, it's there. He's there to walk with you and to help you leave the wreckage of your past behind. He will make you brand new!

24 August We got another homework assignment from our pastor. Say the verse of Philippians 4:13, 10 times every morning and every night. "I can do all things through Christ who strengthens me." If you emphasize a different word each time, it's easy to keep track. It also brings more meaning to the verse. When I do this, I am strengthened. I am so thankful for a pastor who challenges us to do more, be better, climb higher, and succeed in our Christian walk.

Today's song is, "Whom Shall I Fear" ~ Chris Tomlin. This song reminds me that God's on my side and nothing formed against me will stand! He holds the whole world in His hands. Sometimes you have to be reminded that God is on your side. You get to looking at the circumstances, the stuff of life that is happening and you feel so small. Like a grasshopper. Numbers 13:33 talks about it, "There we saw the giants (the descendants of Anak came from the giants); and we were like grasshoppers in our own sight, and so we were in their sight." When you see yourself as small, inadequate, and wimpy, others will see you that way too. Especially your enemies! So you need to shake off that grasshopper complex and see yourself the way God sees you! He says to be strong and courageous. (Joshua 1:6) He says you are more than a conqueror. (Romans 8:37) He says you are the head, not the tail. (Deuteronomy 28:13) Check out the incredible list of who you are when you choose to obey God in Deuteronomy 28: 1-14. These are things you can say aloud each day. Remind yourself who you are. Remind yourself who is on your side. Don't mope and complain. Don't pick fights. Don't sob and cry. Stand up and declare that your God is bigger than any giant of doubt, deception, or discouragement that tries to stop you. Some one said that you should not tell God how big your problem is, but rather tell your problem how big God is. Philippians 1:6 says, "Being confident of this very thing, that He who has begun a good work in you will complete *it* until the day of Jesus Christ;" Be confident that God is working in you. He will not leave you. So be strong today. Be courageous. And, remind yourself that you can do all things through Christ who strengthens you!

25 August Back in "the day" my husband and I were great fans of a particular musical artist. We thought he was awesome! He was a great musician, vocalist, and man of God. Then he was a guest at our church and we got to take him to lunch! Wow! It was like a dream. My son got to sit next to him in the van as we traveled to the restaurant. I was thinking, "That is so amazing!" We had a great meal and great conversation. It was quite an experience. Some one else may have seen it as just a regular lunch. For awhile, I was star-struck. Then I realized that he was a person. It wasn't right to idolize him. Here's the thing, the "Wow" was the part of him that loved and served God. It was the God in him that was awesome. He used his gifts and talents to proclaim the good news of Christ. That's what made him so amazing. Still, I will never forget that day.

Today the song is, "How Great Is Our God" ~ Chris Tomlin. This song tells of the greatness of God. He wraps Himself in light and darkness tries to hide from Him. He is a great and awesome God. There are so many things and people you can get your eyes on and think, "That is so amazing" You can idolize an athlete, a performer, an actor. You can long for a possession, a place, or a status. But all those things and all those people will eventually come up short. You will realize that they are just regular folks who eat lunch like you, or regular things that corrode and rust. Matthew 6:19-21 (MSG) says, "Don't hoard treasure down here where it gets eaten by moths and corroded by rust or—worse!— stolen by burglars. Stockpile treasure in heaven, where it's safe from moth and rust and burglars. It's obvious, isn't it? The place where your treasure is, is the place you will most want to be, and end up being." Wow. What do you treasure today? Take another look. Give it another thought. Make a definite choice. Treasure God. He is so great. There is none like Him. He is awesome. He is amazing. He is unforgettable.

26 August In explaining the importance of proper health care for my back, the chiropractor told me to remember that back pain is accumulative. It may seem like a little thing today, but over time, it can get worse if not treated properly. Sometimes I do that with more than my back. I wait, thinking it will get better on its own. However, without proper treatment, it very well may get worse. Like laundry. I can ignore it all I want, it's not going away. The piles just get bigger!

Today the song is, "Today Is The Day" ~ Lincoln Brewster. This song celebrates that today is the day the Lord has made, I will rejoice and be glad in it. I won't worry about tomorrow; I'm trusting in what God has to say. Today is the day! It's easy to put things off until tomorrow or next week or next month. You think that maybe then it will be easier. Many times it is not. If something can keep you from accomplishing the goal, or completing the task, or building the 'whatever' this month, something else will keep you from it next month. It's time to get to it. Today is the day. Put God first. Treat Him properly – praise Him, thank Him, study what He has to say, obey His words – Today. Your life will not get better on its own. You need God. 2 Corinthians 6:2b says, "Behold, now *is* the accepted time; behold, now *is* the day of salvation." It's today. Address today. Be intentional about today. Do it today. Be it today. Get it today. Give it today. Decide today. Don't worry about tomorrow. Matthew 6:34 (MSG) says, "Give your entire attention to what God is doing right now, and don't get worked up about what may or may not happen tomorrow. God will help you deal with whatever hard things come up when the time comes." There you go. Be about what you need to be about today. Stop procrastinating, start stepping out and stepping into all that God has for you!

27 August There's a particular leader in our company that simply personifies confidence. If you look up "confidence" in the dictionary, her picture should be there. Amazing leader, exceptional speaker, bold, gracious, loving, godly are all words that describe her. She is a tall woman and she stands up – every inch. Head held high, smiling and when she takes the stage, she owns it. She's an excellent example of Luke 1:37, "For with God nothing will be impossible!" She inspires me to reach for more.

Today's song is, "Gold" ~ Britt Nicole. This song is a reminder that whatever you've been told, you're worth more than gold. Hold your head up high; it's your time to shine. It will show from the inside out. You are worth more than gold! Confidence comes when you know who you are. When you know your value. You are one in billions, uniquely crafted by God in your mother's womb. There is no one exactly like you. Even if you are a twin, the two of you are different. You are rare and it's the rare things that are precious and valuable. Oscar Wilde said, "Be yourself, everyone else is already taken". How can you be a better version of yourself? Today, how can you be amazing? You may have some one you can emulate, but you will never duplicate them because you are one of a kind and so are they. See your worth today. So valuable that Jesus gave His life for you! Start to talk like it more. Act like it more. Walk like it more. Work like it more. Worship, love, and live like it more. You are you. Be you. You will touch lives no one else can. You will make an impact like none other. Your time to shine is now. Hold your head up high and own it!

28 August The Christmas section of the store is like a drug to me. I can feel my adrenaline pumping when I walk down those aisles. It's so exciting to look at all the decorations and ornaments. It's the lights and the sparkles. Oh, and the snowmen, and the Nativity sets, and the trees. It's so amazing. I like to look at every single thing there. It's definitely the place where I will be distracted by something shiny!

Today's song is, "Speechless" ~ Israel & New Breed. When I hear this song, I want to fall to my knees and seek God and His grace. I need it and I receive it. He leaves me speechless. God's presence in your life is even better than the high of seeing all of the Christmas decorations in the store. It's so amazing. It will take your breath away. And in that presence, there is grace. You need God's grace daily. It's unmerited favor. You don't deserve it. Did you ever have someone say, "Oh you didn't have to do that" when you gave them a gift? I usually respond, "I know. If I had to do it, it wouldn't be a gift. It would be an obligation." Grace from God is a gift. He doesn't have to give you grace. You aren't entitled to it on your own. You receive it because of your relationship with Him. Psalm 84:11 says, "For the Lord God *is* a sun and shield; The Lord will give grace and glory; No good *thing* will He withhold from those who walk uprightly." No good thing will He withhold! Did you see that? Here's the condition – from those who walk uprightly. Psalm 15:2 (MSG) says, "Walk straight, act right, tell the truth." SO act right and tell the truth. Grace will be extended to you. Then be thankful for the grace of God. Be careful not to cry, "Unfair!" when you see others receiving His grace. Rejoice with them. That is maturity. Today, seek God, His presence, and His grace. You will find something even more exciting than a sparkly ornament or a beautiful tree. So much so that it will take your breath away.

29 August When we get ready to go camping, we gather all the gear and supplies from the garage, house, closets, and kitchen, then pack it tightly into the car. All of it. It's a lot of stuff, but it's everything we need for a pleasant visit to the campground for the weekend. There are a couple of checklists we use to make sure that nothing is forgotten. Sometimes, I am uncertain we have everything. I say, "Did we forget something?" When we do, town is only a few miles and we can go get it. There's some work involved, but we love every minute. Okay, except the bugs. I am not always good with the bugs. But everything else, love it!

Today the song is, "Everything I Need" ~ Kutless. This song reminds me that God is strength in my weakness; He's the refuge I seek. He is everything in my time of need, He is everything I need. The great thing about God is that He doesn't leave something behind if you need it. Life may be hectic. Are you getting prepared for a transfer or an event, a move or a new season and you have some uncertainty or you are anxious? Be patient. God is working on your behalf. He's helping you pack your life with all you need to have a successful journey. James 1:4 says, "But let patience have *its* perfect work, that you may be perfect and complete, lacking nothing." When God is leading you, you won't lack a thing! (Psalm 23:1) Be confident today as you embark on the next step of your life that God will be and have everything you need. He is your strength. Your refuge. He will carry you. There may be a few bugs that show up, but He's got some great repellant, Deuteronomy 28:7 (MSG) says, "God will defeat your enemies who attack you. They'll come at you on one road and run away on seven roads." So you don't have to worry today. God really is everything you need.

30 August I've been thinking and reading about purity lately. It's that no compromise attitude. It's the decision you make before you are in a situation so that you will know how to approach it when it comes. It's saying, "No" when you know something isn't right. It's not walking so close to the edge that just a mere nudge will knock you into the water. It's choosing one spouse, one pastor, one church, one vision and committing yourself to it. It's going along with what God directs versus what the world thinks is right. It's being yourself, but respecting yourself enough to know when enough is enough. It's being able to look in the mirror and say, "I did the right thing." and "I did my best."

Today the song is one that we sang when I was in our church youth choir. It is based on 1 John 1:5, "This is the message which we have heard from Him and declare to you, that God is light and in Him is no darkness at all." I am uncertain of the title or writer, but I am sure of this – there is no darkness in God. No compromise. No "maybe so's" or "kinda sorta's" Matthew 5:37 says, "But let your 'Yes' be 'Yes,' and your 'No,' 'No.' For whatever is more than these is from the evil one." God has given you a guideline and a challenge, if you will. Choose. Deuteronomy 30:19 says, "I call heaven and earth as witnesses today against you, *that* I have set before you life and death, blessing and cursing; therefore choose life, that both you and your descendants may live;" God wants a definitive answer. No messing around. Spend your time dwelling on what's pure and right. Philippians 4:8 says, "Finally, brethren, whatever things are true, whatever things *are* noble, whatever things *are* just, whatever things *are* pure, whatever things *are* lovely, whatever things *are* of good report, if *there is* any virtue and if *there is* anything praiseworthy—meditate on these things." Keep your mind and heart right. Stay positive. Think about what is best for you and those around you. Stay out of situations that could cause you or others to be harmed physically, mentally, or spiritually. Pursue purity in your life. Stay away from the edge of compromise and you won't fall in. Do the right thing and do your best.

31 August When my sons were just learning to communicate, I could usually discern what they were saying because I knew them and their "codes". (Moms learn the codes early on). Then, not really allowing things like grunting or crying, I often said, "Use your words to tell me what you want." One way or another, they would make themselves understood. The words were sometimes accompanied by pointing, loudness, running to a thing or person, or by a tug on my sleeve. Whether they needed attention or a cookie, they would find a way to make it clear. When the message was received, there was rejoicing on all sides. And maybe a snicker doodle or two!

Today the song is, "You Are"~ Colton Dixon. This song proclaims that if I had no voice, or no tongue, I would dance for God. When the day comes that I see God's face I will shout His endless, glorious praise. Exodus 15:2 says, "The Lord *is* my strength and song, and He has become my salvation; He *is* my God, and I will praise Him; My father's God, and I will exalt Him." Nothing should stop you from giving God the praise He deserves. Not circumstances, nor disabilities, nor negative people. When you really know and love some one, you find a way to communicate. God knows you. He has the code to how you talk to Him and what you need. There is a key to what you say. Your faith comes by hearing, but your faith is released by saying. Let God hear what you need today. Speak to Him in the way you know how. You may be new to this faith walk. God doesn't expect you to take on a new language just to talk to Him. If Ye Olde English is not your "deal", then it's not His either. Just be yourself. Be real. Be genuine. Make yourself known to God as He has made Himself known to you. When that message is received, there will be rejoicing on all sides!

1 September My oldest son's birthday is today. The years have flown. We spoke this morning of his birth and it seems like yesterday and yet it also seems like a lifetime ago. For him, I guess, it was. He has grown into a fine young man. He is the level-headed one. Strong. Decisive. Bold. He wasn't a Boy Scout, but adopted one of their themes, "Be Prepared." I love our mom-son chats. I am proud of who he is today. A man of integrity, resourcefulness, and abilities. He's definitely not my baby any more, but he will always be my son and I love him.

Today's song is, "Blink" ~ Revive. This song talks about how time passes and when it's all said and done, no one remembers how far we've run. What matters is how we've loved. So, I don't want to miss a second, because in a blink and a flash it passes. There's no stopping time no matter how tightly I try to hold on to it. When you look at the years past, they have flown so quickly, yet you often feel that you still have time to live, to dream, and to do all you want in the future. The key though is, start now. Now is the best time to live, dream, and do all you want. Someone said that you should live like you were dying. Perhaps it would be better to live like you are living! Be alive. Intentionally take on each day with enthusiasm. Not fearing death, but relishing life – embracing all you have and all you aspire to become.

I had a dream that we went back in time to get a friend who died prematurely. Though our initial goal was frivolous at best, in telling this person about his untimely demise, it changed something in him and he vowed to live better, take better care of himself, and make the most of all that was placed before him. Unfortunately, it was just a dream. Don't let time pass today without you making the most of it. You can't go back. You need to go forward. You have the time to do all which you truly want to do. Yes you do. You don't want to look back and say, "Where did the time go?" You want to smile and say, "We certainly made the most of it, didn't we?" Seek God today, His plan and His purpose. Be strong. Be decisive. Be bold, prepared, and resourceful. You will love your life and you will not regret how you have lived it.

2 September Periodically, I do a evaluation of myself. But sometimes I focus too much on my faults. What I've missed, messed up, or failed. I realize that without God I am nothing. But I also realize that I am fearfully and wonderfully made. I am God's workmanship created for good works in Christ. I am more than a conqueror. I am victorious. There is so much more. My focus needs to be on those things instead.

Today's song is, "Forever Reign" ~ Hillsong. This song talks about how amazing God is. He is good when there's nothing good in me. He's peace, joy, life, light and hope. His love will always be enough. Take a look at your life today. It's not all about you. It's not you on your own. You are not the Lone Ranger. (When you think about it, even he had Tonto.) When your life is a mess or you feel like a failure, realize that God has made you more. Falling doesn't make you a failure. Not getting back up when you fall does. Maybe you've been knocked down today. Maybe you blew it. Dry your tears. Wipe off your pants. Stand up. Try again. But remember – God is on your side. Communicate with Him. He is your peace today. He's your joy. Your life. Your light. Your hope. His love will always be enough for you. There isn't anyone like Him. He's amazing. Focus on Him today and you will never be a failure.

3 September Rick Bayless talks about the difference between a party and a fiesta in his book, <u>Fiesta At Rick's</u>. He says, "What I discovered is this: 'party' is to 'fiesta' as 'lunch' is to 'Thanksgiving dinner.'" He explains the fact that lunch meets nutritional needs just as Thanksgiving dinner does, however, "By its sheer magnitude, Thanksgiving dinner leads us to marvel at its heartening bounty, at the beauty of natural ingredients and handmade preparations." It's a part of a tradition bringing people together and brings about a feeling of nurture by spending time with those who share a history with us. Fiesta! It's so much more than just a party.

Today's song is, "La Buena Vida" ~ Ken Reynolds, Lucia Parker. This song celebrates, exclaiming that I like living the good life, the high life – where all things are possible in Christ. This song is "Fiesta!" It's a grand celebration of all the benefits of living your life in Christ. It's so much more than believing. So much more than a prayer or a hymn or a mere gesture of faith. It is the realization of the awesomeness of God, leading you to marvel at His greatness and all that He has created. It's fellowship with Him. Being near and spending time with Him. Philippians 4:4 (MSG) says, "Celebrate God all day, every day. I mean, *revel* in him! Make it as clear as you can to all you meet that you're on their side, working with them and not against them." Rejoice, relish, and savor God's presence in your life today. Celebrate. God is with you. Romans 8:31 says, "What then shall we say to these things? If God *is* for us, who *can be* against us?" You can't help but win today with God on your side. So rejoice! Fiesta! It's so much more than just a party. He deserves your highest praise!

4 September A reporter asked a neighbor who lived in the area where a horrific crime took place, "What will you do now?" He replied, "We move forward from here." What a great attitude. He knew he could not change the past, but he could have a better perspective of the future, its potential, its promise. The incidents of recent weeks will be imbedded in memories of all involved, but they do not have to dictate the weeks to follow or be a focal point for the survivors.

Today's song is "Moving Forward" ~ Israel Houghton. This song is a declaration that since Christ has brought me to a moment, a life of freedom in Him, I am moving ahead. Moving away from my past and moving forward. My past is over and my life is completely new because I have surrendered to Him. You have heard the phrase, "forgive and forget" How hard is that? On your own, I would say, "impossible." Some things are just seemingly permanent, engraved in your mind. But with God all things are possible. Even forgiving and forgetting. He can help you get through your past. The hurt. The mistakes. The betrayal. The devastation. The loss. All that has been wrong about who you were becomes less than a memory to God when you come to Him and accept the salvation that His Son paid for – with His life. Psalm 103:8-12 (MSG) says, "God is sheer mercy and grace; not easily angered, he's rich in love. He doesn't endlessly nag and scold, nor hold grudges forever. He doesn't treat us as our sins deserve, nor pay us back in full for our wrongs. As high as heaven is over the earth, so strong is his love to those who fear him. And as far as sunrise is from sunset, He has separated us from our sins." God doesn't bring the past back and throw it in your face. To Him, it's gone. If your past is haunting you, it's your enemy, the devil, which is bringing it to your remembrance. Do not confuse where those thoughts are originating. Today, take a look at your focal point. Is it rooted in the past, the lost self? Or is it rooted in the future, redeemed self? Time to go forward. Time to move ahead. Time to relinquish what is past and leap, grasp, and take firm that which is your future. Seek God. Jeremiah 29:13 says, "And you will seek Me and find *Me,* when you search for Me with all your heart." Put your heart into it. God has a new thing for you. Move forward from here.

5 September Picking up stuff that's too heavy for me really isn't a good idea. Hurting my shoulder has slowed me down a bit. But my husband, sons, and friends are here! I am so glad that I have people around me to help me get my projects done. It's nice to have their assistance when I need it.

Today's song is, "Everything I Need" ~ Kutless. This song reminds me that God is strength in my weakness and the refuge I seek. He is everything I need. Even a little injury can slow you down or even stop you. It can keep you from accomplishing all God has for you. But you have a choice. You can whine about it, or win in spite of it! Walk in wisdom yes, and seek help when you need it. God is there to be your strength in weakness. 2 Corinthians 12:10 (MSG) says, "Now I take limitations in stride, and with good cheer, these limitations that cut me down to size—abuse, accidents, opposition, bad breaks. I just let Christ take over! And so the weaker I get, the stronger I become." God is more than enough to make up for your shortcomings. He is more than enough to get you through. He is more than enough to strengthen you. He is more than enough. Don't ever discount His power, His love, and His mercy for you. Rest in Him today. That weakness you have will be strengthened with time, faith, persistence, wisdom, and power in the Lord. So be glad today and carry on. Don't be a whiner, be a winner!

6 September Reunions, homecomings all take us back to our past. We see how everyone has changed. Who is married, has children, become famous perhaps. We see the weight loss and gain, the aging with grace and the aging with not so much grace. Some we think have not changed a bit. Being locked in somehow to the things that were. The 'good ole days'. Those events are fine for an evening. But for me, I wouldn't want to stay there. There is so much more up ahead. So much more to do. So much more to grow and accomplish.

Today the song is, "Moving Forward" ~ Israel Houghton. This part of the song speaks to me today that I'm not going back, I'm moving ahead. I am declaring that my past is over because I am a new creation in Christ. The past is just that. The past. You can learn from it, grow from it, and it was a part of where and who you are today. But you can't go back. You shouldn't want to go back. God has so much more for you in your future. My pastor says that people who have no hope in the future return to their past. They are searching, groping for something back there that they can hang on to. In reality, it's time to reach forward. Jeremiah 29:11 says, "For I know the thoughts that I think toward you, says the Lord, thoughts of peace and not of evil, to give you a future and a hope." So, today, look to the past as a springboard for your future, not a bed to return to. Do not long for the 'good ole days', for your future is so much brighter. So much better. So much richer. You may have some regrets, but you can't go back and redo it. You can do something new though. Let God do something new in you. No matter how much hair you've lost or weight you've gained, no matter if you have become famous or not, there is much more to do, to grow, and to accomplish. So, go. Go forward.

7 September No matter how late I stay up, it seems that once the sun rises that it's time to get out of bed. Today happened to be the morning after a very late night of good clean fun at my sons' birthday party. I realized how blessed we are with great family and friends. As I grabbed my first cup of coffee and looked out the back door over the beauty that is our land and the family farm, this song was almost loud enough in my head to prompt me to look for the choir! It's a children's song from long ago…

Today's song is, "Rise And Shine" listed as Traditional. This is a good morning song! Rise and shine and give God glory! Sometimes when you are very tired, you just want to cover your head and say, "Just awhile longer, then I'll get up." But God has a brand new day for you to see, experience, and live! Lamentations 3:22-23 (MSG) says, "God's loyal love couldn't have run out, his merciful love couldn't have dried up. They're created new every morning. How great your faithfulness!" That's His mercy, His grace, new each morning. Each day you get a fresh start. So wipe the sleep out of your eyes. Give yourself a stretch. Fix some coffee or a fruit smoothie and get yourself going in the mornings. You don't want to miss anything God has for you. There are opportunities just waiting for you to discover! It's exciting. So rise and shine! Give God some glory and realize just how blessed you are!

8 September When the boys were little, just babies in fact, we'd have them reach high and would ask, "How big are you?" Then with arms outstretched we would say together, "So Big!" It was a game to show how they were getting to be "big" boys, over two and a half feet tall! Now at around six feet tall, they are "So Big!" Grown up that is, adults. But more than just big, they are great! I love my sons.

Today's song is, "How Great Is Our God" ~ Chris Tomlin. This song declares that Our God is great. Join with me in proclaiming it! All will see that He's worthy of all praise. Today, you should realize that God is great. He's so big that nothing is impossible with Him. Matthew 19:26 says, "But Jesus looked at *them* and said to them, 'With men this is impossible, but with God all things are possible.'" No matter what you are going through, God is bigger. He's got a solution to your problem. An answer to your question. A way around your obstacle. He can make streams in the desert. (Isaiah 35:6) He can make the crooked places straight. (Isaiah 40:4) In other words, God can change your situation! 2 Corinthians 4: 16-18 (MSG) puts it this way, "So we're not giving up. How could we! Even though on the outside it often looks like things are falling apart on us, on the inside, where God is making new life, not a day goes by without his unfolding grace. These hard times are small potatoes compared to the coming good times, the lavish celebration prepared for us. There's far more here than meets the eye. The things we see now are here today, gone tomorrow. But the things we can't see now will last forever." So what you see is temporal, it is changeable. That's your situation, your circumstance. What is not seen is the eternal God, He doesn't change. Proclaim God's greatness. Stretch out your arms to Him today and when you ask Him, "How big are you, God?" He will say, "So Big!"

9 September When our cats were kittens, their momma took care of them in a blanket lined cardboard box in our garage. Later they paraded through the kitchen to a vacant dog house right outside the back door where they stayed while Mom hunted and brought them back food. That was their little world. As they grew, they discovered there was a whole lot more to the farm than just that old dog house. Venturing out, wandering, hunting, and playing on vast acreage is their life now. It's so much bigger than the box where they were born.

Today the song is, "Make It Loud" ~ Martha Munizzi. This is an amazingly energetic song. It incites celebration to make it big and make it loud, shouting all around the world that there is no other god like our God! You have heard songs that just make you want to jump, shout, and dance – this is definitely one of those! There really is no other god like our God. A wimpy response will do no good. Make it big and loud. Shout it out. Celebrate! Time to get out of your own little world. Today you must think globally. What kind of an impact can you make in the world by your testimony? By your involvement? By your outreach to another people, another country, another culture? How can you venture out today? It's fine and good to enjoy your space, the place where you grew up. But even better to explore the vast acreage of society that is hungry for a good God. For a healing God. For an abundant God. Mark 16:15 (MSG) says, "Then he said, 'Go into the world. Go everywhere and announce the message of God's good news to one and all. Whoever believes and is baptized is saved; whoever refuses to believe is damned.'" Notice that it's your job to announce and the job of the people to believe or refuse. So, who can you tell? And how? Acts 1:8 says, "But you shall receive power when the Holy Spirit has come upon you; and you shall be witnesses to Me in Jerusalem, and in all Judea and Samaria, and to the end of the earth." Your power to share comes from the Holy Spirit. He gives you the strength to carry out Jesus' admonition to go into the entire world. So venture out today, away from the familiar and into a place where you can make a difference with your story of how God has been good to you. Step out of your box. What is waiting for you is so much bigger!

10 September When I started my beauty consulting business, five of my close friends basically said, "Don't talk to me about it." I was flabbergasted. To not have support of those friends was surprising. I've had days where "No" was all too common. Other days I was leaving messages, wondering if anyone would talk to me – ever. Then drama at home or school or the neighborhood. Then the busyness of all of it that could have me overwhelmed, frazzled, crazy, and finally crying. The rough days. There will be rough days. That's when I need God's grace the most.

Today the song is, "Speechless" ~ Israel Houghton & New Breed. This song looks to God for His grace, entreating that I need it. And I receive it – His unmerited favor. All days are not rough days or tough days or dramatic days. There are good days and great days and amazing days too! God's grace is for the race you are in. His hand on your life is what will pull you through the messy, horrible days and ride with you when you coast down the middle of those amazing days. Honestly, your focus will make all the difference. What are you looking at today? How tough life is? Or how great God's grace is? Tell Him you need His grace. Declare it. Believe it. Receive it. It will take your breath away – you will be astonished. God can do so much more for you than you can imagine. (Ephesians 3:20) Your job is to keep pressing forward. Philippians 3:13-15 (MSG) says, "I'm not saying that I have this all together, that I have it made. But I am well on my way, reaching out for Christ, who has so wondrously reached out for me. Friends, don't get me wrong: By no means do I count myself an expert in all of this, but I've got my eye on the goal, where God is beckoning us onward—to Jesus. I'm off and running and I'm not turning back." Keep focused on the goal. Your goal. Your abundant life in Christ. Then you will realize that when the tough days come, He's there. Just keep moving ahead and the amazing days will be here before you know it!

11 September Historically, September 11th was a horrendous day for America. Terrorists killed over 3,000 people by using airplanes as weapons. Buildings fell. My family witnessed the live television coverage of the 2nd plane going into the New York City World Trade Center Tower. It was mind numbing. It was a pivotal incident, splitting the nation's timeline. Recounting of events soon became either 'Pre – 9/11' or 'Post – 9/11'. Devastation, death, deception, defilement, and desecration all happened that day. But out of the ashes, the country rose. The leadership was resolved. Strength came. People united. Healing began. It will never be as it was. Our quest going forward is to make it better than it was.

Today's song is, "Our God Is Greater" ~ Chris Tomlin. This song says that our God is greater and stronger. He shines in the darkness and we rise out of the ashes because of God. There is none like Him. Evil exists because we live in a broken world. Not everything is 'hunky-dory' all the time. Regardless, our God is greater. Greater than all the hurt, the pain, the devastation, the death. He is bigger. Things will happen. They may happen at the hands of men, or weather, or mistake, or accidentally. Complete immunity would be excellent, but life will continue to hold both good and evil, triumph and loss. How you deal with it makes all the difference. Who you look to. What you say. How you pray. That is what separates you from those who have no hope. God is your hope. He is light in the darkness. He helps you rise from the ashes. His hand is upon you when you feel like all is lost. When your mind is numb. When you don't know what is next. God is next. He loved you so much He gave His son (John 3:16). The birth of Christ was so significant that it split the timeline of the world. History is recorded as 'B.C.' (Before Christ) or 'A.D.' (anno Domini – The year of our Lord) And Christ died yes, but on the third day He rose again! Life, strength, healing, and hope! Things were never as they were again. Our quest is to go forward with God. He is greater than anything that could ever happen.

12 September There was a time when I was very afraid of crossing bridges. Termed gephyrophobia, it is an irrational concern stemmed from any of a variety of reasons and emerges when confronted with the necessity to go across a bridge. Though mild, my case brought on anxiety and a bit of panic. To overcome it, I prayed. When approaching, crossing, and getting to the other side, my voice and heart reached to God to get me there. He did. The most important thing is that I didn't let it stop me. I kept going. I crossed each bridge as I got to it. Even though my fear encroached, I felt the fear and did it anyway. I know God was always with me. I am an over-comer.

Today's song is, "Today Is The Day" ~ Lincoln Brewster. This song celebrates that today is the day God has made. I will rejoice and be glad. I trust God, so I won't worry about tomorrow. Psalm 118:24 says, "This *is* the day the Lord has made; we will rejoice and be glad in it." There are a lot of opportunities in life that are new experiences or scary experiences. Challenges. Projects. Goals. Tests. Trials. These are all occasions where you could be fearful. Someone said that fear is False Evidence Appearing Real. Many of your fears will never materialize. Nevertheless, fear can creep in or even jump on you in a situation where you may least expect. But remember God. You can trust Him. He will get you across the rivers that rage in your life. 2 Timothy 1:7 says, "For God has not given us a spirit of fear, but of power and of love and of a sound mind." He did not create that fear in you. He is your peace today. Philippians 4:7 says, "And the peace of God, which surpasses all understanding, will guard your hearts and minds through Christ Jesus." And Philippians 4:6 & 7 (MSG) says, "Don't fret or worry. Instead of worrying, pray. Let petitions and praises shape your worries into prayers, letting God know your concerns. Before you know it, a sense of God's wholeness, everything coming together for good, will come and settle you down. It's wonderful what happens when Christ displaces worry at the center of your life." Wow. Here is your fear buster! Let God know your concerns. Your praise will shape your worries and He will settle you down. So today, be encouraged that God is with you at every step of your life. Every challenge, every project, goal, test, and trial. And know that when something comes along, you will be able to cross that bridge when you get to it.

13 September I discovered during my years in youth ministry and as a school principal that when you acknowledge and appreciate someone, you touch their life. When you acknowledge and appreciate their children, you touch their heart. Also, when you meddle with someone, you can get their anger. But, you mess with their kids, and you can get their wrath! Becoming a parent ignites the warrior spirit in a person. It's a realization of how precious and valuable those children really are. You want to take care of them, meet their needs, stand up for them, help them, and champion their causes. That's how I feel about my sons, because I love them.

Today's song is, "Everything I Need" ~ Kutless. This song directs my attention to God for strength in my weakness and for the refuge I seek. He is everything I need. When you do something for God, that's great. When you do good deeds for others, God's children, that's fantastic. He loves it when you think of someone else. Matthew 25:37-40 says, "Then the righteous will answer Him, saying, 'Lord, when did we see You hungry and feed *You,* or thirsty and give *You* drink? When did we see You a stranger and take *You* in, or naked and clothe *You?* Or when did we see You sick, or in prison, and come to You?' And the King will answer and say to them, 'Assuredly, I say to you, inasmuch as you did *it* to one of the least of these My brethren, you did *it* to Me.'" You touch His heart because you've affected His children. Also, God wants to take care of you, His child. He loves you. He can be your strength, your refuge, your help, everything you need. Psalm 46:1 says, "God *is* our refuge and strength, a very present help in trouble." He knows you are precious and valuable. Isaiah 43:4 says, "Since you were precious in My sight, You have been honored, And I have loved you; Therefore I will give men for you, And people for your life." In The Message it says, "I paid a huge price for you: all of Egypt, with rich Cush and Seba thrown in! *That's* how much you mean to me! *That's* how much I love you! I'd sell off the whole world to get you back, trade the creation just for you." That's God. That's His warrior spirit that would do whatever it takes just for you! Know your value today. Know that God is on your side. He is a loving parent. He will stand up for you. He will champion your cause.

14 September We wed on September 14th. It was a commitment to each other that our love is for all our life. There is no other option for us. Our marriage has been solid. An example. Our relationship strong. A message of hope. In a world where responsibility seems obsolete and longevity seems irrelevant, we emerge. Stable, accountable, durable. Together, my husband and me. We have modeled this union to others. Many have shared with us the impact our example has made on their lives. It's not because of us, though. It's because of the God in us that makes all the difference. Ecclesiastes 4:12 speaks of the power of three. Husband, wife, and the Lord together. A cord not easily broken.

Today's song is, "We Can Change The World" ~ Hawk Nelson. This song is an encouragement that when we work together, we can change the world. We can make a difference. Living a life of example is a responsibility. Your choices change. You take other options when you are walking the path of righteousness. It's not a time to say, "Look at me, I'm an example of how great a Christian should be." It's a time to conduct yourself with respect, responsibility, commitment, honor, and integrity. People will see. You do not have to 'show them'. The 'God' in you should shine out. Matthew 5:16 says, "Let your light so shine before men, that they may see your good works and glorify your Father in heaven." They notice. You may never know who is watching you. Your deeds. Your conversations. Your attitude. We have taught our children – Don't say it if you don't want it repeated. Great advice. Think about your life today. What are you portraying? Have you inspired others? Do they want to be like you? You are like a stone dropped into the water, impacting people in all directions. A ripple effect, one thing or person leading to another. Never think that it doesn't matter what you do. It does. Never think that you don't matter. You do. God has placed you here to make a difference. You can change the world.

15 September

We left the house early in the afternoon to be gone until evening the next day. Our sons later returned home and slept through the night. Cat cries woke them around 6 am. But where was the sound coming from? It seemed to move as my younger son looked through the house. Unknowingly, we had shut our cat in our walk-in closet. Now, this 13 pound cat had managed to lift the vent cover on the floor of the closet and get into the duct work! He was searching for a way out! My son pulled up another cover in the master bath and went for a flashlight. Upon his return, he saw that the cat had popped his head up and was wiggling free of the vent. Quite a rescue!

Today the song is, "Me Without You" ~ Toby Mac. Today, the bridge speaks, that the Lord rescued me and I belong to Him. He saved me and remade me. That cat was stuck in a place where he did not want to be. He was in the dark. No food. No water. Alone. No way out. But he didn't just lay down and pout. He made some noise. He did what he knew to do. He pulled things off the shelves, he turned over the hamper, he searched for anything that could help him. Then he found a way where there was no way, lifted up that vent cover and through sheer determination, he went to where he could be heard and didn't stop until some one came to get him out. His cry for help was answered! Have you ever felt like you were that cat? You are stuck in a place where you don't want to be? You can't see a way out? You feel like you are in the dark? Hopeless. Helpless. Alone. God wants to be your rescuer today. Don't just lie down and pout. Cry out. Cry out to God. 2 Samuel 22:7 says, "In my distress I called upon the Lord, and cried out to my God; He heard my voice from His temple, and my cry *entered* His ears." God will hear your cry today. He will help you. He will make a way. (Isaiah 43:16) So keep searching today. Keep looking. Keep trying. Do not give up. Your rescuer is here. Stay with it. Be determined to find your way out and with God's help you surely will!

16 September I just made a simple comment without further thought. However, when repeated out of context, the supervisor caused an uncomfortable rift between me and the other person. It baffled me as to why she would say that, but I could not un-say it. Further explanation would only make it worse. So I was upset. I felt betrayed. Disrespected. My flesh wanted to lash out. Get back. Get even. But my spirit prevailed. I chose to forgive and let it go. I learned from it: 1. Be careful who you trust. 2. Be careful to be clear in what you say. 3. Be careful how you respond when you forgot to do #1 and #2.

Today the song is, "Losing" ~ Tenth Avenue North. A request to God in this song asks Him to give me grace to forgive others. It does happen. People are people. They say things, break your trust, misunderstand, and betray you. Sometimes they mean to be hurtful. Sometimes they don't care. Sometimes they are just immature. But, thank God for His grace! He has forgiven you. Just so, forgive others. Ephesians 4:32 says, "And be kind to one another, tenderhearted, forgiving one another, even as God in Christ forgave you." And in The Message it says, "Be gentle with one another, sensitive. Forgive one another as quickly and thoroughly as God in Christ forgave you." It says quickly and thoroughly. Don't let unforgiveness linger. Like a splinter in your hand, it will start to fester. It gets sore and infected and it hurts you! It does not cause pain to the board from which it came. In the same manner, unforgiveness does not hurt the other person, it hurts you. Forgive a person entirely. Let it go. You will be better for it. Remember your responsibility in the matter and learn from it. So, if you are dealing with a betrayal today, pray. God will give you the grace to forgive. The grace to go on. 2 Corinthians 12:9a (MSG) says, "My grace is enough; it's all you need." His grace is enough. And, once you get that splinter out, then you can heal.

17 September When crime came close to our lives there was a fine line between being cautious and being terribly afraid. It can be unsettling. I began to question unfamiliar sounds, people, and situations. Constantly thinking, "What will I do if...?" I became a prisoner of my own concerns. It's definitely smart to be aware, but being fearful can be paralyzing.

Today's song is, "We Won't Be Shaken" ~ Building 429. This song declares that whatever will come our way, fire or pouring rain, we won't be shaken. When dealing with a situation that can really shake you to the core, God is the one who can stabilize you. You need to dig in, stand firm, and declare that you will not be shaken. When your life is built upon the Rock – Jesus, you will be secure. Matthew 7:24-25 says, "Therefore whoever hears these sayings of Mine, and does them, I will liken him to a wise man who built his house on the rock: and the rain descended, the floods came, and the winds blew and beat on that house; and it did not fall, for it was founded on the rock." You can stand strong today when the storms of life come. And they will come. God is your refuge, so don't worry today. Philippians 4:6 (MSG) says, "Don't fret or worry. Instead of worrying, pray. Let petitions and praises shape your worries into prayers, letting God know your concerns. Before you know it, a sense of God's wholeness, everything coming together for good, will come and settle you down. It's wonderful what happens when Christ displaces worry at the center of your life." This is the perfect word to stand upon. Bathe your situation in prayer today. God will settle you. He will give you His peace today. Know that whatever comes, you will stand, because of Jesus as Lord in your life. You will not be shaken!

18 September I labeled something this morning so when it left the house that it had a better chance to be returned. It's just irritating when something goes missing due to a misunderstanding or carelessness. I think, "If I just would have put my name on it, I would still have it. It wouldn't be lost." That's my stuff. Honestly though, it's just stuff. The items of my life are far less important than the people. Brooding over a lost book or vase or jacket doesn't do much to bring them back. So when I feel that selfish attitude rise up, I put it in check. Life's not all about me and my stuff, after all.

Today's song, "Jesus, Lover Of My Soul" ~ Passion. This song reminds me today that it's all about Jesus; my praise is for Him, His glory and fame. It's not about me, as if He should do things my way. I surrender to His ways. Focusing on all that is about you limits your vision. You can become narrow-minded and self-serving. It is far more beneficial to focus on God. His will done brings you far more blessing than any possession. Also, a "Look at me" attitude exhausts, annoys, and bores others. It is not a good picture of a loving, giving God. So, today check your focus. Is it about you and your stuff? Your incidents, hurts, or situations? Or is it about what you can do, give, and make happen for others? Are you pointing people toward God? Or trying to bring more attention on you? In John 12:32 Jesus says, "And I, if I am lifted up from the earth, will draw all *peoples* to Myself." He was referring to physically being lifted, but also think about Him being spiritually lifted as well. Meaning exalted, honored, revered. Lift up the Lord and people will be drawn to Him. Drawn to believe. Drawn to follow. Be a catalyst for belief today. Take your eyes off yourself and your stuff and look to God. You will not be lost.

19 September When you receive Christ into your heart it's like filling your pot with water. When you receive the Holy Spirit in your life, it's like turning up the heat! The first is presence, the second is power!

Today the song is, "Build Your Kingdom Here" ~ Rend Collective Experiment. This song reminds me that the church is really the people. It asks God to increase in us, unveil why we're made, and to ignite in us a fire of hope. We need the power of the Holy Spirit in us to build God's Kingdom. All too often you think of the church as a building, the ornate sanctuary of the traditional, the simple wood floor and pews of the country chapel, or the sleek design of the contemporary house of worship. That's merely architecture. The true church is the people. When inspired by Christ and empowered by the Holy Spirit, the people make the difference in this broken society. As a Christian, you can bring hope to a dying world. Christ in you is the hope of glory. (Colossians 1:27) The Holy Spirit is an aspect of God that many do not know. He is one person of the trinity which is God, Jesus, and The Holy Spirit. One God, three parts. The Bible talks of baptism in water and the Holy Spirit. Mark 1:8 says, "I'm baptizing you here in the river, turning your old life in for a kingdom life. His baptism—a holy baptism by the Holy Spirit—will change you from the inside out." Today, increase your dimension in the Lord by inviting the Holy Spirit into your life. Or increase your relationship with the Holy Spirit through prayer. In Acts 2:17 Peter recounts a passage from Joel that says, "'And it shall come to pass in the last days, says God, that I will pour out of My Spirit on all flesh; Your sons and your daughters shall prophesy, Your young men shall see visions, Your old men shall dream dreams." This was first experienced in Acts 2:1-4. The same is available to you as a Christ believer today. You may be full of God, but maybe it's time to turn up the heat! It's great to enjoy His presence, but even greater to experience God's power. So remember, it's not in the building today where you will find God, you will find Him in the people of God. In yourself as a believer. You are the church.

20 September I was at a business meeting, chatting in the lobby, when one of the executives approached me and asked if I would lead in prayer to open the meeting that day. "Yes", was my confident answer. I was honored. Then a young woman nearby said, "What did she ask you?" When I told her, she wondered if I was nervous about praying in front of hundreds of people. I said, "No" and smiled. She teared up. "Is everyone here a Christian?" "A lot of us are." I replied. She began to cry and told me that she was once close to God but had drifted away. I prayed with her that morning; I was blessed to be able to share with her about God's willingness to welcome her back to Him.

Today's song is, "All Over The World" ~ Jermaine Rodriguez. This song is about transformation and declaration. Since my life has changed, been made new in Christ, I'm going to shine His light all over the world – telling others that He brings hope to a dying land, like rain on the desert. When you find out something great, you should share it. A sale, a deal, a recipe, a resource, a method, a message, or an opportunity can help others when you tell them. Letting people know that God has done something in your life can help them. Share your story. Focus on the result. You may have had a horrible tragic life that God completely changed. Or you may have had a relatively uneventful journey with regard to life drama and He transformed your attitude and your outlook. Don't ever feel that your story is too sensational or too mundane. When you share it, you reach out and touch hearts. No matter what you have done or haven't done, Christ died for you. He will change you, heal you, and give you eternal life. John 3:16 says, "For God so loved the world that He gave His only begotten Son, that whoever believes in Him should not perish but have everlasting life." That's your promise. This is your commission, to share the hope that you have been given in Christ. To share the message. To be a light. To be an example. People will notice. They will ask. You will be able to share with them, so that they too will experience God's forgiveness and His willingness to welcome them back to Him.

21 September "It's a spider bite." I thought. The red spot on my leg was not getting better so I went to my doctor. Not a spider bite. But he gave me some cream to put on it. Days later, it was still red and sore. I was puzzled. Then one morning I rubbed the area, now raised more, and a very small granule emerged. I removed it and… it was an alien! No, it was just like a small rock, oddly enough. From that point on, the spot started to heal and was completely better in a matter of days.

Today the song is, "Healing Begins" ~ Tenth Avenue North. This song talks about the brave face you don when things get tough and you won't admit there is hurt. When you come to where you are broken within, that is where the healing begins. That is where the light meets the dark. And the light dispels the dark. There are times when you want to be strong and mighty, but you feel weak and needy. You want others to think you've got it all together when you worry that you'll fall apart. Only when you get alone with God in that quiet place and admit you are broken, the hurt emerges and He can remove it. That is where your healing begins. It's a process. Bit by bit. Day by day. Healing. Restoration. Renewal. Strength returns. Faith rises. The darkness, what the devil has meant for evil in your life, God turns it around for your good. Genesis 50:19-21 (MSG) says this, "Joseph replied, 'Don't be afraid. Do I act for God? Don't you see, you planned evil against me but God used those same plans for my good, as you see all around you right now—life for many people. Easy now, you have nothing to fear; I'll take care of you and your children.' He reassured them, speaking with them heart-to-heart." God is still there in the hurt and the pain. He will take care of you and your family. Be encouraged today or encourage someone else that God loves and will heal that wound, no matter how deep, no matter what caused it, no matter what lies within. Darkness in your life will be dispelled with the light of the Lord and your enemies, hurts, problems, and even aliens have to leave! And if you are hurting today, reach out to some one and do a good deed. That is how you begin to overcome. Romans 12:21 (MSG) says, "Don't let evil get the best of you; get the best of evil by doing good." You'll be well on your way!

22 September Last week our biggest cat was out in the front yard fighting with a stray. By the end of it, he was out in the field wounded and I had to go get him. This week, he came bounding out of the field after a successful rabbit hunt. Spoil in tow; he looked as if to be grinning and saying, "Look, I got it! I am a winner!" It was quite a contrast from wounded and spent to victorious and proud!

Today the song is, "I Won't Go Back" ~ William McDowell. This song tells that I've been changed, healed, freed, and delivered. And I have found joy, peace, grace, joy, and favor in my life. I have waited for this change, this moment, and I won't let it pass me by. I will not go back to the way it used to be before God changed my life. When you know you are a winner, the weight of the world drops off your shoulders and you can run the race God has given you! Isaiah 40:31 says, "But those who wait on the Lord shall renew *their* strength; they shall mount up with wings like eagles, they shall run and not be weary, they shall walk and not faint." Your strength is renewed when you seek God. Wait on Him for your direction and instruction. Let Him change you. Change your attitude. Change your perspective. Change your mind. Be determined to not return to the failures of the past. The hurts. The let downs. Decide to go forward only. Getting stronger, more confident, more full of faith. Remember, although life may sometimes be a bloody battle, leaving you wounded, be of good cheer, you can overcome. Your victory can be as close as the next field over! Then you can smile and say, "Look, I got this! I'm a winner!"

23 September I'm not certain what really compelled me to join a professional fraternity in college. It was mostly musicians. I was an actress and a mime. But I had this overwhelming need to belong. This was a group of people out of my regular circle and I longed to be included. So, I pledged. But I was a casual member, not fully engaged in the mores of the organization. It was a great group of professional women, but my heart was not in it. So, even in belonging, I didn't really feel like I belonged.

Today's song is, "I Belong To You" ~ William McDowell. This song conveys the message that I've been captured by a love I cannot explain. It's God's love. I surrender my life to Him. I belong to Him. He has changed my life. So many times in your life you can find yourself in a place where you feel like you don't belong. Yearning to be a part of something bigger than yourself, you may even do something out of the ordinary, not characteristic of you or your beliefs, just to be included. God has a purpose and a place for you to belong. You can be positioned geographically for God's best for your life. The people there, are your people. Your group. Your connections. The ones you are called to influence. It may be for a season or it may be for a lifetime. Frederick Buechner said, "The place God calls you to is the place where your deep gladness and the world's deep hunger meet." There is a need that you can help fill. There is a hurt you can help heal. It will bring joy to you when you are in the right place. Psalm 18:16-18 & 20b (MSG) describes what happens when you open your heart to God, "But me he caught—reached all the way from sky to sea; he pulled me out of that ocean of hate, that enemy chaos, the void in which I was drowning. They hit me when I was down, but God stuck by me. ... He gave me a fresh start." He will take you to a place and make you complete. He will stick by you. He will rewrite your life. That's exciting! Be compelled to belong to God today. Direct your overwhelming need to be a part of something bigger than yourself to be a part of God's plan. Do not be a casual member of God's family. Be active. Daniel 11:32b says, "But the people who know their God shall be strong, and carry out *great exploits*." Be strong. Do exploits for God. Make a difference in the world. Long to be included in all God has for you. As your heart is changed, you will be able to affect the change of heart in others. It will bring you gladness. That's where you belong.

275

24 September Our conference instructor said, "Raise your hands as high as you can. Now reach a little higher." We did. He wondered why we didn't reach that high in the first place. It was because we thought we were reaching as high as we could. But that was not the case. We can reach higher.

Today the song is, "Gold" ~ Britt Nicole. This song is for everyone all over the world, no matter what you've been told, you're worth more than gold. Hold your head high, it's time to shine. Don't be ashamed, your real self shows from the inside out. You can do more than you think you can. You can try one more time. You can try a little bit more. No matter what others say, within you lay the seeds of greatness. They are just waiting to be watered, nurtured, and harvested. You have the ability to increase.
1 Chronicles 4:10 says, "And Jabez called on the God of Israel saying, 'Oh, that You would bless me indeed, and enlarge my territory, that Your hand would be with me, and that You would keep *me* from evil, that I may not cause pain!' So God granted him what he requested." Jabez asked God to bless him and enlarge his territory. Territory is capacity. What can you do today to enlarge your capacity? The Chinese philosopher, Laozi said, "A journey of a thousand miles begins with a single step." What step will you take? You may not know the end from the beginning, but God does. He will lead you. Isaiah 46:9b-10 (MSG) says, "I am God, the only God you've had or ever will have—incomparable, irreplaceable—From the very beginning telling you what the ending will be, All along letting you in on what is going to happen, Assuring you, 'I'm in this for the long haul, I'll do exactly what I set out to do,'" You can trust God to do what He said He will do. He is faithful. But you have to take the steps. You have to reach for it. So step out today, then keep stepping. Think about where you want to be a year from now. You are worth more than you think you are. You can do more than you think you can. Ephesians 3:20 (MSG) says, "God can do anything, you know—far more than you could ever imagine or guess or request in your wildest dreams! He does it not by pushing us around but by working within us, his Spirit deeply and gently within us." So dream wild today. Dream big. You are worth more than gold!

25 September Really, only part of the chorus of the song came to me this morning. The word "Holy" was all I could seem to hear. So, to find this song today I searched "holy" and that didn't work. Knowing its popularity, I just listened to the local Christian music station and finally after almost an hour and a half they played it. I listened on-line and there was the title and artist! Yay, technology!

This morning's song is "After All" ~ David Crowder Band. This song says that I can't comprehend God's infinite beauty and perfect love. Even when I sing about Him with all that's within me, it won't be loud enough. Heaven and earth are full of His glory. He is holy. 1 Samuel 2:2 says, "No one is holy like the LORD, For *there is* none besides You, Nor *is there* any rock like our God." That word, "Holy". It just played over and over in my head. I believe that's the part God really wanted me to hone in on. Like He was saying, "Remember, I AM HOLY." I know the song and always note this part when I hear it. I reminds me of a scene from The Lion, The Witch, and The Wardrobe or Prince Caspian by C.S. Lewis where they are going into battle. It's powerful! When I hear it, I feel powerful and victorious, like I can do anything. That's my hope for you today. Remember, God is holy. Keep your eyes on Him and your focus on what He wants for your life, your destiny. You are powerful! You are victorious!!! You can do anything.

26 September There was a debate as to who was the true owner of that coveted memento. Was it her or me? It was not worth a fight. Our relationship was so much more important. So we worked it out. I'm so glad that maturity wins over pettiness most every time.

Today's Song, "Forever Reign" ~ Hillsong. This song proclaims that I'm running to God's arms. The riches of His love will always be enough for me and nothing compares to His embrace. He is the light of the world and He will forever reign. No matter what I have or do not have today, God's riches are enough. The want of things can never replace the desire to have a close relationship with God or others. The key is what is really important today? Who is important today? You want to make your decisions today with these questions in mind. Will you choose correctly? Maybe. Will you be right? Possibly. Who will benefit or be hurt by what you decide? Today, take a look at all you are considering. Be mindful of who it affects. Will you be better on the other side of your decision? I certainly hope so. Selfishness keeps you from God's best. Matthew 6:19-21 (MSG) says, "Don't hoard treasure down here where it gets eaten by moths and corroded by rust or—worse!—stolen by burglars. Stockpile treasure in heaven, where it's safe from moth and rust and burglars. It's obvious, isn't it? The place where your treasure is, is the place you will most want to be, and end up being." Be selective about your treasure today. What is really worth it? Worth your time? Your attention? Your investment? Your commitment? Remember that God is good when there is no good in you. He is peace when you are paralyzed by fear. He is Lord. In His presence you are made whole. Your relationships are more important today than things. God's riches are enough.

27 September When my boys were little, they would call out in the night occasionally. "Mommy? Mommy!" It was my signal to come to their aid. Whether it was a drink of water or a tucking in with 'blankie' and 'doggie', I was there to comfort them, calm them, and remind them that they were loved.

Today's song is "Forever Reign" ~ Hillsong. When just a part of this song came to me today I knew it was the same song as another day and yes, it was yesterday. But the only part I heard today was the bridge which says that my heart will sing no other name but Jesus. It's a totally different part of the song that I didn't pay attention to before. The name of Jesus is like no other name. Philippians 2:9-11 (MSG) says, "Because of that obedience, God lifted him high and honored him far beyond anyone or anything, ever, so that all created beings in heaven and on earth—even those long ago dead and buried—will bow in worship before this Jesus Christ, and call out in praise that he is the Master of all, to the glorious honor of God the Father." His name is powerful. It's comforting. It grounds you. It calms. It strengthens. It stirs you. Jesus. Saying His name reminds you of His love, His sacrifice, His ability. His name is above the names of depression, sickness, debt, despair, regret, betrayal...anything that may come your way. His name is "Above" - my pastor spoke recently about the word "above" not only meaning in *importance*, but also as in *a covering.* So, Jesus has got you covered today. Calling on Jesus is your best move. Your claim on His name will make you victorious no matter what you are going through.

28 September Our cousin is one of those people who, when you are in her presence, she draws you in. She is genuinely interested in you, what you have been doing, and what you have to say. We feel good just being around her. She has a gentle loving spirit. She is great at making you forget your troubles and focus on the positive things of life. It's always a blessing to visit with her and her husband.

Today's song is the same as the last two and I am thinking, what else do you want to show me, God? So there's more from "Forever Reign" ~ Hillsong. This song affirms that God is present. Being with Him makes you whole. He is God. He is genuinely interested in you. He is gentle and loving. He will help you forget your troubles. Let go of everything else. There are too many times when you can feel inadequate, undeserving, or unworthy. Even the most confident people have their moments. But in His presence you're made whole. That means there is no lack. Whole means that every piece is in place. Psalms 23:1 (CEB) says, "The LORD is my shepherd. I lack nothing." That is so incredibly clear. You can be confident, safe, and full of peace, your needs met and your future secure when the Lord truly is your shepherd. "Shepherd" - He leads and guides and protects the sheep. They do not follow the voice of a stranger. Stop listening to the *strangers* of this life. They do not have your best interest in mind. It may be people or simply thoughts, lies of your inadequacy or being unloved, hopeless, helpless, or wounded. He is God, let go. It's time to let go of the lies in your life, your hurts, your past, all that has led you to feel lack and turn to God. The holding on is holding you back. When your focus is on your lack, it will grow. Focus on God. You will grow.

29 September Years ago, I had a friend who was thinking about leaving her husband. He had not been unfaithful or abusive. What could I do to help? I went to spend some time with her and talk it out. Thankfully, she stayed and their marriage is strong and happy today.

Today's song is "One Thing Remains" ~ Jesus Culture. This song says that God's love never fails and it never gives up. It will never run out on me. A marriage relationship is designed to be 'until death do us part'. Matthew 19: 4-6 (MSG) says, "He answered, "Haven't you read in your Bible that the Creator originally made man and woman for each other, male and female? And because of this, a man leaves father and mother and is firmly bonded to his wife, becoming one flesh—no longer two bodies but one. Because God created this organic union of the two sexes, no one should desecrate his art by cutting them apart." This is a specially crafted relationship. It's meant to be strong and solid. It's meant to last. Other relationships with people can be for a reason, a season, or for life. Our relationship with God can start for a reason, last through your seasons, and continue through your life. The thing about God is that His love is unconditional. He is not going to give up on you even when you have given up on yourself. Even when others stop believing in you, God still does. He's not going to run out, He won't quit loving you. Remember that you will always have God's love. Even on the tough days and the dumb days. He's there for a reason, a season, and for life. Your choice is if you will stay with him. So, commit to your relationship with God today. If you are going through a rough time, talk it out through prayer. You will feel God's loving arms and His assurance that He will never leave you. He will never forsake you. With Him, you can be strong and happy.

30 September I was awake a lot during the night after a long but awesome day at a business conference and a long drive home. The three cups of coffee I had at the restaurant was at least partly to blame, I'm sure. This time, same song every time I woke up and again this morning… "Your Great Name" ~ Natalie Grant. Specifically it says that Jesus is the lamb that is worthy. If you look up the full lyrics to this song, it is powerful. It talks about the name of Jesus and the power and greatness of His name.

Using the name of Jesus when you pray piques the ears of God. Why? Because Jesus paid the price, He is your advocate. In His name you can claim your authority. In Acts 3, Peter took his authority in the name of Jesus and spoke to the lame man, who was then healed. When a kid goes to his brother and says, "Mom says I can do that" or a co-worker says "Per the boss, I am going to do this" they use "in the name of" to do those things and to let others know they have the authority to do so. Just so, you can use the name of Jesus and do things in His authority. This doesn't not give you carte blanche or genie-like abilities. These things you proclaim must line up with what God said in the first place, in His Word. Check the Bible for claims on your authority in Jesus today. His name is great. Don't take it for granted or abuse it. Use it correctly; you will see great things in your life. His name truly is great.

1 October Traffic can be challenging. I left early with an extra time buffer, but I was confronted with a slow-down due to an accident which blocked the highway up ahead. I saw that I had to go another way if I was ever going to make it. I had to make it work. As soon as I could exit, I headed off on the side roads toward my destination. Thirty additional minutes later, I arrived - late. Detours can be unpleasant.

Today's song is "I Give Myself Away" ~ William McDowell. This song reminds me that my life is not my own. I belong to God and I give myself to Him. Have you given yourself to God today? Are you becoming the person He has destined? The question is not what are you making of yourself, but rather who is God making you to be? I think too many times we are so wrapped up in self ambition, wanting to "make it happen" in our lives that we forget to consult the very one who planned our life out from the beginning. These words today are telling you to give it up. Meaning give up trying to do it all, fix it all, be it all on your own. Time to give yourself completely to God and let Him take care of the details. This certainly doesn't mean that you should sit around and pray, "God just do it all for me, I give myself to you." It means seeking God, communing with God, having a conversation, reading what He has to say, listening with spiritual ears. It means having a relationship with God.

God's plan is the best plan, but if you choose to go your own way, He will let you. That's the kind of God He is. Then when you wonder why things are happening a certain way, don't say, "Well, God is in control" and blame him for your decision to go on without Him. The amazing thing about God is His gift to us of that free will. Today, decide to seek God; decide to listen to Him; decide to follow His plan for your life. You may find some traffic in life. You may have a slow down. But you will be better by taking God's route, because the detours can be unpleasant.

2 October When I am in a crowd and my husband speaks, I can pick him out. I know his voice and I can locate him amidst the clamor of the people. It's easy to sort through because I know him so well, we've spent time together. Years together! So, it stands to reason that if you spend time with God you will know His voice when He's trying to get through.

There is a young woman at our church that sings this song in our worship set and she really conveys the passion of the lyrics. The song today is "I'm not Ashamed" ~ Ricardo Sanchez. This song declares that I am going to worship Jesus like nothing else matters, because I'm not ashamed of His name. Think this morning...When you worship, are you thinking about who is watching, how you're feeling, what is next, or other things of life? Or are you really focused on Jesus like nothing else matters? The noise of your life and in this world starts to drown out the message that He wants to get to you today. But you must draw your attention toward Him and listen to His voice. John 10:27 says, "My sheep hear My voice, and I know them, and they follow Me." And John 10:5 says about the 'sheep' (which are believers), "Yet they will by no means follow a stranger, but will flee from him, for they do not know the voice of strangers." It matters who you are following today. It matters what draws your attention. Pure focus, concentration, dedication in worship will set you up to hear the Lord. Don't be ashamed to engage. Seek Him, He's there in all the noise, in all the crowd - Speaking to you.

3 October Have you ever had a phone call or message un-answered, or an invitation to which no one responded? I have. Sometimes I send it out and hear nothing. I begin to wonder. Did their phone not work? Is my mail lost in the post office or message out in cyberspace? When you are expecting something and hear nothing, the silence can be deafening. Then just when I think that maybe I am the only one left on earth, I get a reply. I celebrate! Sometimes it's the little things in life that are exciting.

Today's song is "God's Not Dead" ~ Newsboys. This song reminds me that my God is not dead. He's definitely alive, living on the inside of me. Sometimes you may feel like you're not hearing from God. He seems silent in your life. You wonder. "Did He hear me? Is He out there? Will He speak to me today?" Psalm 18:6 says, "In my distress I called upon the LORD, and cried out to my God; He heard my voice from His temple, and my cry came before Him, *even* to His ears." God hears you today. Whatever your situation, when you call, it reaches Him. But, when you don't think you have an answer, rest assured it's on its way. Realize that He is not dead and you need to be still and know that He is God. Psalm 46:10 says, "Be still, and know that I *am* God; I will be exalted among the nations, I will be exalted in the earth!" Just stop and listen. Be quiet. He will reply in His time. His answer will lead you and direct you to the destiny He has created you for. Then celebrate! God's got some great things in store for you!

4 October A while back, I had a health issue that concerned me to the point I thought I might die. As it turned out, I am fine. But, I have to tell you, going through that really changed my perspective. Suddenly some things became more important and others not so important. I evaluated my life. What I have been doing, what time have I wasted and what I have been taking for granted.

Today's song is, "Good to be Alive" ~ Jason Gray. This song says that I want to live like there's no tomorrow and love like I'm on borrowed time. It's really good to be alive. James 4:14 says, "Whereas you do not know what will happen tomorrow. For what is your life? It is even a vapor that appears for a little time and then vanishes away." We can't take our days for granted. When we do, the result could be procrastination, carelessness, recklessness, apathy, or complacency. What have you been putting off today that you really should pursue? In what areas of your life have you spent wasted time? Who have you ignored? Have you neglected your health or the people you love? Have you continued destructive habits? Have you passed up opportunities? Today, reflect and decide to live like you are on borrowed time. Remember to be thankful for each day, because it's a gift.

5 October It was a cool, stormy morning here and staying in bed sure sounded good. Yet, the song on my heart compelled me to be about something more than myself. Some days it's easy to be selfish. I think, "What about ME?" I want my right to feel and do as I please. It sounds so reasonable. Unfortunately, it can be destructive. My pastor reminded me that when I have a need, I should plant a seed. Meaning that when I get out of myself, give myself away, God can use me to help and enrich someone else's life and in turn, God will help me, enrich my life.

Today's song is "I Give Myself Away" ~ William McDowell. This song talks about giving myself away so God can use me. Jonah, in the belly of the whale saw a turnaround to his situation when he began to praise God. He got out of himself and then got out of the whale! Jonah 2:9-10 (MSG) says, "But I'm worshiping you, God, calling out in thanksgiving! And I'll do what I promised I'd do! Salvation belongs to God! Then God spoke to the fish, and it vomited up Jonah on the seashore." He changed his perspective, his focus, and his attitude. It was no longer all about him. One of my mentors gave an illustration: Imagine a spotlight over your head. When you are focused on yourself, the spotlight is on you. When you focus on others, the spotlight is on them. With light in your face it's hard to see. With light on others, your path is also lit. Romans 12:3 says, "For I say, through the grace given to me, to everyone who is among you, not to think *of himself* more highly than he ought to think, but to think soberly, as God has dealt to each one a measure of faith." It's not all about you. It's about the lives you can touch, impact, change by your focus on them and what God has for them while working through you. Philippians 2:13 says, "for it is God who works in you both to will and to do for *His* good pleasure." He is working in you. He is working through you. So today, give yourself away, so God can use you. Seek to be a blessing and you will be blessed.

6 October A few years ago we gave away one of our kittens to some friends. When it was taken from their yard by a neighbor (accidentally) I felt like it had been taken from me and I wanted justice! Well, I needed to let go. I had given the kitten away. It wasn't mine any more. Eventually, realizing their mistake, the people (who lived out of state) made amends the following year with an offspring from the one which was taken. So it was a happy ending.

Today's song, I'm Forgiven ~ Sanctus Real. The song says, I'm forgiven. I don't have to carry the weight of who I've been. Have you ever heard someone say, "God will forgive you, but you have to forgive yourself."? When you do or say the wrong thing because of selfish or wrong motives, seeking God, asking forgiveness and letting go are all important to getting on with your life. Sometimes that "letting go" part is tough. Philippians 3:13 says, "Brethren, I do not count myself to have apprehended; but one thing *I do,* forgetting those things which are behind and reaching forward to those things which are ahead," You must be a forward thinker if you are going to grow. Even the plants reach for the sunshine. There is a time to lay down the hurts of the past, any regrets, or errors and reach for God. When you give things to God, whether it's your mistakes or your concerns, even your dreams, you need to let go of them. God has much more capable hands and He knows just what to do with them.

Today, if you are feeling you still need to own your past and continue toting it around, realize that it's time to stop carrying the weight of the guilt and let go. You deserve more; you deserve all God has for you, so stop rehearsing it, and nursing it. You're forgiven. Step on to the next thing, so you can have your own happy ending.

7 October I was talking to a friend and we were sharing what God had been showing us. One thing that's very important to me right now is to be aware, pay attention to the things and the people in my life. The things I have been missing. Time is wasted, opportunities pass and I didn't see them because I just wasn't looking.

Today's song "Give Me Your Eyes" ~ Brandon Heath. This song asks God to give me His eyes to see everything that I keep missing. Sometimes you may just bump along from day to day. You deal with things when they happen. You are too busy putting out 'fires' because you failed to make plans or create strategies to deal with life situations. It's an easy way to get overwhelmed. When you are looking at only what is in front of you, you will miss so much of what is going on around you. Your personal perspective makes things look big. Look outrageous. Look impossible. You can also feel very alone. You may have no idea of how things will work out. It's like doing a maze in a puzzle book. At first it may look confusing. Impossible. Too hard. But check out the end and mentally work your way back to where you start. You know you can do it. Just go forward. The walls aren't so permanent. The times when you feel lost are minimal because you know it will turn out well. Why? You got the big picture. Psalm 139:1-5 (MSG) says, "GOD, investigate my life; get all the facts firsthand. I'm an open book to you; even from a distance, you know what I'm thinking. You know when I leave and when I get back; I'm never out of your sight. You know everything I'm going to say before I start the first sentence. I look behind me and you're there, then up ahead and you're there, too— your reassuring presence, coming and going." God knows you and everything around you. He can figure things out for you. Pray that God will give you His eyes today to be aware and to gain His perspective. The problems aren't as big when you have a higher view. The tasks aren't as impossible when you can see through His eyes. It really is all how you look at it.

8 October After waking at 4 am, I heard this song in my heart and I thought, "It's the same song as one last week, I am sure there is a different one." So I eventually drifted back to sleep thinking that when I woke up, it would be a new song. No, just after 7am – The same song. Here's what I'm hearing today... I Give Myself Away ~ William McDowell. This song says that I give myself away so God can use me.

Parents, especially moms (I think because I am one) give their lives away when they have children. There is a self sacrifice involved to manage family, career, and personal growth. I heard the definition of a mom once: A mom is someone who when there are five people and four pieces of cake says, "That's okay, I didn't want any cake today." As a mom, I give out of love. It's not a bad thing. Giving yourself away can enrich the lives of others and in turn also enriches you. I don't feel less because I am a parent. I feel more.

Giving of yourself involves trust. Remember this scripture, "Trust in the Lord with all your heart, don't lean on your own understanding. In all your ways acknowledge Him and He will direct your path." (Proverbs 3:5-6) Trusting God, trusting that it's worth it, trusting that good will come out of each situation, trusting that you will be better for your giving is what God needs. When you trust, you are putting yourself in His hands and you are safe. One of the many things I trust my husband is his ability to drive. When I am riding with him I trust that we will be safe even in severe weather. I don't want to grab the wheel or tell him how to drive (most times) I trust him. Just so - Trust God. Don't grab the wheel or tell him how to drive. He knows the path, He will direct. Walk in it today. Trust and give. You will be better for it.

9 October We went on vacation one summer and saw a show at the outdoor mall with fire and water. The production was amazing with great bursts of flames and numerous spouts of water. It was like a fountain on steroids! It was totally over and above what we expected to see. All of it was choreographed with music and lights. Spectacular!

Today's song, "All My Fountains Are In You" ~ Chris Tomlin. This song asks of God to open the heavens and come as Living Water. All my fountains are in God. The song is based on Psalm 87:7. The fountains refer to the water coming forth from the ground as an oasis in the dry land and streams that never will run dry. You may be in a in a desert place today, but push forward to the sound of the rushing stream, a fountain which is the Lord. The refreshing that comes with the water is wonderful. Like a cold drink from the garden hose on a really hot day - only multiple times better! When your fountains are in Him, God is your re-freshing. He's your oasis in a dry land. There will be a continuous flow there. Your part is to keep pressing on to the water even if things are rough, dry, or hard. Finding that fountain of His love, His Word, and His presence is life-giving. Ephesians 3:20 says, "Now to Him who is able to do exceedingly abundantly above all that we ask or think, according to the power that works in us." When you seek God for your oasis, He responds with an amazing production of grace, favor, and miracles! What God can do in your life will be totally over and above what you expect.

10 October I think this song must be a reminder for me to be prepared for people to let me down sometimes. That they may talk bad about me or lie or do something completely inappropriate, deceitful, or downright dirty. I need to be ready to forgive them.

Today's song "Feels like I've Been Losin' " ~ Tenth Avenue North. The part of the song that really interested me today asks God to give me grace to forgive people, because I feel like the one losing. No worries for those of you who know me personally. People for the most part are super kind to me. This is one of the times when I really need to share with those of you who are struggling with forgiveness and have been wronged. You have had a chip on your shoulder and you think someone should "Pay". Anger wells up within you. Unforgiveness doesn't hurt the person it's directed to, it hurts the one who chooses to not forgive. Matthew 6:14 (MSG) says, "In prayer there is a connection between what God does and what you do. You can't get forgiveness from God, for instance, without also forgiving others. If you refuse to do your part, you cut yourself off from God's part." It does take grace. God's grace gives you the power to do that which you'd rather not do. You can do it! Take a look at what you haven't forgiven of someone today. Ask God for His grace to forgive and to let go of it. You'll breathe easier, walk lighter, and once again see victory for yourself. And His love through you will change lives.

11 October It's important to take advantage of every day. Not to get through the day, but to get from the day. A day wasted is a day you can't get back. I don't want to spend my days; I want to invest my days!

Today's song "Every Day" ~ Clint Brown. This song declares that every day of my life I will give glory to God. I am thankful today. I woke up feeling pretty good. My family is here, my home is nice, and my opportunities are vast. This is a day of potential. I just have to give God the glory for that. I Thessalonians 5:18 says "In everything give thanks for this is the will of God in Christ Jesus concerning you." Don't thank God for everything, because every thing is not from God. Give thanks IN everything. No matter what happens today, God is still God. He loves you. He wants to see you prosper and succeed. He wants the best for you. Just like parents want the best for their children. However, sometimes they make bad choices. Sometimes they make mistakes. Sometimes bad things happen to them. But that doesn't mean you love them less or want less for them. Your heart may ache when things don't go well for your children. Can you imagine how God feels about you? He loves you so much He gave His only son, to die. Being thankful, appreciating God today is the least you can do. To give Him the glory for the things He has done, but also for just being who He is. You want your family to love and appreciate you for who you are, not just for what you do. Because what happens when you don't come through for them? Will they still love you? The answer should be, "Yes!" Just so, you must still love God even when things don't go your way. When it's not an easy road. He still loves you and face it, you need Him. Give God the glory every day for the rest of your life - it will be the best of your life. It's a great investment.

12 October 3:18 a.m. My husband is quietly snoring beside me in bed. The cat is scratching at our bedroom door and I refuse to get up and let him in. I listen to the rhythm of my husband's breaths. It's calming to me.

Here's the song for today, "God gave me You" ~ Blake Shelton. This song expresses thankfulness that God gave me a person who, in spite of my failures, will be with me in all the seasons of life.

We got back together after our second breakup on Thanksgiving weekend of 1980. We said we weren't going to break up again over something minor. All these years later, we are more in love now than then. Steve is provider, protector, and stabilizer. He is like a buoy in the ocean. Even when he's knocked around by the wind and the waves, he stays strong, in place, anchored. God gave me a wonderful husband. He is a gift. I must remember that. Taking care of that relationship is so important. Ephesians 2:8 says, "For by grace you have been saved through faith, and that not of yourselves; it is the gift of God," His grace is yours. Salvation belongs to you. It is a gift. Your job is to receive it, open it, and use it. Don't leave God over something minor. He is provider, protector, and stabilizer for your life. It's a relationship to not be taken lightly or for granted. God is the anchor for your faith today. You can count on him.

See the relationships in your life as gifts today. You will treat them differently. They are precious. If you don't have the relationships you desire, change something. Yourself. Your surroundings. Your knowledge. Your relationship with God. When you change, things will change for you. So today, cherish your gifts.

13 October Last night I brought one of our cats inside. He was injured and I just wanted to make him comfortable so I held him for awhile. Relaxing in my lap he soon fell asleep. He was safe. I knew he was going to be alright, but I wanted to give him some extra attention.

The song today "Forgiven" ~ Sanctus Real. The part conveying that I'm a treasure in the arms of Christ, because I'm forgiven, speaks to me today. You can rest in the arms of Christ and be safe and know you are valued. Psalms 91:2-7 (MSG) says, "Say this: 'GOD, you're my refuge. I trust in you and I'm safe!' That's right—he rescues you from hidden traps, shields you from deadly hazards. His huge outstretched arms protect you—under them you're perfectly safe; his arms fend off all harm. Fear nothing—not wild wolves in the night, not flying arrows in the day, not disease that prowls through the darkness, not disaster that erupts at high noon. Even though others succumb all around, drop like flies right and left, no harm will even graze you." He is here today with His loving arms to care for you. When you are forgiven, the things of the past need not hinder you or make you feel guilty. You can't dwell on them. It's time to move on. You don't have to fear. You don't have to worry. Rest in His arms today. If you need to seek forgiveness, do so. It's time to move on. God's got great plans for you. Don't be held back by your past mistakes. God forgives and forgets. You don't have to live a life of regrets. This can be your turning point.

14 October 4:30 am. The cat wakes me again this morning. Sigh. Yet, this song washes over me and I drift back to sleep. "I've Found a Love" ~ Ben Cantalon. This song acknowledges that I've found a love greater than life itself, and a stronger hope to which nothing compares. Once I was lost; but now I'm alive in Christ.

Whether you will believe it or not, the world is in a real mess right now. People are worried, out for their own interests, disgruntled, disillusioned, and sad. God has been put on the back burner. Society is plagued by corrupt commerce, greed, division....on and on. It can be upsetting. 2 Timothy 3:1-5 (MSG) says, "Don't be naive. There are difficult times ahead. As the end approaches, people are going to be self-absorbed, money-hungry, self-promoting, stuck-up, profane, contemptuous of parents, crude, coarse, dog-eat-dog, unbending, slanderers, impulsively wild, savage, cynical, treacherous, ruthless, bloated windbags, addicted to lust, and allergic to God. They'll make a show of religion, but behind the scenes they're animals. Stay clear of these people." It may seem hopeless, but it is not. God is a hope that is greater than any trouble of this life. When you have found the love in Christ, you have hope. Hope in the future. It gives you power in the present. You can be strong and alive in Him. The love of God casts out fear. No matter what man can do to you, you can withstand. Even in the "evil" day -when everything seems to be going wrong- you can be grounded, steadfast, and at peace. Hope in Him can be compared to nothing else. It's the best route to take. Seek Him today in the turmoil. You will sense His love and find new hope.

15 October As I watch the dawning of a new day with a breathtaking view of the sun rising, I think of my blessings. Tall trees silhouetted against a gold and blue sky...amazing. Beautiful. I can watch it change. The horizon is getting brighter each moment.

Today's song is "Overcome" ~ Desperation Band. This song includes the statement that we will overcome by the blood of the Lamb and the word of our testimony. This is from Revelation 12:11. The New King James Version in the Bible includes additional words... "And they overcame him by the blood of the Lamb and by the word of their testimony, and they did not love their lives to the death." They overcame him (Satan) in his attempt to destroy the church. Christ Jesus was their victory. They stayed with and upheld the truth of Christ and were not afraid to die for it. There is an attempt these days to crush the people of God. It is by the words of your testimony, sharing the Good News of the Gospel of Jesus Christ that will keep you strong. What is your story of victory today? What has the Lord done for you? Hold fast to that when trials and persecution loom on your horizon. You will overcome. Tell others your story. Share the strength that comes. Remind yourself of your victories, your blessings. Know that you are an overcomer. Proverbs 4:18 says, "The path of the righteous is like the light of dawn, which shines brighter and brighter until full day." Even when things seem darkest, realize that your future in the Lord is bright!

16 October We were blessed to spend a lovely night at a 99 year old mansion. It was once in disrepair. Left for ruins until someone bought it. They restored it and made it even better than it was when it was first built. It's comfortable, gorgeous, and welcoming.

Today's song "I'm Not Who I Was" ~ Brandon Heath. This song echoes of a break up, but I look at it differently. When I look in the mirror I don't see the woman of my youth. I see maturity, seasoning - the effects of the spice of life. Reflecting, I realize there have been so many great things happen so far and I look forward in anticipation of the years to come. More importantly, I am changing on the inside. I am not who I was. When there is renewed faith and awareness of God's presence and hand on your life, He changes you. Being who you were yesterday or last week is not growth. Philippians 3:13-14 says, "I count not myself to have apprehended: but this one thing I do, forgetting those things which are behind, and reaching forth unto those things which are before, I press toward the mark for the prize of the high calling of God in Christ Jesus." When God touches your life, though you may have been left for ruins, He will restore you. He will make you better. The goal should always be continued growth. To be progressively becoming better as a person, stronger, more confident, wiser, and bolder. Resting on your past - who you were, will never propel you into your future. Your destiny has been prepared by God, but it's your decision to walk in it. Time to take a look at your improvement plan today. It should be serving you well. It should include God. It should embrace maturity and seasoning, but also be full of new things, new goals, and new adventures. Just make sure that tomorrow you can say, "I'm not who I was".

17 October In the summer time around where I live, people like to go to 'the lake' on weekends. It's a time for them to get away, launch their boats, sit around, swim, and do lake stuff. Sometimes they are there through Sunday and miss church. Soccer games in this area are also prevalent on Sundays. Sometimes people attend games and miss church. Don't get me wrong, the lake and soccer are great; just don't forget God in the process.

Today's song "You are God Alone" William McDowell. This song reminds me that He is God alone and before time began, He was on the throne. Good times, bad times, always there. Through all the things that are going on in your life, the events, the people, and the distractions - God is reminding you that He is God alone. He is at the front, the top, the beginning, and the most important. You can't put Him at the end of the line today. You need to pay attention to Him, why? Because He is jealous? Yes. He wants to be your one and only God today. Exodus 20:3 (MSG) says, "No other gods, only me."

What you are spending the most time, effort, and attention on is your priority. Essentially, it is your god. You have to take a look and be mindful of your focus. With your priorities right, everything falls into place. With them out of order, everything can fall apart. When you seek Him first, all the other things are added. Matthew 6:33 says, "But seek ye first the kingdom of God, and his righteousness; and all these things shall be added unto you." But it's not about what you want today; it's about whose you are. He should be your God. Him alone.

18 October I am proud of my sons. They have great character; they know how to be good friends and diligent workers. I get excited when they get a "new toy" which right now is a car, bass, camera equipment, and such. They make good decisions. They are responsible. They are so much fun to be around. Even at five years apart in age, they get along well with each other. I try not to gush over them too much. They're guys. It's not always cool. But I'm still "Mom" and I can't help it. I love them so immensely!

Today's song "Amazed" ~ Lincoln Brewster. This song finds God who dances over me while I am unaware. He sings all around, but I never hear the sound of it. This song is from Zephaniah 3:17 in part the Common English Bible says, "He will create calm with His love" What a great bond that you can have with God. That He loves you, calms you with his presence in your life, and He rejoices over you with His singing. The New King James Version says, "The LORD your God in your midst, The Mighty One, will save; He will rejoice over you with gladness, He will quiet *you* with His love, He will rejoice over you with singing." Can you just imagine, God - So proud, dancing over you? So excited when you do something awesome, help some one out, or make a great decision? How cool is that? That is amazing! His love is so great for you; He just can't help but celebrate! You may be unaware of His constant presence today. Be still for a moment, know He is God. He is there. He loves you immensely! Be calmed and smile, His warmth will embrace you and you will know He is dancing over you!

19 October We planted some shrubs in the back yard. They looked quite nice. When our sons came home I wanted them to see what their dad and I had done but, it was dark already. Things don't look quite the same with a small flashlight. From the house, we couldn't see them at all. Were they still there? In the morning as the sun came up, we saw that, yes, they were still there! It will be exciting to see what they look like in the future!

Today's song "You are God Alone" ~ Phillips Craig & Dean. This song again today talks about how in the good times and bad God is on His throne. Whether you can see God or not, He is there. He is on the throne; He has a plan for your life. You may be having a good day or a not so good day. That doesn't change Him. His character, His love for you stays the same. Jeremiah 29:11 says, "I know the plans I have in mind for you, declares the LORD; they are plans for peace, not disaster, to give you a future filled with hope."

You can count on things in your life changing. It's up to you how they change. You can walk in God's plan for you or not. You can recognize His Sovereignty or not. You can be confident in His word or not. It's your choice. If you find yourself getting worried about the future, you can just look to God. Rest in Him. That is where your peace will lie. It's not in others, in a good novel, in a hobby, or sport. It's in Him. God is unchangeable, unshakable, and unstoppable. You need that stability in your life too. The key to a good solid structure is a firm foundation. Without it, the building will lean and fall. Maybe not at first, but over time and great will be its fall. Take a look today, God is there. Through good times and bad, He is there. When things are changing, He is there. When things are not changing, He is there. He is a firm foundation. With Him you can stand. You can be strong. It will be exciting to see what you look like in the future!

20 October I'd like to say that everyday I feel bold, strong, powerful, and successful. The truth is, some days I just don't. This morning I woke up feeling let down. Like I've missed it – especially yesterday. Here's the key though: It was yesterday. Today I have another chance to be who God has called me to be. I have a chance to move in the direction that I am destined to go. I don't have to sit on the regret of yesterday. As I push it aside, the day will dawn and I can look forward, not back.

Today's song "Feels Like I've Been Losing" ~ Tenth Avenue North. Though this is about forgiving others, you need to forgive yourself today for not living up to your potential and making the most of each opportunity. You may feel like you've been losing – But you are not a loser! A rough time or a bad day or a regretful statement does not indicate your whole life's story. It will not always be smooth sailing, but you must use the winds of change to direct your ship. Truly, that is what makes life exciting.

I remember when we went to the ocean in the summer. Though navigating the waves at the beach was sometimes a chore, it was fun. We were challenged to stay afloat and when taken under to pop back up again. The next day when we chose to swim in the pool, it was so boring. Not a wave, nor a challenge. We longed for the ocean again. Long for your ocean waves today. Do not stay on the beach. Do not run away. There is a challenge in the things of life. When you're taken under, pop back up! Take a breath and go again. You are not a loser today. Keep at it, continuing to look forward and soon you will be victorious.

21 October It's a clear, crisp day here and I am looking forward to what the day has in store for me! I look at all God has created in the world around me and it makes me smile. Not too long ago, we spent time with friends at their lake house. What a beautiful setting. The trees were so colorful and the water was amazing. A slight cool breeze was gently blowing and the warmth of the sun was relaxing. Just a couple years ago, that site was a bunch of trees and rocks. Our friends were just going to put a dock and storage shed there, but now there is a lovely house (which they plan to expand) and a porch and a dock and a pavilion and a fire pit and, and, and…. It's a great place!

Today's song "Beautiful Things" ~ Gungor. This song is a reminder that God makes beautiful things out of us. When you think about who you are now, be excited about who you are becoming. You can also take a look back to see what you were. God has been taking a bunch of 'trees and rocks' in you and turning it into something beautiful. There is much yet to come! You are going from simplicity to complexity, from adequate to superb, and from mediocre to outstanding. You know you're not there yet. It's a journey. Pressing forward is the only acceptable direction to go. Stretching and reaching for more of yourself, but most importantly, more of God. It's not how big you are, it's how big He is in you. This is the day to seek more, ask more, knock more and you will have more, do more, and be more. You may feel like you are in an ugly place, but God will make a beautiful thing out of you.

22 October It's another great morning here, kind of a sleepy, relaxing time. For a few minutes at least! When it's time to get up and even the sun isn't up yet, it takes extra effort. But it's a new day. A new day to be alive. A new day to live a blessed life!

Today's song, "My Redeemer Lives" ~ Nicole Mullins. This song declares that I know my Redeemer lives. It is a fact that our Savior, Jesus, died and rose again. He lives! Other "saviors" "prophets" "redeemers" of other various religious groups died and stayed in the grave. But Jesus rose! He wasn't just a leader, He is Savior. He wasn't just a martyr, He was a ransom. He didn't just live His life. He died for us! And God used His arm, His mighty power, to raise Jesus; and the same spirit that raised Christ from the dead dwells in you! Romans 8:11 (MSG) says, "It stands to reason, doesn't it, that if the alive-and-present God who raised Jesus from the dead moves into your life, he'll do the same thing in you that he did in Jesus, bringing you alive to himself? When God lives and breathes in you (and he does, as surely as he did in Jesus), you are delivered from that dead life. With his Spirit living in you, your body will be as alive as Christ's!" Because, if you have accepted the price that Jesus paid for you, He has quickened your mortal body and brought you to life. You now have the ability to live an incredible and blessed life. Remember the difference today that sets Christianity apart in that our Redeemer lives! Your life can be a testimony to what Jesus has done. Walk in His goodness today and don't forget to share it with someone. It's a new day. Live a blessed life.

23 October Last night before I went to sleep I had a searing pain in my foot. There was no apparent cause. The pain and burning sensation was so intense that I could not relax, I could not sleep. I was desperate to do anything to get relief.

Today's song "Like a Fire" ~ Planetshakers. (I couldn't seem to locate the actual version for today's song. Planetshakers does a worship version.) Based on Jeremiah 20:9 in part says that His word is in my heart like a fire, shut up in my bones, and I am weary of holding it in. This song was first an old Gospel tune. It's a powerful, energetic melody. "Like a fire shut up in my bones." The fire of God, His word inside of you must be so intense, so searing that you become desperate to get it out. The indescribable joy, the hope for the future, the sense of victory that comes with knowing an answer to the issues of life – are all ready to be shared. Mark 16:15 says, "And He said to them, "Go into all the world and preach the gospel to every creature." It's your commission to go and tell. When something is big inside of you, you just can't help but let it out. What is big inside of you today? Is it worthy of sharing? Will it change someone's life? Don't relax. Do not sleep. Do what you can to get it out. It's that fire of God, His love, His strength, His joy that permeates your soul. Tell some one your story today. It could change their life.

24 October Stirred awake this morning about 4 am, I heard this song again but, a different part rang clear to me than what was brought to mind on a previous day.

Today's song is, "My Redeemer Lives" ~ Nicole Mullins. This song asks who taught the sun where to stand in the morning and who told the ocean that it can only come so far? The answer is God. He set it all up. There are things in our lives that we set up all the time. We installed a microwave when we built this house. It worked for several years, but then it didn't work anymore. I don't really know what happened. We set it up to work....stuff just happens sometimes. So when God set this whole thing up, the Earth, the Sun, the seas, the sky, the people, the animals, the plants, the rocks....He intended for it to all work. However, stuff happened. People made choices that affected the whole scheme of things. Mistakes were made, sin committed, things were a mess.

So God sent His Son. The next generation. Repairs were made. A price was paid. A chance for things to work again. Now people can choose separation or reconciliation. Essentially it's a life or death deal. You can live within the way it was set up to work or go your own way. Proverbs 14:12-13 (MSG) says, "There's a way of life that looks harmless enough; look again—it leads straight to hell. Sure, those people appear to be having a good time, but all that laughter will end in heartbreak." Yikes. It's a big deal to do your own thing. And it isn't a good thing. Seeking God pays much better dividends. The Message also says in Matthew 6:33, "Steep your life in God-reality, God-initiative, God-provisions. Don't worry about missing out. You'll find all your everyday human concerns will be met." He's there and it's all there for you. Don't panic. Press in. You will have peace and you will see that it will work!

25 October Ever get sick and tired of being sick and tired? Honestly, I really have to get to a point of real discomfort before I am willing to make changes. I guess that's the norm. People say, "If it ain't broke, don't fix it." That is such bad advice. My son reminded me that even if things are good they can always get better. We can always do better, have better, and be better. That attitude of improvement is what we all need.

Today's song, "Good to Be Alive" ~ Jason Gray. This song says that I won't take it for granted or waste another second. All I want is to give God a well lived life and to say "thank you" to Him. How many days have been wasted? How many opportunities missed? How many times will you say, "I wish I would have..."? This is the day to change. This is the day not to waste. This is the day to make it better. To make you better. You are not promised tomorrow and 'Someday' is not a day of the week. What have you been putting off? What circumstances are you waiting for? Sometimes you have to just take a breath and do it. Get the help. Get the knowledge. Get the resources. Get it done. Live your life well and you will have little regret. Besides, it feels great too!

Then, be thankful. Gratitude is an attitude. No one wants to be around grumblers and complainers. Decide now to be constantly thankful. It opens many doors. Especially be thankful to God. I Thessalonians 5:18 says, "In everything give thanks, for this is the will of God in Christ Jesus concerning you." Each day is what you make of it. Make the most of today and be thankful. Make the changes you need to make and don't waste another second.

26 October Life. There is such value in life. The life of an unborn child. The life of an infant. The life of a child. The life of an adolescent. The life of a young adult. The life of an adult. The life of a senior adult. All ages, all situations have value. Honoring life is so vital to our literal existence, but also vital to fully living.

Though the same song has come to me again today, I have found there is more to see in it. "Good to be alive" ~ Jason Gray. Part of this song says that the life that we have been given is made beautiful in the living.

We helped to care for my aging mother-in-law for several years. It was not easy. It was emotionally draining. Many times it was a hassle. But without a doubt, we valued her life. Exodus 20:12 says, "Honor your father and mother so that you'll live a long time in the land that God, your God, is giving you." When I found myself questioning our effort, God reminded me to honor my mother-in-law. That is when things changed. My first effort in honor was to get her a dozen roses. Now bringing roses in from our garden reminds me of her. How much would you miss by whining and complaining about taking care of another person? How selfish are you to dismiss those who you 'have no time for'. Is it inconvenient? Yes. Does it cost something? Yes. Is it hard? Yes. Do we have to make adjustments? Yes. Is it worth it? Yes!

We are all part of a tapestry in this life. Each person, each piece is important. Different sizes, different colors, different backgrounds all add to the complete work that God has created. It is up to each one of us to reach to others. Philippians 2:1-4 (MSG) says "If you've gotten anything at all out of following Christ, if his love has made any difference in your life, if being in a community of the Spirit means anything to you, if you have a heart, if you *care*— then do me a favor: Agree with each other, love each other, be deep-spirited friends. Don't push your way to the front; don't sweet-talk your way to the top. Put yourself aside, and help others get ahead. Don't be obsessed with getting your own advantage. Forget yourselves long enough to lend a helping hand."

27 October The sun isn't quite up yet and the house is fairly quiet. I anticipate a great, productive, fun day. As I write this morning my body is tired, but my mind and spirit active. So, body – Catch up!!

Recently I caught a glimpse of a big dream coming to fruition. I thought, could this really happen? It was so exciting. Yet it was a little terrifying because I didn't feel ready for it. How sad would it be when the opportunity arrives that preparation falls short?

Today's song, "You, You Are God" ~ Walker Beach. This song says to God that I am here, a life You've changed. How many times have you set a goal and believed that you could achieve it and yet here you are with the goal still seemingly out of reach? You charted, you planned, you told others...did all the 'right' things. Here's the problem. You didn't change what you were doing. Mental ascent will not get you thinner. Or richer. Or more successful. Real change in your life has to be real. Making a decision, planning it out, believing it all figures in, but the real test is: What are you doing differently that will take you closer to your goal today?

You may have some big dreams and they may seem so far 'out there' most days. Realizing that each day you could bring yourself closer to them by what you choose to do makes all the difference. Then choose to do. Job 8:7 says, "Although your former state was ordinary, your future will be extraordinary." Let your mind and spirit be active. Today, get ready for your dream. When it arrives you can be excited and snatch the opportunity that is meant to be yours.

28 October I remember when I was a child memorizing 1 Corinthians 13:4-7. Love is patient, Love is kind... It's that list of all the things 'love' is. Many times I have heard it read at weddings. What I missed early on was the first part of that chapter essentially conveying that without that love, nothing else matters.

Today's song, "Don't Have Love" ~ Holly Starr. This song reminds you that you can have money, cool friends, and a ring on your left hand, but it will never be enough if you don't have love. You see the famous, the glamorous, celebrities, moguls, successful entrepreneurs and you find yourself wanting. However, with a closer look, the grass may not always be greener. The stuff of life and having the stuff is not a problem as long as the stuff does not have you. Pursuit of your dream is one thing, but the sacrifice of love for family and friends and especially God in that pursuit is a price too high paid. 1 Timothy 6:17-19 (MSG) says, "Tell those rich in this world's wealth to quit being so full of themselves and so obsessed with money, which is here today and gone tomorrow. Tell them to go after God, who piles on all the riches we could ever manage—to do good, to be rich in helping others, to be extravagantly generous. If they do that, they'll build a treasury that will last, gaining life that is truly life." Right priorities and perspective are keys to a full, successful life versus empty success of merely material goods. Check the root of your pursuit today. Success will never be enough if you don't have love.

29 October There's some frost on the ground this morning. A cool nip in the air. My husband calls this "Snuggle Weather". Yep, he's a romantic. I just love that feeling of curling up on the couch together with a warm drink and a fire in the fireplace, holding hands, and snuggling. It's that safe comfort. It's calm and peaceful.

One month ago this song came to my heart just as today. "One Thing Remains" ~ Jesus Culture. It reminds me that God's love never fails. It overwhelms and satisfies my soul. I'll never have to be afraid. There are many things going on in the world. In the realm of finances, energy, weather, society, leadership, environment, technology-things are changing rapidly. Some are good changes; some are not so good changes. The climate and the anticipation of the future can be nerve wracking because of the element of mystery involved. It can be scary. It can be really scary if you don't know God. His love. His care. Even when you fail, His love never fails. You don't earn His love. He loves you. Period. You don't have to be afraid. You can have an overwhelming satisfaction knowing that love. It's that warm, fuzzy feeling. Joshua 1:9 (CEB) says, "Don't be alarmed or terrified, because the Lord your God is with you wherever you go." No matter what happens, you can be sure that He loves you. You can hold His hand today and you do not have to be afraid.

30 October I was awake for awhile last night, thinking of some little things. They were starting to unnerve me. They were the 'what-if' things. Some things I could fix, others not. None of it worth losing sleep. Getting caught up in the minors steals me from what I can do that's major. I can become "me" focused. Whether I'm spending energy in self-praise or regret, it stalls my progress from what really matters most.

Today's song, "This is the Stuff" ~ Francesca Battistelli. This song starts in frustration and then changes to realization that in the middle of my little mess sometimes I forget how big I'm blessed. There are so many areas in which you are blessed today. You need to remember that. Sometimes it could be hard for you because you want everything to be right. If it's less than the best situation you think you have failed some how. Does God still want you then? Yes. Can God still use you then? Yes. Seeing what is right and good help you get through the dumb stuff of life. Romans 11:29 says,"For the gifts and the calling of God are irrevocable." He's not going to take it back. He has called you specifically to what He has planned. Don't discount it. Don't get distracted. Don't pout. Don't fuss. Keep the majors major and the minors minor. Know your priorities. Matthew 6:32-33 (MSG) says, "What I'm trying to do here is to get you to relax, to not be so preoccupied with *getting,* so you can respond to God's *giving.* People who don't know God and the way he works fuss over these things, but you know both God and how he works. Steep your life in God-reality, God-initiative, God-provisions. Don't worry about missing out. You'll find all your everyday human concerns will be met." God wants to take care of you, but you need to put Him first. Today, in all the stuff of life, remember to look and see that you are blessed!

31 October I was thinking about my mom today. She passed away several years ago. Before she died I got to pray with her and she renewed her relationship with Christ. It is my belief that because of that decision she was pleasant in her last months and fairly happy. (Something that is often uncommon with dementia patients). One of her favorite scriptures was, "I will lift up mine eyes unto the hills, from whence cometh my help. My help cometh from the LORD, which made heaven and earth." Psalm 121:1-2 (KJV)

Today's song is, "Oh Praise Him" ~ David Crowder Band. In this song, it says to turn your gaze toward Heaven and raise a joyous noise. The sound of salvation comes with the sound of those rescued. It's so easy to look at all the things going on around you, shrug your shoulders and say, "Whatever". It can be overwhelming at times. It can be disheartening. It can be confusing and it can be depressing. Why? Because you are looking at people. People can be a resource, but people should not be your source. Luke 21:28 (KJV) Says, "And when these things begin to come to pass, then look up, and lift up your heads; for your redemption draweth nigh."And in The Message it says, "When all this starts to happen, up on your feet. Stand tall with your heads high. Help is on the way!" Hope for rescue gives you strength to endure. Be confident that help really is on the way today. You may not anticipate the package in which it arrives, but nevertheless it shall arrive in due time.

1 November I wouldn't say that I am a huge sports fan. If my sons are interested, then usually I am too. If they are on the team then definitely, Mom is a huge fan! Generally though, I am not the go-to person for the game or player stats. However, if our team is in the finals or play-offs, that is when I will watch and cheer. Really, isn't everybody a big fan when their team is winning? It's an emotional surge. People become passionate about what they normally don't even give a second thought.

Today's song, "Feels like I've Been Losing" ~ Tenth Avenue North. This song points out that there is love and there is hate. We all have a choice that we will make. Emotions are running high right now. There is a lot happening. People are becoming passionate. There is an excitement in the air. Opinions. Feelings. Intensity. In the midst of all, how do you respond? Feel like you have to choose a side? You do, but it's not the side you think is a choice. Joshua 24:15 (MSG) says, "If you decide that it's a bad thing to worship God, then choose a god you'd rather serve—and do it today... As for me and my family, we'll worship God." That's the choice you make. Sometimes things just make you feel yucky, bad, distressed, and dark. Staying with that situation is not the choice. God is light and in Him there is no darkness at all. God is the right choice. It's life vs. death. Tired of the bickering? Choose God. Finished with the fighting? Choose God. Done with discouragement? Choose God. Choose. Choose. Choose. Jesus is the Way, the Truth, and the Light – That's how you get to God. Think you are there? Know you are there? How is that playing out in your life? Do others know your choice? Do others know you serve God? I've heard in church while my pastor was teaching, someone said, "Make it plain!" That's how we need to be with our choice. Make it plain to others so they too will see how great a choice that is. It means life vs. death to them. Stand and be counted among the faithful. The rewards are great. People will be drawn. You will make a difference. That's really why we are here.

2 November I think the season change I enjoy the most is the one from summer to fall. There are so many colors on the trees. It's the time of the year I got engaged to my sweetheart. It's the anticipation of the winter, always followed by the sweet breath of spring. It's the cycle of change.

Today's song. "Whatever You're Doing (Something Heavenly)" ~ Sanctus Real. I feel like this whole song is me today. Specifically, that whatever God is doing inside of me feels like chaos but I believe He's up to something that's bigger than me. A lot can be changing in your life. With an attitude of improvement, there are a lot of areas where you need to grow. The more you grow, the more you want to grow. It's inertia. Get in motion and remain in motion. But with the exhilaration of growth there is the overwhelming feeling of trying to keep up with yourself and what God is doing in you. It feels like chaos sometimes.

My son is a juggler. When I look at all the clubs he throws flying around, I think, "How does he keep track of all those?" Then I remember there is a pattern to what he's doing. He didn't immediately get it all going from the first day he picked them up. It took practice. Sometimes he drops them. Sometimes he gets tired. Sometimes he tries new things. Sometimes it just seems crazy. But, a lot of times it's simply amazing! It's an accomplishment that can make him feel proud. If the changes in your life are like those clubs, you need to find the pattern, practice, try new things, and realize that even when things seem crazy, there's a lot of 'Simply Amazing' in your life that can make you feel proud.

Don't be afraid of change today. It may be uncomfortable; you may not master it at first. Give yourself a chance. Isaiah 43:18-19 (MSG) says, "Forget about what's happened; don't keep going over old history. Be alert, be present. I'm about to do something brand-new. It's bursting out! Don't you see it?" Get excited. The season is changing!

3 November There was a young man several years ago that was selling for a fund raiser. Going door-to-door, he would meet the residents on the porch by holding out the order form at arm's length and then stare at them without uttering a word. He may have been shy or afraid, or both. I believe he received some 'sympathy' sales, but his technique did not reap much in selling.

Today's song, "Top of my Lungs" ~ Phillips, Craig & Dean. This song announces that at the top of my lungs I sing Hallelujah! I'm not ashamed to praise God's name. 2 Timothy 1:7 (CEB) says, "God didn't give us a spirit that is timid but one that is powerful, loving, and self-controlled." People will not be won to the Kingdom of God by timidity. Being kind, patient, gentle, and loving are all parts of the 'fruit of the Spirit' described in Galatians 5:22, true. However, we are also instructed to be strong and courageous, knowing that God is with us always. (Joshua 1:9) You can pray for wisdom, confidence, boldness, power, and strength. Weakness is not a part of it. Standing up for what you know is right makes a difference in the lives of others. Some one said that if you don't stand for something, you will fall for anything. Know what you believe today and be ready to share it. Who will benefit by your silence on the matter? Do not be ashamed of what you have to say in regard to God, His promises, His blessings, His redemption, His soon return. Be moved with compassion in regard to the people you meet and do not let intimidation stop you. Holding them at arm's length and staring will not reap much. You have life to share. Share it.

4 November When I was in elementary school there was always great anticipation for the best part of the day...Recess! Waiting for the teacher's signal at the ringing of the bell, we would walk through the door in an orderly fashion then tear out running in reckless abandon. We would laugh and yell and run and play. Chasing, tagging, hopping, jumping, hanging, swinging, spinning, twirling. What fun! Then we would return to class to learn some more. I really liked school. I liked learning. I liked hanging out with my friends. I liked working hard and getting good grades. And I liked recess.

Today's song, "Good to Be Alive" ~ Jason Gray. The song says, that I want to live like there's no tomorrow, not taking it for granted or wasting another second. Sometimes when you think about "living like there's no tomorrow", you can remember the personal growth class question, "What would you do if you knew this was your last day on earth?" You may be thinking...Have fun, be with people I love, enjoy each moment. Work isn't on that list. Here's the thing, though. You can't spend everyday just playing around. Your time can be wasted, spent, or invested in the activities you choose to do. 2 Thessalonians 3:10b-13a (MSG) says, " 'If you don't work, you don't eat.' And now we're getting reports that a bunch of lazy good-for-nothings are taking advantage of you. This must not be tolerated. We command them to get to work immediately—no excuses, no arguments—and earn their own keep..." Yes, that is the Bible there. Working is profitable and necessary. Working definitely has benefits. However, you can't be so work focused that you don't enjoy life. There's a phrase you may have heard, "All work and no play makes Jack a dull boy." Think about it, what if school didn't have recess? Boo! But, all play and no work would make Jack a dope. The work and the play have to be balanced. Working and accomplishing a goal gives you a sense of well being and self satisfaction. Remembering to take a break, have fun, laugh or play now and again helps to keep you balanced and reduces that stress in your life. Take a look at the balance in your life today. How's that working for you? Good? Then keep going. Not so good? Change something immediately. Make each day count for something. No taking it for granted. No wasting allowed.

5 November Do you ever hear a song and it takes you back to a place in your life? I've had that happen. It transports me right to that moment. I can practically see, smell, and hear the people and the place, but mostly how I felt at the time. It can be emotionally overwhelming. There are a few worship songs that have that kind of effect on me. They immediately bring me back to a place right in front of God. They cause me to weep. They cause me to focus. The stuff of life fades and there we are, just God and me. Today's song is one of those songs.

"Speechless" ~ Israel & New Breed. This song talks about God's grace and how I need it and I receive it. I'm so amazed that when I see it, I am speechless...He takes my breath away. We sang this song in church recently and I could just feel it start from the inside of me and come to the surface. It was my utter dependency on God. I sang it with all my heart. It made me ache for God. I cried. It took my breath away. He took my breath away. Those amazing moments can draw you right into the presence of God. He breathes life into you and you are nothing without Him. Without grace, where would you be? Nowhere. Humility will overwhelm you. With you as nothing and Him as everything, you know you can accomplish anything. That unmerited grace, and favor in your life helps you to achieve more than you ever dreamed. Time to tap into that today. Lay aside the stuff that overwhelms you and let God overwhelm you today. The stuff, it will leave you spent. But, God will leave you revived.

6 November Years ago when my oldest son was only about two years old we took a cave tour. There was a 200 step open staircase that spiraled down to the cave floor. I carried my son. I held him tight and told him not to wiggle. He wrapped his arms around my neck and we made it down all 200 steps. We were safe and had a great time. My son trusted me because I am his mom. Our relationship made all the difference.

When I got up extra early this morning, I anticipated a day of excitement, but my spirit was so peaceful. Today's song, "I Worship You, Almighty God" ~ Don Moen. This song focuses on worshipping God Almighty. There is none like Him. He is the Prince of Peace. I want to give Him praise, He is my righteousness. When you set aside time to praise God and worship Him, you get closer to Him. You feel safe and secure. You trust Him. You trust Him like my son trusted me. Psalm 91:1-2 says, "He that dwells in the secret place of the most High shall abide under the shadow of the Almighty. I will say of the Lord, He is my refuge and my fortress: my God; in him will I trust." Today, realize that you have to dedicate yourself to God. Keep your eyes on Him. People will let you down. People are crazy sometimes. People choose foolishly. People can be hateful, vengeful, selfish, and stupid. But, you must love them anyway. It's God that girds you with strength today. Put your trust in Him. Daniel 3:17-18 (MSG) says, "If we are thrown into the blazing furnace, the God whom we serve is able to save us. He will rescue us from your power, Your Majesty. But even if he doesn't, we want to make it clear to you, Your Majesty that we will never serve your gods or worship the gold statue you have set up." The furnace was not God's will for the men; it was the actions of the King that brought them there. The will of God was to deliver them. Their resolve was to serve God no matter the outcome. That is what's right to do. When you are in the furnace, realize that it is not God who put you there, but God wants to deliver you. He's your peace today, your righteousness, your refuge. Stay in His arms. Do not struggle. Hold on tight. Times can be great. Your relationship with Him makes all the difference.

7 November When I was a teen, I had a couple friends that were fun to be around and I felt great when I was with them. Well, it was great for awhile. They weren't exactly a good influence on me and before long I was drawn off my moral compass and was no longer "myself". Thankfully I had another insightful friend that took time with me to help me see what my life was becoming by being associated with them. When I finally walked away from those relationships, my life became realigned and I got back on track. I shudder to think what my life would be today if I would have continued my relationship with them.

Today's song, "We are Never Ever Getting Back Together" ~ Taylor Swift. Frankly, this song surprised me today. However, I am learning not to fight with the song that comes to me. I knew God had some thing to show me. This is a pop music 'break up' song where she tells him that they are never, ever getting back together in a relationship.

We were in youth ministry for about 13 years. Time and time again we saw young people influenced by their friends. You could tell what path they were on by the friends they kept. 1 Corinthians 15:33 says, "Do not be deceived: 'Evil company corrupts good habits.'" In other words, you become like who you hang around. This works for adults too. If the friendships you have today are taking you where you don't want to be, or not taking you to a place you want to be, you need some new friends. Take a look at your friends today. Are they taking you up or bringing you down? You will be most like the five closest friends you have. If that is the picture in your dreams and it aligns with your goals then that's fantastic. But if it does not, it may be time to take a serious look. It may be time to break it off. Making new friends can open up a whole new world of possibilities. Jeremiah 29:11 says, "I know the plans I have in mind for you, declares the Lord; they are plans for peace, not disaster, to give you a future filled with hope." His plan will include the right friends for you.

8 November For Mother's Day I wanted to go see "The Avengers" It's a superhero movie with Iron Man, Captain America, Hulk, Thor, Black Widow, and Hawkeye. It's a hybrid of adventure and humor. Just what any mom might want to go see on her special day. It's a far cry from the traditional flowers and brunch. But that's me. I'd have to say that Iron Man is my favorite. However, the unleashed power of the Hulk is quite amazing. It is something he can choose to control, but when the transformation comes, he is unstoppable!

Today's song, "Redeemed" ~ Big Daddy Weave. This song proclaims that I am redeemed because Jesus set me free. Now I can shake off the heavy chains and wipe away all of the stains. I'm not who I used to be before I gave my life to Christ. Wrapped up in the chains of the cares of this world can leave a person helpless, hopeless, and defeated. You get busy with work, society, media, trends, information, and technology. They can all envelope you in a web of chaos, confusion, restriction, fear, or limitations. You may struggle, strain, and strive in vain to break loose. Weeping is futile. But God. God can make the difference. How? When you decide to praise Him. Praise Him in spite of your circumstances. Praise Him in spite of the world situation. Praise Him. Acts 16:25-26 says, "But at midnight Paul and Silas were praying and singing hymns to God, and the prisoners were listening to them. Suddenly there was a great earthquake, so that the foundations of the prison were shaken; and immediately all the doors were opened and everyone's chains were loosed." Paul and Silas were imprisoned. They were in chains. It was a hopeless situation. Then in the midnight hour, their darkest moments, they chose to praise! Then the power came! The chains came off! They were redeemed! God set them free! Like the Hulk, they became unstoppable! The jailer was saved and all of his family too! That was just the beginning! What can happen in your life today when you begin to praise God? Praise Him for who He is and for what He's done. Chains will fall, doors will open, and the potential is there to live abundantly! Don't be who you used to be. Be the new you. Renewed, redeemed, and unstoppable!

9 November On occasion, we will purchase an item and bring it home or have it delivered. The box says, "Some assembly required". So the fun begins! My husband is a detail oriented, methodical, read-all-the-instructions type guy. I like to look at the pictures (often captioned in a foreign language) and try to figure it out. Working on these projects can be mutually frustrating. In our years we have assembled then re-assembled when we discovered something backwards or in the wrong place. We have called in reinforcements, our sons. We have thought about hiring professionals. But, in the end, we almost always end up with something lovely and functional. More importantly, our relationship with each other remains intact.

Today's song, "Speechless" ~ Israel & New Breed. This song speaks of God's grace. I need it and I receive it. I'm so amazed that, when I see it I am speechless." You need God's grace today to do the things He has called you to do. You really can't do it on your own. Sometimes it's hard to admit you need help. But you can ask. You have resources available to you for the asking. Reinforcements! Psalm 118:5 says, "I called on the LORD in distress; The LORD answered me and set me in a broad place." Then, Psalm 138:3, "In the day when I cried out, You answered me, And made me bold with strength in my soul." God does hear, but not only hear, He answers! He will set you in a large place, a place of abundance, a place where there is more than what you have now. That is His grace. His unmerited favor. It's the thing He will do for someone who loves Him. How many times have you done something for your family just because they have shown love for you? Lots. There is a relationship there. It should be your desire to give to them. So it is with God. With that relationship comes benefits. It's not a time to give God your shopping list, it's time to build a relationship and His grace can overwhelm you in it. Tap into His grace today. You need it. He will give you the boldness and strength to accomplish all He has planned for your life.

10 November When I was very, very young my mom brought home something called S & H Green Stamps. They were little stamps that the grocery store gave you when you bought your groceries. Some days she purchased my favorite treat, but I had more fun when she let me put the stamps into the little book for her. My mom selected her prize and found out how many stamps we needed. Once we got enough books filled, we could trade them for something! I remember the feeling of collecting all those stamps and the excitement of getting to redeem them! We found some of those old books when we went through her belongings after she passed away. I wonder what else we could have traded them for.

Today's song, "Redeemed" ~ Big Daddy Weave. This song says that I am redeemed. 1 Peter 1:18 (ERV) says, "You know that in the past the way you were living was useless. It was a way of life you learned from those who lived before you. But you were saved from that way of living. You were bought, but not with things that ruin like gold or silver." When mankind fell away from God, got separated by their disobedience, it must have been heartbreaking. But God had a plan. How excited God must have been to have a plan to redeem us! God traded Jesus Christ's spotless life for your damaged, sinful one. It was a prize like no other, but it was also a sacrifice like no other. His son. Died for you. Rose again. Ascended into Heaven. Now sits at the right hand of God. The prize for you – eternal life. For God and you – restored relationship. When you surrender your life to Him, your life will change. Best trade you'll ever make. Here's the thing, if you don't make the trade, you don't get the prize. Whatever in your life is damaged today, make the trade. Whatever has been wounded, make the trade. Whatever has been lost, make the trade. Whatever has been taken, make the trade. Pack up all that stuff that has kept you from your best self and your best life and make the trade. Don't leave the "book of stamps" in the drawer unredeemed. Be redeemed today. Just ask God. He already arranged for your prize, but you have to make the trade. Your life will never be the same.

11 November Zombie Apocalypse. I am relatively certain that it will not happen. Sometimes you get to wondering…is there a chance? It's so silly. But wait, could it happen? No. I have heard that 99% of the things you worry about never happen. You may be thinking, "yes, but there's still a 1% chance!!" Now that's a pessimist!

Today's song, "Good to be Alive" ~ Jason Gray. This song says that I want to live and love, like I'm on borrowed time. Luke 12:25 (ERV) says, "None of you can add any time to your life by worrying about it." Worry does not add to your life. If anything, it takes away. Worry will cost you. It will cost you sleep, relationships, opportunities, confidence, and income. With a very creative mind, you can spin a scenario in detail via worry. More times than not, it never happens that way. Remember getting sent to the principal's office? The class responds in a sing-song, "You're in trouble!" The hall was long, everyone was watching. You could feel it…Doom! That happened to my husband. He reluctantly made his way to the office in grade school. It so happened that he was 'Citizen of the Week'! Granted, it doesn't always work out that way, but worrying does not help.

When your faith rises, worry fades. You can be strengthened. Philippians 4:6 (MSG) says, "Don't fret or worry. Instead of worrying, pray. Let petitions and praises shape your worries into prayers, letting God know your concerns. Before you know it, a sense of God's wholeness, everything coming together for good, will come and settle you down. It's wonderful what happens when Christ displaces worry at the center of your life." What a great way to deal with the worry that comes your way! Pray! Your life will be longer, your sleep will be sweeter, your relationships will be stronger, your confidence will be bolder, and your income will be greater! Then you can kill any zombie that comes your way!

12 November I caught myself standing in front of the microwave oven the other day, waiting for my lunch to heat. Faster, faster! The longest two minutes ever! I really love to cook. Microwaving is helpful, but serves as a shortcut to skillful preparation and the wonderful marrying of ingredients in a slow cook on the stove top. I can almost smell the aroma…the reward of waiting.

So many times you don't want to wait. Don't want to wait in line. Don't want to wait for help. Don't want to wait for much of anything. The virtue of patience runs shallow. You don't want to be inconvenienced. You don't want to give things up. You don't want to sacrifice. You don't want to be uncomfortable. John 15:13 (AMP) says, "No one has greater love [no one has shown stronger affection] than to lay down (give up) his own life for his friends." There is a love that is shown in giving. In letting yourself be uncomfortable for the benefit of others.

Today's song, "How Many Kings" ~ Downhere. This song asks about how many kings step down from their thrones or abandoned their homes? How many great ones have become the least for me? How many gods have poured out their hearts to romance a world that has been torn apart? How many fathers gave up their sons for me? And it answers that only one did that for me. When you look at the extreme sacrifice God made to send His only Son to die for you, you can be humbled. He took the step; He paid the price because He loved you. The original translation of "love" in John 3:16 is "mega-love". That's a lot of love. Here you are to show your appreciation. So today be more thankful, more patient, more giving, more a servant, more uncomfortable for the benefit of others. Strengthen your relationship with God, knowing that He loved you first, before you even knew Him. You should thank Him. You should honor Him.

One more thing. Many in this country have made sacrifices for our freedom. You never want to take that for granted. Pray that you would seek selflessness in a selfish society. Find friends that fought for our freedom. Thank them. Honor them.

13 November I used to hate my name when I was young. It was unusual. People thought they were clever with star references and puns. When I heard the song "Twinkle, Twinkle Little Star" for the billionth time, I thought I would scream. Now that I am grown, I really like my name. It's unique. It makes me memorable. When someone says my name, I know they are talking to me and not another person in the room. They get my attention. No confusion there. Most times there's just one "Starr". My name reflects my outgoing personality. My friends would say that it fits me.

Today's song, "Your Great Name" ~ Natalie Grant. This song reassures that fear has no place at the sound of His great name. The enemy has to leave at the sound of the name of Jesus. There are many names of God. You can do a study on them. There are books written about them. Among them is El Shaddai – The God who is more than enough. Jehovah Jireh – Our Provider. Jehovah Shalom – Our Peace. Jehovah Rapha – Our Healer. God's name tells you about His character. What you call Him is how you see Him today. You can call Him different things in different settings and at different times. When you say His name, He knows you're talking to Him. You get His attention. Psalm 86:7 says, "In the day of my trouble I shall call upon You, For You will answer me." There is power in His name. You can have victory by His name. Your enemies will flee at His name. When you know His name, you know Him. And to know Him is to Love Him. There is no shame in calling out His name. He's a refuge. Help in times of trouble. He's present. Where there is darkness, He is light. Hold on to that when the things of this world get crazy. He is our peace today. We don't have to fear today. His Name is great.

14 November When I got home from a business meeting and all my errands, I quickly changed from heels to slippers and coat to sweat jacket. Yes, much more comfortable! I like dressing for business, but I definitely like dressing for comfort too! I feel content when I am comfortable. I relax. Sometimes I sleep. I take it easy. It can be really nice.

Today's Song, "How Many Kings" ~ Downhere. This song poses a question of how many kings would step down from their thrones. I am very sure that when God's Son stepped down from His throne to arrive on earth in the form of a baby and in a stable no less, He was out of His comfort zone. It was a move made in love for you. It was going above and beyond anything that you deserved. It was an act of humility and greatness all in one. He did it with an end result in mind-reconciliation. Even though being comfortable can be nice, things will only get accomplished when you reach beyond the comfort zone for a greater end in mind. Some one said that your miracle is waiting just outside your comfort zone. How many things would be left undone had you not stepped out? What is left undone now because you have hesitated to step out? God stepped out and rescued you from certain eternal death. He made a way for you to triumph over life's situations, troubles, even curses. That is something for which you should be more than willing to reach! There is a fence around your comfort zone. A hurdle to be vaulted. I Chronicles 4:10 (CEB) says, "Jabez called on Israel's God: 'If only you would greatly bless me and increase my territory. May your power go with me to keep me from trouble, so as not to cause me pain.' And God granted his request." Jabez' territories could not be increased if he did not go out to them. What is interesting about this prayer of Jabez included in Chronicles is that it appears in a long list of genealogy. Among all the names, this is inserted as record of Jabez' entreaty. Because of His desire to get out of his comfort zone, God answered in the affirmative and Jabez stood out among the others in a long list. Jabez is still influencial today. What great examples you have to follow! Jabez and God. Time to step out. Breaching the border of your comfort zone will not only help you, but many others. Some of whom you have not yet met. Stop being content and start reaching for more.

15 November When I am in a new setting I am content to observe. But, when I know the place and the people and find myself responsible to be a leader, perhaps in charge, I most certainly can rise to the occasion. There was a time when I was servicing a wedding of a friend's daughter as a florist. I was helping in what I thought was a minor capacity. At the rehearsal, I was surprised when my friend asked me to coordinate the run-through that night and the wedding the next day. Though there was no phone booth to change in, 'Shy Starr' disappeared and I suddenly became 'Superwoman'! Okay, it wasn't that impressive. However, I got the people in order, worked with our pastor, and we got through all of it beautifully. I was so glad I could help. The best thing was that I had done it before so I could be confident in the task.

Today's song, "Great is the Lord" ~ Michael W. Smith. This song proclaims that the Lord is great and worthy of glory. He is worthy of praise. I will lift up my voice to Him. Honestly, the days of being shy about the Lord are over. It's really time to jump into that phone booth and become the superhero of faith for which so many are searching. You have to realize that you are an example of God's love, faithfulness, and hope for people to see. You need to lift up your voice. How many times have you been in the perfect situation to share the goodness of God and thought, "Wow, they're going to think I am a fanatic or crazy." What? Does that make sense? It's such a bad reason to not share. Psalms 107:2 says, "Let the redeemed of the LORD say so, Whom He has redeemed from the hand of the enemy." What has He brought you through today? What has He done? Time to lift your voice and share, shout even! Great are you, Lord!! As a result, people will be redeemed as well. They will have the courage and strength to endure, and then have victory in their lives. John 12:32 says, "And I, if I am lifted up from the earth, will draw all peoples to Myself." God will draw them. That's His responsibility. Your responsibility is to tell them. Be confident in the task. Don't be shy. You will love the experience!

16 November We built our house in what used to be a bean field. We have a big yard. It would be great to have it all landscaped. Pristine flower beds, shrubs, trees, patios, paths, a trellis...but when I think of accomplishing that beautiful end result, I get overwhelmed. There is the design, the building materials, the plants. Oh, and the funds. It is a veritable mountain of a challenge.

Today's song, "Mighty to Save" ~ Hillsong. This song reminds me that God can move the mountains and He is mighty to save. There are much more vital mountains of circumstances that you face in life every day than the challenges of landscape design. Jobs, family, finances, education, relationships, health. There are, at times, overwhelming situations that will try to paralyze your thinking, your activity, and your faith. Mark 11:23 (CEB) says, "I assure you that whoever says to this mountain, 'Be lifted up and thrown into the sea'—and doesn't waver but believes that what is said will really happen—it will happen." Mountain moving faith does not include doubt. You have to know that God can move that mountain on your behalf. You can be assured of it by knowing Him and by knowing His will for your life. Those answers lie within the scriptures, the Bible. It takes tenacity and a rock solid belief that the mountain will not only move, but be removed! Here's a thought, get serious about your prayer life. Find out what God wants by reading His words in the Bible. Don't doubt. Be confident. He began a work in you, He will complete it. (Philippians 1:6) Don't give up. Though the mountain seems too big, too tall, too rough, too demanding, too cold, too high, too terrifying – You can make it to the other side. The best way to get there is to have God move it out of your way! He is mighty. He can. He will. He has given you authority. Speak to that mountain. It has to listen.

17 November When I was in elementary school I really liked to run. We had the Presidential Fitness Award. One event was the mile run/walk. Ready, go! I took off. I was in the lead. The head of the pack. The flash! That's the way I remember it, at least. At a particular point near the end, I realized that it was not a race. Even though I was #1 by far, I suddenly slowed. Staying ahead of everyone was great, but I no longer had to "win". I just had to finish within a reasonable time. What happened? My purpose changed and I fell far beneath my actual potential. I did get the Presidential Fitness Award that year, but it was so different when my mindset changed from "Be the best." to "Finish within the guidelines."

Today's song, "I'm Not Ashamed" ~ Hillsong. This song says that I will dance for the Lord like nobody's watching and sing for Him like nobody's listening. I won't hold anything back. There are so many things that could hold you back today, make you stop. If you really look at it though, you could narrow it down to fear of failure and simple excuses. As far as goals, accomplishments, showing love, care, compassion, and charity go – it serves no one for you to hold back. Holding back, pulling up, slowing down to just get by does not make you or God look good. Minimum is not excellent. Mediocre is never extraordinary. Adequate is never superb. You will need to reach farther, run faster, jump higher, and do more not only for your personal interests, but to show off a great God that has given you the talents, gifts, and abilities to achieve. Philippians 3:14 (MSG) says, "I've got my eye on the goal, where God is beckoning us onward—to Jesus. I'm off and running and I'm not turning back." It's full speed ahead!!

Now is the time to prepare for the next challenge. What is the next challenge in your life? Are you making excuses? Are you afraid of failure? Are you settling for less than your best? Are you unclear on your purpose? It's time for laser focus. Time to be clear on your goals and purpose. Time to face your fears. Time to make things happen. Time to be all in. Time to go all out. Run full speed. Finish great!

18 November When our cat was just about a year old, she delivered 5 adorable kittens. We named them all and eventually gave 2 away. When they were tiny, their mother led them out to the dog house (we had no dog at the time) and they waited while she hunted a rabbit and brought it back for dinner. Eventually, they learned there was a world beyond the dog house and the ability to hunt was passed on. They became quite skillful in their quests. There are times now when they stay away for a couple days, but they come home. There is shelter here, food here, safety here. When one is injured we offer aid. Cold? It's warm. Hot? It's cool. Hungry? Vittles here. They know that they can always come home and their needs will be met. Yes, I could be the 'cat lady'. But we just had 4, not 54 cats. Thank the Lord!

Today's song, "Everything I Need" ~ Kutless. This song appreciates the love of God that is strength in my weakness and the refuge I seek. He is everything in my time of need. You may have been a Christian for years. Where ever you are in life, you cannot forget that you still need God. He didn't just "save" you and then say, "Okay, kid, you are on your own. I showed you what to do, now do it and you'll be fine. I will see you at the end of your life. Good luck!" No. God wants to continue to be a part of your life. Every day that you have, you can seek Him for your refuge, your strength, your comfort, and your help. You are not abandoned today. With God, you are not an orphan. Psalm 68:5-6a (CEB) says, "Father of orphans and defender of widows is God in his holy habitation. God settles the lonely in their homes;" and Matthew 28:20 tells us He will be with you always. He will be with you, but he will not control you. He will not force anything upon you. If you want to walk away, He will let you. Have you walked away today? Did you think you'd be okay on your own? Time to come back. There's safety in the presence of God. There's nourishment. There's shelter. He wants to take care of you. You can cry. You can talk. You can rest in Him. Press in. He's always been there. You can always come home. If you are close to God today-share hope, strength, and promise with some one for whom you care. They may think God is mad or gone. Let them know He's not. Let them know He's waiting. Let them know He loves them.

19 November Did you ever drive down the road, look off to the side at a billboard and when your gaze returned you found you had drifted over? I have. This happens because we tend to move in the direction where we are looking.

Today's song is "A Mighty Fortress" ~ Christy Nockels. This song affirms that we will keep our eyes on God, our fortress. He is a sacred refuge and His Kingdom is unshakable. We will reign with Him forever. What you look at is important. It will bring you peace, or it could make you panic. There are so many things happening in life it is easy to get distracted. Then you find yourself somewhere far from where you intended and it isn't always clear how to return. You may have taken a detour or a short cut, neither of which are as good as the original route planned for your journey. There's a song I remember from long ago by Helen Lemmel, which says, "Turn your eyes upon Jesus. Look full in His wonderful face, and the things of earth will grow strangely dim in the light of His glory and grace." Looking to the Lord makes all the difference. That focus on Him will cause the cares of the world to fade and what He wants for your life will be visible and bright. Hebrews 12:1-3 (MSG) says it this way, "...It means we'd better get on with it. Strip down, start running—and never quit! No extra spiritual fat, no parasitic sins. Keep your eyes on Jesus, who both began and finished this race we're in. Study how he did it. Because he never lost sight of where he was headed—that exhilarating finish in and with God—he could put up with anything along the way: Cross, shame, whatever. And now He's *there*, in the place of honor, right alongside God. When you find yourselves flagging in your faith, go over that story again, item by item, that long litany of hostility he plowed through. *That* will shoot adrenaline into your souls!" Bazinga! That is a supercharge of reason to be focused today. Don't be distracted. Don't lose sight of where you're headed. That will bring confidence and endurance in all you are going through, reaching for, and attaining. God is solid, a fortress, a refuge, unshakable. Don't let things weigh you down. Rise up and see all God has for you. It will be a memorable journey and an exhilarating finish!

20 November My husband and I dated steadily for five years before we were married. We got engaged on Thanksgiving Eve. He surprised me with the engagement ring just before dinner. The ring was on a ribbon tied around my cat's neck. Sometimes I tell people that I chased Steve 'til he caught me. I remember that wonderful, nervous feeling. Your heart is so full and you are breathless. You want nothing more than to be with that person. Near them. In their presence. Together. Close. Spending time and sharing experiences with them. The common history binds you. Your love grows. It thrives. It deepens. You smile when you think of them. That's how it should be. I am so blessed to have that kind of relationship with my husband.

Today's song, "I'm Not Ashamed" ~ Ricardo Sanchez. This song declares that the Lord loves me and I love Him. Relentlessly, His love is pursuing me. Pursue. Relentlessly pursue. Think about wonderful relationships. They don't just happen. You must pursue them. You hear people say, "Well, if it is supposed to be, it will just work out." Baloney! You must work at any relationship in order for it to be successful. To be close, you must strive to be close. To grow, you must pursue growth. To thrive, you must spend time together.

Your relationship with God should be the same. He is pursuing you today; you in turn must pursue Him. Chase Him 'til He catches you! 2 Timothy 2:22 (CEB) says, "...pursue righteousness, faith, love and peace..." This is the character of God. He desires to be pursued. Matthew 6:33 says, "But seek first the kingdom of God and His righteousness, and all these things shall be added to you." You should seek Him early in the morning. Desire nothing more than to be with him. Near Him. In His presence. Together. Close. The best way to grow that relationship is to spend time with God. Today is the day to start or to increase the time you spend seeking, pursuing God. When you do, you will be blessed.

21 November We ordered a birthday gift for my youngest son one year. It was to be shipped and arrive in time for his special day. So, I waited. And waited. No package. I contacted the company. No reply. I tried again. Still no response. The morning before his birthday, we discovered the package had been left at a door we seldom use. I was so happy to have found it!

Today's song, "How Many Kings" ~ Downhere. This reminds me of the simple arrival of the baby, Jesus, lowly and small, the weakest of all. He was the unlikeliest hero, wrapped in his mother's shawl. He was just a child. And the question, wondering if this is who we have waited for? Things don't always show up in the way you expect. That's what happened when Christ was born. The expectation was for a king, a warrior, a mighty man. The reality was a baby. He was tender, vulnerable, and small. But, He grew and developed into the man that changed the world. You should never dismiss small beginnings. Even a giant oak started out as a small acorn. Christ was the example that a humble genesis can lead to an amazing life. Two things to learn from this today. First, things from God may not come in the form or time frame you expect. Habakkuk 2:3 says, "For the vision *is* yet for an appointed time; But at the end it will speak, and it will not lie. Though it tarries, wait for it; because it will surely come, it will not tarry." Be patient and keep looking. Second, your potential must be developed to be realized. If you don't have it now, it doesn't mean you never will. Dream big. Think big. Expect big. Do not limit yourself or God. You will be so happy to find just what you've been looking for.

22 November If you ever heard of the etiquette pro, Emily Post, my Mother knew her book cover to cover. We would be at my parents' house for holiday dinners and we always ate off of china with silverware, the real silver – ware. The table was pristine and the food in beautiful china bowls. There was a linen table cloth and napkins. It was always so nice. I am thankful that my Mother showed me the proper way to entertain and dine in style. Now, many holidays, we get to have the extended family to our house. And, yes, we use the china.

Today's song, "He Is Exalted" ~ Twila Paris. This song announces that God is the King, exalted on High and I will praise Him. When you reflect on all the things God has done for you, smile to yourself and say, "Thank you, God." The heritage of country and family, your church, your home, your provision and belongings, your friendships, your jobs, and your opportunities are all things for which to be thankful. The direction of that thanks should be to God. Psalm 84:11b says, "...No good thing will He withhold from those who walk uprightly." 2 Corinthians 2:14a says, "But thanks be to God, who always leads us in triumph in Christ." And James 1:17a tells you, " Every good gift and every perfect gift is from above, and comes down from the Father of lights". Then 1 Thessalonians 5:18 says, "In everything give thanks; for this is the will of God in Christ Jesus for you." How could you look at your life realistically and not thank God? You can't. God has been good to you, whether you realize it or not. Whether you acknowledge Him or not. Whether you are thankful to Him or not. There are so many times things could have been much worse for you and your family. But God will cause you to triumph! And for that you can be truly thankful! Take time to thank God today. Change your perspective. It will change your day.

23 November This morning proved to be a challenge for me as I knew the tune to the song, but not the lyrics. Without a shadow of a doubt, this was to be the song today. Finding it was a team effort. I knew that there was a reason I only had the tune. I needed to get help. Those that are closest were able to be there for me. I couldn't have done this without them. Thanks to my family we came up with enough lyrics to identify this 'Song in the Morning'… Today's song, "Right Beside You" ~ Building 429. It reassures you that when the world is on your back and you think that you will never last, or if you're lonely and confused God will be right beside you.

Family. It's a kind of relationship that connects you even when you have just met. It can make you instantly associated though you may not know each other well. You are literally related. I have been amazingly blessed by decent family on both my and my husband's sides. I feel like I can count on them, no matter the time or distance between us. If there is trouble, I know I can turn to someone in the family for help. Friends are great. But, family is blood. There is something about that blood connection.

Hebrews 13:5b-6 (MSG) says, "Since God assured us, 'I'll never let you down, never walk off and leave you,' we can boldly quote, 'God is there, ready to help; I'm fearless no matter what. Who or what can get to me?'" When things get tough, God is there. He will be there when you need help. When you feel lonely. When you are overcome by the circumstances of your life. When you are helpless, hopeless, depressed, and confused. Because of Jesus, there is a blood connection. His blood was shed so we could be restored into our relationship with God. John 3:6 (ERV) says, "The only life people get from their human parents is physical. But the new life that the Spirit gives a person is spiritual." When you accept Jesus as your Lord, God's Spirit changes you. You are truly in the Family of God. You are related, connected, and associated with Him. He will be right beside you. When He's close to you, He'll be there for you. You can't do it without Him. If you are not in God's family yet, time to make the change. If you are, time to bring someone into the family with you.

24 November Several years ago when my mother passed away it was a busy time for me and the family. We flew to Pennsylvania to have her buried next to my father who preceded her in death by 20 years. About two weeks later I sat quietly in my bedroom and looked through her purse. I found her earrings. It was the pair we had searched for so she could wear them last. I cried and said, "I'm sorry, I didn't know I had them." I still have them. In the quietness of that afternoon I had my moments of remembrance.

Today's song, "Heart of Worship" ~ Matt Redman. This song talks about how when the music fades, everything is stripped away and I simply come, longing to bring something that's of worth that will bless God's heart. Vulnerability. Everyone has it. In the busyness of all of life you can lose yourself and not have to feel deeply. But when it quiets down and you are alone, you can simply go to the Lord. Psalms 46:10a says, "Be still and know that I am God." There is purity in those moments where you seek God and you just long to find Him and give to Him something precious. It may be something that until that time you didn't even know you had. In giving of yourself, you get to have so much more. There's a flood of God's love and care. His peace. His comfort. This can be a great need especially when you have lost some one you love dearly. So find your place of quiet, where all is stripped away and you can simply be in God's presence. The thing of great value you have to bring to Him is YOU.

25 November I remember seeing my oldest son for the first time. Just minutes after he was born, my husband brought him to me. That little baby looked at me with deep brown eyes. He was so calm. It's a moment seared in my mind. It was an amazing moment. A breathtaking moment. A moment of intense love for someone I had just met. It was a moment like none other.

Today's song is "Amazed" ~ Phillips, Craig & Dean. This song says of the Lord that I'm amazed by Him and how He loves me. How great is it that God loves you so intensely? 1 John 4:19 says, "We love him, because he first loved us." He first loved you. Even when you have just met Him, you can love Him. He is already in love with you. It's a love so immense that when you needed a savior, He sent His son. His only son.

There is a whole new dimension to life when you have children. You have a greater capacity to love. I know a woman who thought she could not love more than one child, so that is all she had. If only she could know that God gives you the capacity to love each of your children the same, intensely. I do not have a favorite son. They are both the best boys in the whole world. Well, honestly they are now young men. But they will always be my "boys". It's such a great picture of how God loves you. Unconditionally. Constantly. You are on His mind a lot. He wants the best for you. He longs to guide and direct you. He yearns for your fellowship with Him. He's there when you are down and He's there when you are celebrating. It's an amazing love. You have a great opportunity, as well as a great responsibility, to model God's love to your children. Their picture of Him is the one that you as a parent have helped to paint. Think about adding a few carefully placed brushstrokes to the canvas of their lives today. Bridge time and distance with a tender word or touch. It will be worth your time. It can be intense, amazing, and a moment like no other.

26 November We saw a movie awhile back. It was "Red Dawn". It's about an invasion and hostile takeover of America by a foreign nation. There was a lot of fighting, action, shooting, and explosions. I went because the guys wanted to see it. Okay, I was curious too. Afterwards, I'm thinking, "Could that really happen?" Fear crept in and I began to worry about the impending doom! Being prepared is one thing, but being terrified is not the way to live. My active imagination has more than once caused me to lose sleep.

Today's song, "Today is the Day"~ Lincoln Brewster. This song announces that is the day God has made. I will rejoice and be glad in it. I won't worry about tomorrow, because I trust what He says. Turn your focus on what God has for you. Today is the day God has made. What are you doing today? Are you freaking out thinking that a movie scenario will come to pass? Are you crazed over what someone is predicting however misguided it may be? Are you hiding under your blankets? Are you paralyzed with fear? Matthew 6:34 (MSG) says, "Give your entire attention to what God is doing right now, and don't get worked up about what may or may not happen tomorrow. God will help you deal with whatever hard things come up when the time comes." God will help you deal with it. Wow, if more people could just get hold of that. Take it one day at a time. One day. How much can you accomplish in a day? How many people could you reach in a day? This could be the day. Don't spend the day in sorrow or worry or fretting. Spend the day rejoicing, thankful, and hopeful. Your out-look will determine your outcome. You don't know about tomorrow, but you know you have today. You choose how you will spend it. You will not get it back. Spend your day well today. Trust God. He's already seen your tomorrow and He'll be waiting there for you.

27 November I have some big dreams. I will be honest. Things haven't gone exactly as I envisioned. Well, not even close. Somewhere along the line, I got distracted. My life is great. Family. Home. Friends. However, I know there is so much more for me. I just got off track. I have spent too much time doing what I want to do and not enough time doing what I need to do.

Today's song, "Get Back Up" ~ Toby Mac. This song encourages you that when you lose your way, you can get back up again. It's never too late to get back up and shine again. You may have been knocked down, but you are not down forever. Failing doesn't make you a failure, quitting does. Getting off track doesn't finish you, it delays you. If you have been lost or have been knocked down, you can get back up. It may not be easy. It may not be quick. It may not be without resistance. But, you can do it. It starts with a decision. It continues with a commitment. Nehemiah 6:3, in part, says, "I am doing a great work and I cannot come down." Nehemiah was rebuilding the wall of Jerusalem. The gates had been burned and the city was desolate. He made a decision, and then made the commitment to do what he set out to do. He would not be distracted from his work or from his goal.

Are you on track today or have you fallen? Get up. Go up. Try again. Just do it. There is no more time to delay. No advantage in putting off what you need to do. Do a great work. Circumstances may not be perfect. It may go slowly for awhile. Stick with it. You will see progress and eventually victory. Deuteronomy 30:8-9 (MSG) says, "And you will make a new start, listening obediently to God, keeping all his commandments that I'm commanding you today. God, your God, will outdo himself in making things go well for you: you'll have babies, get calves, grow crops, and enjoy an all-around good life. Yes, God will start enjoying you again, making things go well for you just as he enjoyed doing it for your ancestors." God wants to reward the work of your hands, but you must work. The seeds of greatness are inside you. It's up to you to bring them to fruition. Be excited about your future. Reach toward it. Regretting your past is not productive. You may have been knocked down, but not out! It's a new day. You can shine again.

28 November While attending a business function early in my career, I was cordial to a woman on the elevator. We chatted briefly and both exited at the same floor. To my surprise, she was the keynote speaker, an executive in our company. I was so thankful that I had been nice to her and had not been rude or complained about anything. You really never know who is in your presence, watching and listening.

Today's song, "Jesus in Disguise" ~ Brandon Heath. This song says that you were looking for a king you would never recognize, it was Jesus in disguise. There are so many times you can be sure that God has been watching over you and acting on your behalf. Jesus is keeping Him informed. He knows who you are. He knows what you are doing. Your actions speak of your character, your integrity, and your faith. You need to be mindful and not think that it doesn't really matter. Matthew 25: 34-40 says, "Then the King will say to those on His right, 'Come, you who are blessed of My Father, inherit the kingdom prepared for you from the foundation of the world. For I was hungry, and you gave Me something to eat; I was thirsty, and you gave Me something to drink; I was a stranger, and you invited Me in; naked, and you clothed Me; I was sick, and you visited Me; I was in prison, and you came to Me.' Then the righteous will answer Him, 'Lord, when did we see You hungry, and feed You, or thirsty, and give You something to drink? And when did we see You a stranger, and invite You in, or naked, and clothe You? When did we see You sick, or in prison, and come to You?' The King will answer and say to them, 'Truly I say to you, to the extent that you did it to one of these brothers of Mine, even the least of them, you did it to Me.' " How you respond to others is a reflection of your response to Jesus. Therein lies your inheritance. If you want all God has for you, then you need to keep yourself in check. Keep your attitude right. Not be offended. Stay generous. Stay kind. Be a giver, not just a taker.

29 November Last winter there was a snowfall in the middle of the day. I was at work out in the country. I'm talking rural. The snow was wet and slushy. The road home was hilly and curvy. Although I was apprehensive, I left work and headed for home. I made it the first few miles then I embarked on a steep hill. My determination to go forward was fueled by my fear of sliding backwards. Finally, I reached the crest. There was a short side road at the top of the hill. I pulled off and called for help. My phone barely had reception there. Help arrived and I was delivered to my house safe and sound.

Today's song, "I Need A Miracle" ~ Third Day. In this song be reminded that no matter who you are and no matter what you've done, there will be a time when you can't make it on your own. When you are desperate, know you're not the only one praying that you need a miracle. You have to get to a point where you know you can't make it on our own before you can truly get help. When I was in my car, I had to get over to the side and wait. Continuing to struggle would have been futile. I had to be willing to receive help. I had to ask. Then I had to believe that my friend would come and help me. So it is with God. When you find yourself in a position of desperation, stop blaming God. It wasn't His fault. Pray. God will hear you and He will respond. Believe beyond a shadow of a doubt that He will answer. Jeremiah 33:3 says, "Call to Me and I will answer you, and I will tell you great and mighty things, which you do not know." This is a promise you can count on. There are things you won't know until you pray. There are strategies you won't know until you pray. Then your response will determine the outcome. It does no good to have a recipe for a cake if you are unwilling to mix the ingredients and put it in the oven. So what good is it if you ask God to help you, but will not do what He has asked you to do? No good. An unwilling person cannot be assisted. Trying to go it on your own today? Stop. Pray. You may go through pain, desperation, and heartache. The operative word is "through". Don't camp out in your problems. Don't nurse your wounds. Don't rehearse your woes. Snap out of it and seek God. He's got the answers and He's got the plan. Prayer will make you stronger on the journey. Before long you will find your miracle come to pass.

30 November My childhood home had two huge sweet-gum trees in the front yard. One was especially great for climbing. I loved to climb it. It really wasn't the 'girly' thing to do, but I did it. When I was mad, I'd climb the tree. When I was stressed, I'd climb the tree. I could get away if I'd climb the tree. The higher I went, the better I felt. I wanted to get away from the ground, the norm, the stuff that was hindering me. I could set myself apart. I could get a better perspective from way up there. I could see the rooftops. I could feel the breeze in my hair. It was great. Some days I miss that tree.

Today's song, "Only the World" ~ Mandisa. This is a reminder that it's only the world I'm living in. This is the day I've been given. I'm not giving in, because it's only the world and I know the best is still yet to come. The junk of life cannot overtake you unless you allow it. There is more than just what is on the surface. You do not have to go along with 'whatever happens'. Please. You have the power to rise above what is happening. Romans 12:2 says, "And do not be conformed to this world, but be transformed by the renewing of your mind, that you may prove what *is* that good and acceptable and perfect will of God." That renewal of your mind will take you to the next level in your life. You won't have anything new if you don't learn anything new or do anything new or look at or listen to anything new. Remember that you are not bound by what people, government, or media has to say. John 17:16 says, "They are not of the world, just as I am not of the world." If you read the entire chapter you will see it is a prayer that Jesus prayed. He distinguishes His followers from the rest by saying that they do not belong to this world. By virtue of their faith, they have a life in eternity. That's a much bigger picture than just what is on this earth. It's powerful to see that you have so much more to do, have, enjoy, and accomplish. Set yourself apart. Don't let the stuff of the world get you down. It's only the world. The best really is yet to come.

1 December "They grow up so fast" I heard that often when my children were little. Now I see it's true. My young adult sons are such a blessing. It seems like yesterday that they were little boys wrestling in the yard. Well, they're wrestling still, but not little boys any more!

Today's song, "Blink"~ Revive. This song says that it happens in a blink and a flash. It happens in the time it takes to look back. I can try to hold on but I can't stop time. Life can move quickly. It's naive to think you have "all the time in the world" to accomplish your dreams, to love your family, to get your priorities straight, to build your faith, to reach other people, to mend fences, to build new ones. James 4:14 (AMP) says, "Yet you do not know [the least thing] about what may happen tomorrow. What is the nature of your life? You are [really] but a wisp of vapor (a puff of smoke, a mist) that is visible for a little while and then disappears." It's time to make each day count. Stop waiting and wishing. Time to start doing. It will be gone before you know it. The opportunity will be upon you and if you are not prepared, it will pass you by. There are so many great things inside of you waiting to be birthed. Standing idle or wrestling with all the details of your call, procrastinating, or making excuses will only put you farther from the destiny that God has for you. Your sense of urgency will help you get to the next level of your faith, your mission, your vision, and your goals. You can't stop time, but you can certainly make the most of it.

2 December I was about eight years old and I loved to ride my bike. I bet I rode a thousand miles that summer. Wearing shorts and sandals, I headed out to the store a block away. I took the corner too tight and wiped out! There was some scraped skin and a bunch of tears. My Uncle Frank carried me home. By the next day I was out riding again.

Today's song, "Who am I" ~ Casting Crowns. This song asks who am I, that the Lord would even care to know my name or feel my hurt? My uncle didn't even live in the same state, but the day I needed someone, he was there. He and my Aunt Grace were my 'Godparents'. They were visiting that week. What a great picture of God, being there for you, picking you up, carrying you home when you are hurting. Psalm 34:18 (CEB) says, "The LORD is close to the brokenhearted; he saves those whose spirits are crushed." If you are hurting today, know that God really does care. He thinks more of you when you don't think much of yourself. Hebrews 4:15-16 (MSG) says, "We don't have a priest who is out of touch with our reality. He's been through weakness and testing, experienced it all—all but the sin. So let's walk right up to him and get what He is so ready to give. Take the mercy, accept the help." Jesus knows what you are going through. He's been there. Let Him help. If you know someone who is hurting, share the news with them that the Lord knows them and cares. No one ever has to be alone. He can carry you home.

3 December I heard that no two snowflakes are alike. Each one is unique. I thought, who has looked at all those snowflakes? The next time it snowed, I looked at the flakes that fell on the window of my living room, comparing. Of all the 20 or so snowflakes I looked at, none were the same, so it must be true! After some research in writing this, I have found it to be the case that it is unlikely that any two snowflakes ever formed in the history of snow were ever identical! Staggering, isn't it?

Today's song," How Many Kings" ~ Downhere. This song wonders how many kings stepped down from their thrones and declares that only one did that for me. God is unique in that He sent His only son to live on this earth, sinless, experiencing all temptation that is part of humanity, and then die at the hands of men. What is unique is that this Savior, Jesus, also rose from the grave and ascended into Heaven! Genesis 1:27 says, "God created man in His own image, in the image of God He created him; male and female He created them." You are made in the image of God. You have His characteristics. Don't confuse that with the belief that we are 'little Gods'. That is like saying the mirror is me. It reflects an image and is dependent on what is before it for that image. When God is before you, you reflect His image. He is unique and has made each of us unique as well. There is no one just like you. Even identical twins have differences. There is a particular experience you bring to your life. There is a unique call on your life that only you can fulfill. There is a unique combination of people that you know. There is a gifting, the details of which are yours alone. You are one of a kind! No one can truly ever replace you! You are unique, just like a snowflake. The best way to honor that is to be yourself. There are things only you can do. People only you can reach. It's okay if you aren't as outgoing as someone else, or reserved, or practical, or funny, or coordinated, or organized, or clever, or, or, or! There is no comparison! Your job is to be the best YOU that you can be. Not to make excuses for bad behavior or poor performance saying, "Well, that's just who I am." No, no, no. You live well, improve, learn, be the amazing you that only you can be! That's God's intent and His hope for you in your life today!

4 December When our boys were little, they would plan their Christmas morning sneak. Creeping out of their bedrooms ever so early, they would tip toe to the living room undetected and discover treasures! Santa brought a few things, but the best gifts were from us, their parents. Their wonderment was contagious and the sparkle in their eyes so pure with joy.

Today's song surprised me, it's "Santa Claus is Coming to Town" ~ John Frederick Coots and Haven Gillespie. It says that you better watch out. You better not cry. You better not pout and I'm telling you why, because Santa Claus is coming to town. When things get hectic any time of year, it's important to stop and take a breath. Relax. Focus. Remember the joy in life. Remember that even if things are bad, they could be worse. I heard recently of a woman living in a meager home with dirt floors and not much of anything material. She said that she was so rich. Rich because she knew the saving grace of Jesus. She wasn't pouting or crying that she didn't have this or that. She wasn't demanding that someone "owed her". She was thankful. Grateful. Hopeful. Joyful. James 1:17 says, "Every good gift and every perfect gift is from above, and comes down from the Father of lights, with whom there is no variation or shadow of turning." Remember that the best gifts are from God. Especially the gift of His Son. Be thankful, grateful, hopeful, and joyful. Count your blessings today.

Now, think back to when you were more curious than practical. When you were more adventurous than careful. When you were more inventive than complacent. When your wonderment was contagious. Possibilities were endless and creative imagination was in overdrive. Excitement was a regular part of daily life and not just an annual event. Now is the time to pull from life all that it has to offer. Engage the childlike part of you that makes life exciting. No pouting or crying, anticipate the wonderful treasure that's waiting! Your eyes will sparkle with joy! Then help others experience that excitement too!

5 December My young son said, "What if you had a room full of hotdogs?" I'm not sure what my answer was, but it got me to thinking...what if? Imagination. Thinking big. It opens a world of possibilities. I think a whole room full of hotdogs would be awesome! But don't forget the mustard!

Today's song, "Our God is an Awesome God" ~ Rich Mullins. This song reminds me that God is awesome. He reigns from heaven with wisdom, power, and love. When I think of 'awesome' I think of bigness, something incredible, amazing, out of the ordinary realm. That's God. Ephesians 3:20 (MSG) says, "God can do anything, you know—far more than you could ever imagine or guess or request in your wildest dreams! He does it not by pushing us around but by working within us, his Spirit deeply and gently within us." God can work His awesomeness in you! He can include you as a part of the 'anything' He does. Do you see your life as mediocre today? It doesn't have to be. Get involved with God and let Him get involved with you. Your life can be awesome! Find out His plans for you. Jeremiah 29:11 (MSG) says, "I know what I'm doing. I have it all planned out—plans to take care of you, not abandon you, plans to give you the future you hope for." He uses wisdom, power, and love to affect your life for the good. Look to God. He's got the answer to your problem, the plan for your situation, the strategy for your future. He is awesome.

6 December

Today's song is, "Who You Are" ~ Unspoken. This song says that you can never fall too hard, so fast, or so far that you can't get back when you're lost. It's never too late, so bad, or so much that you can't change. You think it's too late? You've done too much? Too much time has passed? You messed up too bad? You're too far off track? Not true. There's always a chance to change. The key is, don't give up. Get up. Start again. Mend the fence. Turn around. 2 Corinthians 7:10 (CEB) says, "Godly sadness produces a changed heart and life that leads to salvation and leaves no regrets, but sorrow under the influence of the world produces death." Your heart change that results from looking to God will not be full of regret, but continuing to seek what the culture expects or what society deems 'right' as your compass will lead to your demise. With God's help you can accomplish the change you need. Change can mean to adjust, or redirect, but great change takes a turn around. You may need to go in a whole new direction. I told my son when he was learning to drive that if he missed his exit, he could go to the next one and turn around. Then he could be back on the right track soon! Sometimes you need to go back and try again. Sometimes you must forget the past and simply move forward. Philippians 3:13 (CEB) says, "Brothers and sisters, I myself don't think I've reached it, but I do this one thing: I forget about the things behind me and reach out for the things ahead of me." Your future holds great promise. The changes you make will allow you to walk into that future with confidence, boldness, power, and strength. Time to get up, look forward, stand tall, and move on. Turn your errors into lessons. Don't repeat them. Defeat them. When you make the changes in your life, you'll be able to encourage others to do the same in theirs.

7 December There have been several advertising campaigns that encourage you to not accept any substitutes for their products. Settling for less than the real thing was never the best choice. I thought that it's either the real thing or nothing. When I was a teen, name brand was a big deal. Labels mattered. My mom had a fit when I spent $30 on a pair of blue jeans. That was a lot of money way back in the day. I did like those jeans. They were totally worth it.

Today's song, "Glorious Day" ~ Casting Crowns. This song talks of Jesus and in living, He loved me, and in dying, He saved me. He carried my sins away. Jesus was a substitute. One you want to accept. He paid the price for your sins by dying on the cross. It was a debt you couldn't pay. A bridge you couldn't mend by yourself. His love was genuine and immense. Philippians 2:8 says, "And being found in appearance as a man, he humbled himself, and became obedient unto death, even the death of the cross." Jesus stood in your place and hung on your behalf, nailed to a cross-brutally murdered for your redemption. When He died the bridge between you and God was mended. Your choice is to walk across. Accept what Jesus did and reach for the other side. You may not consider often enough the high price paid. His life for yours. You may not realize often enough the great value He placed on your life to think you were worth it. It's important to take more time to be thankful. It's important to not take that for granted. And you need to not diminish your own value. Take time to reflect today. When you pay a price for something, is it worth it? The Lord will always say about you, "Yes, they were worth it." This is one substitute you definitely should accept.

8 December Years ago when the boys were small, we realized on Christmas Eve that we had forgotten to help Santa by picking up some stocking stuffers. We left my mother's house and swung by drug/convenience store and purchased some secret stocking items along with snacks, telling the boys we were going to have a Christmas Eve family party! And so we did. The following Christmas Eve they told us they were looking forward to going to the same store to get the snacks for our annual party. Annual party? Okay, we went along with it and as it happened, we have gone there every Christmas Eve since. It's so silly, but now it's a tradition.

Today's song, "Revive Us Again" ~ Big Daddy Weave. This song praises God, giving Him the glory and asking Him to revive us again. This is really an old hymn, rearranged for a contemporary sound. It's a traditional song. Some traditions are silly. Some traditions are continued even when the original reason is distorted or lost. Some traditions are remembrances. Some traditions are holy. 2 Thessalonians 2:15 says, "Therefore, brethren, stand fast and hold the traditions which you were taught, whether by word or our epistle." This refers to the traditions of the Word of God - to that of Christ. When our traditions are founded in the scriptures, the correct context of the scriptures, then they should be kept. If they are founded on man's ideas, then think again. It may be effort wasted. This advice is concerning your spiritual life. The things you hold dear in your devotion to the Lord should be cherished.

Family traditions are important to create connection and unity with your relatives. These are essential in your family life. They should be thoughtful, silly, memorable, as long as they are meaningful or engaging. Not harmful, degrading, nor irreverent to your faith. Take time to look at your spiritual and family traditions. Are they working for you? Do they enhance your life and the lives of others? Do the people in your life know what they are? Don't neglect them. Think about embracing new ones when your belief or life situation changes. They help your children to be more firmly grounded. Give them a fond memory to have when they are older and can say to their children, "I remember when..." It will strengthen both your present and your future.

9 December Years ago, my son the preschooler was happily playing in the yard one day and in the process misplaced his baseball. He stopped by the open kitchen window and said, "Mommy, I lost my ball." I replied, "Do you know where you lost it?" He said, "No, Mommy, that's what 'lost it' means."

Today's song is, "Fall Apart" ~ Josh Wilson. This song tells God that I want to know Him more. I might start to find Him when I fall apart. When my son realized his baseball was lost, he began to look for it. He searched. He asked for help. He eventually found what he was looking for. So many times you can live your life happily playing along and suddenly realize you are lost. That is not the time to give up. That is not the time to blame others. That is not the time to lash out. It is the time to start seeking. Start searching. Start asking for help. But ask someone who knows what 'lost' means. Talk to some one who has come through what you are going through. Some one who has experienced victory on the other side. Psalm 23:4 (MSG) says, "Even when the way goes through Death Valley, I'm not afraid when you walk at my side. Your trusty shepherd's crook makes me feel secure." You will go through the valley, the low point. You are not supposed to pitch a tent and camp there. I have heard people say, "God will pull you through, but you have to be able to stand the 'pull'". There will be hard times. You may feel like you are falling apart. That is the time to look for God. You will find Him. He wants to meet you where you are. He wants to lead you through. He'll even carry you through if you need Him to. If you are having this experience today, keep going. You will make it. If you aren't going through it, this is a perfect time to encourage someone else. You could be the help they are seeking. You could be the answer to their prayer.

10 December   When my youngest son was four his big brother led him in praying to ask Jesus in his heart. The children's pastor was concerned that our eldest did not know the meaning of salvation because he kept going forward in kid's church each week to be "saved". We explained to him that he only need decide once. Then, we found out that he just went up to get more of the brochures about 'what it means to be saved' so he could give them to the neighborhood children. He was just nine, our evangelist. We appreciated his zeal.

Today's song, "Christ is Risen" ~ Matt Maher. This song asks death, where is your sting? And hell, where is your victory? Then entreats the church to stand in the light, because the glory of God has defeated the night! There is a transformation that comes with knowing Jesus. You are changed. There is no time like the present to make sure of your eternity than now. Romans 10:9 says, "Because if you confess with your mouth 'Jesus is Lord' and in your heart you have faith that God raised him from the dead, you will be saved." It's that simple. It's simple to pray yourself and simple to pray with some one else. You may be thinking, "What's the big deal? My life's okay right now. I will think about it later." Here's the thing, you may not have 'later'. You may not have tomorrow. Your friends may not have tomorrow. Don't put it off. As long as you have breath, you can be forgiven. You can be transformed. You can secure eternity. Death will have no power over you. If you've already made the decision, share it. Tell others what happened to you. Don't be shy. Having Jesus in your life makes all the difference. Right now it dispels the darkness of depression, despair and hopelessness in life. Then when your physical body dies, you will find your home in Heaven. Today, make sure you have made the decision to make Jesus part of your life. Then think of those for whom you care and let them know too.

11 December I've been involved in the ministry of the church since I was a teen. That's how I met my husband. I was a part of local, district, conference, jurisdictional, and national activities with the youth of the church. I loved helping, being a part of something bigger than myself. It was and continues to be a joy to serve. My mom once called me a "church-aholic". Well, if that means I am addicted to serving and being a part of the family of God, so be it.

Today's song, "You Are My King" ~ Chris Tomlin. This song talks about the amazing love of the Lord. I know it's true and it's my joy to honor Him in all I do. Honor is not as common as it should be. There are 172 references to 'honor' in the New American Standard Bible. Yet people do not honor those in authority, their parents, their mentors, their leader, their country. Where is honor? The value of it can be lost in a generation. Parents, teach your children honor. One way to honor God is to serve. Volunteer. I know a lot of people who volunteer and they are phenomenal. Their attitude of giving is profound. They have generous spirits. It's that attitude of pitching in to make things happen. It's the "and then some" principle. Doing more than what is required. Showing up early, staying late. Though I believe it references your employment, this verse applies to volunteers as well. Colossians 3:23 (MSG) says, "Servants, do what you're told by your earthly masters. And don't just do the minimum that will get you by. Do your best. Work from the heart for your real Master, for God, confident that you'll get paid in full when you come into your inheritance. Keep in mind always that the ultimate Master you're serving is Christ." It is the Lord whom you serve, whether it is in the church or at the neighborhood picnic. Whether it is in the grocery store or at the soup kitchen. When you give of yourself without expecting repayment, that is when you are truly enriched.

What can you do today that will be of service to another? What additional difference can you make in this life? What can you do that will give honor to God? It will make Him proud. It will get His attention. Be addicted to serving others. Be part of something bigger than yourself. The joy will be immeasurable and the payoff will be eternal.

12 December There was a bakery near our first home. I often went by for a donut after church. The wedding cake displays were beautiful. I thought they were freshly baked and decorated. But they were fake. Made from Styrofoam and iced to look real. Thankfully, the donuts were genuine and tasty!

Today's song is, "Good To Be Alive" ~ Jason Gray. This song says to God that all I want is to give Him a life well lived. Many times you can make everything look great even when things are a mess. You fake it. You pretend to be real but there's not a lot of substance in who you are. You have a choice to continue the charade or come clean, make amends, and start fresh. A life well lived is a daily commitment. Everyone has things they have regretted doing or not doing. It's not limited to 'those crazy teen years'. It goes on throughout your life. The key is in the decision to live well and make your life worthwhile. I John 1:9 (CEB) says, "But if we confess our sins, he is faithful and just to forgive us our sins and cleanse us from everything we've done wrong." Realize that you aren't perfect, ask forgiveness and move on. Strive to stop doing and saying that which is nonproductive or counter productive in your life. Replace bad habits and don't condone poor behavior. Don't justify. Make the effort to change. Attempt to be more genuine each day. Stop treating your body like a trash dump. Start treating it as a chosen vessel. Stop taking relationships for granted. Start treating relationships as blessings. Stop ignoring your family. Start treating your family as precious. Stop shunning the things of God. Start embracing all God has for you. Life can be more than regret. Your life has great promise. Move through the regrets to the promises. Your future is rich, genuine, beautiful, and incredibly sweet.

13 December It was the morning after a storm and we found a nest in the front yard with baby birds inside. It was sad. We weren't sure what to do. We set the nest where we thought it was safe and went along our way. I can't really remember what happened to them. We just did what we could and hoped for the best.

Today's song is, "Jesus, Friend of Sinners" ~ Casting Crowns. This song talks about reaching out to others with open hearts and open doors. It asks Jesus, the friend of sinners, to break our hearts for what breaks His. Merely noticing that someone has a need is not enough. Proverbs 3:27-28 (MSG) says, "Never walk away from someone who deserves help; your hand is *God's* hand for that person. Don't tell your neighbor 'Maybe some other time' or 'Try me tomorrow' when the money's right there in your pocket." Your heart must be broken for the lost, the needy, and those around you who may be hurting or lonely. You must do what you can to help. Do what you can to reach out. Getting involved by God's leading can make all the difference. When you are nudged to do more, do it. Your part, by God's plan, may be small or large. The key is to be listening with spiritual ears to the prompting of the Holy Spirit. It's that still small voice, that idea, that sense of urging, that compassion. It may be your neighbor, a friend, a family member, a waiter, a clerk, a police officer. Reaching outside of yourself, your world, your bubble of comfort will, in turn, warm your own heart. Making a natural sacrifice of time, gifts, or money will reap a supernatural result. God will honor your open heart and open door. Maybe you can offer someone the best, the love of Jesus. Hebrews 6:10-12 (MSG) says, "God doesn't miss anything. He knows perfectly well all the love you've shown him by helping needy Christians, and that you keep at it. And now I want each of you to extend that same intensity toward a full-bodied hope, and keep at it till the finish. Don't drag your feet..." God notices. You may be the calm to someone's storm. The answer to their prayer. Then be assured that at the time of your need, God will send someone to you as well. My pastor says, "When you have a need, sow a seed." In giving, you will receive. It may not come from where you think, or how you think, but it will come. So reach out today. Pay attention and do what is in your power to do.

14 December I heard this song playing in my heart early this morning. I have kept it in my thoughts all through this day. As I am writing, there are so many reasons to be distraught today. Hurts. Pain. Evil. Heartache. Brokenness. Sickness. Poverty. Sadness. It is a world that has been invaded by sin, disobedience, and revenge. BUT GOD...

Today's song is, "How Many Kings"~ Downhere. This song asks how many gods have poured out their hearts to romance a world that is torn all apart? Romans 5:20-21 (MSG) says, "All that passing laws against sin did was produce more lawbreakers. But sin didn't, and doesn't, have a chance in competition with the aggressive forgiveness we call *grace.* When it's sin versus grace, grace wins hands down. All sin can do is threaten us with death, and that's the end of it. Grace, because God is putting everything together again through the Messiah, invites us into life—a life that goes on and on and on, world without end." Your Hope is in the Lord today. Your peace. Your refuge. Your strength. God's grace is sufficient. Through all the muck and mire of the world's reality, you can have your reality in the spiritual realm. That is, life and health and peace. God's grace, favor, forgiveness, and provision will prevail. Today you have an opportunity to share the light of God's love with those around you. If you are hurting, remember God. Let others know that God is still God and He loves us. Remember the character of God. When you are tempted to blame Him for this or that, think again. Romans 8:28 says, "And we know that God causes all things to work together for good to those who love God, to those who are called according to His purpose." God does not cause all things. God causes all things to work together. For your good. Though things can be torn all apart, He can put them back. Restoration. Better than before. Some say it is always darkest before the dawn. Stick with it. The sun will rise again. Others say that when it is dark that is when men see the stars. Some things become clearer when trials come. Learn from the day. Stay faithful and look to God.

Note: This passage was originally written on the day of the Sandy Hook school shooting in Newtown, Connecticut.

15 December In the night the wind and rain kept me awake. It wasn't so much the storm, but the sound of the rain on the roof and the wind whipping around the house. It reminded me of a popular story. It was a horrifying situation. The tornado was encroaching, Dorothy sought shelter. She was overcome, but she escaped fantastically into a land of sunshine and flowers. Well, the story is not without its witches and flying monkeys. However, in the end we see that there indeed is no place like home and all we ever wanted was right in our own back yard.

Today's song is, "Forever Reign" ~ Hillsong. This song talks of running to God's arms. The riches of His love will always be enough, because nothing compares to His embrace. There's a comfort in being where you are supposed to be. Nothing like coming home. When I was younger, home was with my parents. Before too long, ours will be the "home" to return to for our sons. When things are tough or changing, you may find that you have strayed from the security of home. This may be a place for you. It may be a group of people. It may be a church. It may be a town. It may be all of that. But no matter where you are, you can always be 'home' with God. His arms are outstretched and ready to receive you no matter how far you've traveled away from Him or how long you have been gone. Luke 15:18-20 says, "I will get up and go to my father, and will say to him, 'Father, I have sinned against heaven, and in your sight; I am no longer worthy to be called your son; make me as one of your hired men.' So he got up and came to his father. But while he was still a long way off, his father saw him and felt compassion *for him*, and ran and embraced him and kissed him." This is the prodigal who returned and was celebrated because of his decision to come home. Have you walked away from God in any area of your life today? It's time to go home. Time to admit it and turn around. God is waiting. His compassion is large. His love is immense. His forgiveness is true. Nothing compares to His embrace.

16 December

We have a big ole cat named George. George thinks he can fit in small places. He's too big. Sometimes he lays right on the edge of the couch. I say, "George, you're gonna fall off!" Yep, he falls. Then he gets back on the couch, right on the edge again. He doesn't get hurt when he falls though. The thing about cats is that they land on their feet. It's called the 'cat righting reflex'. It is a cat's ability to turn itself as it falls so it can land on its feet. Cats are able to do this because they have an unusually flexible backbone. For them it can be a life saver.

Today's song is, "Rise Up" ~ Matt Maher. This song encourages you that you need to rise up, when this life has got you down. You should look up when you search and nothing's found. There are times in life where you feel like hope is gone. Things are tough or discouraging. People don't respond how you think they should. You can't get relief. You are tired. You are spent. You are exhausted. You are weary. Things have gotten out of hand and you don't know where it all went wrong. You didn't fit in that place you so wanted to be in. You were living on the edge and you fell off. Those times you feel like staying down, on the ground, in a heap on the floor. You don't want to get up at all. But you must get up. Rise up. Take a breath and go again. Don't give up. Don't quit. Lamentations 3:28 (MSG) says, "When life is heavy and hard to take, go off by yourself. Enter the silence. Bow in prayer. Don't ask questions: Wait for hope to appear. Don't run from trouble. Take it full-face. The 'worst' is never the worst." What is your perspective? Things could be worse. And things can be better. In this life trouble will come. How will you land? How will you deal with it? How flexible are you? You may need some help getting up. You may need some one to lean on, but then get up. Stand up. Stand on your own. Be strong. Be courageous. God is with you. Proverbs 24:16 says, "For a righteous man falls seven times, and rises again, but the wicked stumble in *time of calamity.*" The best place to look when you are down is – UP. Be encouraged today. Help someone else be encouraged. Sometimes it's good to hear some one say, "Everything is going to be alright" because, eventually, it will – if you don't give up. Then next time, turn as you fall, and land on your feet. It could be a lifesaver!

17 December I used to watch a show about extreme home makeovers. They would remodel or rebuild a home in seven days! I thought, 'I could do that at my house!' Sure, if I had about 100 volunteers, a surplus of funds and some designers. I think we'll just take it a little at a time. Thankfully, our projects are not as major as the ones on the show. It can be more of a 'gradual' home makeover.

The song today is, "Who You Are" ~ Unspoken. This song is a reminder that you can change who you are. The world is changing all around you. You can resist the change or move with it. Now, some change isn't good. When morals and standards are compromised in favor of convenience, selfishness, or laziness, that's not good. Increasing in knowledge, skill, or relationships can be good. I'm sure you can come up with a great list on both sides of the page. Things are being invented all the time. Others are being improved. Aside from what's going on in the world, you need to look at yourself. Is it time for a change? Time to reinvent yourself? Time to improve? I think YES. Growing and changing are a part of living. But, you have to realize that change is often gradual. Reinventing is a process. You may tend to try to rush yourself. You want an extreme "me" makeover. However, a little change each day multiplies over time. When you do that, you can look back over the past year and honestly say, "I am a different person." When you live your life this year will it be a repeat or a new adventure? You don't want to do the same year again. You should want to be better and you should want to help others. What kind of positive impact could you have? Colossians 4:5-6 (MSG) says, "Use your heads as you live and work among outsiders. Don't miss a trick. Make the most of every opportunity. Be gracious in your speech. The goal is to bring out the best in others in a conversation, not put them down, not cut them out." You need to make the most of each opportunity to not only be your best, but to bring out the best in others. Being a voice instead of an echo. Being an example instead of a warning. Being a light in a dark world. God has called you to make an impression. What can you do to project God's promises and His goodness to a lost generation? Make a plan, write it down, put it into action. This coming year can be a year of great change.

18 December Hurricanes. They can be devastating. Winds can be up to 200 mph. But, it is in the center of this activity that the eye of the storm is formed. It's a clear area. The size of the storm eye on average is 20-40 miles across. An interesting feature about the eye is that while it is surrounded immediately by a cylinder of thick rotating clouds and rain, the air within the eye can be gentle breezes that are less than 15 mph. The lowest surface pressure of the storm is in the eye, which also has the warmest temperature. The eye of the storm will have limited to no precipitation. When you are in the eye of the storm, you should stay put.

Today's song is," Jesus Be The Center" ~ Israel Houghton. This song asks Jesus to be the center of my life. And declares that He is the center and everything revolves around Him. Did you know that in the midst of chaos, you can be at peace? You can be calm? You can have a place of refuge? When the storm is raging, Jesus is the stillness. You can place yourself in the eye of the storm. A place of gentle breezes. A place of lower pressure. A place of limited rain. Matthew 8:24-26 says, "And behold, there arose a great storm on the sea, so that the boat was being covered with the waves; but Jesus Himself was asleep. And they came to *Him* and woke Him, saying, 'Save *us*, Lord; we are perishing!' He said to them, 'Why are you afraid, you men of little faith?' Then He got up and rebuked the winds and the sea, and it became perfectly calm." Jesus can actually calm the storm of your life today. Your faith in God makes all the difference. People who aren't coping today do not know Jesus. They may know of Him, but that relationship is not a strong one. John 14:27 says, "Peace I leave with you; My peace I give to you; not as the world gives do I give to you. Do not let your heart be troubled, nor let it be fearful." You don't have to be afraid of the things of this life. Jesus has given you peace, just let that peace envelope you. Be calm. Take a breath. Settle yourself. You do not have to be devastated by the storm today. You can be in a place clear of the storm by keeping Jesus at the center of your life. Then, do what you can to bring others along with you so they too can experience that peace.

19 December I really like to watch movies. I especially like the end, how it turns out. When there's 10 minutes or less left, the phone won't get answered. Don't bother me. Gotta see the end! If I know it's not going to end well, I won't watch. I did watch one movie a couple weeks ago that I had already seen. Watching it again was fun because I was sure it ended well.

Today's song is, "Your Great Name" ~ Natalie Grant. This song reveres Jesus, the Lamb slain for us. He is the Son of God and man, high and lifted up. The whole world will praise His Great Name. I heard someone say, "I read the end of the book (the Bible) and we win!" It's so great to know that things will turn out in the end! You must make the most of the time you have. You must reach others. You must make a positive difference. Just because you know it ends well, you aren't exempt from participating in life. You have a responsibility to direct people toward a saving grace that comes from knowing Jesus. Seriously. When you have the answer, it's okay to give it to others. It's not cheating. It's redemptive. John 12:30-32 (MSG) says, "Jesus said, 'The voice didn't come for me but for you. At this moment the world is in crisis. Now Satan, the ruler of this world, will be thrown out. And I, as I am lifted up from the earth, will attract everyone to me and gather them around me.'" The attraction in your life today should be Jesus. He offered His life. He paid. And through all the heart ache, the pain, the disappointment, the blood, sweat, and tears, you can be assured that it will end well. It will end well for those in Christ. Being drawn to Him is to be drawn to eternal life. That is certainly a positive outcome. Who can you share a message of hope with today?

20 December Following a long day at work and travel I find myself settled back in and ready to share the song for this morning. "Jesus Be The Center" ~ Israel Houghton. These words rang clear to me at day's dawn; it reminds me that Jesus is at the center of it all. From beginning to end, it will always be Him. There is a comfort in consistency. Knowing what you can count on. Knowing what is reliable. Knowing WHO is reliable. It's a comfort. Reassuring. We have been at the same church now for over 27 years. Our pastor is consistent. He has been, all these years. Trustworthy. Reliable. Always abounding in the works of the Lord. I am thankful for his example, teaching, training, and encouragement. Hebrews 13:8 (MSG) says, "Appreciate your pastoral leaders who gave you the Word of God. Take a good look at the way they live, and let their faithfulness instruct you, as well as their truthfulness. There should be a consistency that runs through us all. For Jesus doesn't change—yesterday, today, tomorrow, He's always totally himself." Whether you have some one in your life who is that consistent presence or not, you definitely have Jesus. When you feel alone, He's there. When you are hurting, He's there. When you are afraid, anxious, worried, or helpless, He's your help. Reliable. Never changing.

With Jesus at the center of your life, you can be strong. You can withstand whatever the world has to throw at you. It's the trees with the deep roots that hold up when the wind is fierce. Take a look at your center today. Where are your spiritual roots? Do they go deep or are they just below the surface? The depth of your roots will determine how much you can stand. Remember Joshua 1:9 which says, "Have I not commanded you? Be strong and courageous! Do not tremble or be dismayed, for the Lord your God is with you wherever you go." This is the strength you need for each day's trouble. Hold tight to the Lord. Keep Him at the center. Strive to be consistent as an example to others and stay faithful.

21 December I love those Christmas classic cartoons. We manage to watch the comic group of children most years in December. They take a sad little tree and transform it! I love to see the dog dancing. I thought of him this morning when this song came to my heart. It's that illustration of joy that just makes me smile today.

Here's the song, "You Are Good" ~ Brian Johnson. This song says that I dance because God is good. In the sun or rain my life celebrates Him. No matter the circumstances, God is still good. And no matter what you have or haven't done, He still loves you. Romans 8:35 (ERV) says, "Can anything separate us from Christ's love? Can trouble or problems or persecution separate us from his love? If we have no food or clothes or face danger or even death, will that separate us from his love?" Nothing can separate us! It's true! So, how good is that? Very good! When you think of all the reasons He could not love you and yet He does. He has and will continue to love you. He really is good. That's worth dancing about! Feel His joy today. Feel His peace. Know His love. Know His goodness. Celebrate His goodness! And be good for goodness sake!

22 December A few nights ago I had a nightmare. The dream was so scary that it woke me. It seemed real. When I opened my eyes though, I realized that I was home in my bed. Safe. The song today is, "Forever Reign" ~ Hillsong. The part of the song I heard this morning reminded me that the Lord is my peace when my fear is crippling.

We have all been afraid of something at one time or another. Fear can stop you in your tracks. It can consume you if you let it. It could be fear of some animal or place or thing. It could be a fear of failure. It could be fear of doom. (Whatever form it may take) There is a way to not live in fear. I John 4:17-18 (MSG) puts it this way, "God is love. When we take up permanent residence in a life of love, we live in God and God lives in us. This way, love has the run of the house, becomes at home and mature in us, so that we're free of worry on Judgment Day—our standing in the world is identical with Christ's. There is no room in love for fear. Well-formed love banishes fear. Since fear is crippling, a fearful life—fear of death, fear of judgment—is one not yet fully formed in love." Another song says that all you need is love...that may seem ethereal, but true. The key is that God is love. So when you are fearful, look to Him.

An acronym for FEAR is False Evidence Appearing Real. Sometimes fear is unfounded. It is a result of lack of knowledge or experience. I have been working through one of my fears lately. I wanted to face it. I engaged the help of a friend. I've been talking about it – Talking about the solution, not the fear. (Because what you focus on becomes bigger.) I have been learning about it. My knowledge and experience is calming my fear. I know with God's help I can be totally free of this fear. His love super-cedes it. In the scriptures He reminds us to "fear not" about 365 times. One for each day. So face your fears today. Develop love in your life. Seek God in the matter. Let Him settle you. Be strong, be courageous, and be at peace today.

23 December As I was driving to church one morning I saw a hot air balloon on the horizon. I smiled. What a peaceful sight. The people inside must have been having such a good time. It was a brisk start to what was turning into a gorgeous day. Years ago we took a hot air balloon ride. I thought it would be windy up there. It was calm. We did not feel the breeze because we were moving with it. The view was incredible!

Today's song is a classic, "Carol Of The Bells" composed by Mycola Leontovych with lyrics by Peter J. Wilhousky. It's based on a folk chant from the Ukraine. Part of it goes like this... "Christmas is here. Bringing good cheer to young and old, meek and the bold... One seems to hear words of good cheer from everywhere filling the air." There is something about Christmas time that causes people to stop and smile. Many find themselves to be more cheery than usual, more giving than usual, and more festive than ever. People are moved because of the atmosphere. The wind of the world may be fierce, but in it there shines some hope, a flicker of light in the darkness. A spirit of charity and love prevails. I know there are some Scrooges out there, but I say to them – "Bah, humbug! I will not let your negative attitude spoil my journey!" They lack that Christmas cheer. Those people just need more of God's love in their lives. They need hope in the future. They are angry, wounded, and lost. Roman's 5:5 (ERV) says, "And this hope will never disappoint us. We know this because God has poured out his love to fill our hearts through the Holy Spirit he gave us." This is the hope that helps you rise above all the cares of this world. It takes you to a new perspective. It helps you to adjust to the winds of change. It offers you an incredible view! Be the one who shares good cheer to others today. You will help lift their spirits too.

24 December I was so proud to hear of my son's actions last evening. He gave of his personal belongings to some boys in need. They weren't seconds. They were not leftovers. They were nice items. He didn't hesitate. That giving spirit is what we all should strive to keep throughout the year. Not just at Christmas. With our family it's a lifestyle. It's the way we have been taught. What a great gift to see your children catch that example.

This morning's song, "Happy Christmas" ~ John Lennon. In it he asks what have you done now that it's Christmas. Another year is over. A new one has begun. As you reflect upon the past 12 months or so, think, what have you done? Your accomplishments, your failures. Where have you excelled? Where have you fallen short? What have you achieved? What have you put off? You should love the New Year. It's a chance to catch your breath. A time to start fresh. An opportunity to regroup and push forward. Strive to step outside of yourself more. Step out of your own world and strive to help meet the needs of others. Romans 12:10 (CEB) says, "Love each other like the members of your family. Be the best at showing honor to each other." This is not an avenue to seek your own fame by essentially saying, "Look how great I am that I did this for someone." but instead it is a way to show the goodness of God to others. Give them a story to tell. A good story. Point them to God as reason for your generous spirit. Matthew 5:16 (MSG) says, "Now that I've put you there on a hilltop, on a light stand—shine! Keep open house; be generous with your lives. By opening up to others, you'll prompt people to open up with God, this generous Father in heaven." What a great way make a difference with your life! Take a look today at the past several months. What impact do you believe your life has made? How might you adjust that to make the most of the days to come? Colossians 4:5 (AMP) says, "Behave yourselves wisely [living prudently and with discretion] in your relations with those of the outside world (the non-Christians), making the very most of the time *and* seizing (buying up) the opportunity." Each opportunity is important. Do not let them pass you by. Helping, giving, and having the right attitude in it are all keys to reminding people how good God is.

25 December Today as we finished opening gifts my husband said, "We are so blessed." God has been good to us. Then at breakfast as he was praying, we were mindful of the true reason for our celebration- the gift of Jesus. The spirit in our home today is especially sweet. We are thankful. We hold dear what God has done for us and what He means in our lives.

Song for today is, "The Solid Rock" ~ Edward Mote. "My hope is built on nothing less than Jesus' blood and righteousness; I dare not trust the sweetest frame, but wholly lean on Jesus' name…On Christ, the solid rock, I stand, all other ground is sinking sand." Focus today on Jesus. Build your house on the Rock that is Jesus. Matthew 7:24-27 says, "Therefore everyone who hears these words of Mine and acts on them, may be compared to a wise man who built his house on the rock. And the rain fell, and the floods came, and the winds blew and slammed against that house; and *yet* it did not fall, for it had been founded on the rock. Everyone who hears these words of Mine and does not act on them, will be like a foolish man who built his house on the sand. The rain fell, and the floods came, and the winds blew and slammed against that house; and it fell—and great was its fall." I want to be wise today. That is why my family and I have built our house on the Rock. Storms may come. Things may shake. Our house will not fall. We have a firm spiritual foundation. We are in this together and we are in it for the long haul. Examine your spiritual foundation today. Is it solid, immovable, unshakable? Does it have cracks? Does it need help? Shore it up today by taking some time to pray, read some scripture, and reflect on the goodness of God.

26 December My father and my brother both worked for ACF – the railroad car manufacturer. So, of course we always had a train under our Christmas tree when I was growing up. We had little cars and benches and street lights. Little bushes and even a little police call box. When I was wrapping presents this year I saw something on the floor and it was that little red police call box. Where did it come from? Why was it there? It took me right back home to that train set of my childhood. The memory flooded my mind. The feeling of home was a good one for me.

Today's song is "I'll Be Home For Christmas" ~ Bing Crosby. It says that Christmas Eve will find me where the lovelight gleams and I'll be home for Christmas, if only in my dreams. There is something about going home. Something about being home that can ground you. A firm foundation. I was fortunate, my home was good. My upbringing was good. I had two parents who loved me and each other. My siblings were all older. I was the last of four with nearly a 20 year total span between us. Family was important. Every one needs a place that they can call home. It may not be the one of your childhood. It may be the home you've established now with your family. It may be where you went to school. It may be your church. It's a place of grounding for you. A place of comfort and rest. A familiar place. A place not like any other for you. Even if you feel like you have no place today, God has something for you. Psalm 68:6 says, "God makes a home for the lonely..." You can always have a home in God. He is the place of refuge for you. He is the God of peace. This is the place to settle yourself. This is the place to call home, your spiritual home. God doesn't change. He's always there. If you have been away from God, it's time to come home. If you have not sought God for your life, it's time to come home. If you have loved ones who don't know God's unconditional love for them, tell them it's time to come home. Home in God is like no other. Invite Him into your life. Jesus said, "Behold, I stand at the door and knock; if anyone hears My voice and opens the door, I will come in to him and will dine with him, and he with Me." (Revelation 3:20). Everyday let Him into your life. Make Him a part. Your home in Him will always be good.

27 December When I was high school age I was in the church youth choir. I really enjoyed singing. The song today was from that time in my life. I remember the tune and the words but not the title.   Interesting though how it foreshadowed what I would be doing today in writing this.

The song celebrates songs in the daytime and in the night. Songs of devotion and delight and I am thrilled with the melodies ringing in my heart. I find it amazing how faithful God is to me and that each morning a new song is there. I don't have to search or labor over it. I just have to be still. Listen. He hands it to me. Then I get quiet and listen to what He wants me to share. Numbers 11:9 says, "When the dew fell on the camp at night, the manna would fall with it." God fed the people daily with manna. There was manna for that day only. (Except for the day before Sabbath, then two days worth) The word 'manna' means "What is it?" They had what they needed and they couldn't explain it. They knew it was from God. They knew they could get it daily. They had to gather it and prepare it to eat. It wasn't like drive thru fast food. It was provision. A resource. It was their responsibility to work with it. God has given me this provision, this resource to work with each day to feed myself and others spiritually. I can't explain it. I know it's from God. The song is for that day. The story, the scripture, the encouragement is all for that day. Tomorrow's song will be here tomorrow.

What provision has God given to you today? What resource? What can you do to work with it and help others? It may not be what you expected. It may not be what you can explain. But it will be yours uniquely to utilize. God has a purpose and plan for you. Discover it. Develop it. Use it to reach others. Use it to make a difference. It will be in your heart and it will be a delight. It will fit you. It will be a part of you. It will be anointed. It will be your daily bread. Your manna. What is it?

28 December When I was in college I performed in the Central Pantomime Theatre Company. We mimed on campus and we toured. It was something I enjoyed and I was good at it. It was my niche. I was also a member of a professional fine arts fraternity made up of mostly musicians. I thought, "Singing, how hard could it be?" So when recital time came, instead of choosing to mime I chose to sing a song. Though I had practiced and thought I would do quite well, I took the stage and failed miserably. Miserably! I was embarrassed. I cried. For the rest of my college years I stuck to what I was proficient in – Pantomime.

This morning's song is the song I chose for that recital. I thought it was long forgotten... "A Love Song" ~ Chuck Girard. It talks about all the emotions and true feelings of life being what music of love is about. You need to be listening with peace in your heart and no doubt. There is a universality of music that draws people. It invokes a feeling. This love song is a sweet one, but for me brings to the surface some raw feelings. It hurts. It's a sore memory. But it taught me a lesson. That is: Build on your strengths. Romans 12:6 (MSG) says, "So since we find ourselves fashioned into all these excellently formed and marvelously functioning parts in Christ's body, let's just go ahead and be what we were made to be, without enviously or pridefully comparing ourselves with each other, or trying to be something we aren't." Be who you are. Comparing leads to disappointment. Look at your unique gifting. What comes easily? What flows? What works for you? What makes you passionate? What do you love? These are keys to your strengths. Keys to your destiny. Keys to what you should really be investing your time and energy into. When you try to be great at everything, your strengths will suffer and your weaknesses may only increase to mediocre. Don't try to be something you are not. I tell my sons to find something where they can win. Where can you win today? Where can you excel? Pursue it. Use that gift to help others. You don't have to be embarrassed. Stick to it. Listen with your heart and don't doubt. God will show you what it is and how to be great.

29 December When my son was little he asked, "What is a cemetery?" I told him that it was a place where people remember those who have gone on to Heaven. It was a simple answer. True, but not too much detail or theology. I hadn't ever heard it explained that way, but that was my take on it. It satisfied his curiosity for the time being.

Today's song, "Me Without You" ~ Toby Mac. This song admits to God, where would I be without You? I would be packing to leave when I need to stay. How do people cope when bad things happen to them? I can't imagine how they function without God in their lives. You can tell the difference at the hospital and at funerals. The spirit of the place and the spirit of the people is more peaceful when God is a part of their lives. God brings comfort. When you welcome His presence, there is calm. God can give you the ability to, instead of saying, "Why me?" you can say "What now?" He helps you to move forward instead of being a just a victim.

When things are tough, something bad happens, some one gets hurt or dies, look to God. Avoid making up answers without consulting the Bible. People don't die because God needs more angels in Heaven or because God has an empty seat to fill. They die because there is evil in the world. (John 10:10) See what God has to say about it. You may wonder, "Is it His will for life and recovery?" Those questions are answered in 3 John 1:2, "Beloved, I pray that in all respects you may prosper and be in good health, just as your soul prospers." God wants you to prosper and be in good health. And there are more scriptures to answer the questions you have. Search for the verses that apply to your situation. Find encouragement, don't lay blame. Get uplifted, don't be without God. When you are upset or confused, seek Him. If you feel you can't find Him, find someone who knows Him. They can help. And make yourself ready to help others find Him today. Think about where you would be without Him. You'd be packing to leave when you need to stay.

30 December Several weeks ago I woke up in the early morning and I could tell the weather was about to change. The barometric pressure increased. I could feel it. My head began to ache. That physical change in the atmosphere let me know I'd better check to see what was going on. I thought, "I may need an umbrella today!"

This morning's song, "Glorious One" ~ Steve Fee. This song announces that our hands are lifted high, and our hearts bow in reverence to being surrounded by God's presence. When you are in an atmosphere of God's presence, things change. Your heart aches, longs for more of Him. When you honor God, He surrounds you. He feels welcome and offers His presence in your life. You can be in a place where the presence of God is tangible. You really can feel it. It washes over you. You can hardly stand. It's a calming presence. It's a healing presence. It's a covering. The atmosphere that you place yourself in today can be life giving or it can be destructive. It makes a difference where you are and with whom you are. You can create your own atmosphere by the music you select, the space in the room, the words you read, and by your attitude. Being reverent to God puts you in a posture to receive from Him. Isaiah 40:31 (AMP) says, "But those who wait for the Lord [who expect, look for, and hope in Him] shall change *and* renew their strength *and* power; they shall lift their wings *and* mount up [close to God] as eagles [mount up to the sun]; they shall run and not be weary, they shall walk and not faint *or* become tired." Strength comes when you get in God's presence. You are changed in His presence. There is power in His presence. Get into His presence today. Adjust your atmosphere. You may need His umbrella to cover you. You will be energized in your weariness. You will be able to go on when you want to quit. You will know His glory and you will receive what He has for your life.

31 December Fads can be fun. Well, unless you get swept up in the excitement to extremes. Then you find yourself with bunches of bean bag animals or a truckload of rock pets! I remember the 3D pictures fad– Stereograms. I would see them at the shopping mall. Stores displayed them in the windows. At first glance they appeared to be obscure patterns of color, and then when you stared for awhile and focused differently, somehow a hidden picture would "appear". Sometimes I would stop and gaze for a long time and never see it. Other times it became very clear to me. As soon as I saw the hidden picture, it was easier to find it again.

Today's song is "Jesus in Disguise" ~ Brandon Heath. These words rang in my spirit today, to open my eyes wide as I can, even though I may be blind. Perspective. God can give you the ability to see things that are not obvious. Not in plain sight. Is it magic? No. It's spiritual vision. 2 Kings 6:17 says, "Then Elisha prayed and said, 'O Lord, I pray, open his eyes that he may see.' And the Lord opened the servant's eyes and he saw; and behold, the mountain was full of horses and chariots of fire all around Elisha." Elisha's servant was able to see into the spiritual realm. He saw things not visible until Elisha prayed. His focus was changed.

In Jeremiah 33:3 it says, "Call to Me and I will answer you, and I will tell you great and mighty things, which you do not know." God will show you hidden things. You can ask Him. He will give you the strategy and the plan. He will help you change your focus. Once you see what He has for you, it will be easier to see again. You may not see the whole picture all at once. But He reveals steps. Psalm 119:105 says, "Your word is a lamp to my feet and a light to my path." God's Word will direct. It's a lamp to your feet – the immediate, what's right in front of you. And it's a light to your path – projected before you, a glimpse of the future. Seek God today for your direction. He has a great plan for you. There are good choices and there are God choices. Make the God choices. You won't regret it. When what He has is clear to you, you will be able to find and fulfill the destiny for your life.

Note from the Author

My prayer is that you have been inspired this year by <u>Songs in the Morning</u>. God has great things in store for you, so walk in them. Seek His face and do all you can to fulfill His plan for your life. Share His love with others and make a positive difference in this world while you can.

Remember to listen in the stillness of the morning for the song that God would give you for your day.

Blessings,

Starr

About the Author

STARR HIMMEL is married to Steve Himmel. They have two sons, Sean and Ryan. They have been a part of Church On The Rock, St. Louis since 1985. Starr loves family, church, writing and consulting. Her Bachelor of Arts Degree is from Central Methodist College where she majored in Religion and Philosophy with an emphasis in Christian Education. She has experience as a Floral Designer/Manager, K-12 Christian School Principal, Program Director, & Adult Ed. Instructor and Beauty Consultant. Her desire is to help others in their spiritual walk.

48274368R00226

Made in the USA
Charleston, SC
29 October 2015